T0246211

YUKIKAZE'S WAR

Only one elite Imperial Japanese Navy destroyer survived the cruel ocean battlefields of World War II. This is her story. Brett Walker, historian and captain, delves into questions of mechanics, armaments, navigation, training, and even indoctrination illustrating the daily realities of war for *Yukikaze* and her crew. By shifting our perspective of the Pacific War away from grand Imperial strategies toward the intricacies of fighting on the water, Walker allows us to see the war from *Yukikaze*'s bridge during the most harrowing battles, from Midway to Okinawa. Walker uncovers the ordinary sailor's experience, and we see sailors fight while deep-running currents of Japanese history unfold before their war-weary eyes. As memories of World War II fade, *Yukikaze*'s story becomes ever more important, providing valuable lessons in our contemporary world of looming energy shortfalls, menacing climate uncertainties, and aggressive totalitarian regimes.

Brett L. Walker is a historian of Japan, medicine, the environment, and World War II, as well as an experienced captain.

YUKIKAZE'S WAR

*The Unsinkable Japanese Destroyer and
World War II in the Pacific*

Brett L. Walker

Montana State University

CAMBRIDGE
UNIVERSITY PRESS

Shaftesbury Road, Cambridge CB2 8EA, United Kingdom

One Liberty Plaza, 20th Floor, New York, NY 10006, USA

477 Williamstown Road, Port Melbourne, VIC 3207, Australia

314–321, 3rd Floor, Plot 3, Splendor Forum, Jasola District Centre,
New Delhi – 110025, India

103 Penang Road, #05–06/07, Visioncrest Commercial, Singapore 238467

Cambridge University Press is part of Cambridge University Press & Assessment,
a department of the University of Cambridge.

We share the University's mission to contribute to society through the pursuit of
education, learning and research at the highest international levels of excellence.

www.cambridge.org
Information on this title: www.cambridge.org/9781108837293

DOI: 10.1017/9781108938792

First published 2024

Printed in the United Kingdom by TJ Books Limited, Padstow Cornwall

A catalogue record for this publication is available from the British Library

A Cataloging-in-Publication data record for this book is available from the Library of Congress

ISBN 978-1-108-83729-3 Hardback

To my mother, Linda

Because I feel that, in the Heavens above,
The angels, whispering to one another,
Can find, among their burning terms of love,
None so devotional as that of "Mother" …

Edgar Allan Poe

Contents

Preface

Many famous ships, by virtue of their captains and crew, passengers, navigational wherewithal, engineering, construction, charts and electronics, armaments, contagious diseases, livestock, weeds, hitchhiking barnacles, and parasitic bilges have shaped the course of historical events in ways just as powerful as any human idea. This fact is undeniable, so I will not belabor the point.

And ships resemble people, too. They have personalities; some even have attitudes. Like people, they are also born with differing degrees of fortune – some ships are lucky, while others are not. Frankly, writing a biography of a ship is not unlike writing a biography of a person. It involves the same balance of historical context and individual grit. We are a product of our will, to be sure; but we are also products of the ideas and material world that swirl around us and shape us every day. We can't escape these currents, and ships can't, either.

Polynesians settled the South Pacific in large, multi-hulled canoes, with only the stars, waves, and the occasional white tern to guide them. Leif Erikson's Norse ship is said to have brought the Icelandic explorer to North America about 500 years before Christopher Columbus was even a twinkle in Susanna Fontanarossa's eye. Vasco da Gama's *São Gabriel* rounded the Horn of Africa in 1497 and opened trade routes to the spice-rich lands of Arabia. Columbus's *Santa María* crossed the Atlantic Ocean and enabled the European colonization of North America, sadly leading to a holocaust against native populations. Zheng He's colossal Chinese treasure ships visited Brunei, Java, Thailand, the Horn of Africa, and Arabia in the sixteenth century, before China's self-imposed dynastic isolation.

James Cook's *Endeavour* charted islands in the Pacific Ocean from New Zealand to Hawai'i in the eighteenth century, bringing contagions that decimated local populations. Horatio Nelson's *Victory* led the way in the defeat of Napoleon at Trafalgar in 1805, reshaping the map of Europe forever. In the 1830s, Robert Fitzroy's *Beagle* transported Charles Darwin and a copy of Charles Lyell's *Principles of Geology* to South America, including the Galápagos Islands, transforming how we look at natural change and geological time forever. Tōgō Heihachirō's battleship *Mikasa* helped sink the better part of the Russian Baltic Fleet at the Battle of Tsushima Strait, leading to Japan's meteoric rise as a world power at the dawn of the twentieth century. History undeniably changed in the wakes of these ships.

This book is the story of one of these ships, a World War II warship named *Yukikaze*. This Imperial Japanese Navy destroyer navigated through many of the most harrowing naval battles in World War II, where brave young sailors on both sides, confined in cramped galvanized warships, fought valiantly in a life or death struggle for survival and, ultimately, victory over the enemy. Her story provides fresh insights into why Japan waged war in the Pacific, and how the Imperial Navy won and lost key battles.

Yukikaze's story traces dangerous changes in Imperial Navy culture and conduct as the war ground on, particularly Imperial Navy abandonment of conventional naval strategies and tactics in favor of a "kamikaze spirit" that was often resisted by the shipboard rank and file. After the Battle of the Philippine Sea in the summer of 1944, the Imperial Navy waged war less for tactical successes than to preserve honor: to appease the ghosts of its founders, men such as Tōgō Heihachirō and Yamamoto Gonnohyōe, and to satiate Japan's martial heroes, men such as the samurai loyalist Kusunoki Masashige. It's hardly surprising that *kikusui* – the floating chrysanthemum, the Kusunoki family crest – became code for Imperial Navy "special operations" in the final years of the war.

Finally, *Yukikaze*'s war was part of the global story of World War II, highlighting the interconnectedness of the conflict. Historian A. J. P. Taylor, in his landmark *The Origins of the Second World War*, wrote that the Asia–Pacific and European wars "remained distinct"[1] from one another. He continued that the "European war and its origins can be treated as a story in itself, the Far East providing occasional distractions off-stage." Actually, as we shall see, this statement couldn't be further from the truth.

Yukikaze's war was anything but a distraction happening off stage, particularly when viewed through the strategic lens of Japan's need to extract oil from the soil of decaying European empires, such as the Dutch East Indies. In May 1940, Adolf Hitler's blitzkrieg had forced the Dutch government into exile in London. Consequently, the London Cabinet, as the Dutch government in exile was called, abandoned the East Indies and its oilfields, leaving them like an "orphaned child." What *Yukikaze*'s war shows is that the two military theaters constantly overlapped, and nowhere was that more true than at sea.

Yukikaze's war challenges us to reexamine larger questions regarding how we interpret the broader meaning of World War II some seventy-five years later, after most of the men and women who served in that war are no longer with us. Sadly, history departments in the United States have all but abandoned military history in favor of other fields, and this remains particularly true regarding the study of Japan. But, in the wake of Russia's brutal invasion of Ukraine and continuing hostilities around Taiwan, and Japan's Prime Minister recently stating that, "With the security environment in the East and South China seas ... becoming more severe,"[2] Japan has "no time to waste" in beefing up its military posture in the region, it's probably high time for historians to reexamine how war shapes our world.

It's critically important that the horrors of World War II not be lost in the twenty-first century. Today, the postwar consensus for liberalism is fading at the same time that memories of World War II do. As those war memories fade and the global democratic tide begins to ebb, the jagged reefs of nativism and despotism are being exposed in the coastal nadir. Historian Robert Kagan, in *The Jungle Grows Back*, writes that most of human history is about "war, tyranny, and poverty,"[3] and the triumph of the liberal order since World War II has been a "historical aberration." The postwar liberal order "is like a garden," observes Kagan, "it is ever under siege from the natural forces of history, the jungle whose vines and weeds constantly threaten to overwhelm it." There are many ways to tend the garden of the liberal order, and teaching more about World

War II is one of them. It is, after all, in the bloodsoaked soil of World War II that the seeds of the liberal garden first began to germinate.

Yukikaze, as a technology of war, not only shaped history, but also served as a window into it. She fought in what can only be described as a cataclysmic and grotesque eruption of industrial modernity and political ideologies, a global conflict that killed an estimated 70–80 million people and maimed countless more. The historian Eric Hobsbawm called the twentieth century the "age of extremes," and little proved more extreme during this age than the killing during World War II.

Yukikaze's story is not an easy one to flesh out. The Allies, who won the war, kept and preserved copious notes, while the losers' notes, in this case those of the Imperial Japanese Navy, were largely destroyed. Still, historians know the outlines of Pacific battles well, and expertly illustrate them with charts of fleet dispositions, tactics, navigational decisions, torpedo actions, aerial assaults, and gunnery exchanges to help understand the intricacies of often-chaotic engagements on the water. These charts might illustrate that Imperial Navy destroyers launched torpedoes here, at some known longitudinal and latitudinal coordinate; and, consequently, a US Navy vessel sank there, at another known coordinate – the map icon of a wrecked ship designates its watery grave.

But, in large part, historians can only speculate regarding what happened aboard Imperial Navy warships during key confrontations, what sailors thought and why. Many Imperial Navy vessels sank, and their records, including sailors' personal memories, sank with them. Sailors aboard *Yukikaze*, by contrast, survived the war and burned her shipboard records on land after Japan's surrender in 1945, and only a smattering of histories, interviews, and diaries remain to bring her travails to life. Of course, I have mined these, and also augmented them with the copious US Navy action reports that, I hope, help transport the reader back in time to these watery battlefields.

The history that emerges in these pages reveals more than just industrial-scale killing by men in clanking, cranking, and smoking machines. *Yukikaze* shares with us a world in the white-knuckled grip of total war, when entire nations, including their women and children, geared up to fight, and offers suggestions regarding how we might remember the epic conflict today, in a world filled with similar uncertainties. Even after the war, when the big guns quieted, *Yukikaze* and her treasured name navigated through the postwar world in the form of her enduring historical legacies, similarly informing us about dangerous Cold War geopolitics, Japan's postwar popular culture, and the enduring global security challenges in the Taiwan Strait, the most fraught body of water in the world. Ironically, the energy requirements that Japan used to justify its "Southern Operation" in 1941 still persist today, and Japan's Maritime Self-Defense Forces, not unlike their Imperial Navy forebears, plan for new challenges in an age of disappearing oil.

Yukikaze serves as a historical avatar of sorts, a floating, mechanical representation of the complex, multifaceted reasons industrial nations fought World War II, from their political ideologies to their industrial dependency on oil. Her story is a valuable one in our world of lurking energy shortfalls, menacing climate uncertainties, and aggressive totalitarian regimes.

A Note on Sources

In the name of readability, I have reduced the endnotes in this book to a bare minimum, citing only quoted dialogue. But sources other than the ones cited contributed to this book, many of them in important ways. Primarily, this book was inspired by three chapters in Itō Masanori's *Rengō kantai no eikō* (*Glory of the Combined Fleet*, 1962), a book I discovered for the first time as a Reischauer Fellow while perusing the Harvard-Yenching stacks. It piqued my interest in the destroyer *Yukikaze*, and I've been hooked ever since.

Those chapters framed much of the analysis in this book up until around 1944. After that, one of Itō's other histories, *The End of the Imperial Japanese Navy* (1962), framed the analysis of the final two years of the war. I've always respected Itō's work, particularly his close friendships with many in the Imperial Navy. I'm fully aware of some of the problems with his scholarship, and I have meticulously checked his work against other sources. But Itō provided a unique perspective into the Imperial Navy, and I have tried to retain this distinct flavor – he's both historian and primary source.

Otherwise, to track *Yukikaze*'s movements in a long and geographically dispersed war, I referenced her Track Record of Movement (TROM) on Jonathan Parshall's remarkable database www.CombinedFleet .com. I also cautiously used Toyota Jō, *Yukikaze wa shizumazu: Kyōun kuchikukan eikō no shōgai* (*Yukikaze Can't Be Sunk: The Glorious Career of a Fortunate Destroyer*, 1983). Several general histories of the war in the Pacific informed my thinking, including Samuel Eliot Morison, *History of the United States Naval Operations in World War II*, 15 vols. (1947–1962); William Leonard Langer and S. Everett Gleason, *The Undeclared War, 1940–1941* (1953); *Senshi sōsho* (The War History Series, 102 vols., compiled by the War History Office of the National Defense College of Japan), including the translated *The Invasion of the Dutch East Indies* (2015); Paul S. Dull, *A Battle History of the Imperial Japanese Navy, 1941–1945* (1978); Ronald H. Spector, *Eagle against the Sun* (1985); Richard B. Frank, *Downfall* (1999); Ian W. Toll's trilogy, *Pacific Crucible* (2012), *The Conquering Tide* (2015), and *Twilight of the Gods* (2020); Waldo Heinrichs and Marc Gallicchio, *Implacable Foes* (2017); Craig L. Symonds, *World War II at Sea* (2018); Evan Mawdsley, *The War for the Seas* (2019); and Richard B. Frank, *Tower of Skulls* (2020). For Japan's occupation and postwar history, including naval history, I referenced John W. Dower, *Embracing Defeat* (1999); Euan Graham, *Japan's Sea Lane Security, 1940–2004* (2006); and Alessio Patalano, *Post-war Japan as a Sea Power* (2015). I consulted Chen Jiang, *Mao's China and the Cold War* (2001), regarding the Taiwan Strait during the Cold War.

I used numerous histories and reference books on the Imperial Japanese Navy, including Charles Schencking, *Making Waves* (2005); David C. Evans and Mark R. Peattie, *Kaigun* (2012); Mark Stille, *The Imperial Japanese Navy in the Pacific War* (2013); and David C. Evans, ed., *The Japanese Navy in World War II* (1969). I referenced Anthony John Watts and Brian G. Gordon, *The Imperial Japanese Navy* (1971); Hansgeorg Jentschura, Dieter Jung, and Peter Mickel, *Warships of the Imperial Japanese Navy, 1869–1945* (1977); and Eric Lacroix and Linton Wells, *Japanese Cruisers of the Pacific War* (1997). I relied heavily on the *US Naval Technical Mission to Japan* (1945) for data on Imperial Navy vessels, weapons, and other maritime systems. For information on food aboard Imperial Navy warships, I used Fujita Masao, *Shashin de miru kaigun ryōshokushi* (*A History in Photographs of Imperial Navy Provisioning,* 2007). On the US side, the National Archive's "World War II Navy Command Files" contain an absolute treasure trove of primary sources, including World War II Action Reports from Pacific battlefields.

I drew on general histories of wartime Japan, including Saburō Ienaga, *The Pacific War* (1978); John W. Dower, *War without Mercy* (1986); Mark R. Peattie, *Nan'yō* (1988); Haruko Taya Cook and Theodore F. Cook, *Japan at War* (1992); Samuel Hideo Yamashita, *Leaves from an Autumn of Emergencies* (2005); *Sources of Japanese Tradition, 1600 to 2000, Volume Two, Part Two: 1868 to 2000,* compiled by W. Theodore De Bary, Carol

Gluck, and Arthur E. Tiedemann (2006); Samuel Hideo Yamashita, *Daily Life in Wartime Japan, 1940–1945* (2015); and Noriko Kawamura, *Emperor Hirohito and the Pacific War* (2015), among others.

My thoughts on Imperial Navy destroyer names and Imperial nationalism are rooted in such scholarship as Haruo Shirane, ed., *Traditional Japanese Literature: An Anthology, Beginnings to 1600* (2007); H. D. Harootunian, *Toward Restoration* (1970); H. D. Harootunian, *Things Seen and Unseen* (1988); Mary Elizabeth Berry, *Japan in Print* (2006); and Brett L. Walker, *A Concise History of Japan* (2015), among others. I consider Ivan Morris, *The Nobility of Failure* (1974) essential reading when thinking about Japan's tragic heroes.

To recreate an on-the-water perspective, I relied on four autobiographical accounts, in particular: Hara Tameichi, *Japanese Destroyer Captain* (1961); Nishizaki Nobuo, Yukikaze *no notte shōnen: Jūgosai de shussei shita kaigun tokubetsu nenshōhei* (*A Boy aboard Yukikaze: Departing for the Front at Fifteen as a Special Navy Youth Sailor*, 2019); NHK Interview Archive, *Kuchikukan* Yukikaze *Suisokuin:* Noma Mitsue-san (Destroyer *Yukikaze* Hydrographer, Noma Mitsue, October 23, 2011); and Yoshida Mitsuru, *Requiem for Battleship Yamato* (1985).

For individual battles, I used the above general histories, as well as more specific studies (in approximate chronological order), including David Arthur Thomas, *The Battle of the Java Sea* (1968); Donald M. Kehn, *In the Highest Degree of Tragic* (2017); John B. Lundstrom, *Black Shoe Carrier Admiral* (2016); Jonathan Parshall and Anthony Tully, *Shattered Sword* (2005); Craig L. Symonds, *The Battle of Midway* (2011); Richard B. Frank, *Guadalcanal* (1990); James D. Hornfischer, *Neptune's Inferno* (2011); Trent Hone, *Learning War* (2022); W. David Dickson, *The Battle of the Philippine Sea, June 1944* (1975); James D. Hornfischer, *Fleet at Flood Tide* (2016); Barrett Tillman, *Clash of the Carriers* (2005); Anthony P. Tully, *Battle of Surigao Strait* (2009); Mark P. Parillo, *The Japanese Merchant Marine in World War II* (1993); *The United States Strategic Bombing Surveys (Pacific War)* (1987); and Shizuo Fukui, *Japanese Navy Vessels at the End of World War II* (1992), among others.

Historians always build their work on the foundation stones set by the work of others; they sometimes even rearrange those stones, ever so slightly, and this book is certainly no different.

CHAPTER 1

Divine Ships of a Bluewater Navy

The snowy wind, unspeakable weather and so dark ...

The *Kagerō nikki* (the *Mayfly Diary* or *Gossamer Years*, 974)

WE START WITH IMPERIAL NAVY WARSHIP NAMES, including *Yukikaze*'s, and what they reveal about Japanese nationalism in the twentieth century. As they steamed into battle, Imperial Navy warships became emblematic of Japan's divine landscape, over which the Emperor, both head of state and Shinto's chief priest, reigned supreme. Destroyer names, in particular, tapped into ancient Japanese aesthetics, ones often tied to classical poetic conventions, and they often evoked an ancient melancholy that suited wartime. These names, such as *Yukikaze*, resembled the "scripture of the gods" and served as "spirit words" that linked sailors and the Japanese public to the aesthetics of Japan's imperial nationalism.

These warships deserved divine names, given their colossal cost in national treasure. But, if Japan was to become a world power at the end of the nineteenth century, defend itself from predacious great nations, and ultimately become one, it needed a blue-water navy. Starting in the Meiji period, Japan's government spent untold treasure to build this floating divine arsenal, one that could assert Japan's national desires across the sea and help create and defend an empire. These warships became dramatic symbols of the Japanese nation, celebrated on postcards and taught in schoolbooks; they became celebrities of a sort. Their purpose, however, from the beginning, was to defeat the US Navy in a hypothetical war with Japan's Pacific rival.

In the opening months of the war, the Imperial Navy deployed these heroic warships with nearly religious intensity in the idea of an Alfred

Mahan-style "decisive battle" with the US Navy, one that would knock the Americans out of the war. But, ironically, World War II was rarely about decisive battles (though it had some), and the Imperial Navy found itself adjusting to a war over lines of communication, shipping routes, and fuel transports.

Nonetheless, it is with these colossal warships, prides of a nation, mechanical celebrities with their "spirit word" names, and their doctrinal pursuit of a "decisive battle" with the US Navy, that we begin *Yukikaze*'s war.

* * *

Yukikaze means "snowy wind" in Japanese. In 1939, yard workers at the Sasebo Naval Arsenal painted that name in four bold white *kana* characters on the starboard and port beams of a newly constructed warship. The navy-gray vessel splashed into the water on March 24 of that year. With draping garlands of Japanese *sakaki* leaves, rising-sun battle flags, ceremonial bunting, and, dangling from her bow, an ornamental paper *kusudama* bursting with streamers like a giant upside-down tulip, the destroyer *Yukikaze*, fully dressed in signal flags extending from her bow up to the tip of the mast and then down to her stern, prepared for her first sea trial and shakedown. She would need it. Within two years of launching, she plunged into total, unrestricted warfare in the deadliest conflict the world has ever seen. The ferocity of World War II could never have been anticipated.

Guests and dignitaries received two commemorative postcards at *Yukikaze*'s launching, packaged together in a neat decorative envelope. The first is a highly stylized depiction of *Yukikaze* sliding down the slipway (see Figure 1.1). The image evokes a sense of technological progress more than it does a war machine designed to break bones and boats. *Yukikaze*'s bluff red bow looks as if she's on rails, heading inexorably into a limitless, preordained future. Snowflakes float and swirl around her, much as her name, *Yukikaze*, evoked. From her bowsprit, the *hinomaru*, or Japanese national flag, and the *kyokujitsuki*, or the rising sun flag (battle ensign of the Imperial Navy), also wave proudly in the wind, a reminder of the national obligations that transcended the cosmopolitan artistic trends that inspired the postcard's unknown artist. It's nationalistic, but not overly so: it's more celebratory.

Figure 1.1 The postcard reads: "In commemoration of the destroyer *Yukikaze*'s launch." March 24, 1939. Sasebo Naval Arsenal (author's collection).

The second postcard depicts *Yukikaze* under way, with thick lines and rich colors more akin to traditional Japanese woodblock printmaking than to early-twentieth-century Italian futurism. In this postcard, snow blankets the destroyer, a little reminiscent of a winter scene by Utagawa Hiroshige, the Edo-period master. She charges through heavy seas in a snowstorm surrounded by frothing whitecaps, the black exhaust from her funnel blending with the gathering dark clouds in the sky. The rising sun battle flag flutters from her transom (see Figure 1.2). Together, the two postcards

Figure 1.2 The commemorative postcard reads the same as the one in Figure 1.1 (author's collection).

are optimistic, almost light spirited. Nothing in them hinted at the havoc the little warship would unleash in the Pacific in some two years, or the trials and tragedies that would be reciprocated on her by her enemies.

Indeed, nobody fathomed on that early spring day in 1939 that *Yukikaze* would become known as Japan's "unsinkable destroyer," but only after she had survived some of the most harrowing naval warfare of World War II. She was part of what naval historian Samuel Eliot Morison labeled Japan's "perimeter of steel,"[1] a formidable armada of warships designed to defend its southern oceanic empire of natural resources, particularly oil, from Allied attempts to reclaim it. Her role in the world was a violent one, and her history belies her quaint depictions on those two commemorative postcards.

Over the course of the war, *Yukikaze* sailed nearly everywhere in the Pacific. The warship escorted troops during the invasion of the Philippines and launched torpedoes at Allied cruisers at the Battle of the Java Sea. She escorted Midway invasion forces, screened the aircraft carrier *Zuikaku* during the Battle of the Santa Cruz Islands, and her main guns blazed and torpedo tubes hissed during the ferocious night fighting that occurred in the waters around Guadalcanal.

4

Yukikaze fought almost always at night in the Solomon Campaign, including at the Battle of Kolombangara, where by moonlight she and other warships launched Type 93 torpedoes to devastating effect against Allied cruisers. She guarded valuable assets, including Kawasaki-style refueling tankers at the Battle of the Philippine Sea, and tangled with escort carriers twice her size at Leyte Gulf. She escorted flattops, including the super-carrier *Shinano*, when torpedoes struck the carrier and sank her. *Yukikaze* battled submarines and aircraft as well, in numerous locations throughout the Western Pacific, and with several different commanders, each of whom had his own style and all of whom survived the war, much like their destroyer did.

On April 7, 1945, she escorted *Yamato* on the battleship's final suicide mission. A famous US Navy photograph shows *Yamato* vaporizing into a mushroom cloud after sustaining repeated torpedo and bomb hits from hundreds of US aircraft that descended upon the behemoth. *Yukikaze* is the destroyer holding station just to the left, her bow facing the explosion (see Figure 1.3). The photograph speaks volumes about the intrepid little warship. She fought until the bitter end. No longer is her bow facing a limitless horizon, as depicted in her commemorative postcard; now she faces certain defeat and an uncertain future. For the Imperial Japanese Navy, the war was over in that explosive moment, even if the war's story still required two bigger mushroom clouds for it yet to truly be over.

After Japan surrendered, engineers removed *Yukikaze*'s two amidships quadruple torpedo launchers, the two remaining twin 12.7 cm (5-inch) .50 caliber Type 3 naval guns, and the over twenty-five double and triple 25 mm Type 96 antiaircraft mounts and transformed the warship into a toothless refugee transporter, as thousands of demilitarized Japanese troops fled the once-occupied territories of the Greater East Asia Co-Prosperity Sphere. She brought home hungry, desperate, and disheveled men in droves in this manner, with makeshift living quarters erected on her deck, traveling to Rabaul, Saigon, Bangkok, and Okinawa, as well as the eastern coast of Guangdong and the southwestern coast of Liaoning in China.

On July 6, 1947, after designated war reparations, she departed Nagaura Bay bound for Shanghai. As she cleared the breakwater, her white wake fanning outward in the blue water behind her, the crew heard shouts of "Banzai!" and "Japan's best ship!" from yard workers ashore. It proved her last sortie for Japan, but not her last sortie as a warship. As the newly

Figure 1.3 The explosion of battleship *Yamato* on April 7, 1945. *Yukikaze* (Snowy Wind) is the first vessel on the left, then *Hatsushimo* (First Frost) and *Fuyutsuki* (Winter Moon). Official US Navy Photograph, National Archives, Catalog #: 80-G-413914.

renamed *Dan Yang*, she became a cold warrior for the Republic of China, serving for decades after the evacuation of the Nationalists to Taiwan.

Scuttlebutt has it that, after the war, the US Navy had initially drawn *Yukikaze* as war reparations, but acquiesced that the Nationalist Chinese needed her more. Despite her weapons and combat systems being hopelessly outdated, the loving care lavished upon her by her crew caused this ship, even with her systems nearing obsolescence, to be carefully maintained and combat ready. When Allied officers overseeing the transfer ceremony at the Shanghai Wharf inspected the warship, one allegedly remarked, "I've never seen a naval vessel from a defeated nation in this kind of impeccable order!"[2] When the Nationalists succumbed to the Chinese Communist Party and evacuated mainland China for Taiwan in 1949, *Yukikaze* fled with Generalissimo Chiang Kai-shek. Ultimately, she was scrapped in 1970.

At the outbreak of World War II, the Imperial Navy had eighty-two Special Type and First Class destroyers, of which *Yukikaze* was one (Map 1.1).

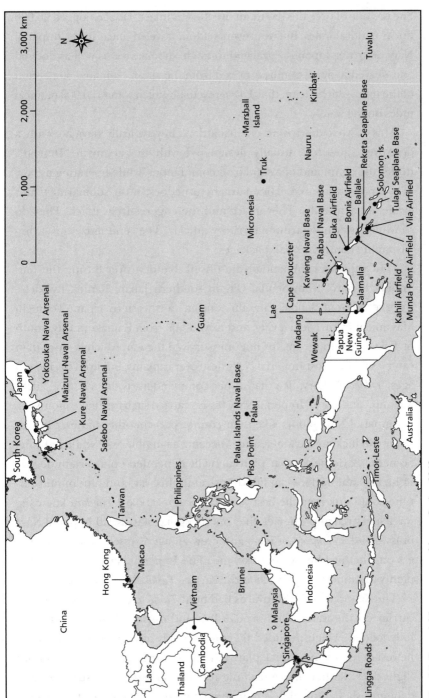

Map 1.1 Imperial Japanese naval bases, Spring 1943

She was one of precious few to survive the war intact. *Yukikaze* logged 96,000 linear nautical miles. But destroyers seldom traveled linear miles. Imperial Navy destroyer captains zigzagged to evade submarines, as well as dodged and weaved to avoid bombs dropped from the air an estimated 30 percent of the time, which meant that *Yukikaze* actually sailed some 120,000 nautical miles on the water.

This is what destroyers do in battle. They typically navigate with a destroyer squadron, usually designated with the acronym "Desron," under the command of a squadron commander, while operating as part of a larger task force. They launch torpedoes, hunt submarines, and evade aerial assaults. They guard and then aggressively attack. They do so while covering maritime territory quickly. They epitomize the saying "dynamite comes in small packages."

Four captains commanded the unsinkable destroyer during the war: Tobida Kenjirō, from Sendai City in southern Japan; Kanma Ryōkichi, from a different Sendai City, this one in northeastern Japan; Terauchi Masamichi from Tochigi City; and Koyō Keiji, from Kamakura City, south of Tokyo. The four captains not only survived the war, which is more than can be said for most Imperial Navy destroyer captains, but lived to ripe old ages. *Yukikaze*'s story, like that of her commanders, is the tale of a "lucky warship," and not all Imperial Navy vessels carried such fortunate monikers.

Imperial Navy sailors, like their counterparts in other navies, came to believe in luck on the water, and it became a tangible asset while fighting. Sometimes, desperate war plans actually depended on a certain degree of luck. Naval warfare can be whimsical in this way, and random misfortune could sink even the best warships. Sailors aboard *Yukikaze* knew she was a lucky warship – in fact, they openly spoke of it, as did Imperial Navy brass – and *Yukikaze*'s officers and crew always assessed new commanders on whether they were lucky, too. The Imperial Navy commissioned plenty of unlucky ships, such as the carrier *Taihō*: they never lasted long.

The Kawasaki Kobe Shipyards had built *Taihō* to be the most powerful carrier on the water. She was 855 feet and displaced over 37,000 tons fully loaded, which included 65 combat-ready aircraft. She sported the newest defenses and a thick plate of high-tensile steel covered her entire flight deck. Rather than a teak flight deck – elegant to be sure, but also dangerously flammable – engineers painted a thick coat of latex over the steel deck covering. Engineers designed her to survive the kind of aerial pummeling that decimated the flattops at Midway. *Yukikaze* had escorted *Taihō* during her shakedown at Tawi-Tawi Island in the southern Philippines. Her officers and crew knew the flattop well.

But the carrier proved woefully unlucky. The US submarine *Albacore* fatally holed her with a single torpedo on June 19, 1944, at the Battle of the Philippine Sea. Imperial Navy planners had meant for *Taihō* to serve as the centerpiece of a newly constructed Combined Fleet, one that could halt the Allied advance in the Mariana Islands. Instead, she sank ingloriously, six and a half hours after her torpedo hit, blown apart by two massive internal explosions, a result of design flaws.

In his novel *Citadel in Spring*, Imperial Navy veteran Agawa Hiroyuki described the carnage aboard *Taihō* when she exploded and sank. In the galley, one sailor had the "bone of a broken leg, jutting up like a crutch,"[3] with "pieces of dark red flesh adhering to it." One sailor's head had "split open like a pomegranate, wedged between the door and the jamb." As sailors abandoned the stricken flattop, their open wounds throbbed in the seawater. Nonetheless, *Taihō*'s demise was relatively peaceful: the "forty-four-thousand ton vessel thrust its stern up into space and slipped beneath the waves in a twinkle of an eye." With her sank the Imperial Navy's dreams of winning a decisive battle against the US Navy before Saipan fell and US bombers could reach the home islands and burn them to the ground. It was good to be a lucky warship in World War II.

"Really,"[4] wrote Itō Masanori, a respected wartime journalist and author of numerous books on the Imperial Navy, including the one that has guided my story, *Yukikaze*'s history remains "miraculous in the entire world of naval warfare." It was a miraculous career indeed. It begs the question of the boat biographer, though: where should we start in telling her story?

* * *

I start with her name. "Snowy wind" is weather that should not be confused with a blizzard. In the Imperial Navy, there was an entire class of destroyers called *Fubuki*, or the Blizzard class. They were built about a decade before *Yukikaze* and her sister ships, between 1926 and 1932. Armed with three twin-mounted 5-inch guns and sporting a flat foc's'le and flared deck, the boats sliced through even the heaviest seas and delivered a serious punch. In historian Morison's estimation, in their day they "led the world's navies in design and armament."[5]

Mutsuki, or the Harmonious Moon class, had preceded them, a name that refers to the first month of the Lunar Calendar. Japan had followed the Lunar Calendar until the Meiji Restoration of 1868, when the country modernized along Western lines. *Hatsuharu,* or the Early Spring class, succeeded the *Fubuki* vessels. After these vessels came the *Shiratsuyu,* or the White Dew class, built until 1937. Then came the *Asashio,* or the Morning Tide class, built for only two years between 1937 and 1939. There is an entire pantheon of Japanese destroyers and many with elegant names, but none celebrated more accomplishments on the water, or more elegant names for that matter, than the *Kagerō,* or the Gossamer class, of which *Yukikaze* was one of nineteen built.

There is a lot to a warship name, and Japan's naming practices reveal something important about Japanese culture, particularly in wartime. The Imperial Navy named destroyers after weather or atmospheric phenomena, ones often with classical poetic references. They named battleships after ancient provinces, or on occasion ancient references to Japan itself, such as *Fusō* or *Yamato.* They named heavy cruisers, such as *Atago* and *Chōkai,* after mountains and light cruisers after rivers and streams. Atago is a mountain near Kyoto with a Shinto shrine where the local avatar protects Kyoto from fire, for example. Chōkai is an active volcano in northeastern Japan. *Atago* was also a *Takao*-class heavy cruiser that the US submarine *Darter* holed prior to Leyte Gulf. It had served as Rear Admiral Kurita Takeo's flagship, and he ended up swimming for his life. *Chōkai* was scuttled following the Battle off Samar, also part of the Leyte operation. In essence, the Combined Fleet, with black smoke belching from its stacks, became a steel maritime reflection of Japan's divine landscape, one rooted in Shintoism.

Two years before Sasebo launched *Yukikaze,* the Education Ministry launched a campaign to highlight Japan's "unparalleled national polity"[6] by tying it to the natural landscape. The *Cardinal Principles of the National Polity,* a highly nativist text, wove Japan's "beautiful nature not seen in other countries" together with its people's unique "national essence." While "Natural features overpower India, and in the West one senses that man subjugates nature," the Japanese lived in "constant harmony with nature." So did their warships, apparently, given their names. Even on the blue expanse of the high seas, the Imperial Navy became a reflection of an exceptional landscape, over which the Emperor reigned supreme. Such names reminded sailors of Japan's unique qualities, the lofty nature of their sacred cause, and their spiritual invincibility on the battlefield. They must have thought, hopefully, that some of the Emperor's divinity rubbed off on them.

Japanese destroyer names linked ships to a divine landscape, and were wistful and poetic, even ephemeral – they named things that were temporary, not long for this world. They reflected the inherent change in the natural world, much like their wavy reflection on the water. They evoked a sense of impermanence, as fleeting as white dew or snowy wind. To this day they evoke a wistful, melancholic quality, even though they were machines of war and unleashed unspeakable terror on the water.

In this manner, destroyer names evoke traditions of Japanese aesthetics that, more than national anthems and flags, tied all Japanese to a common past. To be Japanese is to know this aesthetic, to feel it reverberate inside ancient words that move through the centuries and into one's conscious through shared learning. They evoked connections to Heian-period (794–1185) notions of *mono no aware*, a sensibility that evokes the "melancholic nature of things." *Mono no aware* defined early Japanese poetry, a Buddhist-inspired notion born from the fleetingness of life. Early Buddhism taught that we know only one truth in life – that it's impermanent, and therefore painful – and this melancholy colored Heian life in dark, broody hues. The names of Japanese destroyers conjure this sentiment as well.

Admittedly, *Fubuki*, or a Blizzard, can be dangerous. It's true that not all atmospheric phenomena are wistful and poetic; but still, most Japanese destroyer names evoke scenes of impermanence, beautiful precisely because they are not long for the world. Japanese didn't name their destroyers things like "typhoon" or "tsunami" because the names were never meant to conjure the destruction they could unleash. Unlike a howling blizzard, snowy wind evokes the sense of a late fall day, when blustery winds bring intermittent snowflakes, a signal that winter is coming. It signifies cyclical change: renewal, life, and death. Nothing is stable for long in the world. The Chinese classic *Book of Changes* saw change as the fundamental pattern of the universe. Similarly, the Buddha said, "All compounded things are subject to decay." This proved particularly true of Imperial Navy destroyers during World War II.

Seasonal change and ephemerality have long been poignant emotions in Japanese culture, and served as a frequent theme in classical poetry. Starting in the Heian period, court poets often wrote in *kana* rather than *kanji* script, purposefully choosing a vernacular Japanese rather than classical Chinese style. The *kana* script encouraged a largely native Japanese poetics, which became common in *waka*, a thirty-one-syllable form. In large part, destroyer names conjured this native vernacular, and naval yard workers customarily painted their names in *kana*. Just to name two, *Shiratsuyu*, or White Dew, was a destroyer constructed in the Sasebo Naval Yard and launched in May 1935, four years before *Yukikaze*. Heian poets frequently meditated on white dew because of its impermanence. Few things are more ephemeral in this world than a delicate drop of dew. Certainly, this poem from a tenth-century anthology evokes this idea.

> If the white dew must vanish,
> let it vanish:
> even if it stayed
> no one would care
> to make it a string of gems.[7]

Similarly, a poetry competition from the Kamakura period featured the theme of another destroyer, *Shigure*, or Autumn Showers. Poets in the competition wrote their poetry inspired by the evocative word. The Uraga Dock Company built *Shigure* and launched her in 1936. The warship celebrated a distinguished service record until January 1945 when the US submarine *Blackfin* torpedoed her. Today, she rests quietly at the bottom of the Gulf of Siam; but poetry on autumn showers resonated with Japanese readers.

> When winter comes
> the oak leaves
> in the garden scattered

echo the autumn showers
in a village by the foothills.[8]

The *Kagerō* destroyers evoked these native Japanese sensibilities as well, with celebrated vessels such as *Amatsukaze*, or Celestial Wind, *Isokaze*, or Seashore Breeze, and *Tokitsukaze*, Favorable Breeze. In fact, you need to be either a meteorologist or an expert in classical poetry to know the differences between a Sea Breeze (*Urakaze*), a Beach Wind (*Hamakaze*), a Seashore Breeze, a Favorable Breeze, a First Wind (*Hatsukaze*), and a Valley Wind (*Tanikaze*), all names of *Kagerō* vessels. Similarly, you need training in tidal sciences and Japan's offshore currents to discern the differences between a Black Tide (*Kuroshio*), a Father Current (*Oyashio*), a Swift Tide (*Hayashio*), and a Summer Tide (*Natsushio*) – again, all names of *Kagerō* destroyers.

The name *Kagerō* itself, though written with different *kanji* characters when referring to destroyers, is a homonym for one of the most famous diaries of the Heian period – the *Kagerō nikki*, or *The Mayfly Diary* or *Gossamer Years*, depending on the translator – the dark, broody lament of a lonely aristocratic woman who lived in Kyoto in the tenth century. The third volume contains the melancholic line "The snowy wind, unspeakable weather and so dark,"[9] illustrating the unsettling place of "snowy wind" in Heian writing. The author experienced the weather during an autumn visit to the Kamo Shrine in Kyoto, a "miserable trip" during which time she "caught cold and languished in bed." This is the genesis of *Yukikaze*'s name.

By the late eighteenth century, a handful of Japanese scholars had started rejecting traditional Chinese learning and imported Buddhism, submitting that only by reading early vernacular poetry written in *kana* could Japanese commune with the native Shinto deities of the divine land. Some words proved more powerful than others, moreover, and these became known as *kotodama*, or "spirit words." Scholar Kamo Mabuchi, the son of a Kyoto Shinto priest, wrote that "Yamato, the several islands that have been transmitted to us, is the country blessed with the language of the gods."[10] Motoori Norinaga, another nativist scholar, called such early writings, the very ones evoked by later destroyer names, the "scripture of the gods." Soon, such spirit words became inexorably tied to early forms of imperial nationalism. Indeed, you would be wrong if you concluded that such "spirit words" proved less nationalistic than the masculine bombast of flags, drums, and trumpets. Often, they proved more so.

Destroyer names often resembled the "language of the gods" or the "scripture of the gods," linking sailors to the aesthetics of imperial nationalism, and they proved just as ephemeral. Famously, Admiral Yamamoto Isoroku, on the eve of the Pearl Harbor operation, had cautioned the prime minister that Japan's naval victories would be ephemeral, too. "If you insist on my going ahead,"[11] he warned, "I can promise to give them hell for a year or a year and a half, but can guarantee nothing as to what will happen after that." The admiral proved prophetic as usual. As the war ground on, mercilessly, this sense of impermanence began permeating the cultural fabric of the Imperial Navy as a decisive battle with the US Navy became more elusive. Initially, Japanese victories in the Central and Western Pacific led some observers to diagnose the navy with what they called "victory disease" within the ranks, an infection that culminated with the Japanese defeat at the Battle of Midway in early June 1942. Basically, Japan had come to expect victories on the water. But that soon changed.

With four fleet carriers lost, the fever of the "victory disease" broke after Midway. Then, slowly but noticeably, new spirit words began to enter the Imperial Navy's cultural lexicon, ones that again tapped sensibilities of impermanence. Historically resonant phrases such as "special assault" and "floating chrysanthemum" operations, references to forms of ritual suicide steeped in samurai traditions and imperial nationalism, began to appear attached to naval orders, none grimmer than the final run of battleship *Yamato*. As referenced by Kamo Mabuchi above, the battleship had been named after the Japanese islands themselves. When she got under way for Okinawa in Operation Ten-Gō, or "Heaven-One," war planners had designated hers a special assault operation and Imperial Navy Headquarters ordered that she be given only enough fuel for a one-way trip. It hardly mattered. Most of the holding facilities in its tank farm were long since empty anyway. But, in Japanese culture there is nobility in this kind of futility and failure – long live the tragic hero! – and *Yamato* certainly captures this ethos.

Some scholars, such as Ivan Morris, have linked the "nobility of failure" to traditions of radical Confucianism, where demonstrations of sincerity of the heart, an important virtue, weighed heavier than actual success, even in battle. Many Japanese respect sincere losers more than opportunistic winners. In Japan's samurai traditions, Minamoto Yoshitsune remains an object of adoration, even though his brother, Yoritomo, became the first Kamakura shogun in 1185. Brutally, the latter had forced his younger brother Yoshitsune to commit ritual suicide. Nobody would ever question Yoshitsune's sincerity, willing as he proved to die for it, as well as for his brother's rule. *Yamato*, too – symbol of the entire nation; named after the divine land – oozed sincerity from her every bulkhead and carried such pure motives on her massive, reinforced hull. "Ours is the signal honor of being the nation's bulwark,"[12] mused Ensign Yoshida Mitsuru, a young sailor aboard *Yamato* who survived her final mission. "One day we must prove ourselves worthy."

He did, and *Yamato*'s wreckage now rests quietly at Latitude 30° 22' 0.0016" N and Longitude 128° 4' 0.0016" E. Her barnacle-encrusted hulk still captures the imagination of millions. But her cause was lost before she ever shot a single shell in anger.

* * *

Building these Imperial Navy warships came at the expenditure of mountains of national treasure. When the navy lost destroyers such as *Shiratsuyu* and *Shigure*, cruisers such as *Atago* and *Chōkai*, battleships such as *Fusō* and *Yamato*, and fleet carriers such as *Taihō* and *Shinano*, it proved not only demoralizing and strategically disastrous for the Imperial Navy, but ruinous for the nation. Warships are expensive to build and maintain, and represent multigenerational investments, but they are indispensable for empire building and national defense, particularly for an island nation. It is estimated that *Yamato* cost approximately ¥137,802,000 to build, while *Nagato* cost ¥43,900,000.

The Meiji regime came to this realization, if slowly. Two powerful slogans drove Japan's Meiji period (1868–1912), when the country abandoned its feudal past in favor of becoming a modern nation, with an empire of its own. The first, *bunmei kaika*, or "civilization and enlightenment," symbolized Japan's embrace of Western notions of historical progress and culture, from the Gregorian calendar and clock time to beer and the writings of John Stuart Mill. The second, *fukoku kyōhei*, or "rich country and strong military," represented the importance of privileging an industrial economy over an agrarian one in order to support an army and navy, ones capable of empire building. In the early Meiji years, the Imperial Army received the lion's share of national attention. Indeed, until the Sino-Japanese War in 1895, Meiji leaders exhibited scant interest in becoming a great maritime power. One historian has labeled this period under the direction of the Military Ministry the "army first, navy second"[13] stage of Japan's military development. Mainly, the Meiji regime concerned itself with strengthening its hold on power, not projecting power overseas. This meant conscripting an Imperial Army to maintain domestic order.

In 1893, the year the Imperial Navy came into its own, Japan's countryside shouldered 85 percent of the total tax burden. The toil of farmers built these warships and armed them. One Imperial Navy postcard noted that, alongside ballistics information, a single shell for *Nagato* cost ¥4,250, which would have nearly tripled what an urban worker made annually in 1935. It exceeded seven times what farmers brought in annually. The government taxed the countryside into a place of filth and squalor to build and arm these warships. Often, farmers sold their daughters to textile mills and brothels, only to have them sent home with tuberculosis. Fukuzawa Yukichi, the leading intellectual of his times, observed, in the early Meiji period, "The purpose [of government] seems to be to use the fruits of rural labor to make flowers for Tokyo."[14] Had he lived a decade longer, he might have said "to make warships for the Imperial Navy," such was the high percentage of national expenditures that went to the navy budget.

Unsurprisingly, the countryside carried the burden of conscription, too, what farmers referred to as the "blood tax." The Meiji regime, tapping into European traditions that dated to the French Revolution, submitted that, "If people want freedom, they must take part in military service." Farmers paid a high price for this freedom and, before long, rumors swirled in the countryside that the Imperial Army "will draft young men, hang them upside down, and draw out their blood so that Westerners can drink it."[15] Riots and disturbances rocked the Meiji countryside, nearly 200 such incidents by one count, as a result of excessive taxes and conscription, a hallmark of the bumpy transition to imperial power after 1868.

But the Imperial Navy always relied less on conscription than the Imperial Army did, and so had a different flavor. In 1874, 90 percent of the cadets at the Hyōbushō, the early naval academy, hailed from samurai backgrounds. But still, the Imperial Navy sought anyone "who desired a naval career, regardless of their social and geographical origin,"[16] and implemented an entrance examination to lure in talented young men. By 1891, commoners constituted 21 percent of naval cadets. A decade later, that number had risen to 34 percent. It was a veritable meritocracy.

In 1871, the Meiji government split the umbrella Military Ministry into the Army Ministry and the Navy Ministry. That year, the Imperial Navy commanded 14 warships, manned by over 1,500 personnel, with a total displacement of over 12,000 tons. In 1885, the Meiji government issued wildly popular public bonds to expand the navy. Two years later, even the Imperial family donated generously to the bond effort. Nonetheless, in 1893, on the eve of the First Sino-Japanese War, the Imperial Navy budget was a mere half that of the army, and under 1 percent of the national budget.

But 1893 was a banner year for the Imperial Navy. In that year, it established its own General Staff, one independent from the army. There were objections from the army, of course. One Imperial Army staffer quipped, "the army has been the mainstay of Japan and the navy is an aid to it … The army decides the fate of Japan."[17] But war overseas changed that terrestrial mindset; so did the Imperial Navy's advocacy of the "southern advance" campaign. The southern advance strategy gave the Imperial Navy a raison d'être in a larger, philosophical sense. In 1893, the Colonization Society pitched that, "If Japan wants to secure command of the seas, Japan must extend her trade routes,"[18] and this meant "strengthening her navy." Soon, the navy received as much as the army from national coffers, often far more.

The first battle test of the Imperial Navy came when it confronted China's modern Northern Fleet in the Battle of the Yellow Sea in September 1894. The impressive Northern Fleet had visited Yokohama only four years earlier, and China's maritime progress startled gawking Japanese. In the battle, the Imperial Navy sank eight of ten Chinese warships at the mouth of the Yalu River and then finished the job at Weihaiwei in early 1895. The victory proved decisive. It intoxicated the public and demonstrated to the Meiji government the importance of a modern fleet for national security and protecting Japan's newly acquired colonial interests. The warships also became objects of nationalistic veneration. Many Japanese knew these ships by name.

By 1898, Imperial Navy expenditures exceeded army ones, and represented some 26 percent of the national budget. In the coming decades, Imperial Army and Navy budgets fluctuated, but, as the navy nurtured ties to the Seiyūkai Party and pushed the southern advance campaign, it enjoyed a larger portion of the budgetary pie. It also benefited from ties to Satchō men – predominantly ex-samurai from Satsuma, Chōshū, and other powerful feudal domains – who had orchestrated the overthrow of the Tokugawa shoguns in 1868.

In 1905, in the Battle of Tsushima Strait, Admiral Tōgō Heihachirō, with the "help of heaven and providence,"[19] destroyed the Russian Baltic Fleet after months of indecisive fighting near Port Arthur, securing Japan's victory in the Russo-Japanese War. The Imperial Navy paraded the handsome Tōgō and the glorious fleet in front of the Meiji emperor and the public, orchestrating nothing less than a public relations coup. The Imperial Navy became Japan's salvation, and its ships celebrities. Echoing the discontent over the settlement of the Russo-Japanese War in Portsmouth, New Hampshire, for which President Theodore Roosevelt won a Nobel Peace Prize, one Japanese newspaper trumpeted, "If Japan has failed in diplomacy, the glorious navy has done more than make up for such failings."[20] The next year, the Japanese public celebrated its first Navy Day, an official holiday.

In the navy budget, warship construction represented a substantial portion, and overseas developments often drove Japanese warship development and construction. After the British built the battlecruiser *Invincible* in 1907, for example, Japanese engineers set out to build a superior version of the new fast ocean fighter. But, before the ink had dried on Japan's battlecruiser drawings, the newly launched *Lion* had outclassed *Invincible*. In 1910, the Imperial Navy decided to hire the British naval architect George Thurston to design the first *Kongō*-class battlecruiser, and Vickers Shipbuilding and Engineering, a British company founded in 1871, built the prototype at their shipyard at Barrow. By having *Kongō* built overseas, Japanese engineers could learn the newest in hull design, weaponry, and shipbuilding techniques. She was launched in May 1912. Her sister ships, starting with *Hiei,* Japanese shipyard workers built in home ports. That same year, the Kure Naval Arsenal laid the hull for the battleship *Fusō,* with her six twin 356 mm (14-inch) gun turrets and, after 1933 refits, towering pagoda bridge. Her profile is striking, some say ugly: she looked like a preying mantis. But all agreed she could deliver one hell of a broadside.

In 1912, Japan's shipyards built some of the most famous battlecruisers and battleships of the Imperial Navy, while its budget was 15 percent of national expenditures. By 1917, when the Kure Naval Arsenal laid down the hull for *Nagato,* the navy budget was a full 22 percent of the national budget and towered over Imperial Army expenditures that year. *Nagato* had four twin 41 cm (16-inch) naval guns that fired a Type 91, 1,020 kilogram (2,250 pound) armor-piercing shell over 20 miles – one every 21 seconds. That's about the weight of a 2021 Toyota Prius. Admiral Yamamoto had cut his teeth aboard the cruiser *Nisshin* at the Battle of Tsushima, where Japan sank Russia's Baltic Fleet. Despite being the "father of naval aviation," he always expressed an affinity for capital ships. Not surprisingly, he hoisted his flag aboard *Nagato* on occasion.

The battleship *Nagato* saw no action at Pearl Harbor with Yamamoto's flag aboard, but did cover the withdrawal of the carrier task force as it raced back to the safety of the Western Pacific. The battleship was at the Battle of Midway, but didn't see any action there, either. Later, she fended off aircraft at the Battle of the Philippine Sea. *Nagato* mostly found herself moored or anchored in home waters until the Battle of Leyte Gulf, where she first unmasked her big guns in combat. Like most Japanese battleships, she was named after an ancient Japanese province. The ancient provinces, unlike today's prefectures, evoke a strong sense of imperial authority. Nagato Province is located on the southernmost tip of the main island of Honshu, near the strategically important Shimonoseki Strait, where the Sino-Japanese War was concluded by treaty.

Nagato was the only Japanese battleship to survive the war, but the US military chose to use her, along with a handful of other warships, as a target during Operation Crossroads, a series of nuclear tests at

Bikini Atoll in mid 1946. The US battlewagon *Nevada* met her inglorious fate together with *Nagato* at this Pacific radioactive wasteland. A US Navy crew under the command of W. J. Whipple limped the neglected dreadnought to the atoll at ten knots, her hull leaking like a sieve. *Nagato* sank after the second nuclear blast, the underwater Test Baker, on July 29, 1946. That night, she listed, and finally rolled over and sank. In so many ways, her radioactive demolition symbolized the fate of Japan as well, as her biographer, the novelist Agawa Hiroyuki, cleverly recognized.

Some, such as Japan's Navy Minister Katō Tomosaburō, saw such reactionary warship building as a recipe for disaster. Given its natural resources, he reasoned, Japan could never hope to compete with the US in warship construction. Even with private companies, such as Mitsubishi and Kawasaki, investing in shipyards, they couldn't keep pace with the resource-rich United States. The two ingredients most essential to warship construction were high-grade steel and oil, and Japan had neither.

In 1917, 90 percent of Japan's steel came from the United States. Katō believed that Japan's inability to construct ships at the pace of the United States would "create such a disparity"[21] as to reduce the Pacific Ocean to an "American lake." It didn't until 1945, but this sense of desperation, that Japan needed to do something, and do something quickly, to counter the threat posed by the United States, became an ever-present theme in the build up to war. From Japan's side, the war always had the flavor of being a war of desperation, a desperate need for steel and oil, which is a major thread woven through *Yukikaze*'s war.

Katō's concerns made it necessary that Japan participate in the Washington Naval Treaty of 1921, a post-World War I warship-reduction regime designed to stem a naval arms race among the Great Powers. Katō believed, correctly, that the agreement would put the brakes on Japan's naval race with the United States, making the situation less desperate. Importantly for the next chapter, the stipulations in the Washington Naval Treaty established the international framework for warship design and construction around the world, including in Japan. Nowhere were the influences of the agreement on naval engineering seen more visibly than in destroyer design.

* * *

In the late nineteenth and early twentieth centuries, Alfred T. Mahan, a US Navy officer and historian, ruled the waves of strategic thinking on both sides of the Pacific. Famously, in his *The Influence of Sea Power upon History, 1660–1783*, published in 1890, he emphasized the importance of the "decisive battle" between adversaries, and he quickly became a favorite on course syllabi both at Japan's prestigious Etajima Naval Academy and at the US Naval Academy in Annapolis, Maryland. In his writings, Mahan emphasized decisive battles and blockades, and such thinking drove the procurement practices and strategic thinking of the Imperial Navy. The colossal twins *Musashi* and *Yamato* serve as the ultimate artifacts of this belief in a battle of annihilation with the US Navy, as the carriers *Taihō* and *Shinano* did later in the war.

In some respects, Imperial Navy planners had good reason to adhere to this doctrine. After all, Admiral Tōgō, hero of the Russo-Japanese War (1904–1905), had destroyed the Russian Baltic Fleet at Tsushima in the mother of all decisive battles aboard the battleship *Mikasa*, securing Japan's victory in 1905. It was textbook naval warfare, a classic crossing of the "T" with big battleships slugging it out. Eventually, such thinking led Admiral Yamamoto to his fateful decision to lure the US Navy into an engagement at Midway, and Admiral Chester W. Nimitz shrewdly obliged.

The Etajima Naval Academy would have benefited from balancing its curriculum with the British strategist Julian Stafford Corbett. In *Some Principles of Maritime Strategy*, published in 1911, he pointed out that "Command of the sea ... means nothing but the control of maritime communications, whether for commercial or military purposes,"[22] not necessarily victory in a decisive battle. Indeed, the "object of naval warfare" lay not in the "faith" of a decisive battle, but rather in the "control of communications" – by which he meant the importance of securing shipping lanes. After the war, the US Strategic Bombing Survey concurred, acknowledging that Japan had been "desperately vulnerable to attack on its shipping."[23] Indeed, "Japan's geographical situation determined that the Pacific war should in large measure be a war for control of the sea and to insure control of the sea." Yet, the Imperial Navy remained fixated throughout the war on fighting Mahan-style decisive battles.

Japan had started the war with 6 million tons of merchant shipping of over 500 tons gross weight. (To put this in some context, a 32-foot Nordic Tug pleasure boat weighs about 25 gross tons. A World War II PT Boat, like President John F. Kennedy's *PT-109*, weighed about 300 gross tons. By contrast, the *Oasis of the Seas*, a new Royal Caribbean Cruise ship, weighs 226,838 gross tons.) It then gained an additional 4 million over the course of the war. Of the 10 million tons of shipping, nearly 9 million tons were "sunk or so seriously damaged as to be out of action at the end of the war," noted the US Strategic Bombing Survey. By the end of the war, Japan possessed little more than 10 percent of its former shipping tonnage. Imperial Navy planners pinned the entirety of their war strategy on a decisive battle, and failed to invest in the defense of the territories and shipping channels they had secured at such high cost. In many ways, the story of the two unlucky carriers, *Taihō* and *Shinano*, encapsulates this narrative. They never had a chance.

As the war in the Pacific ground to a conclusion, the conflict revolved around destroying Japan's merchant shipping, tankers, and troop transports, and *Yukikaze*, as always, navigated right in the thick of this oil-covered water.

CHAPTER 2

Torpedoes, Destroyers, and Samurai of the Seas

Torpedo-attack warfare seemed to agree with the character of Japanese sailors
Rear Admiral Tanaka Raizō, the torpedo maestro

YUKIKAZE WAS A DESTROYER, and to appreciate the role of destroyers in World War II we next turn to the history of destroyer design and engineering. We end this discussion with *Yukikaze*'s design, specifically. Many credit the Imperial Navy for having invented the first destroyer, a vessel named *Kotaka*, or Little Hawk. Whether that is true or not, the Imperial Navy certainly understood the effectiveness of these agile little warships. Crucially, the emergence of the destroyer paralleled the emergence of the torpedo. Indeed, not long after its debut, the torpedo became the principal weapon of Imperial Navy destroyers. Eventually, what was first called *Der Küstenbrander*, or "coastal fire ship," emerged as one of the more deadly weapons in World War II, whether delivered from destroyers, cruisers, submarines, or aircraft.

The Imperial Navy began studying complex torpedo tactics as early as the Battle of Port Arthur in the Russo-Japanese War of 1905. In this battle, Japanese destroyers slipped into the Russian harbor under cloak of darkness and launched their torpedoes, to admittedly mixed results. But planners saw the potential. By World War II, the Imperial Navy had become expert at torpedo warfare, as evidenced by two battles in particular. *Yukikaze* participated in neither, so I treat them separately in this chapter – the Battle of Tassafaronga and the Battle of Savo Island, both fought in the waters around Guadalcanal in 1942. Men such as Rear Admiral Tanaka Raizō became legendary in the Solomon Islands for their killer torpedo instincts. These two battles represent clinics in torpedo warfare, and exemplify early Japanese successes on the water.

We end with a look at the Japanese naval engineering that directly led to *Yukikaze*'s construction, specifically destroyer design during the "treaty years," a reference to the Washington Naval Agreement of 1922. Japan's Special Type destroyers became the gold standard for navies around the world. Makino Shigeru, *Yukikaze*'s designer, cut his teeth during the "treaty years," and, even though the Imperial Navy launched *Yukikaze* after the Washington Naval Agreement and its successor agreements had expired, she carried key engineering traits from those years, traits that defined her performance on the water. It wasn't only luck that allowed *Yukikaze* to survive the war. In her day, she represented the pinnacle of destroyer design.

* * *

Destroyers are the smallest of the four principal types of warship that fought on the oceans during World War II (carriers, battleships, and cruisers were the others). She displaced a mere 2,500 tons, while *Yamato*, a super-dreadnaught-class battleship, displaced a whopping 65,000 tons. Nonetheless, destroyers posed serious threats to battleships. Destroyers were lightly armored, but not defenseless by any means. With torpedoes, naval guns, antiaircraft mounts, and depth charges, they carried a diverse array of weapon systems. They were also typically fast and maneuverable. Despite being smaller, in other words, their weapons, specifically their torpedoes, enabled destroyers to wage asymmetric warfare against much larger and better-armored warships.

Interestingly, it was the destroyer that survived World War II to become an indispensable part of today's navies, particularly Japan's Maritime Self-Defense Force. The *Maya*-, *Atago*-, and *Kongō*-class destroyers, for example, all considerably larger than *Yukikaze*, are critical pieces of Japan's maritime defenses. While guided missiles and the Aegis Combat System are the primary weapons of new Japanese destroyers, the emergence of the first destroyers in the nineteenth century paralleled that of the torpedo, an underwater missile of sorts. Consequently, the two must be treated in tandem to fully understand how the destroyer transformed naval warfare.

Basically, the torpedo – aptly called the "Devil's device" by its inventor – revolutionized naval warfare in the nineteenth century because it blew gaping holes in capital ships below the waterline, where they were less armored. Importantly, much smaller, and less expensive, vessels called torpedo boats could deliver the stealthy killers, introducing a style of asymmetric warfare that terrified the admirals of the Great Powers. Originally, naval architects designed destroyers to combat these newly designed torpedo boats, but destroyers later evolved into the Jack-of-all-trades warships.

Early on, the Imperial Navy became attracted to destroyers because their tactics required attributes that Japanese fighting men admired – they required speed, decisiveness, and courage, resembling the legendary fighting prowess of the samurai. In many respects, destroyers relied on battlefield tactics similar to those of the mounted samurai of Japan's medieval period, with warriors dashing to within archery range and then unleashing their arrows on the enemy. In this analogy, destroyers served as mounts and torpedoes as arrows. Often, destroyers fought at night, moreover, catching the enemy by surprise, and they did so with lightning-fast ferocity. These attributes, too, tapped into centuries-old Japanese martial traditions of the *yōuchi*, or "night attack," perhaps none more famous than the bloody finale of the forty-seven rōnin incident. Whereas most US Navy cruisers weren't armed with torpedoes, even Japanese heavy cruisers, such as *Atago* and *Chōkai*, carried quadruple amidships torpedo launchers, and their captains learned to use them to deadly effect. As much as naval aircraft launched from flattops, the effective use of the torpedo came to characterize Japanese naval fighting in World War II.

For a weapon that proved so revolutionary, the torpedo had crude beginnings. Giovanni Luppis, a commander in the Austro-Hungarian Navy, first conceived of *Der Küstenbrander*, or the "coastal fire ship," as a small wooden vessel with a clockwork motor that turned a screw and propelled a pistol-ignited explosive toward its target. Luppis designed the simple device to damage or sink capital ships that ventured near shore to bombard ports or coastal installations. Though clunky, it piqued the curiosity of some Austrian naval officials. But Luppis needed to improve the device, so he visited the prominent marine engineer Robert Whitehead.

Naval engineers had experimented with tethered torpedoes decades before, such as Robert Fulton's designs, but they proved exceedingly difficult to operate. *Der Küstenbrander* was untethered and therefore a dramatic improvement over earlier mobile mines, but the clumsy device still presented obvious limitations, not the least of which was that it lumbered on the surface of the water like a lame duck, making it easy to avoid or shoot out of the water. It also didn't blow a hole below the waterline because it didn't submerge. Not to be dissuaded, in 1864, Luppis decided to visit Whitehead, who had risen to nautical prominence after designing the engines for the Austrian armor-plated frigate *Archduke Ferdinand Maximilian*. Rear Admiral Wilhelm von Tegetthoff had catapulted the warship to stardom by ramming into the Italian Navy's *Re d'Italia* at the Battle of Lissa in 1866. Tegetthoff had even written Whitehead afterwards, "Thanks to your first-class engines I was able to win the Battle of Lissa."[1] Then living in Fiume (Rijeka), Whitehead was the perfect person to consult regarding the possibilities of *Der Küstenbrander*.

Intrigued, Whitehead tried to improve *Der Küstenbrander*, but eventually gave up on the hopelessly clunky device. He did not, however, give up on the idea of a torpedo. The key, Whitehead concluded, was getting the torpedo to travel toward its target underwater. This way, it was stealthier and struck below the waterline, hitting the soft underbellies of the iron-clads. With this principle, he invented his own torpedo. Looking a little like a metal dolphin robot from a 1960s science fiction film, the "Whitehead torpedo," as it became known, was nearly twelve feet long, with a diameter of fourteen inches. It carried its 18 pounds of dynamite at 6 knots and could, with some skill and even more luck, hit its intended target at 200 meters away. In 1868, as Japan began modernizing under the Meiji Emperor, Whitehead managed to stabilize the Devil's device's propensity to whimsically surface and dive with "the secret," as he called it, a rather simple ballast chamber. Impressed enough by Whitehead's torpedo, the Austrian Navy bought manufacturing rights to what they acknowledged was an "imperfect and crude"[2] weapon. But it had potential.

Following the Austrians, the British Royal Navy conducted its own trials of Whitehead's torpedo near Sheerness in 1870. The demonstration occurred aboard the paddlewheel *Oberon*, and Whitehead insisted on the utmost secrecy. As the chairman of the Royal Navy's evaluation committee noted, "As Mr Whitehead had not patented his invention, he was desirous that everything connected therewith should be kept as secret as possible." Earlier in life, Whitehead had had bad experiences with patent offices in Italy. For this reason, the evaluation committee was kept in the dark as to the torpedo's inner workings. Though the trials were plagued by mishaps, one of Whitehead's torpedoes blew a hole "as big as the First Lord's carriage" in the side of the wooden corvette *Aigle*, despite missing by some eighteen feet. Impressed, the British Royal Navy concluded that they needed the Devil's device. The Royal Navy's evaluation committee was "unanimously of the opinion that any maritime nation failing to provide itself with submarine locomotive torpedoes would be neglecting a great source of power."[3] The torpedo was born, and ocean battlefields would never be the same.

Despite these modest beginnings, much like the aircraft would in the twentieth century after Taranto, the torpedo revolutionized naval warfare in the late nineteenth century by introducing tactical asymmetric warfare. Suddenly, small coastal vessels armed with torpedoes threatened to sink, or at a minimum harass or badly damage, large battleships. Basically, the Whitehead torpedo put battleships on notice that a ship a fraction of their size and cost could sink them.

In 1871, the Royal Navy bought rights to the Whitehead torpedo and began manufacturing at the Royal Laboratories in Woolwich. Two decades later, the US Navy acquired the blueprint for the Whitehead torpedo. The machine these navies began manufacturing was a surprisingly complex device. It consisted of a warhead, a compressed air flask, an immersion chamber, and a tail section that housed the engine room and a host of other gears, shafts, and mechanisms designed to keep the torpedo moving forward on course and at the right depth.

By the 1880s, with the Whitehead torpedo traveling over 800 meters at 18 knots, most of the world's navies began fitting torpedo tubes to coastal boats in order to deploy the new capital-ship killer. These "torpedo boats" and "torpedo gunboats," as navies called them, represented a serious challenge for capital ships in coastal waters. The British *Lightning* of 1877 and other early torpedo boats exemplified how smaller, less expensive boats could sink larger battleships with their locomotive payload launched from tubes. But it wasn't long before naval engineers began brainstorming and designing remedies for the torpedo boat.

The Royal Navy experimented with early destroyer designs, but the Yarrow Shipyard in England believed "Japan to have effectively invented the destroyer"[4] with the *Kotaka*, or Little Hawk. This warship was far ahead of her time. In many respects, *Kotaka* was simply a heavy torpedo boat. The London shipyard built *Kotaka* to Imperial Navy specifications. Later, Yokosuka yard workers reassembled her. In 1888, at 203-tons, *Kotaka* weighed more than most torpedo boats, but that was precisely the point. Though heavier, *Kotaka* topped out at nineteen knots, had one-inch-thick steel plates protecting her machinery, four torpedo tubes (two forward and two aft), and four rapid-fire 37 mm (one-pounder) naval guns. With her fourteen-inch German Schwartzkopff torpedoes – of the Whitehead design, but made of bronze rather than steel to resist corrosion – *Kotaka* punched well over her weight.

But *Kotaka* proved one of a kind, because the Imperial Navy ended up choosing smaller torpedo boats of French design instead. The Imperial Navy came to adopt the naval principles of the French *jeune école*, which prioritized fleets of smaller and faster vessels. It procured numerous midsized, lightly armored but heavily armed cruisers, accompanied by fast attack squadrons of torpedo boats. But *Kotaka* had already made a splash. She demonstrated that she could accompany larger warships on the high seas, expanding her usefulness beyond coastal defense. This was precisely the ability that made destroyers different. They not only defended larger warships or convoys from torpedoes, but also eventually largely replaced torpedo boats by becoming dangerous offensive weapons as well.

The British built several classes of torpedo gunboats in the late nineteenth century that inched toward proper destroyers. In 1891, the British Director of Naval Ordnance called for the building of the "torpedo boat destroyer," a vessel designed for "channel protection"[5] and "hunting down the enemy's torpedo boats." With this call came a series of British vessels built by Yarrow and Thornycroft that first carried the designation "torpedo boat destroyer," including the *Daring* class and *Havock* class. Their top speed came close to thirty knots, and one twelve pounder and three six pounders complemented the fixed torpedo tube on the bow and the two revolving tubes just abaft the main exhaust funnel. The French followed the British with the *Durandal* class and the United States with the *Bainbridge* class, and, by the first decade of the twentieth century, destroyers had become a fixed part of Great Power navies.

Speed was essential for destroyers, and the British *Viper* broke thirty knots in 1899 with the first steam turbine in any warship. It is interesting to note that, even by World War II, the top speed of most destroyers had changed little and remained in the neighborhood of thirty knots. The US Navy's *Fletcher*-class destroyers had a top speed of thirty-six knots, while the *Kagerō*-class destroyers went at thirty-five knots.

The British torpedo boat destroyer *Spiteful* was the first warship to use fuel oil instead of coal in 1904, though the practice remained a decade away from becoming widespread. Despite the rapid British advances in destroyer design, the Imperial Navy first used destroyers tactically at the Battle of Port Arthur on February 8–9, 1904. That night, unwilling to expose his six capital ships to the withering fire of Port Arthur's formidable shore batteries, Admiral Tōgō, who was still months away from being immortalized at the Battle of Tsushima Strait, decided to send in his destroyers instead, among them *Kotaka*, and do so under the cloak of darkness. Although torpedo nets saved most of the Russian warships, the Japanese destroyers accomplished enough of their mission to earn their keep. Their action certainly inspired future generations of Imperial Navy officers.

With their speed, energy, and derring-do, it's not surprising that later Imperial Navy admirals, such as Rear Admiral Tanaka, the clever commander of Japan's Destroyer Squadron 2 (Desron2) during World War II, admired the little warships. He believed that the Battle of Port Arthur birthed Japan's study of complex torpedo tactics and night-fighting techniques, as well as its basic fondness for destroyers. "The Sino-Japanese and Russo-Japanese wars indicated that torpedo-attack warfare seemed to agree with the character of Japanese sailors,"[6] he commented. It tapped into the offensive-minded characteristics of samurai warfare.

Imperial Navy cruisers and destroyers became legendary in the Solomon Islands for their night-fighting abilities, and Tanaka, a master at torpedo warfare, orchestrated some of Japan's most brilliant naval victories, including the Battle of Tassafaronga (known as the Battle

Figure 2.1 The cruiser *Minneapolis* after the Battle of Tassafaronga on December 1, 1942. Official US Navy Photograph, National Archives, Catalog #: 80-G-211215.

of Lunga Point by the Japanese) on November 30, 1942. It remains a stinging example of patient, offensive-minded night fighting. On that night, the US Navy's Admiral Carleton Wright, seeking to disrupt the "Tokyo Express" to Guadalcanal, ordered his cruisers to open fire on Tanaka's destroyers while in "The Slot" (New Georgia Channel). Many of Tanaka's destroyers, which didn't include *Yukikaze* on this occasion, were burdened to the gunwales with supplies sealed in buoyant oil drums. Targeting the US cruisers' muzzle flashes, the Imperial Navy destroyers carefully maneuvered and launched their torpedoes at optimum range, sinking the cruiser *Northampton* and mauling *Minneapolis*, *New Orleans*, and *Pensacola* (see Figure 2.1). With Tanaka in command, the Battle of Tassafaronga proved to be among the most humiliating defeats in the US Navy's history.

Japanese skill in such attacks shouldn't have been surprising to US admirals. "Especially after the Russo-Japanese War," Tanaka mused, "tremendous expenditures and effort were put into the production and improvement of torpedoes and craft to use them." As he remembered, "Special emphasis was also placed on the training of skilled crews for handling torpedoes on board the ships." Aboard the cruiser *Jintsū*, Tanaka drew on Japan's histories and traditions of destroyer tactics to lead Desron2 into some of the most ferocious fighting in the Western Pacific.

Japanese officers and sailors viewed night fighting as the great equalizer – the US Navy might have more ships, but the Imperial Navy fought better at night. Before radar transformed night combat in late 1942, night fighting with cruiser and destroyer squadrons had become for Japanese a carefully choreographed affair of lightness and darkness, sound and silence, waves and calm, flares and flags, and coordinated warship maneuvers and navigation. Peering through their big-eye binoculars, keen-eyed Japanese lookouts always scanned the horizon for US ships. Often, these gifted lookouts spotted the enemy before US Navy radar had detected their ships.

The Battle of Savo Island (Japanese name, First Battle of the Solomon Sea), which occurred early in the Guadalcanal saga, is another example of the Imperial Navy tapping into its traditions of torpedo techniques and night fighting to throttle its enemy. Like so much of the naval fighting around Guadalcanal, however, the Imperial Navy enjoyed initial tactical successes on the water, only to ultimately suffer strategic failures in the end. At Savo Island, shortly after midnight on August 9, 1942, Vice Admiral Mikawa Gun'ichi, the task force commander, approached Savo Island in a single column over two miles long. He sought to frustrate the US troop landings at Guadalcanal. His flag was aboard *Chōkai*, the nearly 16,000-ton *Takao*-class heavy cruiser with 5 twin 20 cm (8-inch) guns, 2 twin 12 cm (5-inch) guns, and 8 torpedo tubes housing Japan's deadly "Long Lances," as historian Morison labeled the stealthy Type 93 torpedoes.

Japanese cruisers were formidable, and *Chōkai* was well armed. Six additional cruisers and one destroyer followed Mikawa's flagship as he pressed toward Savo Island. While Imperial Navy cruisers moved within range of the US warships, two picketing US destroyers, *Blue* and *Ralph Talbot*, ghosted past, but failed to spot the stealthy Imperial Navy cruisers. Japanese sailors had spotted them, however. Patiently, Admiral Mikawa held his fire and pressed on. Everything depended on surprise.

Throughout the previous day, Mikawa's cruisers had catapulted reconnaissance seaplanes, trying to determine the precise whereabouts of Admiral Frank Fletcher's aircraft carriers. It turns out they had departed the area; but Mikawa never knew that. As the sun dipped below the western horizon, the methodical Mikawa ordered that all deck-side flammables be thrown overboard.

With hints of Admiral Tōgō's gravitas, he then sent a signal to the other cruisers: "In the finest tradition of the Imperial Navy we shall engage the enemy in night battle. Every man is expected to do his best."[7] He then organized the cruisers in battle formation. The cruisers catapulted more seaplanes to reconnoiter the waters south of Savo Island after dark, a tricky operation, but lighting the target area with parachute flares would be essential for accurate fire. Imperial Navy sailors fashioned long white streamers to signal yards for nighttime identification. With every precaution taken, Mikawa's force coiled for the attack.

The Admiral increased speed to twenty-six knots, but then reduced speed after seeing the picket destroyers in order to minimize his columns' wake. At "high speed our large ships kicked up a wake that would have been hard to conceal,"[8] remembered Ōmae Toshikaze, an officer on the flagship. After passing the second destroyer undetected, Mikawa increased speed to thirty knots.

Then, piercing the silence, a lookout shouted, "Three cruisers, nine degrees to starboard, moving to the right!" A parachute flare then lit the watery battlefield.

"Torpedoes fire to starboard – Fire!,"[9] boomed the thunderous voice of *Chōkai*'s captain, Hayakawa Mikio.

It was twenty-three minutes to midnight. Then the full fury of the Imperial Navy guns opened up, causing the "enemy's backdrop to be brightened by the flames of burning ships, reflecting from clouds, while we moved out of utter darkness."[10] They were in perfect position, using lightness, darkness, and reflections to their advantage as they dashed south around Savo Island in a counterclockwise direction. *Chōkai* launched a second salvo of fish at the scrambling US cruisers, which were not outfitted with torpedoes. It became the kind of battle that the Imperial Navy had trained for since the early twentieth century. This is what the first stage of the decisive battle was supposed to look like, when

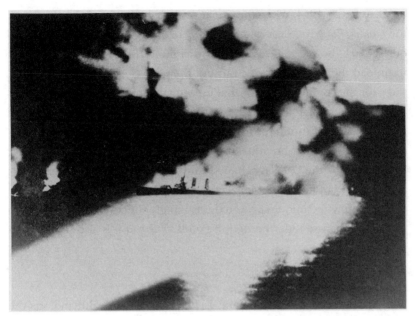

Figure 2.2 The burning US cruiser *Quincy* lit up by Imperial Navy searchlights during the Battle of Savo Island. NH 50346. Courtesy of the Naval History & Heritage Command.

Japan crippled the US Navy with cruisers and destroyers, operating at night, armed with Type 93 torpedo squadrons.

As she changed course to the northeast, with Savo Island to her port beam, *Chōkai* began using her massive searchlights to direct her fire. "The initial firing range of seven thousand meters closed with amazing swiftness. Every other salvo caused another enemy ship to burst into flames," Ōmae remembered. The heavy cruiser *Quincy* came out to challenge the Imperial Navy cruisers. "Though her entire hull from midships aft was enveloped in flames,"[11] recalled Ōmae, "her forward guns were firing with great spirit." Eventually, *Quincy* sank. "She was a brave ship, manned by brave men," concluded Ōmae. "She certainly made an impression on the men of our force" (see Figure 2.2).

After their rapid pass counterclockwise around Savo Island, Mikawa ordered a withdrawal from the target area, rather than attempt to sink the US transports and risk being hammered by US carrier planes when daylight broke. It proved a costly decision, just as it was when, a little over two years later, Admiral Kurita failed to attack the US transports at Leyte Gulf on October 25, 1944. When the smoke settled, the Imperial Navy had sunk the *Quincy, Canberra, Astoria,* and *Vincennes* in a single pass. Despite the serious setback, however, Rear Admiral Richmond Kelly Turner continued to unload the 15,000 Marines, most of them on Guadalcanal, setting the stage for the coming battle for that inhospitable piece of real estate.

It was a strategic loss for the Japanese war effort, as they eventually lost Guadalcanal in one of the turning points of the war, but the tactical victory remained breathtaking, nonetheless. The lessons learned at Savo Island by the US Navy shaped warship and transport deployments at later US landings, particularly those at Leyte Gulf. Imperial Navy night-fighting techniques proved devastatingly effective in the early years of the war, before radar evened the odds. *Yukikaze* was also schooled in this tradition.

* * *

Fought between May 31 and June 1, 1916, the Battle of Jutland was the largest naval battle of World War I, and it was a capital-ship affair. Of the over 150 British combat vessels, 28 were battleships. The Germans had just short of 100 ships, of which 16 were battleships. Navy strategists around the world can be forgiven if they concluded after the epic North Sea confrontation (fought west of Norway's Jutland Peninsula) that the battlewagon was here to stay, but in truth it was the battlewagon's swansong. In general, destroyers saw more action than capital ships in World War I because they guarded critical merchant marine convoys and hunted submarines with the increasing ability to listen underwater. During the Great War, German U-boats had posed the most serious challenge to the British Royal Navy, much as they would in World War II. Initially, destroyers relied on ramming surfaced submarines to combat them. The British destroyer *Badger* rammed the German *U-19* in October 1914, badly damaging the U-boat. The *Garry* sank *U-18* one month later. Though no doubt thrilling, ramming submarines was hardly a recipe for winning wars.

As the torpedo-armed submarine became a greater threat to surface combatants, warships began deploying new antisubmarine countermeasures. The British invented the depth charge, for example, a union of Herbert Taylor's hydrostatic pistol, Alban L. Gwynne's primer, and the sinkable mine. It wasn't long before engineers began fashioning depth-charge racks to the stern of destroyers, preparing them to battle submarines. As a result, the battlefield portfolio of destroyers expanded yet again. In World War I, destroyers became convoy escorts and submarine hunters.

Armed with the new depth charges, the British *Llewellyn* sank *UC-19* in December 1916. In the nineteenth century, naval engineers had conceived of destroyers as the antidote to smaller torpedo boats, but, after World War I, destroyers became an integral part of guarding merchant convoys from submarines and killing them, with guns, depth charges, or reinforced bows for ramming. In World War II, a similar conversion would be made for battling aircraft, including antiaircraft mounts. *Yukikaze* started the war with anemic antiaircraft capabilities, but eventually had an aft gun turret removed to make room for more. The portfolio of the destroyer had expanded yet again.

Following World War I, naval engineers began beefing up destroyers, outfitting them with more armaments. The British *V* class and *W* class emerged as the preeminent destroyers in this context. But the real breakthrough in destroyer design came a decade after the Great War with Japan's *Fubuki* class, what became known in Japan as Special Type destroyers. *Yukikaze* is considered among the Special Type and First Class destroyers, of which there were eighty-two vessels when war broke out. Importantly, the development of the Special Type destroyer is a story of naval architecture that evolved within the limitations of international arms treaties that followed in the wake of World War I.

In the context of the Washington Naval Treaty, vessel tonnage meant everything. Negotiated between November 1921 and February 1922, the victors of World War I (Britain, France, Italy, Japan, and the United States) signed the agreement in order to "contribute to the maintenance of the general peace, and to reduce the burdens of competition in armaments."[12] Specifically, it sought to limit the construction of battleships, battlecruisers, and aircraft carriers – the big ships. The agreement did not limit the construction of other warships, such as cruisers, destroyers, and submarines, but did limit their displacement. It limited the Imperial Navy to 315,000 tons of capital ships and 81,000 tons of aircraft carriers, while the United States and Britain retained 525,000 tons and 135,000 tons, respectively.

This infamous "5:5:3 ratio" irked hawks in the Imperial Navy leadership and similarly outraged the Japanese public. With his opening remarks,

Charles Evans Hughes, the US Secretary of State, "sank in thirty-five minutes more ships than all of the admirals of the world would have sunk in a cycle of centuries,"[13] one newspaper quipped. But Japan's situation immediately after the Great War was tricky. It's true that the treaty placed Japan in a disadvantageous position relative to the US Navy in capital-ship numbers. At the same time, however, it placed limits on how many warships the United States could build. Navy Minister and plenipotentiary to the conference Katō Tomosaburō always feared an unlimited naval arms race with Japan's hypothetical adversary in the Pacific. Japan couldn't hope to compete with the United States in warship construction, but, if Japan could maintain 70 percent of the US warships' tonnage, particularly after President Woodrow Wilson's Big Navy Act of 1916, which precipitated a dramatic increase in the size of the US Navy, that was as good as could be expected.

The hotheaded president of the Navy Staff College, Katō Kanji, adamantly disagreed, however. He argued that the United States, an industrial sleeping giant, could afford to maintain a downsized navy under the treaty because it had the capacity to expand its navy at short notice. Japan, he concluded, did not. Indeed, 90 percent of the high-grade steel Japan used to build warships came from the United States. The elder statesman Katō won the day, however, and Japan signed the treaty. But the hawkish "anti-treaty faction" remained an influential force in the Imperial Navy, shaping its internal political and cultural dynamics for decades.

Regardless, because of the limitations placed on the Imperial Navy in the construction of new battlecruisers, battleships, and carriers, Japan became committed to highly advanced destroyers and innovative destroyer tactics. Imperial Navy planners believed that, if a decisive battle with the US Navy presented itself in some future Pacific conflict, destroyer squadrons, with cruiser support, would play an integral role by holing US capital ships in coordinated nighttime torpedo raids, much like Mikawa at Savo Island and Tanaka at Tassafaronga. Then, with the US ships foundering as their massive bilge pumps divulged countless gallons of oily seawater, Japan's battleships and carriers would swoop in and finish the cripples off with their big guns and aircraft.

The warship that best epitomized this optimistic view of the future destroyer was the Special Type *Fubuki* class, completed between 1928 and 1931. There was variation amongst the twenty Special Type destroyers built, but, starting with the hull, the *Fubuki* boats proved quite seaworthy, with the foc's'le raised and extended aft, and the bow flared, to improve stability and protect the forward gun from heavy seas. Four boilers powering two-geared turbines generated 50,000 horse power and propelled the destroyer at 35 knots, while better fuel capacity increased the warship's range to 5,000 nautical miles. These were blue-water killers.

But it was in armaments that the Special Type destroyers excelled. Three twin Type 3 127 mm (5-inch) guns complemented the three triple torpedo mounts with reloads, meaning that a *Fubuki* destroyer had eighteen torpedoes with which to reach out and touch enemy ships. Originally, two 7.7 mm antiaircraft mounts defended the warship from aerial attack, but this was modified over time. Basically, the Special Type destroyer represented one of Japan's remedies to the Washington Naval Treaty – a destroyer more heavily armed than many Imperial Navy light cruisers, but within specified weight limits. The mission for Japan's naval engineers became to place more weapons on a lighter hull, even if sacrifices needed to be made in basic seaworthiness.

The naval architect who pioneered this push in lightweight warship construction was Hiraga Yuzuru. Hiraga was a career naval officer who, after the Russo-Japanese War, attended the Royal Naval College in Greenwich, England. He graduated in June 1908 and, later, became a professor of engineering at Tokyo Imperial University. He emerged as Japan's leading naval architect in the 1910s and 1920s, primarily focusing on battleships and cruisers, but he also designed the Special Type *Fubuki* destroyers. Hiraga, together with another famous naval architect, Fujimoto Kikuo, had designed the experimental lightweight cruiser *Yūbari* (commissioned July 1923). After a stint as technical director to the Japanese delegation in Washington, D.C. during the Washington Naval negotiations, Hiraga became head of the Imperial Navy's Technical Department and sought to place the armaments of a 5,000-ton displacement vessel on the hull of a 3,000-ton vessel in order to compete with Britain and the United States under the agreement's 5:5:3 apportionment.

The Imperial Navy's Shipbuilding Department undertook these early architectural efforts and produced the cruiser *Furutaka* (commissioned March 1926) and her sister ship *Kako* (commissioned July 1926). Hiraga and Fujimoto's team designed the vessels to counter the US *Omaha*-class and British *Hawkins*-class scout cruisers, and they drew extensively on the innovations of the earlier *Yūbari*. *Furutaka* outperformed her Western counterparts in nearly every category: she bristled with three twin 20.3 cm (8-inch) guns, four single 12 cm (4.7-inch) guns, and a host of .50 caliber antiaircraft mounts. She could also outrun the British ships at thirty-five knots. The British Royal Navy was so impressed by *Furutaka* that it reportedly made a formal request to buy her construction blueprints. After *Furutaka* came the heavy cruiser *Myōkō* – the first 10,000-ton-displacement cruiser built by any navy, but still largely within the design constraints of the Washington Naval Treaty.

Because of the constraints of the treaty, the Navy General Staff began to make increasingly impossible demands on the Imperial Navy's Shipbuilding Department, however. They clamored for more guns on less boat. While the Navy General Staff demanded more armaments and equipment on deck, Hiraga and Fujimoto came to believe that such demands compromised the basic seaworthiness of their vessels. Eventually, the politicization of naval architecture led to two maritime calamities that changed the direction of the Imperial Navy and cast a shadow on Hiraga's otherwise illustrious career. But they also made the Navy General Staff rethink its commitment to the Washington Naval Treaty and international agreements in general.

The *Tomozuru* Incident was the first. The Imperial Navy had begun developing the 600-ton *Chidori*-class torpedo boat to circumvent the Washington Naval Treaty. Because they were small, the treaty did not limit them, and they could be produced in large numbers. On this small platform, engineers mounted three 4.7-inch guns and four 21-inch torpedo tubes. Imperial Navy planners envisioned the *Chidori* as assuming some of the duties of destroyers, including convoy escorting and submarine hunting. On March 12, 1934, one of these torpedo boats, the *Tomozuru*, while steaming at fourteen knots in a strong gale near Sasebo, capsized. An Imperial Navy cruiser later found *Tomozuru* drifting keel up, with the majority of her 113 officers and sailors dead. It led many in the Imperial Navy to question the basic stability of the vessels.

But North Pacific waters were not through testing Hiraga's warships. The real test came on September 26, 1935, when the Fourth Fleet was battered by a strong typhoon off the coast of northeastern Japan during the exercises of the Combined Fleet's Grand Maneuvers. The Combined Fleet had divided into red and blue squads and prepared for a mock battle. Not only were the refitted battleships *Yamashiro* and *Haruna* present, but also the new *Mogami*-class cruisers and *Hatsuharu*-class destroyers graced the fleet. After the red Fourth Fleet had crossed through the Tsugaru Straits, which separates Hokkaido from Honshu, a typhoon with a front stretching for nearly 200 miles descended on the warships. Escaping the eighty-knot blow proved impossible.

With punishing winds and forty- to sixty-foot waves, the warships turned their bows into the storm, quartered the waves, and rode it out. The winds proved relentless and the storm damaged some of the bigger warships, including the carriers *Ryūjō* and *Hōshō*, as well as the cruisers *Mogami* and *Myōkō*. Despite their seven-year unblemished service record, the Special Type destroyers took the worst pounding, however, including the entire bows shearing off the *Fubuki*-class destroyers *Yūgiri* and *Hatsuyuki*. The Special Type destroyers had rolled close to 75 degrees and pitched violently in the waves – after wrinkling and buckling on the forward decks, they sheared at the bows.

The cruel storm damaged nearly every ship in the Fourth Fleet and over fifty men were killed or missing. The calamity forced the Imperial Navy to establish a blue-ribbon committee to reassess its lightweight and top-heavy destroyer and cruiser designs, and repair and reinforce existing vessels. As a result of the ensuing investigation by the Navy General Staff, Fukuda Keiji replaced Fujimoto at the Shipbuilding Department, and Fujimoto died a broken man one year later. Fujimoto had honorably taken responsibility, even though the Navy General Staff had pushed for the heavier armaments over his repeated objections. It also prompted the Imperial Navy to withdraw from the Washington Naval Treaty and its later incarnations. It was from this experience that *Yukikaze* and the other *Kagerō*-class destroyers were born.

* * *

The naval architect Makino Shigeru designed *Yukikaze* and her seventeen sister ships. Born in Nagoya, Makino was a child of the Ship Building Department of the Washington Naval Treaty years – Hiraga, Fujimoto, and Fukuda had all served as his mentors at one time or another. In

1922, Makino had entered Tokyo Imperial University's Engineering School, specializing in naval engineering. Shortly afterwards, he was accepted as a student in the Imperial Navy's Ship Building Department. In March 1925, Makino graduated from university, and two months later the Imperial Navy promoted him to first lieutenant and stationed him at Yokosuka as a member of the Imperial Navy's Technical Department. In 1934, during a stint in France, he graduated from the national marine engineering school at the Cherbourg Naval Base. Between 1936 and 1941, he worked at the Kure Naval Arsenal on a number of projects, including the *Yamato*-class battleships and the *Kagerō*-class destroyers.

Makino drafted the blueprints for *Yukikaze* at a time of global crisis, while the Second Sino-Japanese War raged and Japan eyed oil and other resources in the South Pacific. Presciently, he sought to build a destroyer expert at killing submarines. He also had the luxury of designing ships after Japan had withdrawn from the cumbersome London Naval Conference in 1936, and had allowed the terms of the Washington Naval Treaty to expire in January 1937. The international arms treaty regimes of the 1920s and 1930s were leeward of the Imperial Navy now, but Japanese naval architects had learned certain techniques and design characteristics from working within its weight limitations.

But the key was better stability and seaworthiness, which Makino achieved through new theories on metacentric height, which is the distance between the ship's center of gravity and center of buoyancy. Simply, the metacenter is a kind of theoretical pivot point when the vessel inclines. A vessel is said to have a stable equilibrium when the metacenter is above the center of gravity, and the vessel quickly returns to her upright position after being inclined. She is stiff, in this regard, as opposed to tender. If the center of gravity is above the metacenter, the vessel is said to have unstable equilibrium, and easily capsizes. Clearly, the treaty-era vessels, with their heavy guns and light hulls, tended toward neutral or even negative equilibrium, a condition remedied in the *Kagerō*-class destroyers. He also modified the keel from the earlier destroyers, further lowering the center of gravity in the vessels.

The legacies and lessons of the treaty era were always present in Imperial Navy destroyers, however. Indeed, with *Yukikaze*, the hull constituted only 27 percent of her overall weight, unlike similar US and British destroyers, whose hulls constituted closer to 33 percent of their weight. This allowed 6 percent more weight in armaments, including full complements of Type 93 torpedoes. In order to reduce hull weight, state-of-the-art designing of the bow, stern, and keel became necessary, which required heightened steel strength and innovative welding techniques. In her day, *Yukikaze* was nothing short of a marvel in nautical design.

Makino drew on the earlier experience with the Special Type destroyers to create the *Kagerō*-class boats, the new Super Type boats, which exceeded thirty-five knots in time trials fully armed, which is what mattered. Itō Masanori compared *Yukikaze*'s lines to a nobly sleek "flying swallow,"[14] a warship that had stability, smartness and, finally, speed. Imperial Navy engineers designed and built innovative destroyers after the *Kagerō*-class boats – namely, the *Yūgumo*, *Shimakaze*, *Akizuki*, *Matsu*, and *Tachibana* classes – but few accrued the service record of the *Kagerō*-class warships. The highly experimental *Shimakaze*, with its three quintuple torpedo tubes, could launch a broadside, on either port or starboard, of fifteen torpedoes; but only one was made, and she never proved the workhorse that the *Kagerō*-class vessels did.

The *Kagerō*-class warships proved an excellent example of what a destroyer was capable of accomplishing in speed, armaments, and radius (see Figure 2.3). In turn, they reimagined the relationship between

Figure 2.3 *Yukikaze*, in her original armaments configuration, steaming off Sasebo in December 1939. Courtesy of the Yamato Museum, Kure, Japan.

time and space in creating an oceanic empire and defending it. They became tools of empire, not only of war. Like all warships, *Yukikaze* was never the product of pure, unencumbered nautical engineering and the structural, electronic, and mechanical requirements of an oceangoing vessel. Rather, *Yukikaze* interacted with the international diplomatic and engineering environments as much as she did with the marine one that lapped at her hull every day.

Regardless, with *Kagerō*-class warships in the vanguard, the Imperial Navy could strike with lightning speed, securing the valuable oil and other resources in the South Seas. *Yukikaze* and her sister ships would be the key to Japanese autarchy and independence from US oil. Such destroyers proved instrumental in resolving what became known as Japan's "Southern Question," a topic we turn to next.

CHAPTER 3

Oil Empire and Japan's Southern Advance

It is no exaggeration to say that the Greater East Asian War broke out with oil as the main cause.

The *War History Series*, Japan's official telling of the Greater East Asian War

HAVING EXAMINED IMPERIAL NAVY WARSHIPS, including their names, slice of the national budget, weapons, and strategies, we next turn to why Japan jeopardized these vessels and went to war in the Pacific. In the decades leading up to the outbreak of hostilities in the Asia–Pacific theater, a constellation of factors propelled Japan toward total war: the economic upheaval of the Great Depression, diplomatic responses to US racist and anti-immigration policies, the perceived failures of liberal democracy and the rise of ultra-nationalism, insubordinate Imperial Army officers, myths of racial superiority and the empty promise of liberating Asians from Western imperialism, and the defense of the South Manchurian Railway and other colonial financial assets.

For its part, the Imperial Navy and its supporters conjured their own set of reasons for the push south, but the true raison d'être was always oil. In the Southern Operation, acquiring oil became not only the reason for Japan's push into the South Seas, but also the modus operandi, with specially trained paratroopers deployed to secure important oilfields and refineries. Oil engineers then quickly followed to get the facilities running and the bunker fuel pumping into the fuel holds of warships. Japanese sailors and soldiers died to liberate this oil, not their Asian brothers and sisters, and Allied troops died defending it. The endless thirst of industrial war machines drove Japan southward.

After Japan's conquest of the Western and South Pacific, the Imperial Navy sought to create a "perimeter of steel" to protect its new ocean empire, and keep lines of communication and merchant shipping lanes open. The Allies, for their part, sought to shoot holes in it. This dynamic characterized the first two years of fighting in the Pacific, until the US Navy forced Imperial Army and Navy forces to slowly, and painfully, withdraw northward, back toward the home islands.

But, as Admiral Yamamoto had promised, the Imperial Navy gave the Allies "hell for a year or a year and a half," and that's where *Yukikaze*'s war started.

* * *

By the 1930s nearly all warships burned bunker fuel or heavy oil, rather than traditional coal, and Japan's warships were no exception. The US Navy had started transitioning to oil with the battleship *Nevada* in 1912, and that same year the British established the Anglo-Persian Oil Company to fuel the Royal Navy. Without ready access to oil, the German and Japanese navies continued to burn coal later than most. But there were serious problems with coal.

On warships, coal produced large quantities of ash, called "clinker," and coal dust represented a serious explosion hazard, which made it challenging to stow and work with, particularly when the high seas turned to battlefields. It remained suitable for domestic power generation and industrial purposes, but not for warships. Warships, like all ships, are about efficiency, and coal is inefficient compared with oil – it burns at about 40 percent less energy per unit weight. But there is a more important reason still. Warships can't be resupplied with coal at sea, meaning that coal-burning vessels remained tethered to strategic ports. By contrast, warships can be refueled with oil at sea, making navies truly pelagic in nature. Theoretically at least, with oil as their fuel, warships could remain at sea for months, even years, at a time during war.

With this in mind, starting in the 1920s, Japanese engineers refitted the *Kongō*-class battlecruisers, the *Fusō*-class battleships, the *Ise*-class battleships, and the *Nagato*-class battleships with more compact and efficient oil-burning power plants, which gave warships more space for weaponry and greater range. During the 1933–1934 refit, the oil-burning boilers reduced the weight in the *Kongō*-class warships by nearly 800 tons, while the horsepower remained unchanged. In the case of the *Fusō* and *Nagato* battleships, the refit to oil in 1930 reduced the number of boilers and meant the elimination of the forward exhaust funnel. This single mechanical advancement, a new form of hydrocarbon energy, drove most of the Imperial Navy's South Seas strategies in World War II, particularly the 1941 Southern Operation.

Japan possessed reasonably rich coal deposits that helped fuel its late nineteenth- and twentieth-century industrial development, and what Japan did not have was readily available elsewhere in the empire, particularly Manchuria. But, when battleships converted to oil, everything changed. When *Yukikaze* departed Palau Island, east of the Philippines, on her first mission of World War II, she stowed some 600 tons of fuel oil to power her three boilers. This fuel oil stowed in her hull represented a small fraction of the insatiable appetite for oil that pushed Japan's Imperial Navy southward.

During the refits of the 1930s, the Imperial Navy's Technical Department had standardized boiler design throughout the fleet, with oil as the common ingredient. Whether on giant battlewagons or smaller destroyers, the Technical Department had standardized boiler performance to a "consumption of 16,000 pounds of oil per hour maximum, to generate steam at 30 kg/cm^2 and 350 °C from 95 °C feed water."[1] (Imperial Navy engines were powered by steam super-heated to 350 °C, or 662 °F, about three times the boiling point of water. Engineers used distilled water for "feed water" in such super-heated systems. In terms of fuel consumption, heavy fuel oil weighs 8.25 pounds per gallon, so burning 16,000 pounds of oil "maximum" per hour is approximately 1,939 gallons.) In comparison with US Navy power plants, such as the Babcock & Wilcox boilers that powered the *Fletcher*-class destroyers, which achieved closer to 450 °C with similar oil consumption, the Imperial Navy designs proved relatively inefficient, but they were powerful enough to drive Japanese policies in the South Seas for decades.

In Japanese destroyers, the machinery produced 52,000 horse power with three boilers. *Yukikaze* held 600 tons of fuel, or approximately 145,000 gallons. At cruising speed, she had a radius of about 5,000 miles. As mentioned, *Yukikaze* steamed some 96,000 nautical miles during World War II, closer to 130,000 nautical miles if you count her constant zigzagging to avoid Allied aircraft and submarine raids. At 18 knots, *Yukikaze* alone required well over 3 million gallons of fuel oil to wage her war. Battlewagons such as *Fusō* and *Nagato* consumed over ten times that much oil, and *Musashi* and *Yamato* even more still. Not surprisingly, in the late 1930s, Japan began eyeing the closest source of fuel – British and Dutch Borneo, and the Dutch East Indies. How to tap this oil became known in war planning circles as the "Southern Question."

Yukikaze battling in the South Seas represented a crescendo to decades of Imperial Navy campaigning that started in the Meiji period. Initially, the idea of the southern advance tied the South Seas to Japan's national destiny through the promise of economic expansion, as well as empire and diaspora creation. By the twentieth century, the acquisition of oil for warships had become another powerful reason for the southern advance. In effect, the Imperial Navy and its allies constructed an entire mystique around the South Seas, one that reached a feverish pitch by the early twentieth century and proved instrumental to the construction of a modern navy. Once engineers had refitted most Imperial Navy vessels to burn oil rather than coal in the 1920s, acquiring fuel for the Combined Fleet became a strategically important question, and Imperial Navy planners linked the conquest of the South Seas to Japan's survival in the industrial age.

Unlike the British and the United States, Japan did not have ready access to oil on domestic or imperial soil. The Southern Operation sought to remedy that predicament, though Japanese military adventurists often couched the reasons for war in more ideological terms. At a certain level, all World War II combatants waged a strategic war to secure hydrocarbon energy, particularly oil – aircraft carriers and battleships, Tiger and Sherman tank divisions, and Hurricanes and B-24 Liberators proved relentlessly thirsty machines. As Friedrich von Mellenthin, a staff officer of the German Afrika Korps, acknowledged after the defeat at the second battle of El Alamein, a motorized division without fuel is mere "scrap iron."[2]

In 1941, after the imposition of US, British, and Dutch embargos of Japan, the Imperial Navy faced the very real prospect of commanding a fleet of navy-gray scrap iron. This proved a powerful motivator for war. In this manner, Imperial Navy vessels themselves, their mere existence, played a role in pushing Japan southward. It became an example of an irresistible circular logic: Japan needed a modern fleet to sail southward, but then Japan needed to sail southward to refuel its modern fleet. Essentially, the Imperial Navy spent World War II plundering the South Seas to refuel these thirsty warships, in a maritime front that remained only loosely connected (in a strategic sense) to military affairs in mainland China. Theoretically, going south, in particular securing French Indochina and the Burma Road, represented a way out of the China quagmire, but the Dutch East Indies was all about oil.

Whether liberal, communist, or fascist, the belligerents still required resources to fuel their industrial economies and militaries. This is the meta-rationale for the war, the transnational and trans-ideological quality of the war, and the irresistible series of pushes that drove Japan's strategies in the South Seas. Ideas without energy behind them are only musings – or intellectual scrap iron – and fossil fuels, in particular, powered all ideological sides in World War II. Such thirsty industrial machines as *Yukikaze* became the inertia-driven puppeteers behind the ideological strings, a structural condition of the twentieth-century world industrial economy that powered World War II.

* * *

Decades earlier, with World War I devouring Europe, Japan had started to link much of its future energy security to the South Seas. Indeed, as the belligerents gathered in Paris in 1919 to negotiate the end of the war, Japanese colonies in Micronesia, agreed to in secret with British diplomats, were some five years old already. The Imperial Navy had come to view Micronesia as a critical avenue to oil-rich Borneo and the East Indies. As one Imperial Navy memorandum explained, "The newly occupied territories in the South Seas fill a most important position as a link between Japan and the East Indies, the Philippines, New Guinea, and Borneo."[3] It continued, "Even if our occupation brings no immediate advantage, the islands must be carefully kept in our possession as stepping-stones to the treasure houses of the southern regions."

Yamamoto Miono, an economics professor at Kyoto University, wrote that Micronesia might be but one stop in the "southward advance of the Japanese people."[4] Later, writing in English, the publisher

K. K. Kawakami insisted that Japan needed Micronesia "more badly than any other nation" because of its proximity to Southeast Asia's energy resources. Japanese negotiators knew this, and, in December 1920, the League of Nations, after significant haggling, confirmed Japan's mandate over Micronesia. The United States never joined the League of Nations, and Japan concluded a separate agreement in Washington, D.C. in February 1922. Imperial Navy war planners held true to the idea that Micronesia represented only stepping-stones to the "treasure houses" of the East Indies.

On September 18, 1931, Japan's Kwantung Army instigated the Mukden Incident, which eventually caused Japan to overrun Manchuria and withdraw from the League of Nations in 1933. In 1937, the China Incident (or Marco Polo Bridge Incident of July 7–9, 1937) sparked the Japanese invasion of China proper, which led to the occupation of much of coastal China and the brutal Nanjing Massacre (December 1937–January 1938). But the Imperial Army was not the only army on the move at this juncture in world history: during the next year, the German Wehrmacht annexed Austria (March 1938) and occupied the Sudetenland in Czechoslovakia (October 1938). In response to the China Incident, in July 1939 the United States abrogated the US–Japan Treaty of Commerce and Navigation (1911), which dealt Japan a serious economic blow. In September 1939, the German Wehrmacht and SS Einsatzgruppen began their campaign of rape and murder in Poland in the name of creating Aryan *Lebensraum*, and Europe, following the Asia–Pacific region some eight years earlier with the Mukden Incident, plunged into total war.

Vulnerable to US sanctions and embargoes, particularly related to oil (but also copper and scrap metal), Japan viewed diplomatic relations with the Netherlands as the key to its survival. Asia–Pacific affairs were hopelessly intertwined with the outbreak of war in Europe. In 1934, Japanese negotiators visited Batavia to promote relations between the two nations. The Japanese government also enacted the Petroleum Industry Law in 1934, which allowed the government to license the importation and refining of petroleum. Importantly, it required oil importers to stockpile a six-month supply at all times. Imperial Navy planners worried about private-sector straws in their precious oil reserves. In February 1940,

Japan sought to improve relations with the Netherlands, a diplomatic initiative sparked by growing concerns over diminishing oil imports from the Dutch East Indies – 870,000 tons in 1937, 670,000 tons in 1938, and 570,000 tons in 1939.

When, in April 1940, the Wehrmacht began operations against Denmark and Norway, tension rose between Germany and the Netherlands, and Japan expressed concerns about the war spreading to the South Pacific. In May 1940, when the Wehrmacht crossed the Ardennes and invaded France, the Dutch were quickly defeated and the Dutch royal family fled to London. Once more, on May 11, 1940, Japan expressed hopes that the war would not spread to the South Pacific. Nonetheless, on that very day, the Imperial Navy command ordered the Fourth Fleet, of which *Yukikaze* was a part, to the Palau Islands. Increasingly concerned about oil, on May 20, 1940, Japan demanded from the Dutch government in exile a firm commitment of 1 million tons of oil and 200,000 tons of bauxite (for making aluminum) annually. Eventually, the Dutch agreed to the bauxite number. But they waffled on the oil exports, leaving those in the hands of British and US firms operating in the Dutch East Indies – both Standard Vacuum Oil Company (a joint venture of Standard Oil and Mobil Oil) and Royal Dutch Shell operated Dutch East Indies oilfields. The Allies, it appeared, remained content to dictate the terms of Japan's hydrocarbon future.

At this juncture, the United States moved to contain Japan. Previously, the United States had served as Japan's most generous supplier of oil, but that changed over the course of the next year. In June 1940, the United States announced a machine-tool embargo against Japan. One month later, the United States announced the creation of separate Atlantic and Pacific fleets (two months earlier the US fleet had been moved to Honolulu), and began requiring a license for oil and scrap iron exported to Japan. With the Dutch government in London, the Netherlands had become increasingly dependent on the British and United States. In October 1940, shortly after Japan had signed the Tripartite Pact with Germany and Italy (September 27, 1940), US, British, and Dutch officials met in Singapore to discuss the deteriorating international situation. Japan dispatched a special envoy, but his requests for over 3 million tons of oil proved futile.

In December 1940, Japan dispatched an envoy to the Dutch East Indies again, but these discussions met with similar results to previous ones. In March 1941, Japan had managed to stockpile just under 43 million barrels of oil, primarily from California and Tarakan (off the eastern coast of Borneo). In July 1941, Japan moved into French Indochina, and the United States, Britain, and the Netherlands froze Japanese assets. Reeling from a newly imposed Allied oil embargo on August 1, 1941, Japanese war planners prepared for the Southern Operation – they sought to settle Japan's oil security question once and for all by capturing and holding oilfields, securing island airfields, and then utilizing sea lanes to ship oil to the home islands. It was to be an ocean empire unlike anything the world had ever seen.

News of the US oil embargo rippled through the Japanese fleet. As Hara Tameichi, at this point in the war captain of the *Kagerō*-class destroyer *Amatsukaze*, recalled, on the eve of the Pearl Harbor operation, Imperial Navy planners lectured officers on the "shocking results of the Allied embargo. Japan was running short of such critical supplies as petroleum, iron ore, rubber, zinc, tin, nickel, and bauxite."[5] War planners concluded that "Japan would reach a point of collapse within a year or two if the present situation continued." For aggressive, trigger-happy destroyer captains, it was high time to weigh anchor and sail southward.

* * *

As naval historian Samuel Morison succinctly summarized the Japanese strategy in 1941–1942, "Given free access to the oil and rubber of the Indies, the Greater East Asian Co-Prosperity Sphere could live on its own. Japan proposed to take these regions that yielded products vital to her economy, consolidate her position with a perimeter of steel and then repel any counterattacks offered by the enemy."[6] Similarly, according to Japan's official telling of the Southern Operation in the *War History Series*, "It is no exaggeration to say that the Greater East Asian War broke out with oil as the main cause."[7] This is an overly simplistic conclusion, to be sure, one no doubt clandestinely designed to absolve Japan of its war responsibilities, but, in part, it's true.

In the South Pacific, oil came from Miri and Seria in British Borneo, Tarakan and Balikpapan in Dutch Borneo, and northern and southern

Sumatra and eastern Java, both in the Dutch East Indies. In the East Indies, the best fields were near Palembang in southern Sumatra – at Pladjoe (the Bataafsche Petroleum Maatschappij refinery, a subsidiary of Royal Dutch Shell) and Sungei Gerong (the Nederlandsche Koloniale Petroleum Maatschappij refinery, a subsidiary of American Standard Vacuum Oil Company). The *War History Series* explained that the Southern Operation sought to make a "sudden attack against British Malaya and the US-ruled Philippines in order to set up footholds for a quick conquest of the Dutch East Indies, and while occupying the latter and securing its resources, to establish a defense line along the Sundra Islands."[8]

Famously, much of this ambitious plan hinged on the crippling of the US Pacific Fleet stationed at Pearl Harbor. To achieve this, on November 26, 1941, Japan's combined carrier task force departed the Kuril Islands under strict radio silence and sailed for Hawai'i. The successful surprise attack ravaged the Pacific Fleet, particularly battleship row, and caused President Franklin D. Roosevelt to proclaim December 7, 1941 a "day of infamy." He might well have called it "a year of infamy," given the full ambitions of the Imperial Navy. Pearl Harbor was the most flamboyant part of the operation, but it was only a strategic means to an oil-empire end. Hawai'i, after all, has no oil.

In 1939, the Dutch East Indies produced about 8 million tons of oil. At a minimum, Japan required about 5 million tons per year, but was incapable of producing even a tenth of that amount domestically. The biggest oil prize of all was the Palembang oilfields on Sumatra. With the Dutch royal family exiled in London, the British Expeditionary Force evacuated from Dunkirk, and the surrender and collaboration of the French, "like an orphaned child,"[9] explained the *War History Series*, the "Dutch East Indies was left on its own in eastern Asia."

In December 1941, *Yukikaze* was poised to strike southward. While the aerial muscle of the Combined Fleet steamed toward Hawai'i, on December 6, 1941, she warmed her boilers and began leading Desron16 from the Palau Islands to Legaspi for the invasion of the Philippines – the first of the stepping-stones that led to the oilfields of Borneo and the East Indies. Flanked by *Amatsukaze, Tokitsukaze*, and *Hatsukaze* – all *Kagerō*-class destroyers – at dawn early on December 12, the lookout spotted the conical shape of Mount Mayon, a volcano in Luzon Province. They had raised the Philippines. *Yukikaze* steamed into Legaspi Bay just before day-break and began assisting with minesweeping operations, evading the occasional strafing by US aircraft.

The landings at Legaspi went according to schedule, and the Japanese secured the necessary airstrips to provide critical air support. *Yukikaze* and her column then steamed toward Lamon Bay, just north of Legaspi. There, the destroyer assisted with the troop landings under the command of Lieutenant General Morioka Susumu. This served as part of a pincer maneuver from the north and east designed to seize Manila. *Yukikaze* participated in the eastern portion of this pincer maneuver, arriving at Lamon Bay on Christmas Eve to protect with gunfire and antiaircraft cover some 9,000 men from the Imperial Army as they went ashore. The northern landing occurred at Lingayen Gulf on December 22 with the Forty-Eighth Division under the command of Lieutenant General Tsuchihashi Yūitsu.

At the head of Lamon Bay, a US P-40 Warhawk fighter strafed *Yukikaze* and one round penetrated her fuel tank. Oil started trailing in the wake of the destroyer: a serious vulnerability, particularly given the number of US submarines and aircraft patrolling the Philippines. *Yukikaze*'s com-mander, Captain Tobida Kenjirō, immediately ordered that the vessel zigzag in order to evade detection. Then, another round from a US air-craft hit one of *Yukikaze*'s torpedo tubes, but did not detonate the Type 93's payload. When the battle for Lamon Bay concluded, medical per-sonnel onboard the destroyer treated six of her crew with minor injuries, and sailors pounded wooden bungs into her wounds to stop the leaking. She then steamed back to Legaspi.

After the fighting, the Imperial Army's liaison officer aboard *Yukikaze* said to Captain Tobida, "She's a lucky ship alright!"[10] Captain Tobida responded enthusiastically, "From this point forward, let her good luck in battle last an eternity!"

On New Year's Eve, *Yukikaze* came abeam the 10,000-ton repair ship *Akashi*, the only dedicated repair ship in the Imperial Navy, in Davao Harbor, where engineers properly welded her bullet holes. *Akashi* com-pleted the repairs in three days. Eventually, General Douglas MacArthur fled Luzon with his family by torpedo boat on March 11 to the north coast of Mindanao, where Flying Fortresses evacuated them to Australia. Japan now controlled the Philippines.

After Pearl Harbor, the Japanese sinking of the British *Prince of Wales* and *Repulse* (December 10, 1941), the capture of Manila (January 2, 1942), and the fall of British Singapore (February 15, 1942), Japanese war planners could basically step on whatever stones they desired in order to capture the "treasure houses" of the South Seas. In 1941, the Dutch East Indies extended over about three times the total area of the greater Japanese Empire. The South Pacific, particularly around the Malaya Barrier and in the Solomon Islands, was a fluid world, always in motion, one driven by tides and currents and well suited for highly skilled naval operations. In this watery world, oilfields and airfields served as the keys to Japan's advance southward, which took the form of a massive pincer movement, with Central and Eastern Invasion Forces.

On December 16, 1941, while *Yukikaze* was in the Philippines, the Central Invasion Force captured oilfields and refineries in British Borneo, part of a comprehensive campaign to subdue the vast right flank of British Malaya. However, as General Kawaguchi Kiyotake and his men approached, they discovered that the evacuating British had destroyed the Lutong refineries and pipelines and sabotaged the oilfields at Miri and Seria. On January 12, other elements of the Central Invasion Force moved on the Tarakan oilfields in Dutch Borneo. As General Sakaguchi Shizuo and his men discovered, the retreating Dutch had set both Tarakan oilfields ablaze by the time Japanese troops secured them. In Lingkas, for example, fire had destroyed all but just over 12,300 tons of heavy oil. The Dutch had destroyed some 700 oil wells in Tarakan's Pamoesian and Djoeata fields as well. Japanese troops, in retaliation, brutally executed European prisoners of war the next day. Next, Sakaguchi and his men occupied Balikpapan on January 23–24, only to learn that the Dutch had destroyed the refineries there five days earlier. Once again, European prisoners of war paid for oil with their lives.

Yet, even with many of the wells and refineries ablaze, Borneo could produce 35 percent of Japan's oil needs. Tarakan's high-quality oil was allegedly burned directly in warship boilers, even though engineers later determined that the high-sulfur content made engine steel brittle. The Balikpapan oil center – the "Ploeşti of the Pacific," as it was called, a reference to the Romanian region that provided the German Wehrmacht with critical oil supplies – processed some 5.2 million barrels of crude oil per year, as well as aviation gasoline, diesel and motor fuel, kerosene, and other lubricants. It was crucial hydrocarbon real estate: enough to keep the pistons of Japan's war machine pumping for years. The Central Invasion Force of the Japanese pincer then moved toward Java, captured Bangka Island, and eyed the rich oilfields of Palembang on Sumatra, which could produce enough oil to fuel Japan's war machine on their own.

* * *

While Palembang's oil was a worthy prize, claiming it required pioneering tactics: the capture of Palembang became one of the first surgical paratroop raids conducted by any belligerent. The key to the plan was the element of surprise by specially trained forces – to penetrate behind enemy lines and secure the sprawling airstrips, oilfields, refineries, and storage tanks before the retreating Dutch destroyed them. Once secured, an Oil-Drilling Unit would follow the advance team of paratroopers in barges up the Moesi River: these engineers would get the wells, refineries, cracking facilities, and other infrastructure up and running as quickly as possible. The war effort depended on it.

The Japanese military had already organized itself to exploit the oilfields and refineries once it had seized them. War planners formed the Oil-Drilling Unit, originally assembled in September 1941, under the direction of Ōkubo Tōru and two officials from Nippon Oil Corporation. On the ground, the Oil-Drilling Unit consisted of Nagahata Yoshinobu, the unit's commander, about 10 officers, and about 150 engineers. The unit first saw action on December 16 in British Borneo. Given the number of oilfields, Japanese war planners eventually had to divide the unit into three separate groups. Nagahata commanded the first group, which war planners eventually shifted from Miri and Seria in Borneo to Palembang. The second group, led by Katō Shunji, rebuilt oilfields in northern Sumatra. Meanwhile, a third group remained in Borneo in the Miri and Seria sector. Since much of Japan's war effort hinged on getting oil facilities pumping, Palembang showcased this effort.

On the morning of February 14, some 329 men jumped from their Kawasaki Ki-56 transport planes in the jungles to the west and south of Palembang and scrambled into position. There they awaited the equipment, supplies, and ammunition that came with the second wave of cargo planes. The paratroopers charged with securing Palembang's (Pangkalanbenteng) Airfield completed their drop by 11:26, while the paratroopers charged with taking Palembang's Pladjoe and Sungei Gerong oil facilities completed theirs four minutes later.

Bill Taute, an officer on the scene, later recalled that initially the Allied forces thought the Japanese planes were "friendly aircraft, our own aircraft."[11] However, the aircraft then "circled slowly round." It was "then we realized there were fighter aircraft with them which looked like Japanese Navy Zeros. And then the parachutes began to drop and they were different colours ... They fell beyond the perimeter of the airfield and where we were, we were between them and the airfield." Immediately, Mitsubishi Ki-21 planes began dropping equipment and supplies as scheduled, while other planes strafed targets and suppressed enemy defenses. By just after noon, after downing one Allied aircraft and chasing off nine others, the Air Groups began returning to their base at Kluang Airfield in Malaya.

In large part, Japan's paratroopers succeeded in catching the Allies by surprise. Kōmura Takeo commanded the main force of some 180 men to secure Palembang's airfield; they had landed some 3 kilometers southeast of the airstrip. Outnumbered and outgunned by Japanese paratroops, all Taute and his men could do was "ooze around in the jungle until you could see a Japanese, which we did occasionally, and then you could shoot him and then he'd fall out of the trees."[12] Allied pilots had been preparing to bomb a Japanese convoy in Banka Straits, not knowing that the convoy served as the main body of the invasion force. Terence Kelly, a British pilot, insisted "I am certain we had no idea there was an invasion fleet ... that we had no idea an invasion of Sumatra was imminent."[13] By 21:00, after heavy antiaircraft fire and sporadic fighting, Japanese troops had assembled at the main office at Palembang's airfield, though the Dutch had destroyed fuel drums and aircraft. Over the course of the next two days, Japan's Special Forces gradually strengthened their control of the airfield.

Back at the refinery, in the early afternoon, Japan's paratroopers secured all the distillation units and raised the Rising Sun flag at the central distillation tower. Finally, at 14:10, after stiff resistance by Allied machinegunners, Japanese paratroopers entered the central distillation unit and began closing the pipe valves and putting out fires ignited by the retreating Dutch. Yet, because the Japanese paratroops were relatively few in number, Dutch units launched several counterattacks, and bullets ripped new holes in oil tanks and pipes. Both sides lobbed mortar shells and grenades into the refineries, which ignited even more fires.

The Allies sought to destroy all the oil facilities before the main Japanese invasion force arrived, recognizing their importance to Japan's effectiveness. One Allied soldier explained how they weaponized the landscape by turning the river into an inferno. After preparing explosives, he recalled, "all the men save half a dozen ... withdrew to Palembang. The charges were then set off and ... by the time [Japanese] invasion barges began to reach the refinery the ensuing blasts of the petrol and diesel oil tanks flooded out onto the river and the burning fuel carried downstream on the six-knot current engulfed the best part of a section of the invasion force."[14]

On February 15, an Allied time bomb detonated in the Sungei Gerong refinery, and flames enveloped the entire facility once more. A. H. C. Roberts, another soldier, remembered the Japanese invasion in this manner: "We had reasonable success wiping out the first attack. But the Japs saturated the area with more paratroops and an invasion force up the river. On orders from the Dutch we slowly fell back to the river bank allowing the Japs to occupy the refinery. We suffered many casualties in the process."[15] He went on to recount that the Japanese "commanded the area all around them by setting up machine-gun posts on top of the storage tanks filled with high-octane aircraft fuel. What we didn't know, and neither did the Japs, was that incendiary bombs had been planted in all the storage tanks. These were all ignited at the same time and we beat a hasty retreat to the other side of the river but even there the heat was intense."

P. H. S. Reid recalled that "The oil refineries were mainly burnt out and suffered from explosions during the fighting with paratroops especially when at Pladjoe (Shell) refinery, a Dutch Kapitein Ohl launched a

68 grenade attack and set the place in flames; Sungei Gerong N.K.L.M. was destroyed by means of a time fuse bomb." Although the Allies fought desperately to keep oil out of Japanese hands, as Reid was forced to acknowledge, it was not long before the Japanese "had the refineries partly working."

The Japanese secured 250,000 tons of oil in the operation, at the cost of thirty-nine men. The Dutch successfully destroyed about 80 percent of the Sungei Gerong facility, but Japanese paratroopers managed to save most of the gasoline tanks at the Pladjoe facility. The paratrooper attack at Palembang quickly became a celebrated engagement in Japan, with artists such as Fujita Tsuguharu and Tsuruda Gorō depicting the "divine soldiers" of Palembang, with parachutes that "bloomed like flowers" descending from the Sumatran sky. In reality, carbon from burning oil painted the skies black over Palembang.

The next day, the Japanese commander wrote to his superiors that tankers should be dispatched immediately to ship the 150,000 tons of crude oil and 400,000 tons of refined oil from the Pladjoe refinery "to the homeland."[16] The commander explained at the time, "It is required to urgently dispatch a large number of engineers who can handle the distillation and cracking installations because all the main Dutch engineers have fled." Meanwhile, the Sungei Gerong refinery remained ablaze, with "no prospect of when the fire will be extinguished." Only about 70,000–80,000 tons of refined oil was secured from the Sungei Gerong refinery.

"As such is the situation," the Japanese commander concluded, "I am of the opinion that it would be better if fuel for operations and other needs during the southern operation be supplied from Palembang as a base, so that the supply [of oil] from the homeland can be reduced as much as possible." Like a marauding cavalry of old, the Japanese military proposed that its naval machines would live off the industrial hydrocarbon landscape as it advanced forward into the South Seas.

But the Allies nearly neutralized Japanese efforts at Palembang on February 19. Allied planes, operating from a secret airstrip, attacked the Palembang airfields and oilfields, which set the Pladjoe oil tanks ablaze. For three days, despite the efforts of Japanese fighter planes, Allied planes attacked the Palembang facility. With most Japanese fighter aircraft diverted away from Sumatra for Java operations, the Allied raids erased most of the gains painstakingly made by Japanese paratroopers. Japanese operations planners proved unaware of the second airstrip and paid dearly for the intelligence lapse. In these late-February raids, Allied planes destroyed nearly 30 oil tanks, including the precious 100-octane gasoline tanks.

Japanese war planners attempted similar paratrooper tactics to secure the oil facilities at Balikpapan, where Allied engineers transported oil from fields in Samarinda and Sanga Sanga in pipelines to Balikpapan, where it was refined and stored.

* * *

On January 11, *Yukikaze* had "served as the tip of the brush" for the push south to Manado on the northern tip of Celebes Island. While they were anchored, Allied planes bombed the destroyers, and *Yukikaze* received several dangerous near misses. Sailors remembered that "It was terrifying the way the ship trembled like in an earthquake"[17] as the bombs fell. These proved anxious times.

Two days later, an Imperial Navy reconnaissance plane reported "Large number of enemy subs heading north." *Yukikaze* served as flagship for Desron16 – with the destroyers *Tokitsukaze, Amatsukaze,* and *Hatsukaze* in the vanguard, followed by the cruiser *Jintsū* and the destroyers *Sazanami* and *Ushio* in the rear – which went out in pursuit of the enemy submarines. The submarines turned out to be a pod of whales, however. This sparked nervous laughter among *Yukikaze*'s officers and crew. Pygmy blue whales move between Celebes and the Banda Sea in September through December, likely making such sightings commonplace during naval operations.

Manado became an important communication terminal between Guam and the Yap Islands, since it possessed a telegraph station and an outstanding harbor. Although the assault on Palembang remains more famous, paratroopers also captured Manado. Paratroopers, led by Horiuchi Toyoaki, a fitness freak who had spearheaded gymnastics training for the Imperial Navy, had traveled nearly 400 miles from Davao to complete the assault.

From Manado, the same squadron steamed south to Kendari, and, on January 24, helped secure what many considered the finest airstrip in the Dutch East Indies. At the same time, Japanese forces secured the oilfields around Sanga Sanga. On January 31, *Yukikaze* assisted with the landing on Ambon Island, due east of Kendari and the eastern tip of the pincer movement descending on Java. On February 20, *Yukikaze* escorted the Japanese invasion force to Timor, an island in the Lesser Sunda Islands under the jurisdiction of the Dutch and Portuguese. Both jaws of the Japanese pincer then prepared to take Java and annihilate the Allied presence in the region.

On March 8, 1942, with much of the ABDA Command fleet resting quietly on the bottom of the Java Sea and Sunda Strait after the Battle of the Java Sea (Japanese name, Battle off Surabaya), the Dutch East Indies formally surrendered to Japan. Japan's war planners then began erecting a massive maritime and island defensive perimeter to guard their prize – a 32 million square mile oceanic empire, one built to extract natural resources. In six months, Japan had acquired 70 percent of the world's tin supply and almost all its natural rubber supplies. In the East Indies, Japan had gained access to higher annual oil production than California and Iran combined (well over 7 million tons). Japan also mined 1.4 million tons of coal from Borneo and Sumatra. Japan exploited gold, manganese, chromium, and iron in the Philippines; tin from Thailand (allied to Japan); and oil, silver, lead, nickel, and copper from Burma – and slave labor, some of it POW labor and some of it betrayed native populations, extracted it all. With military operations complete in early 1942, war planners estimated 1.7 million tons of oil coming from what had formerly been the Dutch East Indies.

But just because Japan had conquered a vast hydrocarbon empire by the summer of 1942 didn't mean that the Japanese could make good use of it. The Allies did not intend to allow Japanese war planners to realize their dreams of energy independence – oil still needed to move from the South Seas oilfields, refineries, and ports to the home islands, and it did so in poorly escorted, lumbering tankers. This proved a significant vulnerability for Japan. After President Roosevelt approved unrestricted air and submarine warfare against Japan only hours after the attack on Pearl Harbor, the Japanese military suffered a major setback when, on May 8, 1942, the US submarine *Grenadier* torpedoed *Taiyō-maru*, a 14,503-ton transport vessel, while she made way for Singapore. The *Taiyō-maru* turned out to be a big prize: she carried the renowned hydraulic engineer Hatta Yoichi, who had designed the Chianan Irrigation Canal and Wushantou Reservoir in Taiwan, as well as a number of oilfield technicians bound for Borneo and Sumatra. The human talent so desperately needed to get the refineries working again was now in Davy Jones's Locker.

This battle also revealed just how effective submarines would be in disrupting Japan's lines of communication. When *Grenadier* surfaced in the early morning hours of May 8, rough seas blew in from the northwest, making spotting difficult. The submarine submerged and hunted all day by periscope. That afternoon, *Grenadier* spotted smoke and identified a convoy of about six or seven vessels, including a "larger liner."[18] The submarine launched four torpedoes at the unsuspecting vessels; the crew then heard the report of two explosions. The submarine immediately commenced evasive tactics. That evening, *Grenadier*'s crew heard more explosions and they accurately identified the "old Taijo maru" as one of the ships hit. *Grenadier* then dove. "Vessels could be heard going ahead fast, stopping to listen, and probably firing depth charges … depth charging continued until 2300 ranging from very close aboard to several miles," the commanding officer recalled. But the damage had already been done; the *Taiyō-maru* had sunk. Only early the next morning did *Grenadier* surface after a twenty-one hour dive and commence charging her batteries. (Until the German Navy invented a "snorkel" that allowed combustion engines to run underwater, World War II-era submarines used diesel engines while running on the surface and batteries while running underwater. Because the diesel engines also charged the batteries, this could only be done while the boat was surfaced.)

* * *

In one fell swoop, the Imperial Navy had conquered the South Seas, ignominiously evicting its Western European colonial masters. *Yukikaze* and her fellow destroyers proved instrumental in the Southern Operation, serving as the "tip of the brush," as Itō Masanori worded it, in the strokes that painted the maritime boundaries of Japan's new empire. Many circumstances fueled Japanese empire creation, and the hunger for energy independence proved a powerful one. With the South Seas oilfields and refineries secured, Japan would no longer need to bow to the political demands of the United States, her heretofore hydrocarbon master.

But securing and holding South Seas oilfields and refineries, and transporting those resources to the homeland, proved a complicated undertaking. Japan's war effort in the Pacific depended on its ability to do so. The Imperial Navy enjoyed some early successes, but, as the war ground on, and the mirage of the decisive battle with the US Navy faded into the logistical reality of protecting tanker convoys, Japan's hopes of autarchy were dashed and replaced by the oil slicks that became commonplace markers of a failed maritime strategy.

CHAPTER 4

Conquest of the South Seas

All ships were assumed to be enemy ships
     Captain A. L. Maher, surviving senior officer of the US cruiser *Houston*

T HE FINAL ASSAULT of the Dutch East Indies began on February 18, when General Imamura Hitoshi departed French Indochina with fifty-seven troop transports for the invasion of Java, the final phase of acquiring the "treasure houses" of the East Indies. An Allied naval task force, led by a Dutch admiral, lay in wait. On February 27, the Allies intercepted the Imperial Navy task force approaching from Makassar Strait at the Battle of the Java Sea. The main action lasted throughout the night as Rear Admiral Karel Doorman tried to sink the troop transports headed for Java.

Sporadic fighting occurred over the course of the next several days, with the Allies suffering a stinging defeat. Admiral Doorman went down with his flagship, *De Ruyter*, during the battle. *Yukikaze* launched torpedoes as part of a massive coordinated salvo and, later, nearly sank the US submarine *S-37* with depth charges. The action ended at Sunda Strait when the Imperial Navy sank the US cruiser *Houston* and the Australian light cruiser *Perth*. The Allied task force delayed the Imperial Army troop landings by one day, but at the cost of its annihilation.

The Imperial Navy outgunned the Allies at Java Sea, but it still served as an impressive victory. To understand how the Imperial Navy waged war in the South Seas, we examine the navigational and celestial charts, cloud atlases, tide machines, binoculars, hydrophones, sonar, and other equipment that enabled Japanese sailors to be successful on the water in these early months of the war. When warships fought on the water, they didn't just suddenly appear in front of each other, guns blazing. They constantly scanned the horizon with "big eye" binoculars, looking for smoke, periscopes, or other evidence of warships and submarines.

But it wasn't just enemy vessels that concerned them. They read the clouds to anticipate weather. If there was no land for coastal navigation or dead reckoning, they used the stars to guide them. They also used sextants to determine their position. They watched birds, and looked for changes in water color. In the Solomon Islands, they relied on nautical charts to identify shoals and reefs. Sonar scanned the underwater environment for enemy submarines. Hydrophones listened for twisting screws. This was a world before GPS, and sailors aboard these warships needed to be solid mariners in order to successfully wage war. It wasn't just the enemy they needed to worry about.

* * *

For US submarine *S-37*, the sortie to the Java Sea on February 26, 1942 was plagued by mishaps. When Lieutenant James R. Reynolds assumed command of the boat, she hid "in the stream" at the Surabaya Naval Yard (on the eastern side of Java, south of the Madura Strait) as an air raid precaution. She couldn't get under way anyway. "Many important parts were still in the navy yard shops"[1] and scheduled maintenance and repairs remained incomplete. The vessel was in no condition to do battle, particularly with the numerically superior Japanese.

Once the submarine had returned to her moorage when the air attack threat had passed, dockworkers and the crew began assembling the parts aboard in order to get under way. But, once making way, the newly installed starboard engine cooler overheated and, late during the night of February 27, the electrical steerage failed. The engine cooler required even more work, delaying the boat's departure until after daylight, when the submarine might be spotted by Japanese reconnaissance planes or, worse yet, bombers. Captain Reynolds lamented that "It was obvious that daylight would arrive with the battery and air banks still uncharged."

At the western entrance of the Surabaya Naval Yard, *S-37* held station in order to get everything charged. That morning, after crews had worked around the clock, the starboard engine came on line to assist with the charging. It was risky holding station because Japanese warships were in the vicinity and planes roamed overhead everywhere. During practice evasive dives, Captain Reynolds noted that "exhaustion of the crew was indicated by several mistakes made on their diving stations." But, once crew had repaired the starboard engine, S-37 followed the pilot vessel through the protective minefield and out into the Java Sea. It was a frustrating start to a dangerous mission – to confront the Japanese southern invasion force bound for Java, which *Yukikaze* spearheaded.

S-37 submerged in the early afternoon having exited the Surabaya Naval Yard roads. Captain Reynolds set course for northwest of Madura Island, assuming the Japanese invasion force would be there by now. He was hunting troop transport vessels in order to stymie the invasion. About forty-five minutes later, S-37 spotted the Allied task force sent to confront the Imperial Navy and the Japanese invasion force. The submarine identified itself with yellow smoke and then changed course to parallel the Allied warships. When the warships circled around the entrance to the Surabaya Naval Yard, Reynolds assumed no battle was imminent and proceeded with his patrol. That evening, he and the crew observed lantern flares and "tracers of large caliber shells," and watched from about fifteen miles away, looking for the Japanese transports.

The Imperial Navy flares impressed Captain Reynolds. "These flares are apparently launched by aircraft and hang at almost constant altitude as if carried by a helium balloon." The flares dropped by seaplanes catapulted from cruisers were key ingredients to Japanese night-fighting prowess. At 02:45, after spotting two heavy cruisers with three escorting destroyers, S-37 prepared her torpedo tubes, flooded the forward trim, and submerged. "When back at periscope depth," lamented Captain Reynolds, "there was nothing left in sight." The heavy cruisers, likely the fast-moving *Nachi* and *Haguro*, and their escorting destroyers had vanished.

Around noon on February 28, S-37 came across a "boat with improvised sails," filled with Dutch sailors. On investigation, Captain Reynolds and the crew learned that they were survivors from the Dutch cruiser *De Ruyter*, which the Imperial Navy had sunk the previous night. S-37 took two US sailors aboard, and then passed food, water, and cigarettes to the Dutchmen, and continued the hunt for the Japanese convoys. "To have taken the other survivors aboard," concluded the captain of *S-37*, "would have precluded the performance of my mission." The Dutchmen in the makeshift sailboat would have to fend for themselves.

* * *

The Imperial Navy had sunk the cruiser *De Ruyter* during the Battle of the Java Sea. On February 18, with fires still burning in Palembang, General Imamura Hitoshi had departed French Indochina for the invasion of Java. This operation represented the final phase of acquiring the "treasure houses" of the Dutch East Indies. High seas were one of the obstacles facing the invasion force, but Allied resistance proved another. On February 27, the Allies sortied a naval task force to destroy the transports, led by Dutch cruisers *De Ruyter* and *Java* and strengthened by the US heavy cruiser *Houston*, a favorite vessel of President Roosevelt. They planned to attack the Japanese under cover of darkness.

The heavy cruisers *Nachi* and *Haguro* led the Imperial Navy's task force, with *Yukikaze* holding the center of Desron16. Rear Admiral Tanaka, the torpedo maestro, oversaw the destroyers from *Jintsū*. At about 10,000 meters from the enemy vessels, *Yukikaze* and her column launched their torpedoes in a battle that raged throughout the day and night (see Figure 4.1). They cheered, "banzai!" as columns of dark water rose near the enemy warships. It was their first taste of the fighting that lie ahead. Spotter planes launched from the two cruisers had greatly aided the Imperial Navy.

The cruiser *Houston* had been less prepared. "No day doctrine had been formulated,"[2] wrote A. L. Maher, the surviving senior officer from *Houston*. "A night encounter had been planned, and for that reason the only undamaged HOUSTON plane had been left at port." Meanwhile, "The enemy had an observation plane in the air immediately upon contact, and this plane remained on the lee side beyond anti-aircraft range throughout the action." It proved a costly oversight by the Allies.

The Allied task force also suffered from serious communication problems. As Maher lamented, "The fleet had been together only one day, and since it consisted of ships of four nations the doctrine, training, communication, and gunnery standards were all different." Making matters worse, the incoming fire from the Imperial Navy task force proved

Figure 4.1 Iizuka Reiji's "Torpedo tubes trained on enemy ships" postcard (author's collection).

"extremely accurate," landing in tight groupings. Over the next two days, the Allied task force was decimated, with *Kortenaer, Electra, Jupiter, De Ruyter, Java, Exeter, Encounter,* and *Pope* all sunk. Rear Admiral Karel Doorman, the Dutch commander of the Allied task force, went down with *De Ruyter*. The four remaining US destroyers fled to Australia.

When the sun rose on the morning of February 28, the crews of destroyers *Yukikaze* and *Hatsukaze* began fishing Allied sailors from the waters. These men were covered with oil, and it proved difficult to discern that the sailors hailed from Britain, the Netherlands, and throughout Indonesia. Captain Tobida of *Yukikaze* quickly ordered crew to interrogate the Allied prisoners. Of the forty-some prisoners slouching on *Yukikaze*'s deck, Captain Thomas Spencer, a British gunnery chief from *Electra*, was the highest-ranking among them. It turned out that Ensign Yamazaki Takio had studied English while in school and was able to talk with Spencer.

"What is your name?,"[3] he first asked. Captain Spencer offered his name to Ensign Yamazaki's delight, but would reveal no military plans. He did talk about his birthplace in Scotland and revealed that he had graduated from Dartmouth, the Britannia Royal Naval College.

Spencer explained, "If I ever return to England on a prisoner exchange, I will receive a medal of honor! The reason is I endured hard fighting as a gunnery chief during the sinking of the *Bismarck* and the sinking of the *Prince of Wales*. Even now, surely, in fighting with the Japanese navy, we damaged several ships and sank one or two cruisers."

It is true that *Electra* had escorted *Hood* when the celebrated battlewagon hunted *Bismarck* in the North Atlantic, only to be sunk by a fateful shot. *Electra* had also rescued British sailors from *Repulse*, when Japanese planes sank it and the *Prince of Wales* together at the outset of the war in the Pacific. It was now that Ensign Yamazaki revealed that not a single Japanese warship had been lost at the Battle of the Java Sea, much to Spencer's disbelief.

While Ensign Yamazaki was interrogating Spencer, *Yukikaze*'s spotters kept a keen lookout for any signs of Allied submarines, such as *S-37*, which strangely had failed to join the melée the day before. The prisoners remained on deck. *Yukikaze*'s orders were to deliver them to a prison ship, the Dutch vessel *Op ten Noort*, a 6,000-ton hospital ship, which *Amatsukaze* and *Yukikaze* had escorted to Bawean Island earlier. But en route, suddenly, while on deck, the prisoners began singing, dancing, and gesturing to Japanese sailors, expressing their gratitude for saving them from drowning. They signaled that they had nothing against the Japanese or Japan's war effort. Predominantly "colored men"[4] from the British and Dutch empires, the captured men felt "liberated" from their colonial masters.

In a sense, they had been: the Japanese had liberated them from the firm grip of European empire. Sadly, they had no idea that their new colonial masters, though promising Asian liberation, proved just as rapacious. The Imperial Navy was far less concerned about liberating "colored people" than it was about liberating fuel oil from Indonesian wells. On March 4, her prisoners on board, *Op ten Noort* steamed to Makassar, on Celebes Island, and arrived the next day, where she spent the next eight months providing medical facilities for Allied prisoners. Such vessels became known as "hell ships" over the course of the war because of their appalling conditions.

Aboard the submarine *S-37*, Captain Reynolds recalled, "Sighted a light cruiser of the JINTSU class with four DD's bearing 055T"[5] in the late afternoon that day. *Yukikaze* was one of those four destroyers. It proved excellent ship identification work because Admiral Tanaka's *Jintsū* led *Yukikaze*'s column. When Captain Reynolds next raised the periscope, he saw the destroyers heading for him at high speed – Japanese lookouts had spotted him. He changed course, but the destroyers still charged ahead, so he dove to 140 feet. "The first depth charges landed at 1631,"[6] and *S-37* made evasive maneuvers. "Forty minutes later, heard six bombs explode in the water at some distance," wrote Captain Reynolds.

Later, he "faintly heard a heavy explosion." He observed that Imperial Navy destroyer captains often approached "from the direction of the sea currents" because they had been "coached on to the mud stream which we probably made on landing" on the seafloor. It is an interesting tidbit – Imperial Navy destroyer captains no doubt looked for mud being kicked up from the ocean bottom to identify the whereabouts of their targets. During the action, Captain Tobida thought he had killed the submarine. He wrote in his report for the day "Conclude reliable signs of one enemy sub sunk."[7] *S-37* had actually slipped away, but barely.

The Imperial Navy attacked another Allied submarine on March 1. Destroyers *Amatsukaze* and *Hatsukaze* engaged *Perch* that night. Captain Hara Tameichi remembered that, once lookouts had confirmed the enemy submarine, *Amatsukaze* "raced headlong for the target. At 2,700 meters, *Amatsukaze* came around to port, bringing all guns to bear directly on the submarine."[8] Captain Hara yelled "Shine searchlight! Open fire!" Following the salvos from the two destroyers, *Perch* "blazed fiercely." Once *Perch* submerged, the two destroyers dropped depth charges and combed the area. "Our sonars did not pick up any targets," recalled Hara, "but the area smelled strongly of heavy oil," so they left the scene. But they had only damaged *Perch*, which hid in 147 feet of water. Destroyers *Sazanami* and *Ushio* finished the job the next day when *Perch* resurfaced. Following the attack, *Ushio* rescued the submarine's stricken crew out of the water in a rare example of mercy. The war was still relatively young, and the hunger for revenge less prominent.

The end of the Allied defense of the Malay Barrier came that night. In the waning hours of February 28, there was no wind, the seas were calm, the moon was full, and silvery, glowing clouds punctuated an otherwise inky black sky. *Houston* and *Perth*, having escaped the melée at the Java Sea and refueled in Batavia, encountered an Imperial Navy task force at the entrance to Sunda Strait, despite having been told by aerial reconnaissance that the narrows were "free from any enemy forces."[9]

The Imperial Navy task force was landing troops at Bantam Bay, when *Houston* and *Perth*, main batteries blazing, engaged the enemy forces just before midnight. As Gunnery Officer Maher remembered, "Due to flashes of gunfire difficulty was experienced in following the movements of the PERTH until she was observed to be in a sinking condition." Once the *Perth* went down, it made targeting easy for *Houston* because "all ships were assumed to be enemy ships." While evading torpedoes, *Houston* began receiving "many direct hits from gun fire."

Maher recalled that "Much debris was flying about" when *Houston* received a devastating hit in the port-side engine room. Then a shell smashed into turret number two. As if the repeated Imperial Navy attacks were not enough, the "proximity of the ship to shoal water and the strong current running were additional hazards to maneuvering." Maher explained that, "Because of the overwhelming volume of fire and the sheer rapidity with which the hits were being scored on the HOUSTON, it was impossible to determine in many instances whether a shell, torpedo, or bomb hit had occurred." After once countermanding the abandon ship order, the orderly abandonment of the listing cruiser began around 00:33 and the warship sank at 00:45. Gunnery Officer Maher, the senior-most surviving officer, believed that the Japanese captured a total of 268 US sailors after the sinking.

* * *

The South Seas represented treacherous water to fight on. Jagged coastlines gashed by narrow straits with fast tidal currents and clusters of small islands provided the archipelagic framework for Indonesian waters, ones always in motion. Dangerous shallows punctuated by deep trenches hint at the rugged mountainous seafloor that lies below the blue surface, a product of plate tectonics. Powerful currents drive Indonesian seas from the nearby South Pacific and Indian Ocean, whipping up strong waves. Tidal nodes are located throughout these waters, as are areas of strong tidal fluctuations, residual circulations, internal waves, and even the periodic rogue wave. As naval historian Morison acknowledged, "Netherlands East Indies waters are as tricky as any in the world."[10]

It's a dynamic environment in which to wage war. In these waters, both US and Japanese warships used the heavens above for understanding tides and for celestial navigation, and meteorology in the atmosphere for wind and weather. They observed the surface of the water for waves, tides, and currents, and sounded the subsurface and seafloor spheres, looking for dangerous shoals and reefs, as well as lurking enemy submarines.

In the eighteenth and nineteenth centuries, over thirty British, Dutch, German, and US expeditions had surveyed Indonesian waters. These expeditions sought to observe hydrographic conditions, monsoon-driven tides in the Java Sea, and the general climate of the region. In 1923, the Dutch physicist F. A. Vening Meinesz mounted a gravimeter to the submarine *K II*, measuring seafloors for the first time. In this manner, Dutch submarines surveyed the ocean trenches surrounding the Indonesian archipelago, mapping its depth and topographical contours. One of those trenches, the Sunda Trench, separates the Andaman Sea and the Indian Ocean northwest of Sumatra, where the Australian–Capricorn tectonic plates subduct under parts of the Eurasian plate. It's a geologically active region, part of the Pacific's legendary "ring of fire."

In 1929–1930, Commander P. M. van Riel oversaw one of the most comprehensive oceanographic surveys of Indonesian waters during the *Snellius* expedition, sponsored by the Society for Scientific Researches in the Dutch Colonies and the Royal Dutch Geographical Society in Amsterdam. Importantly, Riel identified the tidal transport in Indonesian waters to be directed mainly by the Indian Ocean. He also contributed important hydrographic and seafloor topographical information. Physicist Johannes Paulus van der Stok had access to this information and, more importantly, logs from Dutch naval vessels operating between 1814 and 1890, and published them in his *Wind and Weather, Currents, Tides, and Tidal Streams in the East Indian Archipelago*. This pioneering text served as a foundational maritime aid in the early twentieth century. In fact, the US Navy reproduced this book in the 1940s to aid in naval navigation in this strategically important region.

Imperial Navy navigators were familiar with Stok's text and the hydrographic complexities of southern waters. Imperial Navy navigators also had access to Dutch, British, and US nautical charts of the area. Since the turn of the century, particularly after World War I, when Japan received mandates in the South Pacific, the Imperial Navy had frequented

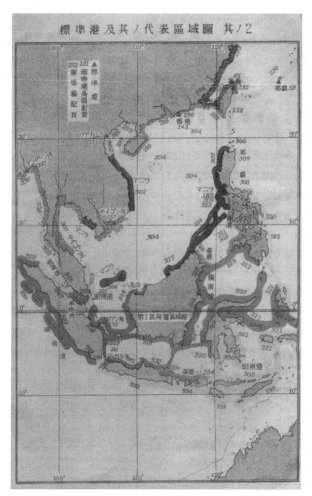

Figure 4.2 A 1944 Imperial Navy tide book. This reference map standardized major ports with their accompanying tidal zone boundaries. Coastal areas in blue, for example, corresponded to Manila's high and low tides. Yellow represented Singapore, red represented Tinnanpo, red stripes represented Hong Kong, and blue stripes represented Bako. Black numbers were page numbers for standard times of high and low tides, while red numbers were page numbers for more detailed tidal information (author's collection).

Indonesian waters on training cruises. By December 1941, when *Yukikaze* fired up her boilers and steamed west from the Palau Islands for the invasion of the Philippines, the Imperial Navy's information on tides for the East Indies, as well as such ports as Shanghai, Hong Kong, and Singapore, came from the Hydrographic Department of the British Admiralty, the displaced colonial masters of much of Asia (see Figure 4.2).

Otherwise, the Imperial Navy relied on the ability to predict tides in an additional twenty-nine ports, including those in Indonesian and Solomon waters, using Lord Kelvin's elegant tide-predicting machine, an early analog computer of sorts. Even then, however, British ports remained the baseline for most Imperial Navy tide information. In 1926, Arthur Thomas Doodson, a preeminent British tide scientist who later helped plan the tidal dimensions of the Normandy landings, explained that the tide-predicting machine "sums a number of harmonic variations, transmitted vertically to pulleys, round which passes a wire or chain which is fixed at one end and carries a recording pen at the free end."[11] It then draws a tide graph. The machine is "unrivalled in accuracy and cheapness," he wrote, and could be found in nine countries by 1926, including two examples in Japan (a third machine was apparently destroyed in Japan's Great Kantō Earthquake of 1923).

The accuracy of the machine depended on the number of "constituents," represented by pulleys and gears, the machine incorporated into its calculations. "For some ports," noted Doodson, "especially those situated in estuaries, a machine with, say, eighty constituents would be required." This is because seafloor contours, coastal shapes, depths, rivers and estuaries, and other littoral factors drove the nature of high and low tides. For Japan's oceanic empire of archipelagos, littorals, estuaries, coastlines, and even open expanses of pelagic blue water, such tide-predicting ability was essential to conducting complex naval operations, particularly nighttime raids in shallow Indonesian waters and around the Solomon Islands, and maintaining the fluid southern boundaries of the Greater East Asian Co-Prosperity Sphere.

In general, predicting tides proved an integral part of battle strategy during World War II, when amphibious landings became essential to taking or retaking territories in the Atlantic and Pacific theaters. The early Allied amphibious assaults on Dieppe in August 1942, on North Africa in November 1942, and on Tarawa Island in the Pacific in November 1943 presented numerous tide-related logistical challenges that, when combined with stubborn German and Japanese resistance, cost thousands of Allied lives, and portended bloody amphibious fighting ahead. A neap tide (a weak to moderate tide, created when the tide-generating forces of the sun and the moon oppose each other) in November 1943 meant that

US Marines had to wade ashore to Betio, on South Tarawa, rather than land with especially designed assault vehicles, which required four feet of water. It cost the Marines dearly. The French coast near Normandy, site of the Allied amphibious landings to retake "Fortress Europe," experienced six-meter tide variations, at low tide exposing expansive beaches that Allied landing forces would have to traverse, making them easy targets for German machinegunners. Tide-prediction machines proved essential to the Normandy landings.

Lord Kelvin's first tide machine, built in London in 1872 by Légé Engineering Company, had pulleys and gears for ten tidal constituents. When the Allies landed in North Africa in November 1942, they used a tide-predicting machine designed by Rollin Harris and completed in 1912 by the US Coast and Geodetic Survey – a thirty-year old "brass brain," as it was called. For Normandy, Doodson used a modified version of Lord Kelvin's original 1872 machine, and a forty-constituent machine designed by Edward Roberts in 1906 for the Bidston Observatory's Liverpool Tidal Institute.

After careful analysis, Doodson and his team of calculators pinpointed the time of the most favorable tidal conditions to avoid the considerable German coastal obstacles placed to deter the landings. Operation Overlord planners concluded that just after low tide was best, so that demolition crews could remove the obstacles for the next wave of landing craft and soldiers. The Allied invasion took place on June 6, 1944, and changed the course of the war. In Japan's oceanic empire, reading tides proved equally important. Tide-predicting machines allowed Imperial Navy navigators and war planners to render ports and coastal environments legible, facilitating naval supremacy and the maintenance of Japan's oceanic empire.

Imperial Navy warships also relied on nautical charts for navigation, ones that mapped depth soundings, coastal areas, island outcroppings, reefs, and other hazards critical to safe and strategic navigation. Nautical charts proved particularly important for coastal navigation and what is called dead reckoning, where protractors, compasses, and optics, such as the mounted "big eye" binoculars made by the companies Nikon and Tokyo Optics, were essential. Before the start of the war, Japan's optics industry relied on overseas connections for research, development, and production, importing everything from polishing materials such as commercial grade sands and wet stones to low-expansion glass, such as Corning's Pyrex, and Canada balsam (a natural resin used to glue lenses) produced by the German company Merck. Once the war broke out, optics makers scrambled to find most of the material in Japan or the empire, and moved the optics manufacturing facilities to the Kure Naval Arsenal. Japan's naval optics proved to be some of the finest in the world, allowing Japanese spotters to identify Allied warships from miles away. US Navy officers often credited them with the Imperial Navy's unrivaled night-fighting abilities.

Most Imperial Navy nautical charts were of British, Dutch, or US origin and, along with the history of Japan's optics industry, illustrate the early international cooperation that built the infrastructure of the Imperial Navy – which was certainly less parochial than its cousin, the Imperial Army. Early on, the Imperial Navy had acquired numerous British Admiralty charts. The nautical charts used for the sortie from Davao Harbor to Manado Bay on northern Celebes, for example, through the Celebes Sea, were probably based on British Admiralty Chart No. 2575, published originally in December 1857 and substantially corrected in April 1904. Rear Admiral Kimotsuki Kaneyuki, an accomplished meteorologist and head of the Imperial Navy's Hydrography Office, then oversaw the translating, updating, and publishing of the charts in November 1904. This chart became Imperial Navy Chart No. 674, though it never contained depth soundings.

The Imperial Navy relied on celestial charts as well. Tide books began with a table of the "moon's age"[12] and the "time of the moon's upper transit (135°)" because, in the purest sense, knowing tides depended on knowing the location of the moon. But blue water and nighttime navigation also depended on knowing the locations of celestial bodies. With a "Tenzu (Chart of the Heavens)," such as Imperial Navy Chart No. 1001, published on January 15, 1891, when the Hydrography Office was under the direction of a younger Captain Kimotsuki Kaneyuki, the heavens were rendered legible. A "Chart of the Heavens," a sextant, a compass, and a Pacific Ocean chart allowed warship navigators to fix a vessel's position without coastal sighting or dead reckoning, which was instrumental to successful sorties to such faraway targets as Hawai'i and Midway.

Closer to Earth, instruments designed to feel atmospheric conditions aided sailors in successfully gauging incoming weather. Barometers read lows and highs in atmospheric pressure, helping to anticipate changes that might aid naval tactics. A sudden drop in barometric pressure could bring foul weather and signal an incoming gale or a more localized squall, for example. Squalls proved common in the Solomon Islands, and could provide helpful cover for warships evading aircraft or danger-ously scatter columns trying to hold an attack formation (see Figure 4.3).

Naval battles are popularly depicted as won and lost during exchanges between big guns and torpedoes, of warships crossing the "T" and sink-ing their adversaries. But making marine environments legible proved equally important in World War II, particularly in the watery world of the Philippines, Indonesian waters, and the Solomon Islands. *Yukikaze* relied on these navigational aids as much as any warship, and the ability of her crew to expertly navigate was one reason why she survived the war – it wasn't all luck.

* * *

Later in the war, on May 14, 1944, as *Yukikaze* safely entered the Tawi-Tawi anchorage, in the southernmost Philippines, after escort duties from Lingga in the Dutch East Indies, an encounter occurred near the strategic anchorage between Imperial Navy destroyers and the US submarine *Bonefish*. On that day, *Inazuma*, *Hibiki*, and one additional destroyer steamed to the southwest of Tawi-Tawi Island en route for the refineries of Balikpapan with a small convoy of tankers. *Bonefish* sighted the convoy, managed to approach undetected, and put at least one tor-pedo into *Inazuma*, sinking the destroyer.

Only one month earlier, the US submarine *Harder* had sunk her sister ship, *Ikazuchi*, southeast of Guam, evidencing the toll submarines wreaked on Japanese shipping and thin destroyer escorts in 1944. Normally, the sound gear aboard an Imperial Navy destroyer, its passive sonar, should have detected *Bonefish* speeding in the waters east of Sibutu Island, try-ing to catch the convoy. As the commander of *Bonefish*, Captain T. W. Hogan, reported, "The near escort, a HIBIKI Class DD, passed very close aboard ahead of me. His high speed must have blanked his sound gear as he did not detect me although I was making high speed to close the

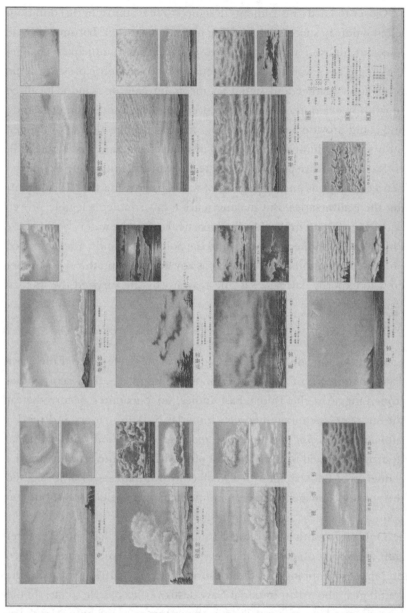

Figure 4.3 An imperial Navy "Illustration of Cloud Formations" from 1938. Reading the atmosphere could be just as important as reading coastlines and tidal currents. Courtesy of the Gaihōzu Digital Archive, Tohoku University, Sendai, Japan.

gap."[13] *Bonefish* fired five torpedoes in the direction of the convoy, judging its fourteen-knot speed from the "size of the target's bow wave."

Bonefish claimed to have hit a tanker with three torpedoes, but the notoriously unreliable Mark 14 torpedoes apparently malfunctioned. Instead, the fourth torpedo appears to have struck *Inazuma*. When *Hibiki* charged at the submarine, *Bonefish*'s commander ordered an emergency dive. The destroyers then pursued *Bonefish*. The commander heard the first "heavy" depth charge as the submarine dove. "Commenced heading out of the passage to the Northward," wrote *Bonefish*'s commander, "taking advantage of the current." Meanwhile, the two destroyers "continued dropping depth charges, all astern of us, but they worked Northward also." The navigators aboard the two Imperial Navy destroyers also knew the tides and currents in Sibutu Passage and continued dropping depth charges accordingly.

"They would stop and listen then speed up and drop one or two charges," noted *Bonefish*'s commander. At this time, "they were not echo ranging." *Hibiki* began fishing Japanese sailors out of the water, while the other destroyer continued the hunt. "One destroyer commenced echo-ranging astern of us. He was the only one heard after this time. He appeared to commence a systematic sound search of the area, working to the Northward." But *Bonefish* slipped away to the east.

In the submarine-infested waters near the Tawi-Tawi anchorage, *Yukikaze* spent the coming days escorting runs to the refineries of Tarakan and guarding the newly constructed carrier *Taihō* in her shakedown operations. It proved dangerous duty: on June 9, for example, the sharpshooting *Hardin* sank *Yukikaze*'s sister ship *Tanikaze* in Sibutu Passage. Normally, such training exercises occurred in safer home waters, but a serious lack of oil and aviation fuel forced *Taihō* to conduct her operations near the source of Japanese oil in Balikpapan. For days, *Yukikaze* came and went from Tawi-Tawi anchorage, keeping a careful watch for US submarines that, like *Bonefish* and *Hardin*, hunted in the area. At dusk on May 22, while returning from escort duties, *Yukikaze* encountered strong currents at the mouth of the anchorage and kissed a coral reef, damaging a fin on one of her propellers.

The Imperial Navy nautical chart depicts the Tawi-Tawi anchorage as a veritable fortress encircled by menacing coral reefs. A US chart from

1930 served as the basis for the Imperial Navy chart of Tawi-Tawi. Chief navigator Taniguchi and Captain Terauchi aboard *Yukikaze* would have been familiar with these charts and the local tides – the Imperial Navy tide book for 1944 has Tawi-Tawi Inlet flooding strongly to a 5.1 meter high on the evening of May 22, 1944 – and these strong tide-driven currents got the best of *Yukikaze*. Conducting proper repairs proved impossible because the undeveloped harbor had no dry docks, and the damaged propeller reduced *Yukikaze*'s speed to a sluggish, and quite dangerous, twenty-five knots (see Figure 4.4).

The consequence was that *Yukikaze* missed the main action of the Battle of the Philippine Sea on June 19–20, 1944, which turned out to be mainly a duel between aircraft anyway. The Combined Fleet had assembled at Tawi-Tawi and on June 13 decamped for the Philippine Sea with the carrier *Taihō* serving as the flagship. Her speed reduced, commanders relegated *Yukikaze* to tanker escort duty, a sad consolation for a warship bred for a decisive battle of annihilation with the US Pacific Fleet. Once the tankers had refueled the fleet before the battle, *Yukikaze* escorted the Kawasaki-type oilers back to the Philippines and then the Kure Naval Yards. In the ensuing battle, US submarines and planes sank the new carrier *Taihō* and the stalwart *Shōkaku*, decimating Japan's poorly trained fliers in the process.

When Imperial Navy destroyers chased *Bonefish* north through Sibutu Passage, or navigated in shallow waters, they carried a Type 93 Model 2 Hydrophone, which engineers had developed from the US Navy's MV-type Hydrophone, first introduced to Japan in the 1930s. In 1920, US Navy sound physicist H. C. Hays had trumpeted the virtues of the hydrophone, explaining that it aided warships by "hearing and locating a moving propeller-driven vessel at ranges varying from 2 to 10 miles"[14] and by "accurately determining the direction of submarine sound signals." It also aided in navigation. For Imperial Navy destroyers involved in antisubmarine warfare, being able to hear the subsurface environment, and know the depth of the seafloor, was more important than being able to see the surface environment. Sailors aboard destroyers became highly sensitive to the underwater aural world that surrounded them and discerned different sounds from one another.

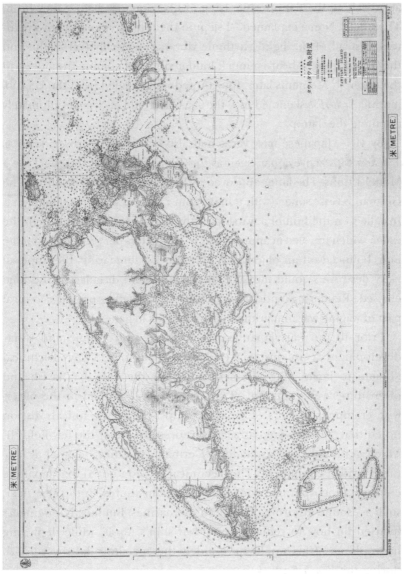

Figure 4.4 Imperial Navy nautical chart of Tawi-Tawi Inlet where *Yukikaze* fouled her propeller on May 22, 1944. "Fuirippin shotō Sūrū sōtō" ("Philippine Islands, Suru Archipelago," TAWITAWI ISLAND and APPROACHES). Imperial Navy Chart No. 692. Courtesy of the Gaihōzu Digital Archive, Tohoku University, Sendai, Japan.

Take this telling example. In the early morning of November 29, 1944, while *Yukikaze* escorted the carrier *Shinano* with two other destroyers, Hydrophone Operator Noma Mitsue actually heard the torpedoes approaching the flattop while lying in his hammock before they hit it. That night, Noma explained, "I slept in the torpedo department's quarters. Instead of the light, rhythmic vibration I usually feel in the gut, the 'zoon, zoon,' I heard a much louder vibration coming from deep in the water."[15] Moments later, four torpedoes launched from the US submarine *Archerfish* slammed into the starboard side of *Shinano*, ultimately dooming the flattop.

By 1944, Japanese navy yards had also equipped destroyers such as *Yukikaze* with active sonar, such as the Type 93 Model 3 and the Type 3 Model 1 units. The latter appeared in 1943 and was developed from the German *S-Gerät* sonar (with a maximum range of about 6,000 meters). Installed on the hull of a warship, active sonar sent a ping through the water, which traveled at approximately 343 meters per second. When the ping bounced off an object, say a lurking US submarine, the Imperial Navy destroyers could measure the location and distance by the time elapsed. Rendering underwater sound waves legible proved a critical part of waging war in maritime environments in general.

Prior to the war, Japan had prioritized hydrophone and sonar development, a circumstance evidenced by, as the US Navy Technical Mission to Japan noted immediately after the war, the "lavish and often unnecessary amount of space allocated to them in the otherwise cramped quarters of Japanese ships."[16] The Technical Mission noted that "Sonar would appear to represent one of the few fields in which generous use was made of German assistance," as well as captured British equipment. The Technical Mission noted that Japanese engineers incorporated some "anti-sonar measures" into their fleet, such as "sound-absorbing paint" on submarines. But mostly, engineers focused on how to reduce their "own ship's noise" while deploying hydrophones (this would have aided the speeding destroyer *Hibiki* during the *Bonefish* attack).

* * *

With the destruction of *Houston*, and by using all the navigational tools available to it, the Imperial Navy had largely accomplished its goals: landing its invasion force and securing its military hold over the oilfields of Sumatra and Java. Between March 29 and April 25, 1942, *Yukikaze* participated in the defeat of the Allied stronghold of Ambon, and then proceeded to Papua New Guinea to secure such cities as Buna, Sorong, Ternate, Manokwari, Serui, Sarmi, and Hollandia. Charged with escorting landing forces, the operations went smoothly for the most part, though *Yukikaze* faced some fighting at Sarmi and Hollandia. Mostly, the Imperial Army landing forces disembarked without incident. Like the Philippines months before, the Japanese conquest of the South Seas was complete, and all well ahead of schedule.

CHAPTER 5

Escorting Catastrophe at Midway

It's a disgrace that the skies over the imperial capital should have been defiled without a single enemy plane being shot down.

Admiral Yamamoto Isoroku in a letter to Admiral Koga Mineichi

O N THE EVENING OF APRIL 17, 1942, Japan's Navy General Staff went to bed masters of the Western Pacific and South Seas. They had largely manhandled the Allies at every turn in the war, exceeding even their own inflated expectations. The Pearl Harbor operation had been a success, even if the US Navy's carriers had remained unscathed. Japanese aircraft had attacked the British Royal Navy's *Prince of Wales* and *Repulse*, sending the behemoths to the bottom of the ocean. The Imperial Army's invasion of Malaya, including impenetrable Singapore, had been successful, with many of the troops triumphantly entering the city on bicycles.

The invasion of the Philippines also went according to plan, punctuated by the Bataan Death March (April 9–17, 1942), as had the taking of Borneo and Celebes. The Battle of the Java Sea, where the Imperial Navy sank much of the Allied task force, including President Roosevelt's adored *Houston*, cleared the path for the conquest of the Dutch East Indies. With a small handful of exceptions, everything the Navy General Staff touched had turned to gold. Creating a 32 million square mile oceanic empire is never an easy undertaking, but things were going remarkably well.

The defeat at Midway, Admiral Yamamoto's much desired decisive engagement, changed all that. Unlike most treatments of the legendary battle, we examine the Midway operation not from the flight decks of the big flattops, but from the bridges of troop transports and their screening cruisers and destroyers. These were the Imperial Army troops that sought to occupy the small atoll in the middle of the Pacific Ocean, and change the course of the war.

But we begin with the daily operations and routine maintenance aboard *Yukikaze* and other Imperial Navy warships, the vital work that kept them ready for combat operations, such as Midway. These routines kept warships ready for battle, and elevated the morale of sailors. Imperial Navy sailors studied such booklets as the *Rules for Navy Hand Signals* and *Essential Knowledge for Navy Sailors*, which contained information on knots and lines, as well as the timeless, inspirational words of the Emperor, which served as a reminder of whose warships these young men sailed aboard. *Yukikaze*'s sailors paid particular attention to her torpedoes and launching systems, as their effectiveness could be the difference between life and death. But they also had to keep antiaircraft batteries, the main guns, and other systems in working order.

Warships were machines, but they were also floating villages, with infirmaries and their accompanying medical personnel, dental facilities, galleys, baths and toilets, and sleeping quarters for officers and sailors. They reflected terrestrial social hierarchies and Japanese culture. Warships became small, floating reflections of Japan, ones that, like Japan the nation, changed for the worse as the war dragged on (see Map 5.1).

* * *

On April 18, 1942, after breakfast, members of the Navy General Staff received an alarming report from patrol boat No. 23, the *Nittō-maru*. Unbelievably, the converted fishing boat reported seeing three enemy carriers just over 700 miles east of Tokyo. The vessel then went eerily silent.

"The fleet staff plunged into activities at once,"[1] remembered Admiral Ugaki Matome. Immediately, "We issued an order to activate Tactical Method No. 3" against the intruding carriers. The Navy General Staff ordered Admiral Nagumo Chūichi's task force, currently off Taiwan and fresh from conducting raids in the Indian Ocean, to intercept the US warships at once. Conventional thinking said that no carrier-based plane

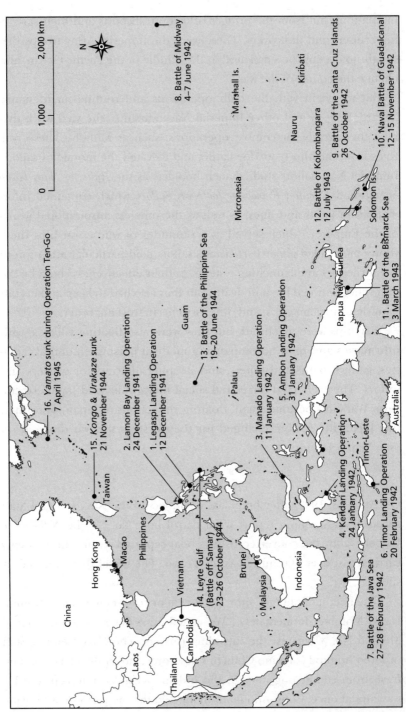

Map 5.1 Yukikaze's landing operations and battles, 6 December 1941–7 April 1945

China

Hong Kong

Macao

Philippines

Vietnam

14. Leyte Gulf
(Battle off Samar)
23–26 October 1944

Brunei

Malaysia

Laos

Thailand

Cambodia

Indonesia

Timor-Leste

Australia

7. Battle of the Java Sea
27–28 February 1942

6. Timor Landing Operation
20 February 1942

4. Kendari Landing Operation
24 January 1942

5. Ambon Landing Operation
31 January 1942

3. Manado Landing Operation
11 January 1942

Palau

Guam

13. Battle of the Philippine Sea
19–20 June 1944

1. Legaspi Landing Operation
12 December 1941

2. Lamon Bay Landing Operation
24 December 1941

15. Kongo & Urakaze sunk
21 November 1944

16. Yamato sunk during Operation Ten-Go
7 April 1945

Taiwan

Micronesia

Marshall Is.

Nauru

Kiribati

Solomon Is.

Papua New Guinea

11. Battle of the Bismarck Sea
3 March 1943

12. Battle of Kolombangara
12 July 1943

9. Battle of the Santa Cruz Islands
26 October 1942

10. Naval Battle of Guadalcanal
12–15 November 1942

8. Battle of Midway
4–7 June 1942

N

0   1,000   2,000 km

could be launched from such a distance, not even half that distance, so the US warships could still be intercepted before they launched their attack package. But, as it would turn out, this was not a conventional raid.

"At 13:00 we received news of an enemy air raid on Tokyo," recalled Admiral Ugaki. But it was too late to retaliate because the US carriers had slipped eastward into the darkness, just as ghostly as they had appeared. "This is more than regrettable, because this shattered my firm determination never to let the enemy attack Tokyo or the mainland," confided Ugaki. He conceded that "this is one up to the enemy today." If the Doolittle Raid shattered Admiral Ugaki's hope in sparing Tokyo the ravages of war, Admiral Yamamoto, Commander of the Combined Fleet, was rendered singularly distraught by the raid.

Yamamoto wrote to a colleague, "I was distressed to hear that Tokyo finally had a raid."[2] He said, "I feel it was just enough of a taste of the real thing to warn the people of Tokyo against their present outlook." In a letter to Admiral Koga Mineichi, who succeeded Yamamoto as Combined Fleet Commander one year later, Yamamoto shared, "one has the embarrassing feeling of having been caught napping just when one was feeling confident and in charge of things." He continued, "it's a disgrace that the skies over the imperial capital should have been defiled without a single enemy plane being shot down." The enemy had bombed the capital of Imperial Japan, a country that no foreign power had ever conquered.

It was indeed a daring attack. It was actually something that Ugaki and Yamamoto could admire. When James Doolittle, leader of the attack, had applied for aeronautics school in 1917, his letter of recommendation writers gushed about his potential as an aviator. At the time, Doolittle was an aspiring mining engineer and senior at the University of California, Berkeley. An associate professor of Physical Education wrote of the young Doolittle, "I have observed his work in boxing, wrestling, gymnastics, and acrobatics, and feel sure that he has the type of aggressiveness and courage to make him a first class aviator."[3] Nearly twenty-five years later, as Doolittle's Mitchell B-25 lumbered off the flight deck of the carrier *Hornet* deep in the Pacific, he tapped into that "aggressiveness and courage" to change the course of the war. It was the spring of 1942, and the Imperial Navy had largely pummeled the Allies in the Pacific.

The Doolittle Raid represented an attempt to strike back, if largely symbolically. But the Imperial Navy appreciated symbolism.

"This force is bound for Tokyo,"[4] announced Admiral William Halsey days earlier, over the loudspeakers of the *Enterprise*, the second carrier of what became Task Force 16, as it sailed toward Japan. The sailors cheered loudly. *Enterprise* provided air cover for the preoccupied *Hornet*, whose flight deck remained crowded with the Mitchells. The US Navy needed a morale booster, and Doolittle's fliers delivering 500-pound bombs over Japan's largest cities proved just the ticket. That morning, after having been reported by the picketing *Nittō-maru*, the *Hornet* had increased speed to 30 knots and turned into a freshening breeze over 600 miles from Japan, while the *Nashville*, under Admiral Halsey's orders, engaged the *Nittō-maru*. By 08:21, Captain F. S. Craven of the *Brooklyn*-class cruiser reported "enemy vessel on fire"[5] and, four minutes later, "enemy vessel sunk."

With waves "breaking over the deck" of the carrier, sixteen Mitchell B-25s with five-person crews successfully took off and made their way toward their intended targets. The bombers dropped their payloads in the dark 6 hours later, killing close to 100 people and injuring hundreds more. Never a raid with much strategic value, the Doolittle Raid was meant to get into Japanese heads. It certainly got into Admiral Yamamoto's head (see Figure 5.1).

With the aid of a fortuitous tailwind, all but one of the bombers made it to China, where they crash-landed or the crews bailed out after over 2,000 nautical miles of flight. The remaining bomber flew to Vladivostok in the Soviet Union. Three airmen were killed in action; Japanese soldiers captured eight more and executed three of them. Of those five remaining men, one died in captivity, while the remaining four survived the war. As Yamamoto pondered the implications of the Mitchells dropping their 500-pound bombs on *Shinkoku*, or the "divine homeland," he became even more resolute that it was time to annihilate the US Navy in a Mahan-style decisive battle once and for all. Otherwise, the homeland and the Emperor, whom many saw as a living god, would never be safe from US planes. Meiji leaders had promoted this national myth surrounding the bespectacled Emperor, astride his majestic white horse Shirayuki (White Snow, a California transplant),

Figure 5.1 James Doolittle takes off in his Mitchell B-25 from the carrier *Hornet* some 650 nautical miles from the Japanese home islands. Official photograph of the National Museum of the US Air Force, VIRIN: 420418-F-0000D-003.JPG.

and now US planes threatened the Divine Sovereign who stood at the center of the modern Japanese state.

Yamamoto became determined to annihilate the US Navy at the small atoll of Midway, about 1,500 miles northwest of Hawai'i. Imperial Navy General Headquarters had green-lighted Yamamoto's scheme weeks earlier, and the Doolittle Raid only cemented Yamamoto's resolve for the MI Operation. It also convinced the Imperial Army to participate. The war in the Pacific would pivot on the outcome of the Midway assault; the gambler Yamamoto had designed it that way, and *Yukikaze* would be a part of that fateful roll of the dice in the Central Pacific.

* * *

One week after the Doolittle Raid, *Yukikaze* lowered her anchor into the waters off Davao, in the Philippines, and made preparations to depart the next morning for Kure, Japan, where she would dock for maintenance.

Since decamping the Palau Islands, she had been out for over four months and badly needed supplies and routine maintenance. The crew also needed a break. Many of the crew hailed from central and western Japan, and they could visit families. After the engagement in the Java Sea, the destroyer had spent March and early April escorting landing forces in western New Guinea in the Dutch East Indies. Those missions were now complete, the South Seas were in Japanese hands, and the war had entered a new phase for Imperial Navy planners.

After New Guinea, life aboard *Yukikaze* had returned to some semblance of bustling, combat-ready normalcy. The thrill of roaring engines, firing main guns, concussive depth charges, bursting antiaircraft fire, and the compressive punch of torpedoes leaping from their launchers during battle gave way to the daily affairs of keeping watch for periscopes and routine chores aboard the warship, a constant battle against the saltwater environment that proved at least as formidable as the enemy. It was also important to guard against fatigue and maintain the mental and physical fitness of the sailors. The crossing to Davao and then Kure proved a momentary respite for *Yukikaze* before the storm of war returned to rock the warship in the Solomon Islands, particularly around the strategically vital island of Guadalcanal.

In the Davao Gulf, topside activities, such as washing and drying laundry, and idle conversations about the battles already witnessed characterized life aboard the destroyer. Lookouts constantly scanned the horizon for enemy ships and aircraft, or the menace of a submarine periscope; but otherwise life aboard the warship calmed. The wind whistling through the mast, waves lapping against the steel hull, and the cry of seagulls brought familiar sounds – sailors no doubt became lost in thought of the past and the hopeful future.

Sailors in any navy, however, are rarely idle for long, because warships need constant attention, and *Yukikaze* proved no exception. Even when not being targeted by enemy ships, planes, and submarines, warships are always under assault from the wind, the sun, and the saltwater world they float atop. Barnacles and sea vegetation sought to grow on *Yukikaze*'s hull, slowing the vessel, obstructing her through-hull valves and sonar gear, and jamming the steerage. To combat this, the Imperial Navy used a hot plastic Venetian antifouling paint, a knockoff of Italy's Moravian paint, produced by Toa Chemical of Osaka, among other commercial chemical companies.

Unlike the US Navy, where a warship might be at sea for years in the Pacific, Japan's area of naval operations actually decreased over the course of the war, and long-lasting antifouling paints became less necessary. Moreover, as metals became scarce, Japanese chemists began replacing the cupric oxide and Paris green (copper), litharge (lead), and red mercuric oxide (mercury) with more readily available chemicals and ingredients. But, periodically, bottom painting still needed to be done at dry dock at Kure. Topside, sailors painted *Yukikaze* with an anticorrosive paint, laced with zinc oxide and zinc dust, in order to keep rust and corrosion at bay. Usually this was done while the ship was at dock, but sailors needed to touch up chipped paint as part of their routines.

Meanwhile, torpedo men repeatedly oiled their deadly fish so they didn't rust or corrode. The Torpedo Chief checked and rechecked the launchers so that they could be used at a moment's notice. Torpedo men trained the Imperial Navy Type 92 torpedo launchers, weighing eighteen tons with their massive steel splash shields, which, confusingly, fired the Type 93 oxygen torpedo, on enemy warships with a ten horsepower air motor that required careful maintenance. Otherwise, men trained the torpedoes with hand wheels, which took valuable time in combat. Almost daily, torpedo men practiced their firing protocols in order to be ready for action. The torpedo, World War II's underwater missile, served as *Yukikaze*'s principal weapon.

These quadruple launchers fired their torpedoes with compressed air. They leapt from their tubes at forty feet per second, splashing into the water before gliding, with no wake or warning, toward their target at fifty knots by burning kerosene fuel in pure oxygen. The maximum range of the "Long Lance," as historian Morison nicknamed the Japanese torpedo, was forty kilometers. Robert Whitehead might have invented the "Devil's device," but Japanese engineers perfected it. Warships equipped with the Type 93 torpedo, such as destroyers and cruisers, needed oxygen-generating equipment to fuel the finicky and fragile devices. Alternatively, torpedoes could be launched with powder, but the explosion produced a flash that betrayed the location of the warship during night battles. In large part, the Imperial Navy was built to fight at night, and compressed air aided their ability to do so.

The Type 93 torpedo represented one of the engineering marvels of World War II. A mixture of oxygen and kerosene powered the 9 meter (29.5 feet) and 2,721 kilogram (6,000 pound) underwater missile toward its target at about 50 knots. The warhead alone weighed 490 kilograms (1,080 pounds), and the torpedo could travel some 22,000 meters at its highest speed setting, or approximately 13 miles. Torpedo men had to be highly skilled to hit their targets. If *Yukikaze* sought to hit a US Navy cruiser running at 30 knots at 24,000 meters when firing abeam, for example, torpedo men would need to lead the cruiser by some 13 kilometers (8 miles). While launching at targets 8,000 meters away, they needed to lead their target by nearly 5 kilometers. And those firing solutions don't include compensating for sea conditions, such as wind and tide.

Once loaded, torpedoes could be fired from the bridge with the push of a button, or fired from the launcher itself. Aft of each torpedo launcher was a watertight box that needed to be repainted with anti-corrosion paint and maintained – it held one reload of torpedoes, the difference between life and death in battle. Typical of Japanese torpedo technologies, a ten horsepower air motor moved the steel fish from the magazine to the launcher. If this lifter failed, the torpedoes had to be loaded by hand, which could take upwards of ten men with traditional block-and-tackle pulleys. In principle, the air motor could reload torpedoes in as little as three minutes, but any mishaps or mechanical failures delayed the reload time, which was often the case in rough seas. Importantly, to ensure that it would function properly in the saltwater environment in which *Yukikaze* fought, torpedo men doted over this complex machinery, making sure the wheels, gears, tubes, compressed air, and fuels were always ready for combat. They rehearsed combat and studied drills during their spare time. It was fulltime work. The life of the destroyer depended on it, and hitting an enemy vessel speeding at thirty knots twenty kilometers away with torpedoes traveling at forty knots in rough seas was as much an art as it was a science.

In rough seas, saltwater splashed over the bow, dowsing the forward main gun in corrosive saltwater. Engineers designed and launched destroyers such as *Yukikaze* with three twin 12.7 cm .50 caliber (5-inch) gun turrets. One turret was mounted forward, the other two aft, because of space constraints forward of the bridge, and weight-distribution concerns. In August 1943, Kure yard workers removed the more-elevated aft turret, called the "X-Turret," and replaced it with two triple 25 mm antiaircraft mounts. Earlier, Kure workers had added twin 25 mm machine guns to the bandstand forward the bridge. As the war progressed, and *Yukikaze* gained experience on the water, the need for beefier antiaircraft capabilities came to far outweigh the need for main guns used for surface combat.

Weighing over four tons, the 12.7 cm guns hurled shells some eighteen kilometers. A 100-horsepower motor moved the heavy turrets according to the fire-control solution inputted by the chief gunner and gunner's mates. Unlike US Navy warships, where radar eventually drove most fire control, Imperial Navy warships relied on old-school techniques, where specialists, such as *Yukikaze*'s Chief Gunner Ishikuma Tatsuhiko, calculated target speed, course, and range to render accurate flight time, as well as vertical and lateral deflections. They inputted these values manually to the sights and fuse receivers. Then, they let the shells fly and watched for a hit, or waited for a report from a spotting aircraft to pinpoint the whereabouts of the miss.

The motors that moved the turrets needed to be maintained as well. So did the Type 16 depth-charge projector, with its depth charges and their finicky fuses. Plunging at twenty-two feet a second, Imperial Navy depth charges were not unlike the Allied versions, though the Japanese proved less advanced with magnetic and acoustic innovations. The depth-charge projector was located just behind the aft-most gun, and the depth charges needed constant attention to make sure they were secured and ready if an enemy submarine was sighted, such as during the engagement with the elusive *S-37* in the Java Sea months earlier.

The 25 mm machine guns proved an only modestly effective antiaircraft deterrent, but they were ubiquitous on Imperial Navy warships and antiaircraft crews fussed over them. The venerable 25 mm machinegun was modeled after the French Hotchkiss machinegun, with several Imperial Navy modifications. It shot a 250-gram projectile at a rate of between 180 and 200 rounds per minute, with a muzzle velocity of 900 meters (2,950 feet) per second. It was air-cooled, so often sailors draped wet cloth or clothing over the barrel in an attempt to cool it during rapid firing. The machinegun itself weighed 95 pounds, but the triple mount, of which *Yukikaze* had four by the end of the war, weighed upwards of 4,000 pounds. The 25 mm mount killed best within 2,000 meters distance, but only after expending an average of 1,500 rounds, which were often in increasingly short supply as the war dragged on.

Often poor accuracy was a result of antiquated sights. Manufacturers built the 25 mm with a mixture of sighting technologies, including the Le Prieur mechanical lead computing sight, open-ring sights, or optical-ring sights. Usually, Japanese systems possessed only fifteen-round magazines, which made engaging enemy aircraft even more precarious. Normally, each barrel needed replacement after about 20,000 rounds (otherwise, the projectile tumbled and became less accurate), but that number increased as Japan felt the squeeze on raw materials and manufacturing. When not being replaced, the barrels needed to be carefully oiled, and the rifling in the barrel had to be inspected and cleaned. This, too, was fulltime topside work for the chief gunner and his mates.

Then there were the guts of the destroyer. As the shipboard electronics became more sophisticated, so did the need for more onboard energy to power them. The saltwater environment assaulted electronics constantly, and corrosion of vital power connections and grounds became a daily concern. Like all Imperial Navy destroyers built after 1935, *Yukikaze* possessed a 220-volt, three-phase AC power system with inline distribution. Rather than rely on one unit, as destroyers had in the past, engineers distributed multiple units throughout *Yukikaze*, placing them in well-armored locations. This combination of turbo and diesel generators powered all shipboard electronics, such as lighting, VHF radio, search radar, radar-detecting devices, hydrophones and sonar, telegraphs, telephones, electric blowers for ventilation, aluminum water heaters for tea, electric sterilizers, sometimes refrigeration, and a host of other equipment.

All shipboard communication moved through these power lines, along with voice tubes and runners, so telecommunications within the vessel was checked routinely. Although Imperial Navy warships had

り 眠 き げ ら 安　　　（活 生 軍 海）

Figure 5.2 Imperial Navy sailors in hammocks aboard a warship, part of a postcard collection titled "A day in the life in the navy" (author's collection).

lighting, it was woefully inadequate by US Navy standards. In 1945, after Japan's surrender, a US Navy Technical Mission, which surveyed Japanese equipment, commented that "Lighting throughout the ships is inadequate, and, except in compartments provided with ports, the officers and crew lived and worked in perpetual and depressing gloom."[6] In these gloomy, cramped spaces, men slept in tightly lined up hammocks, which swayed with the vessel's constant yawing, pitching, and rolling (see Figure 5.2).

There was also the routine maintenance of sailors, including basic hygiene, such as bathing, and dental and medical attention (see Figure 5.3). The sea is hard on people, just as it is on equipment, and the quality of a ship's ability to fight comes down to the fitness and preparedness of her officers and crew. During World War II, the Imperial Navy drew on the Navy Dental Corps to supply qualified dentists, the bulk of whom were well trained in modern techniques at Japan's dental colleges. Some had practiced in civilian clinics before the war. Despite their qualifications, however, in general the Imperial Navy was perennially understaffed, particularly with oral surgeons, as more recruits entered the service. The Imperial Navy had a little over 250 dentists, creating a

上甲板の帆布風呂 （海軍生活）

Figure 5.3 Imperial Navy sailors bathing on the deck of a warship, part of a postcard collection titled "A day in the life in the navy" (author's collection).

ratio of dentists to sailors about 1:7,000, or roughly 224,000 teeth per dentist. That's a lot of teeth to inspect for one dentist.

Obviously, the Imperial Navy could little afford to supply every warship with dentists, and, as the smaller fighting ships, destroyers didn't have them. Cavities and gingivitis were relatively common on warships, and sailors had to wait to make port to receive care. More concerning was that face injuries became a reality of naval warfare, and oral surgeons were needed to care for disfiguring wounds. Much like the situation with antifouling paints, Japanese dentists had fewer precious metals such as gold as the war ground on, and used more acrylic resins for tooth fillings.

The need for adequate medical personnel proved even more pressing than dentistry, given battlefield traumatic injuries, the infectious diseases of the South Pacific, and just the routine medical care of the men in the service. The Navy Medical Corps deployed physicians to hospitals and dispensaries at such imperial bases as Singapore, Batavia, and Rabaul. Doctors also found themselves afloat, tending to sailors on warships in sick bays. Typical of destroyers, *Yukikaze* had one physician aboard, as well as one or two hospital corpsmen, who cared for the 240 or so sailors aboard the vessel. During battle, officers from different departments might wear the armbands of "Special Navy Medics" and provide battlefield medicine, such as when an officer from *Yukikaze*'s accounting department by the name of Maruyama treated Torpedo Specialist Nishizaki Nobuo for bullet wounds to his thigh during Operation Ten-Gō in 1944. Imperial Navy battleships, by contrast, had between three and six physicians, one dentist, five or six noncommissioned medical officers, and upwards of ten hospital corpsmen aboard. Compared with those of destroyers, the medical facilities aboard a battleship were luxurious. Often, the sick bay had a capacity of between twelve and thirty-two people, a treatment room, an operating room, an X-ray room, a lab, a general ward, and a recovery room.

Destroyers had a small sick bay devoted to dispensing medical treatment and pharmaceuticals, but sailors had to recover in their hammocks. *Yukikaze* might have had a small electric instrument sterilizer, a steam vacuum sterilizer, a water heater, and a small wooden cupboard with simple medical supplies, as other destroyers did. She might also have had a metal box with instruments for laparotomies, as well as supplies for ear cleaning, sinus treatments, moxibustion, mouthwash for gingivitis, and saltwater for gargling. There were also plenty of cod-liver oil pills to go around. To treat the war wounded, Japanese physicians used forms of hemostasis, such as bandaging, as well as glucose, intravenous saline, and cardiac stimulants. Often, individual sailors carried their own sterilized bandage kits as well. Indeed, Torpedo Specialist Nishizaki, during Operation Ten-Gō, ended up digging bullet fragments from his own thigh with a pair of tweezers, as the medical staff was overwhelmed at the time. US planes had repeatedly strafed *Yukikaze*'s deck.

On destroyers, it wasn't just the sick bays that were cramped – living quarters aboard Imperial Navy destroyers were rather Spartan, too. This was a fighting ship, after all. Officers might have a bathhouse, with tile floors and porcelain urinals, toilets with wooded seats, and well-ventilated quarters with ports looking to the outside. But the average sailors pissed in long metal troughs, usually alongside men bathing in simple tubs. The officers' galley was usually neat and compact, with wooden cabinetry for stowing dishes and cups. It might be outfitted with an electric water heater for making tea and coffee and a simple coal-fired cooking stove. Similarly, the crew's galley had a coal-fired range, as well as a large ten-gallon aluminum rice cooker mounted in brick with an open hearth for coal. Some destroyers had refrigeration for keeping fresh foods and medicine, while others did not. Most food came from a can, as food spoils quickly at sea.

Providing food for officers and crew aboard an Imperial Navy warship was a full-time affair. Before the war, officers and crew aboard battleships ate fairly well. In fact, it was one of the allures of navy life, particularly for young men from poor rural households where white rice was seen as a delicacy. A May 24, 1926 breakfast menu aboard the battleship *Nagato*, for example, included white rice and ground barley, miso soup with a leafy vegetable, onion, and fried tofu, as well as daikon radish marinated in miso. Lunch consisted of white rice with ground barley, beef curry with potatoes, daikon radish, sweet potato, and onion, along with daikon radish marinated in miso. Finally, dinner came with the same white rice and barley mixture, grilled mackerel, *kon'yaku*, and daikon radish. This would've been borderline lavish for young Japanese men from the grinding poverty of the countryside, where millet and barnyard grass were commonly eaten instead of white rice. In fact, the Imperial Army and Navy became so reliant on white rice to recruit men into their ranks that many developed beriberi, a thiamine deficiency, as a result of the change to their diet. Before World War II, far more men died from beriberi than enemy bullets. In large part this is why barley was added to the galley's menu (see Figure 5.4).

As the war progressed, however, the Imperial Navy was not immune from serious food shortages that ravaged the homeland. When *Yukikaze* docked at the wharf in Saipan on May 26 (Japan time), she took on such provisions before the Midway operation. The sailors were still eating relatively well in 1942. But, as the war dragged on, sailors usually ate unpolished rice, a weak fish-paste soup with daikon radish sprouts, and pickled daikon radish, and drank tea. Cooks served no seconds, and servings became increasingly small. As a result, many sailors became malnourished, visibly emaciated, and lost the capacity to fight effectively, particularly at night, when endurance was key.

Often, naval histories are brought to life with accounts of the dramatic ocean battles that decided the outcome of wars, but it was the daily task of caring for ship and crew that consumed the most time. Every day,

事 炊 の 内 艦 （海 軍 生 活）

Figure 5.4 Imperial Navy cooks preparing fish during the times of plenty in a warship galley, part of a postcard collection titled "A day in the life in the navy" (author's collection).

officers and crew ate, drank, used the toilets, brushed their teeth, bathed, cleansed their sinuses, washed and dried their clothing, required medicine, and combed their hair, all in an attempt to stay healthy aboard a tightly bounded, galvanized world surrounded by corrosive saltwater. Life aboard a destroyer was cramped and mundane in this way, drawn out by the monotony of lengthy ocean crossings. Until, that is, it wasn't, when the main guns started blazing, or depth charges were launched, or the fish were in the water streaming toward their US Navy targets with the Torpedo Chief impatiently watching his stopwatch. Then, it was anything but mundane.

* * *

Japan's Imperial Navy sailors didn't possess radar-driven fire control and, though their torpedoes proved ferocious, their main guns remained largely inferior to Allied guns. Their ships were dark and their food increasingly lacked taste and nutrition. They had sparsely equipped sick bays, few doctors, and even fewer dentists. They had little to no big entertainment, other than the odd sumo wrestling tournament or kendo match on the deck of a battleship. They opened care packages from home when the mail managed to reach them, and if they were lucky received *haramaki*, or "belly wraps," handmade with 1,000 stitches by young women back home. These were said to stop bullets, but they of course didn't, and Japanese men kept dying on the fronts. They fought in distant, lonely, exotic waters for a cause that became increasingly abstract against an enemy that only became stronger as the war progressed.

When the war broke out, Japanese sailors were among the best-trained seamen in the world. Gunners, torpedo men, engineers, and navigators committed to memory such booklets as the *Rules for Navy Hand Signals*. The Navy Ministry Office of Education published this particular booklet, which covered the basic hand signals required to operate a vessel at sea, as well as more specialized hand signals for artillery, torpedoes, and mine laying. It also contained the basic hand signals related to the engine room and those used in the case of emergencies. Along with their usual shipboard duties, familiarizing themselves with hand signals became an important part of advancement within the service (see Figure 5.5).

Sailors also read numerous booklets devoted to rank advancement. The booklet devoted to the technical knowledge required for a seaman fourth class, for instance, a rank among the enlisted men, was an example of the kind of knowledge required to move up the chain of command into the ranks of petty officers and possibly even flag officers. Seamen studied ship construction and design, vessel stability, and the main parts of a ship and its lifesaving equipment, including lifeboats, the operation of davits, grappling hooks, and oars. They learned the proper method to tie mooring lines to cleats and bollards, the scope required to properly anchor a vessel, the deployment of drogues and sea anchors in heavy seas, nautical knots and line care, the mechanical advantages of block and tackle, reading a compass, including the difference between variation and deviation, and many of the other masteries that created Marlinspike seamen within the Imperial Navy. They were not only brave fighting men – Japanese sailors also proved as knowledgeable as any on the water.

Despite such widespread expertise, what supposedly made the Imperial Navy sailor superior to his Allied counterpart was his spiritual strength. Throughout the war, Japanese wartime propaganda contrasted the needy, pampered individualism of US sailors to the spiritual superiority

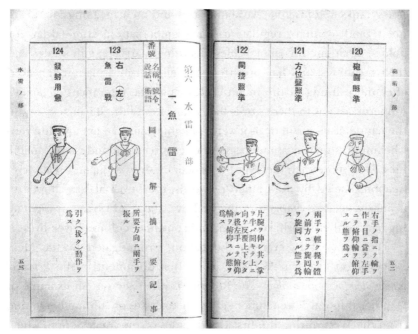

Figure 5.5 The beginning of the section on torpedo launching in the *Rules for Navy Hand Signals* (*Kaigun tesaki shingō hō*, Kaigun-shō Kyōiku Kenetsusai [Tokyo: Kaigun-shō Kyōiku Kenetsusai, 1937]) (author's collection).

of Japanese sailors. That strength, propaganda emphasized, emanated from the Emperor, the wellspring of Japanese national life. When *Yukikaze* arrived in Kure on May 2, 1942, after the crossing from the Philippines, sailors disembarked and many returned to their homes with stories of South Seas battles, or others stayed in nearby travel lodges to rest. While on land, some pulled from their sailor's duffle a copy of *Essential Knowledge for Navy Sailors.* Thumbing through the booklet, the words reminded them, page after page, of their unique relationship to the Emperor, the essence of what it meant to be Japanese. The Emperor loomed large in the hearts and minds of Japanese sailors. His official portrait adorned most warships. If there was adequate time, officers transferred his portrait before a warship sunk, just as his portrait was taken from the carrier *Akagi* as she burned in the Central Pacific after the Battle of Midway.

The *Essential Knowledge for Navy Sailors* was first produced in November 1920 and revised nearly every year, almost thirty times in all. In this booklet, sailors could reference information on principal Imperial Navy ports; ranks and insignia; naval uniforms and their meanings; naval etiquette and manners; regulations on disembarkation; criminal law for sailors; discipline for sailors; rules regarding marriage; gun salutes and their meanings; and flag protocols. But all that information appeared after the printing of the Imperial Rescripts, the utterances of Japan's Emperors. It was in these words that sailors found the spiritual strength, the nationalistic fortitude as it were, to fight against an enemy with overwhelmingly superior numbers, natural resources, and industrial capabilities. Even more than the Type 93 torpedoes, this was Japan's real secret weapon. Fueled by the Emperor's words, the Imperial Navy hoped to achieve a decisive victory over the US Navy, and send US sailors hightailing back to their lavish, jazz-laden, and consumer-culture-driven lives.

The Imperial Rescript on Education, promulgated by the Meiji Emperor on October 23, 1890, is the first document in the *Essential Knowledge for Navy Sailors*. The Rescript is often seen as an example of Confucian moral retrenchment after the excesses of cultural borrowing from the West during the first two decades of the Meiji period, which started in 1868. But the 1890 Rescript also reflects the basic values of nineteenth-century universal humanism. In many ways, the fledgling Imperial Navy had served as a poster child of such cultural cosmopolitanism, built as it was in the likeness of the British Royal Navy. In 1870, Imperial Decree had designated the British Royal Navy as the model for Japan. Three years later, Lieutenant Commander Archibald Douglas had arrived in Japan with a thirty-four-man naval mission. Douglas oversaw instruction for several years at Japan's fledgling Naval Academy at Tsukiji, where he instructed his Japanese counterparts in the traditions and formalities of the Royal Navy.

The cultural borrowing had extended into the realm of engineering as well. Japanese naval engineers learned from their experiences working with Vickers and other prominent British shipbuilders. *Kongō*, the first innovative battlecruiser of that class, was built by Vickers & Sons in Barrow-in-Furness, in England. But she then served as a template for Japanese yard workers to build her sister ships in Japan. Japanese yard workers built *Hiei, Kirishima*, and *Haruna*, at Yokosuka, Nagasaki, and Kobe, respectively. These warships ruled the waves in their day. This represents a microcosm of Japan's borrowing after the

Meiji Restoration of 1868 – ideas born abroad morphed to fit their new Japanese context, just as warships did.

Historians call this process cultural borrowing, and among the foreign ideas that Japan borrowed were thoughts on the "social contract" by Jean-Jacques Rousseau and musings on democracy by Thomas Jefferson. A fascinating discovery illustrates the pervasiveness of these borrowed Western ideas in late nineteenth-century Japan, particularly regarding individualism and human rights. In 1968, Irokawa Daikichi, a historian and Imperial Navy veteran, took students to an old house in Tokyo's Tama District and discovered there a bundle of political writings inscribed on traditional Japanese *washi* paper, what became known as the "Itsukaichi Constitution." The authors of the "Itsukaichi Constitution," likely commoners, had crafted the progressive document from imported Western ideas, including musings on constitutional government. With such political philosophies floating around Japan, it's not surprising that, after years of agitation by Japan's newly formed political parties, the Meiji Constitution was promulgated by the Emperor in 1889, and followed one year later by the Rescript. Japan held elections for the first time, with about 5 percent of the population able to vote.

But Western thought promoted individualism and human rights, which chafed against traditional Confucian values of family and loyalty. Meiji public intellectuals such as Fukuzawa Yukichi had concluded, after their studies of Western life, "my creed is that a man should find his faith in independence and self-respect."[7] Confucian teachings, by contrast, were responsible for Japan's "obvious shortcomings" in the nineteenth century, thought Fukuzawa. He believed that "studies in number and reason in material culture" and "independence in spiritual culture" lacked in traditional Confucian education. Vickers & Sons could help with the "studies in number and reason" related to naval engineering, but many in the Meiji government sought to curb the enthusiasm for Western ideas, particularly individualism.

In this regard, the Imperial Rescript on Education in 1890 sought to clarify the relationship of the individual subject to friends, family, and the state, while emphasizing that loyalty to the Emperor trumps all. Spiritual culture was not about independence and individualism, but about the individual's relationship to family and the Imperial State – what became known as the *kazoku kokka,* or "family state." In the new imperial Confucianism, "loyalty" and "filial piety" transcended generations and provided the glue that held this devotion to the Imperial State together, the Rescript instructed. "This is the glory of the fundamental character of Our Nation."[8] In a rehearsal of the Cardinal Confucian Relationships, the Rescript beseeched, "be filial to your parents, affectionate to your brothers and sisters; as husbands and wives be harmonious, as friends true." The loyalty and filial piety the sailor demonstrated toward his family permeated his relationship to the state. "Always respect the constitution and observe the laws," the Rescript stated, "should emergency arise, offer yourselves courageously to the state." Given the daily recitation of the Rescript in the classroom, historians assume that this mindset was implanted in many young sailors, and the reason they enlisted – they offered themselves "courageously to the state" in the "finest traditions" of their forefathers. In other words, the Imperial Rescript on Education clarified why sailors served aboard warships, and provided the moral adhesive that held the little fighting microcosm together. It was the spiritual fuel that powered the Imperial Navy into battle.

When Japanese sailors fought, in other words, they fought with the ferocity of a man defending his family. Crazed fanaticism might be one way to describe Imperial Army banzai charges, such as the one on Saipan on July 7, 1944, that left 4,000 Japanese dead; but so might passionate devotion to family and the Imperial State, a devotion articulated in the Rescript. The "savage, ferocious fighting"[9] in the Pacific Theater, depicted with such gut-wrenching candor by US Marine Eugene Sledge, was born, on the Japanese side, from a manipulation and corruption of this intense devotion. On the US side it was born from the need to survive in the face of it and make it home alive.

Take this heartfelt exchange between Torpedo Specialist Nishizaki, a young sailor who joined *Yukikaze*'s crew during the Mariana Islands campaign, and his friend Hydrophone Operator Noma. Both men hailed from Mie Prefecture, and they became friends aboard the destroyer. On April 7, 1945, as the Second Fleet navigated through the Inland Sea with the battleship *Yamato* on her suicide mission to Okinawa, many of *Yukikaze*'s sailors gathered above deck to gaze upon Japan's mountains, perhaps for the last time. It was a "Floating Chrysanthemum" operation, after all, a suicide mission. There, Nishizaki ran into Noma.

"Hey, Nishizaki,"[10] said Noma, "it's finally come, hasn't it. Is this our farewell look at Japan? The next time we meet, will it be at the Yasukuni Shrine?" Founded by the Meiji Emperor in 1869, the Yasukuni Shrine houses the souls of Japan's war dead.

Nishizaki answered, "No, I'm certain that we'll survive and return home."

In his heavy Nagoya accent, Noma responded, "We're still pure, in the midst of the springtime of our youth. How can we die before we've partaken in liquor, tobacco, or women?"

Nishizaki said, "If we come back, it'll correspond to the Buddha's birthday."

But then Noma looked at Nishizaki with a serious expression. "Anyway, Nishizaki, we fight for our families."

Nishizaki remembered being caught off guard by these words. "At the time," Nishizaki later wrote, "of course we fought for our country, but Noma thought the same as I did. I felt a glow in my chest, and I became even more resolved." Later, Noma claimed in interviews to have fought for "the country where his mother lived,"[11] not for the Emperor, but clearly, in the milieu of Japan's Confucian "family state," the two had become largely indistinguishable. The Imperial State was family; and family was the Imperial State.

Following the Imperial Rescript on Education in the *Essential Knowledge for Navy Sailors* was the Imperial Rescript to Soldiers and Sailors. The Meiji Emperor had presented this particular Rescript to military leaders at the Palace on January 4, 1882. It reaffirmed what would later be codified in the Meiji Constitution – the Imperial Army and Navy served under the direct authority of the Emperor. "Loyalty," the Rescript explained, remained the "essential duty" of the soldier and sailor. The Rescript asked the straightforward rhetorical question, "Who that is born in this land can be wanting in the spirit of grateful service to it?"[12] The Rescript warned against party politics and offered "duty" and "loyalty" as an alternative to participatory government. "Remember that," the Rescript cautioned, "as the protection of the state and the maintenance of its power depend upon the strength of its arms, the growth or decline of this strength must affect the nation's destiny for good or evil." Finally, don't be led astray by "popular opinions or meddle in politics, but with single heart fulfill your essential duty of loyalty, and bear in mind that duty is weightier than a mountain, while death is lighter than a feather." The divine words of the Meiji Emperor and his predecessors weighed heavily on soldiers and sailors as they performed their duties: they must have felt the weight of that mountainous duty as they cast aside their natural fear of death in battle.

During World War II, US production replaced warships at an astonishing pace. In August 1945, the US Navy operated 6,768 ships, including 28 aircraft carriers, 23 battleships, 71 escort carriers, 72 cruisers, and 232 submarines. As US Navy warships once sunk came back like Buddhist reincarnates bigger and better than before, and as Imperial Navy galley stores emptied and 25 mm antiaircraft ammunition ran dangerously low, Japanese sailors came to rely more and more on words such as duty, filial piety, and loyalty. These concepts came to be what men lived for as the war outlook became more and more grim, which it decidedly did after the defeat at Midway.

* * *

"I woke up at 05:00 and departed the Furumori Travel Lodge,"[13] wrote Gunnery Chief Ishikuma Tatsuhiko in his diary on May 22, 1942 (Imperial Navy warships kept Tokyo time during operations, and Midway was no exception). "I returned to the ship on the scheduled train." *Yukikaze* "left Kure Harbor at 08:20. The weather was fair with no waves. We swiftly transited the Inland Sea and shot through the Morojima Channel. War was coming quickly. We executed all kinds of drills in preparation for battle."

"At 11:00 AM," he continued, "we calibrated a discrepancy in the magnetic compass." There are two types of discrepancies with a compass. Compass variation is the distance between true north and magnetic north, while compass deviation is the influence that shipboard attractors have on a compass. Typically, the compass wouldn't be calibrated for variation. Rather, that would be noted on charts while navigating. Ishikuma's reference is likely to compass deviation. "After 13:30, we rendezvoused with the oil tankers *Nichiei-maru* and *Akebono-maru* and stationed ourselves appropriately as escorts." Together, the vessels then navigated the Bungo Channel and the Western Waterway. After a brief submarine scare that afternoon, "bearing 147° at 14–15 knots we departed mainland Japan." *Yukikaze* then sailed for Saipan, the staging area for the occupation forces in the "MI operation." Admiral Yamamoto was about to have his decisive battle with the US Navy at Midway.

The next day, Ishikuma wrote, "The seas grew heavier. Many people became seasick. The new third-class sailors proved particularly suscepti-ble. The course was south. But in order to smooth the ride, the ship's heading was changed 30°. Starting at 13:00, they executed drills with the *Akebono-maru.* The shortest distance separating the ships was thirty-five meters. It went smoothly." He added, "As we proceeded south, the air temperature climbed. Sunset was at 19:05."

On May 24, the wind freshened and the seas grew even heavier. The ship's heading was changed an additional 40°, again to smooth the ride. With the sunrise at 05:05, battle preparedness was switched from night to daytime. At 09:40, *Yukikaze* undertook gunnery drills, and Ishikuma reported that the shells scored over 90 percent of the time. "That after-noon," he confided, "I spoke with Captain Tobida about life aboard a destroyer." He continued, "We received frequent reports of enemy sub-marines in the vicinity of Ogasawara, Saipan, and the Taiwan Straits. It rained in the evening." He then turned in for the night.

On May 25, "It rained in the morning and the heavy seas subsided. The ship's heavy pitching also lessened. The temperature heated to twenty-seven degrees. Starting in the morning, we wore our heat-shedding clothing. I could tell we were in the South Seas from the color of the water and the shape of the clouds." The destroyer *Tokitsukaze* and the tanker *Nichiei-maru* split off and headed to Guam to join Desron7. Ishikuma studied the disposition of the forces to consume the time. He studied emergency fire and water damage control in the late afternoon.

While on duty that evening, he spoke with Captain Tobida about naval academy days – the benevolence of the Academy Principal, the wisdom of the Head Teacher, the courage of the cadets. That night, *Yukikaze* sailed the South Seas at thirteen knots. On the morning of May 26, the crew awoke to see Saipan emerging from the clouds. Several mer-chant vessels and a handful of warships tugged on their anchor chains in front of the harbor. *Yukikaze* entered the Saipan anchorage at noon; but later that afternoon relocated to the newly constructed wharf, where she

refueled and the sailors loaded food and other provisions for the coming mission. The next morning she returned to the anchorage. There,
the officers and crew celebrated Navy Day. (Navy Day was celebrated
on May 27 between 1906 and 1945, a commemoration of the Battle of
Tsushima Strait.) The Chief Navigator delivered a lecture on the upcoming "MI operation." That night, Ishikuma enjoyed a "pleasant dinner"
with Captain Tobida.

Saipan served as the staging area for the Imperial Army occupation
component of the MI operation. As part of the Second Fleet Escort
Force, commanded by Rear Admiral Tanaka, Imperial Navy planners
had tasked the force with escorting the main Midway invasion body –
some 2,800 soldiers (the 28th Infantry Regiment), commanded by
Colonel Ikki (often rendered Ichiki) Kiyonao. Once again, *Yukikaze*
found herself following the cruisers and destroyers under Rear Admiral
Tanaka's command, including Captain Hara's *Amatsukaze*. The mission
had a decidedly different flavor from the Pearl Harbor Operation, however. Hara recalled that, upon leaving Saipan, "I felt that something was
wrong with this operation, and my heart was not buoyant."[14]

The next morning, May 27 at 07:20, *Yukikaze* weighed anchor and
eased herself out of the Saipan anchorage for patrol duty. On conclud-
ing her patrol, *Yukikaze* and the occupation fleet departed Saipan that
evening around 17:00. The destroyer *Hatsukaze* experienced engine trouble, which delayed the departure by an hour. *Yukikaze* first headed on a
course of 270° and then adjusted her course to 230°. By 19:00, *Yukikaze*
was headed 180° as she made her way around the western part of Saipan.
She then made a complete turn and headed for Midway. Gunnery Chief
Ishikuma wrote "sixteen destroyers to the left, and another eighteen to
the right. The occupation force transports followed the speeding destroyers and cruisers." Though an exaggeration of the total number of warships involved, it made his heart swell with pride. They were on their way.

The occupation force and its destroyer escort charged from the south
toward Midway. During his free time, Chief Gunner Ishikuma continued
to study fleet dispositions and oversaw gunnery exercises and maintenance. The days were long, often starting at three in the morning and
ending well after dark. As the sun rose on May 28 at 04:41, *Yukikaze* commenced Evasive Pattern Alpha to avoid lurking submarines. By the end

of the day, Saipan was 240 miles behind them. The sun rose on May 29 at 04:23. It was twenty-seven degrees. *Yukikaze* took on fuel oil with some of the other destroyers, taking a half hour to pour fifty-two tons into her tanks. As the fleet started to head north, the temperature became colder. That evening, Ishikuma watched the cruisers *Kumano*, *Suzuya*, *Mikuma*, and *Mogami*, part of Rear Admiral Kurita Takeo's Second Fleet Occupation Support Force, slicing the waters in a line northward at 60°, the same course as *Yukikaze*. The fleet looked so powerful as it sailed toward its rendezvous with destiny.

The sun rose on June 1 at 03:25. *Yukikaze* was on a course of 55° following Evasive Pattern Epsilon. At around 10:30, the destroyer *Hayashio* signaled, "Spotted what appeared to be a floating mine." Then, the signal came that a submarine had been detected bearing 200°. *Yukikaze* began sweeping the area and launched two depth charges in a shallow sandbar of about 125 meters of water. Later, she poured an additional eighty-two tons into her fuel tank. That night, as the temperatures dropped, the occupation force and its escorting warships sailed to within about 850 miles of Midway.

The sun rose at 02:33 on June 3. At 06:13, lookouts spotted a lone enemy PBY Catalina flying boat, bearing 50° off *Yukikaze's* starboard bow. At 13:25, nine B-17s, bearing 170°, appeared through the cloud cover and, without hesitation, the fleet began evasive maneuvers to avoid the bombs. Twelve minutes later, *Yukikaze* opened up with her guns. Within two minutes she ceased fire, having expended some twenty-one shells. It was their first engagement with enemy aircraft near Midway.

On June 4, the day of the Midway attack, the sun rose at 02:15. *Yukikaze* spent the morning preparing for air raids. Then, *Yukikaze* received a radio transmission that Admiral Nagumo's Carrier Strike Force was attacking enemy carriers about 240 miles northeast of Midway. After that, they waited for word of the results of the battle. Then, unexpectedly, they received word of the unthinkable.

"*Akagi* is engulfed in flames," came the radio report, "and Admiral Nagumo's flag had been transferred to light cruiser *Nagara*."

Chief Gunner Ishikuma recalled, "Judging from later transmissions … over a hundred enemy aircraft had descended on carriers, *Akagi*, *Kaga*, and *Sōryū* and they were ablaze." *Yukikaze* and the Second Fleet forces retreated to the northwest. Later, they learned that enemy aircraft had attacked *Hiryū* while the carrier fled to the north.

Then, orders came over the radio, "transport fleet to evacuate westward. Second Fleet Torpedo Squadron take station southeast and search for the enemy." In response, a handful of destroyers remained to guard the transports, while the other warships charged to the northeast to engage the enemy. "At 23:00 that night, we came across a burning light in front of us," wrote Ishikuma. "As we got closer, the shape of the vessel could be made out as the burning *Akagi*." Flames engulfed Admiral Nagumo's former flagship, and *Yukikaze*'s crew heard her teak deck pop and crackle as it burned. Four destroyers scurried about the burning hulk, trying to rescue surviving airmen and sailors.

* * *

Admiral Nagumo of Pearl Harbor fame had launched the air raid on Midway Atoll at 04:28 (Local Time) that morning. A half hour later, the cruiser *Tone* launched her No. 4 floatplane to reconnoiter for the US carriers, one of several planes catapulted to do so. The attack on Midway began two hours later. While returning, the flight leader of the attack, Tomonaga Jōichi, radioed at 07:00, "there is need for a second attack wave."[15] Fifteen minutes later, the Admiral ordered a second attack on Midway Atoll, which required prepping the available aircraft, some seventy-seven in all, including forty-three Nakajima B5N2 torpedo bombers on *Kaga* and *Akagi* and thirty-four Aichi D3A1 dive bombers on *Hiryū* and *Sōryū*, as well as their Zero escort. It proved a fateful decision. At 07:28, *Tone*'s No. 4 aircraft reported, "See ten ships probably enemy. Bearing 10° from Midway. Distance 240 miles. Course 150°." Admiral Nagumo had started fitting his planes with bombs for land use when he needed to be preparing them with armor-piercing bombs for the coming battle with the US carriers. But he had just found that out.

Admiral Nagumo signaled to his warships, "Prepare to carry out attacks on enemy fleet units. Leave torpedoes on those attack planes, which have not as yet been changed to bombs."[16] But Nagumo was still uncertain as to the composition of the enemy forces. The flagship contacted *Tone*'s No. 4 aircraft. At 08:09 the crew of the search plane reported that they could see five cruisers and about five destroyers, but then added at least one "ship that looks like a carrier" eleven minutes later. Meanwhile, the Midway attack planes finished landing on the carriers by 09:12. Crews began prepping them for a second attack on Midway. This is an extremely vulnerable moment – aviation fuel hoses, ammunition, and bombs littered the hangar and flight deck of *Akagi* and *Kaga*. Below, in the hangar deck, crews, in their haste, failed to properly stow torpedoes and bombs. Time was everything now.

Meanwhile, twenty Grumman F4F Wildcat fighters, sixty-seven Douglas SBD Dauntless dive-bombers, and twenty-nine Douglas TBD Devastator torpedo bombers were on their way from the carriers *Hornet* and *Enterprise*. Admiral Nagumo received messages from his reconnaissance aircraft of inbound carrier-based planes. He knew they were coming and could wait no longer. He signaled to *Kaga* and the other warships, "We plan to contact and destroy the enemy task force." The Carrier Strike Force changed course to the northeast at 09:18. It wasn't long before the US torpedo planes descended on the carriers. Mitsubishi A6M Zeros in combat air patrol mowed them down. Of forty-one torpedo planes from the *Yorktown*, *Enterprise*, and *Hornet*, the three US carriers on the scene that day, only six returned and not a single torpedo touched a Japanese flattop, though the US torpedo planes did prevent Admiral Nagumo from spotting his planes on the flight decks. Importantly, however, the Zeros were now out of place and too low to meet the incoming dive-bombers.

The Dauntless dive-bombers brought hell to Japan's Carrier Strike Force. At 10:26, a bomb, dropped by Lieutenant Richard Best, rocked the flagship *Akagi* (see Figure 5.6). It proved a fatal blow. Eventually, the officers and crew abandoned *Akagi* and completed the ritual transferal of the Emperor's portrait at 17:15 (she sank the next day). *Sōryū* sank at 19:20 and *Kaga* at 19:25. *Hiryū* went down at 03:15 early the next morning, but not before delivering a fatal blow to the US carrier *Yorktown*, which a Japanese submarine later finished off. Midway was a stinging defeat that reshaped the contours of World War II in the Pacific.

That night, *Yukikaze* departed the area of the burning *Akagi* and proceeded westward to rendezvous with the remainder of the Main Body. Admiral Yamamoto ordered the bombardment of Midway by the Second

Figure 5.6 The carrier *Akagi* during operations in the Indian Ocean. Photograph taken from an Aichi D3A Type 99 carrier bomber immediately after takeoff. Courtesy of the Yamato Museum, Kure, Japan.

Fleet coming up from the south, but ultimately changed his mind when he realized they would be vulnerable to air attack the next morning. As they turned away, heavy cruisers *Mogami* and *Mikuma* collided. Eventually, US carrier planes from *Hornet* and *Enterprise* mauled the badly damaged *Mikuma*, betrayed by the telltale trail of fuel oil gushing from her ruptured portside tank. She sank, but *Mogami* miraculously survived the attack, even though she, too, was badly mauled.

About this time, a plea from the struggling *Mogami* came over the wireless, "We are under attack from enemy planes. Speed nine knots. It appears that enemy air squadrons are still in the area."[17] Then another plea, "We are receiving a second attack. Unable to navigate."

While the Main Body zigzagged westward, commanders ordered *Yukikaze* eastward, and at daybreak of June 7 she discovered the badly damaged *Mogami*. She took on some of the sailors and proceeded to the southeast to seek out the enemy, but was eventually ordered to return to the Imperial Navy base at Truk. She arrived June 13, but was quickly dispatched to Guam before heading to the Hashirajima anchorage, about twenty miles south of Kure, on June 24, 1942. *Mogami* successfully limped back to Truk, arriving on June 14. Yamamoto's decisive battle was over.

* * *

Japan's defeat at Midway was devastating, and shifted the Pacific War to Guadalcanal and the Solomon Sea, where the war intensified for destroyers. Colonel Ikki Kiyonao's forces – the "Ikki detachment" – once slated to occupy Midway, were diverted there to try and retake Guadalcanal after the Japanese lost it to US Marines. Rear Admiral Tanaka would become legendary in the fighting around Guadalcanal. For *Yukikaze*, the war, with all its merciless ferocity, was just getting under way – Midway wasn't the end of something, but rather only the beginning of Japan's long, torturous defeat.

CHAPTER 6

Barroom Brawl at Guadalcanal

Tow her with all your might!

Combined Fleet Headquarters to Admiral Abe Hiroaki

AFTER THE THROTTLING AT MIDWAY, the Imperial Navy limped back to the Western Pacific to lick its wounds. *Yukikaze* changed captains during this interval and began operations around the strategically vital Guadalcanal. Midway was important, but Guadalcanal was more so.

In the Solomon Islands, only three locations proved suitable for airfields, and Japan controlled two of them in 1942. After the loss of four fleet carriers, the Japanese needed them more than ever. And Japanese war planners wanted the third on Guadalcanal. It wasn't long before Imperial Army engineers began construction of an airstrip on Guadalcanal. This airstrip quickly became the object of US strategic desires, particularly if lines of communication were to be maintained with Australia. On August 7, 1942, US Marines came ashore to take the island and its primitive airstrip.

That night, however, Imperial Navy warships attacked Allied warships at the Battle of Savo Island, which we discussed earlier. The nighttime raid sank four Allied cruisers. Nonetheless, US engineers began making improvements to what became Henderson Field. Between August 7, 1942 and February 9, 1943, Japanese and American forces fought ferociously over this precious piece of strategic real estate. Repeatedly, and by today's standards inexplicably, Japanese commanders threw inferior numbers of Imperial Army troops at entrenched US Marine positions, a tactic based on the belief of the spiritual superiority of the Japanese fighting man. It was a notion rooted in the myths of racial superiority that, at least in part, undergirded the war in the Asia–Pacific theater. It was a conceit that proved disastrous.

The Naval Battle of Guadalcanal, debatably the most intense naval engagement of the entire war, in any ocean, occurred at this juncture. On November 12–13, 1942, US Navy and Imperial Navy forces engaged in close combat in rapidly changing weather conditions, and the outcome helped determine the fate of Guadalcanal. The subsequent evacuations of Imperial Army troops from Guadalcanal, conducted by destroyers, proved one of the most daring rescues of the war. *Yukikaze* was on the front line for both.

* * *

On June 23, 1942, the Imperial Navy relieved *Yukikaze*'s captain, Lieutenant Commander Tobida. For six months he had slept less than three hours a day in order to keep the destroyer afloat and her crew safe. Lieutenant Commander Kanma Ryōkichi would serve as *Yukikaze*'s new captain. After disembarking, Tobida was promptly escorted to the hospital with severe exhaustion, though he did overcome his illness and survive the war, just as all of *Yukikaze*'s captains did.

As her new captain settled into his Spartan quarters, *Yukikaze* departed Yokosuka with the transport *Nankai-maru* to the forward naval base at Rabaul. Then, on July 14, the Navy General Staff embedded *Yukikaze* into the newly formed Third Fleet, as part of Desron 10. As *Yukikaze*'s crew saw it, the new captain and the Third Fleet represented perfect fits for the tenacious little warship.

Captain Kanma was no newbie to fighting in the Western Pacific. When the war started, he had served as captain of the *Kagerō*-class destroyer *Isokaze*, a warship that would fight alongside *Yukikaze* to the bitter end of the war. On December 8, 1941, *Isokaze* had escorted Major General Takumi Hiroshi's detachment during the Imperial Army's landing at Kota Bharu on the Malaya Peninsula, minutes before the first bombs fell on Pearl Harbor. Initially, well-fortified Allied positions had pinned down the Takumi detachment on the beachheads. Then, to make matters worse, Allied Lockheed Hudson aircraft pummeled the detachment from the sky. In particular, the transports took a heavy beating. During the raid, sixteen Allied bombs set the transport *Awajisan-maru* ablaze and she sank. Royal Australian aircraft descended on the transport *Ayatosan-maru* and set her ablaze as well, but emergency crews extinguished her fires.

Nearby, *Sakura-maru* took seven bombs but managed to stay afloat. Though bombs fell all around her, *Isokaze* remained undamaged during the Allied raid. Not unlike the destroyer *Yukikaze*, Captain Kanma's *Isokaze* gained a reputation as a warship that couldn't be touched in battle. In the summer of 1942, *Yukikaze*'s crew whispered rumors of such invincibility throughout the warship. Captain Kanma would be a perfect fit. As the new Gunnery Chief Morita Takashi put it, "This ship's reputation as being lucky is the result of its lucky captain. The battlefield doesn't matter: we'll leave untouched."[1] That conceit would certainly be put to the test in the coming months in the waters around Guadalcanal.

* * *

On the night of November 12, 1942, an Imperial Navy Raiding Force, under the command of Rear Admiral Abe Hiroaki, approached Guadalcanal from the north. Abe's warships included the fast battleships *Hiei* and *Kirishima*, as well as one cruiser and eleven destroyers. Its mission was to conduct a naval bombardment of Henderson Field on Guadalcanal in anticipation of a major Japanese offensive to seize Henderson Field and retake the island. As *Hiei* and *Kirishima* approached Lunga Point, on the north coast of Guadalcanal and near the airstrip, destroyer patrols searched the area some ten kilometers in front of the two battlewagons, now preparing to rain a fiery hell down on the US Marines dug in there. *Yukikaze* held station about 1,500 meters from *Hiei*'s port beam. Suddenly, a squall of increasing ferocity clobbered the fleet, reducing visibility to zero, and even prominent landmarks to the west, such as Savo Island and Cape Esperance, disappeared in the curtain of rain, wind, and storm clouds.

At 00:10 on November 13, Admiral Abe, concerned about running aground, ordered, "Prepare entire squadron to simultaneously turn 180° to starboard to new heading."[2] Though he valued the cover provided by the storm, Abe had decided to turn around until the weather was more favorable. Even his catapulted search seaplane left for Bougainville, rather than try to find big *Hiei* in the squall.

Normally, on the bridge of an Imperial Navy warship, commanders received orders to "prepare" for a certain maneuver, or *yōi* in Japanese, and then, about one minute later, to "execute" that maneuver, or *hatsudō*. When Abe's command to "prepare" was not immediately followed by an order to "execute," even some four minutes later, the commander of the forward sweeping destroyers, Rear Admiral Takama Tamotsu, became convinced that the wireless operator aboard his destroyer, *Asagumo*, had somehow missed the order.

In the dead of night and in the middle of a violent squall, Takama impatiently turned *Asagumo* 180° to the north. Seeing this, commanders aboard destroyers *Murasame* and *Samidare* became confused and shouted, "Hard to starboard!" They too came hard about. When lookouts aboard destroyers *Yūdachi* and *Harusame* saw the other ships turning to the right, they decided to continue straight, convinced that the order to "execute" had yet to arrive from Admiral Abe. They continued on their southerly heading. As a result, the Fourth Torpedo Squadron, essentially *Hiei*'s escort, fell out of formation and became dangerously dispersed, leaving the big battleship exposed.

It was at this point that Admiral Abe's order to execute came through. But, of the five destroyers tasked with being the feelers for the fleet, three had already turned north. Without warning, the battlewagon *Hiei*, one of the most beloved warships in the Imperial Navy fleet, found herself short of escorting destroyers, and at night. No sooner had Admiral Abe ordered the northward turn than the squall blew out and the sky cleared, revealing a starry night. Immediately, Abe ordered the fleet south again toward Henderson Field to complete the bombardment mission. But, at this point, the ships had fallen out of formation. This context is important for understanding what happened next.

As the fleet steamed south, a US squadron, commanded by Rear Admiral Daniel J. Callaghan, began heading north in order to intercept Abe's bombardment mission. At 01:42, the two fleets met. Because *Hiei*'s destroyer screen had dispersed, she received little advanced warning and spotted the enemy for herself at under 9,000 meters. Suddenly, the warships found themselves gunwale to gunwale. When *Hiei* illuminated her searchlights the *Atlanta* and *Barton*, a *Benson*-class destroyer, fired directly into *Hiei*'s bridge. In fact, the warships were so close at this precise moment that *Hiei* could not lower her big guns enough to be effective. *Atlanta* and *Barton* lit up *Hiei*, as well as the destroyer *Akatsuki*. These exchanges represented the opening salvos of one of the most smash-mouthed naval battles of World War II, a "barroom brawl after the lights had been shot out,"[3] as one US observer described the Naval Battle of Guadalcanal (Japanese, Third Battle of the Solomon Sea). It was one of the most important naval engagements in the Pacific, and *Yukikaze*, as usual, found herself on the front line.

* * *

After the Midway fiasco, *Yukikaze* had spent most of the late summer and early fall of 1942 training near Kure in Japan's Inland Sea. Even after the sinking of four fleet carriers at Midway, the Imperial Navy still possessed a powerful surface fleet. On September 2, *Yukikaze* escorted the carrier *Un'yō* from Saipan to the heavily fortified base at Truk north of Rabaul. During this time, the focus of the war in the Pacific shifted toward the Solomon Islands, particularly Guadalcanal. *Yukikaze* and elements of the Combined Fleet sortied toward the Solomon Islands in late October for the next chapter of World War II in the Pacific.

Guadalcanal was an unlikely place to invite so much mayhem. But both the Japanese and the Allies viewed the island as strategically valuable. For the US Navy, control of the South Pacific was key to retaining lines of communication with Australia. With precious few flattops in 1942 and the US committed to a "Europe first" timetable in World War II, the Allied strategy in the South Pacific depended on the ability to create a protective umbrella provided by land-based aircraft. In the Solomon Islands, only three places proved suitable for proper airfields, and Japan controlled two of them in 1942 – Rabaul (on New Britain) and Buka (just north of Bougainville).

The Japanese began eyeing the third, on Guadalcanal, on May 18, when Captain Miyazaki Shigetoshi, commander of the Yokohama Air Group stationed at Tulagi (about 50 kilometers north of Guadalcanal), reported that the coastal plane of Guadalcanal was suitable for an airfield. Within weeks, Japanese engineers had arrived, set up camp, and built a primitive wharf to receive heavy equipment. On June 20, thick smoke blanketed the island from burning cogon grass in order to clear foliage for the runway. On July 6, over 2,500 Construction Unit men had arrived, as well as their earthmoving equipment. With an airstrip on Guadalcanal, the Japanese could potentially own the skies over the southeastern Solomon Islands and northern Coral Sea, making it exceedingly difficult for the US Navy to operate and, eventually, threaten lines of communication with Australia.

US war planners knew this. In response to the Japanese presence in the Solomon Islands, the US launched Operation Cartwheel on July 2, which included "seizure and occupation of the New Britain–New Ireland–New Guinea area"[4] and the expulsion of the Japanese from the fortified base at Rabaul. The seizure of the Santa Cruz Islands and Tulagi was slated to be the first order of business; but when, on July 4, a US reconnaissance plane reported the Japanese work on the airstrip, Guadalcanal became the newest object of Allied strategic desire.

Realizing the island's value, six days later, Vice Admiral Robert L. Ghormley, Commander South Pacific, received orders from Admiral Nimitz to seize Tulagi and evict the Japanese from neighboring Guadalcanal. Operationally, Ghormley gave Rear Admiral Richmond Kelly Turner command of the Amphibious Force: he oversaw the logistics of the transport vessels, their escorts, and the US Marine landings on Guadalcanal. Eight cruisers and a modest destroyer screen comprised the escort for the Amphibious Force. Vice Admiral Frank Jack Fletcher oversaw the carrier task force to the south, which was positioned to provide air cover during the day. Nighttime was a different matter altogether, however – the night belonged to the Imperial Navy.

The landings on Guadalcanal began on August 7 four miles east of Lunga Point and were uneventful, though the Japanese fought tenaciously at Tulagi and other nearby smaller islands. But on Guadalcanal, by sunset, 11,000 US Marines had waded ashore, established a beachhead, and begun enjoying the coconuts. To some, it was an eerily quiet entry onto a battlefield that would be drenched in buckets of blood in the coming weeks. The next day, US Marines pushed the Japanese Construction Units working on the airstrip into the surrounding jungle. Meanwhile, the fifteen

US transport vessels, along with their escorting cruisers and destroyers, held station south of Savo Island. The next night, concerned about fighter support and fuel supplies, Admiral Fletcher ordered his carriers southeast and away from Guadalcanal, withdrawing air cover for Turner's transports and escort warships, which were badly behind schedule. That night, while Fletcher's powerful carrier task force withdrew from Guadalcanal, Vice Admiral Mikawa, aboard his flagship *Chōkai*, conducted his night-fighting clinic at the Battle of Savo Island, discussed earlier. In the nighttime brawl, the Allies lost four heavy cruisers – *Astoria, Canberra, Quincy,* and *Vincennes.* With no air support, Turner wanted out, and, by the evening of August 9, his Amphibious Force, and those escort ships Mikawa had not sunk the night before, had vacated the scene.

Turner's departure left Major General Alexander Vandegrift and his leathernecks to fend for themselves on Guadalcanal. After the US landing, the Marine Engineer Battalion began improving the rough airstrip, which, at this point, was merely cleared ground and a graded surface. Adding to the labor, Vandegrift ordered that the airstrip be lengthened. Despite the backbreaking work, by August 12 an amphibious Catalina had landed on what became known as Henderson Field.

Meanwhile, in Rabaul, not long after the US landing on Guadalcanal, General Hyakutake Harukichi was placed in command of the Seventeenth Army, and he oversaw Japanese Guadalcanal operations. About 17,000 US Marines had landed on Guadalcanal; but Hyakutake erroneously estimated the number to be far fewer, maybe an expeditionary force of 2,000 men. He therefore dispatched a regiment under the command of Colonel Ikki Kiyonao, whom Japanese war planners had originally slated to occupy Midway, to evict the Marines and retake Henderson Field. Crammed into six destroyers, the Ikki detachment departed Truk on August 18 and successfully landed on Guadalcanal. Three days later, Ikki attacked with an echelon of 916 men the Marines at the Battle of Tenaru River, where they were quickly overmatched and decimated. Ikki likely took his own life, as did several of his officers. Meanwhile, US planes began landing on Henderson Field one after another, particularly after the US Navy's Seabees had improved the airstrip even more. Never would an airstrip be destroyed and rebuilt on so many occasions.

Ikki's slaughter didn't stop Japanese war planners from trying to beef up the Imperial Army presence on Guadalcanal. In fact, it only spurred it on. With Henderson Field, US planes might rule the skies during diurnal hours, but during the nocturnal hours the Imperial Navy ruled the seas. Rear Admiral Tanaka, aboard *Jintsū*, and other commanders, including Mikawa, continued to land Japanese forces on the island under the cover of darkness. In this way, the fighting around Guadalcanal took on a circadian quality by the fall of 1942. But, because the night landings used fast but cramped destroyers instead of slower but more spacious transports, they delivered a trickle rather than a steady flow of Imperial Army reinforcements and supplies. The Imperial Navy even loaded some supplies into drums, tied them together, and then threw them overboard where the current delivered them to the hungry Seventeenth Army. Though clever and resourceful, the "Tokyo Express," or what the Japanese dubbed "Rat Transports," never delivered adequate troops or supplies. The Japanese troops on Guadalcanal barely hung on.

But the war escalated around Guadalcanal all the same. On August 24, the Imperial Navy, in support of the landing of an additional 1,500 Japanese troops on Guadalcanal, launched a full-scale attack on US Naval forces in the Battle of the Eastern Solomons (Japanese, Second Battle of the Solomon Sea). The battle involved large numbers of surface vessels on both sides, and the Imperial Navy lost the light carrier *Ryūjō* during the engagement when planes from the US carrier *Saratoga* discovered her.

In this engagement, *Yukikaze* found herself in Desron10, part of Rear Admiral Abe's Vanguard Group. The battle proved largely indecisive and anticlimactic (unless you were aboard *Ryūjō*, of course), but the US Navy did manage to prevent the landing of Japanese transport vessels, again forcing Japanese planners to rely on nighttime Rat Transports. This too little, too late rhythm became a prominent theme of the Japanese effort on Guadalcanal. But the more men, planes, and warships lost around Guadalcanal, the more the strategic value of the inhospitable island seemed to increase for both sides, and the fighting only grew more ferocious.

Still acting under the assumption that only 2,000 Marines guarded Guadalcanal, Rabaul next threw Major General Kawaguchi Kiyotake at

Henderson Field. Thanks to the nightly transports, Kawaguchi's forces had been building since late August. General Hyakutake had offered an additional battalion, but Kawaguchi felt he had adequate forces to expel the Marines. With his 6,000 men from the Seventeenth Army, Kawaguchi launched his attack on the night of September 12. He concentrated his forces on a grassy ridge south of the airstrip known as Lunga Ridge.

By early morning of September 14, Kawaguchi's men, after wave upon wave of terrifying bayonet charges, reluctantly admitted defeat. The next morning, the grisly scene of hundreds of dead bodies dotted the grassy ridge. The putrid smell followed. By the time Kawaguchi had retreated to Kokumbona to the west, nearly half his men were dead. It had taken weeks to build up the Imperial Army forces by Rat Transports, and they had been lost in a single night's fighting. This, too, became a familiar pattern in the Pacific.

* * *

Both Ikki and Kawaguchi had launched attacks against dug-in US Marine positions, where they were seriously outnumbered. In terms of overall numbers, Ikki had one man for every seventeen Marines, while Kawaguchi had about one for every three. The Marines had better artillery because barnacles actively colonized most of the Imperial Army artillery on the bottom of Iron Bottom Sound. Plus, the Marines controlled Henderson Field and, therefore, the skies above Guadalcanal. The Imperial Army proved repeatedly outmanned and overpowered. In part, faulty intelligence explains this circumstance, while the inability of the Imperial Navy to safely escort troop transports proved important, too. The Imperial Army had also enjoyed early successes in the war fighting with smaller numbers of forces. But the Imperial Army's cult of spiritual superiority also poisoned the ability of Japanese war planners, particularly in the army but also in the navy, to think rationally about military operations around Guadalcanal – and it probably cost them the island. In a few words, Imperial Army planners sold lives far too cheaply on Guadalcanal.

Both Ikki and Kawaguchi were approximately fifty years old when they fought on Guadalcanal. Kawaguchi graduated from the Imperial Japanese Army Academy in 1914, and Ikki did two years later. The bulk of the formative education of both men occurred in the years immediately after the Russo-Japanese War (1905) and the beginning of World War I, when the Imperial Army underwent important cultural shifts. Both men grew up in a highly masculinized and militarized environment, to put it mildly.

As young boys in school, their teachers likely instructed arithmetic by counting battleships and taught grammar through imperial military edicts. Ethics teachers discussed "the meaning of the imperial edict declaring war"[5] and "the exploits of valiant Japan and our valiant military men." Other topics might include the "special behavior of children during the war" and the "duty of military service." Scientific topics included "searchlights, wireless communication, land mines and torpedoes, submarines, military dirigibles, Shimose explosives, military carrier pigeons, heavy cannon, mortars, machine guns, the Arisaka cannon, and military sanitation." Schools taught music through military songs. To these young men, their personal connection to Japan's Imperial State was characterized by military service, military duty, and military sacrifice. That's all they knew – they lived and breathed war. On Guadalcanal, they ultimately died from it.

While young Ikki and Kawaguchi were schoolboys, Imperial Army brass revised Japan's military codes. More than previous army codes, they emphasized the "spirit" of the Japanese soldier. In many ways, this emphasis on spirit undermined rational thinking among Japan's war planners. It made them tactically lazy. When Ikki and Kawaguchi confidently committed their men to such overwhelming odds, they tapped into the ethnic conceit of the spiritual superiority of Japan's fighting men. This is what they had been taught at the military academy. Impatiently, Major General Kawaguchi had even turned down General Hyakutake's offer of another battalion to overwhelm Lunga Ridge and take Henderson Field. The victory against the Russians in 1905 had birthed the serious revisions of Japan's military codes: the adoption of the Infantry Manual in 1909, the Army Education Regulations in 1913, and the Field Regulations in the next year.

The emphasis on "spirit" emerged as a prominent feature of the Imperial Army's new strategic doctrine. Elevated phrases such as "the attack spirit,"[6] "absolute sincerity," "sacrifice one's life to the country," and "absolute obedience to superiors" came to permeate Imperial Army doctrine. It was as if Yamamoto Tsunetomo, the author of the eighteenth-century martial classic *Hagakure*, had drafted Japan's modern strategic doctrines with his own ink and brush. But the *Hagakure's* insistence that the "Way of the warrior (bushido) is to be found in dying"[7] proved out of synch with World War II. World War II was an industrial war of attrition, with industrial-scale killing, and offered little spiritual redemption in death. The *Hagakure* emphasized the overwhelming power of the "death frenzy"[8] in battle because "even dozens of men cannot kill a man in a frenzied state already determined to die." But on Guadalcanal US Marines proved they could kill such a man, over and over again in fact, and the Imperial Army's reliance on such medieval fighting philosophies sealed its fate on the inhospitable island.

In the Imperial Army, surrender was not an option. The 1908 army criminal code stated plainly, "A commander who allows his unit to surrender to the enemy without fighting to the last man or who concedes a strategic area to the enemy shall be punishable by death."[9] The 1941 Field Service Code, endorsed and signed by General Tōjō Hideki himself, explained, "Do not be taken prisoner alive." Such élan might have had some place during Yamamoto's time, when hand-to-hand combat was more commonplace, but, in the highly mechanized context of World War II, it simply threw young Japanese men into the meat grinder. No matter how loudly Ikki and Kawaguchi shouted "Banzai!" and no matter how ferociously they charged dug-in US Marine positions on Guadalcanal to demonstrate their "spirit," they proved no match for the red-hot lead that awaited them.

Such assumptions about the Japanese fighting spirit remained deeply rooted in the racial biases of Japan's ethnic nationalism, and they extended to the civilian population as well. In the late 1930s, for example, the Ministry of Education built a Spirit Culture Institute in order to "perfect and unify the entire nation with one conviction."[10] This perfect national unity could be accomplished because Japan's national polity wasn't comprised of competing branches of government, such as judicial, legislative, and executive, but rather functioned more as a single body, with the Emperor serving as the spirit-mind. In Japan's national polity, wrote Itō Hirobumi, architect of Japan's Meiji Constitution of 1889, "sovereignty is one and indivisible. It is like the human body, which has limbs and bones, but whose source of spiritual life is the mind." The

Imperial Army and Navy channeled the Emperor's "spiritual life" in the battlefields of the Western Pacific, and nowhere more courageously, and hopelessly, than on Guadalcanal.

The Yamato race viewed itself as superior to others because of its relationship to the Emperor, himself a descendent of the gods, and therefore its ethnic purity. In 1942, one popular Japanese monthly explained that "brightness,"[11] "strength," and "uprightness" made the Japanese the "superior race in the world." In turn, Japan's creation of the Greater East Asian Co-Prosperity Sphere built a natural racial hierarchy that placed Japanese at the top because of their "spiritual and physical purity." It was exactly this imagined superior "spirit" that became strategic doctrine in the Imperial Army, but the façade was shot through with holes on battlefields across the Pacific.

Insofar as the minds of its participants drive history, and not the invisible currents of its material context, this was in the minds of Japanese men as they threw themselves against Marine positions on Guadalcanal in an attempt to take Henderson Field and win the war. But the material reality of US lead told an altogether different story. In the final analysis, Japanese fighting men obeyed a vertical hierarchy of loyalty, one that led directly to the Emperor and the Imperial State, while horizontal feelings of camaraderie motivated US Marines on the battlefield. Where those vertical and horizontal lines crossed, the axis as it were, was where human nature converged in all fighting men – when soldiers, whether Japanese or Allied, cried out for their mothers as they bled out on battlefields across the Pacific.

* * *

On September 15, 1942, the US Navy received a bloody nose when the Japanese submarine *I-19* fired a spread of four torpedoes at the US carrier *Wasp* south of Guadalcanal, sinking the flattop a little over six hours later. Two of the torpedoes found their mark on the starboard side of *Wasp*, one of them near the gasoline stowage tanks and the other near the forward bomb magazine. Observers on the cruiser *San Francisco*, which screened *Wasp*, commented that the forward explosion looked "painfully similar to the one seen when the *Arizona*'s forward magazine blew up on December 7th."[12]

Figure 6.1 The US carrier *Wasp* south of San Cristobal Island shortly after submarine *I-19* torpedoed her on September 15, 1942. Official US Navy Photograph, National Archives, Catalog #: 80-G-391481.

Captain Charles McMorris, of the *San Francisco*, wrote, "She continued to burn, the flames working aft all the time, and explosions were heard at frequent intervals." It wasn't enough that fires broke out throughout the stricken carrier, but "free gasoline pouring from the ruptured tanks onto the surface of the water was ignited, and soon WASP was completely enveloped in flames." A mere thirty-five minutes after the torpedoes slammed into *Wasp*, Captain Forrest P. Sherman gave the order to abandon her. She had become a floating inferno (see Figure 6.1).

On October 11, one month later, the US Navy returned the favor at the Battle of Cape Esperance (Japanese, Sea Battle off Savo Island), when Rear Admiral Norman Scott crossed the "T" of Rear Admiral Gotō Aritomo's escort force in a reversal of the results of the Battle of Savo Island. The US lost the destroyer *Duncan*, while the Imperial Navy lost the destroyer *Fubuki* and the cruiser *Furutaka*. Gotō was mortally wounded aboard his flagship, the cruiser *Aoba*. Nonetheless, the US tactical victory at Cape Esperance failed to keep the Rat Transports from landing more forces that night. Slowly but surely, the Japanese continued to use destroyers to build up their forces on Guadalcanal in preparation for a major offensive to retake Henderson Field.

On October 13, the US 164th Infantry Regiment reinforced the Marines on Guadalcanal. That day, the Japanese began daily raids and nightly bombardments in order to soften up the US positions in preparation for another offensive. In the mother of all naval bombardments, just after midnight on October 14, Rear Admiral Kurita maneuvered the battleships *Haruna* and *Kongō* into position to fire over 900 14-inch Type 3 incendiary shells on Henderson Field. "The Bombardment,"[13] as it came to be known, resembled the "arsenal of the underworld," according to one US Marine.

In the early morning of October 15, Japanese transports unloaded about 4,500 members of the Seventeenth Army until US planes mounted an attack against the transports, forcing the Japanese to beach three of them and abandon the area. Nonetheless, Japan's war planners had elevated the Guadalcanal campaign to principal importance, above even the Papua operation. Every night, the Rat Transports unloaded some 900 reinforcements on the island. The orders out of Tokyo were straightforward at this juncture. "After reinforcement of Army forces has been completed,"[14] they stated, "Army and Navy forces will combine and in one action attack and retake Guadalcanal Island airfield. During this operation the Navy will take all necessary action to halt the efforts of the enemy to augment his forces in the Solomons Area."

In the next phase of the Guadalcanal campaign, General Maruyama Masai oversaw a carefully choreographed push that required capturing Henderson Field before US planes could be launched against the Imperial Navy, which provided cover for the Imperial Army troop transports.

On October 23, General Maruyama launched his bid to retake Henderson Field, and cruel fighting raged on Guadalcanal between the US 7th Marine Regiment, the US 164th Infantry Regiment, and Japan's Seventeenth Army. While the Imperial Army approached Henderson Field, *Yukikaze* sailed southward with the Combined Fleet. Admiral Nagumo, of Pearl Harbor fame and now Midway infamy, commanded the Main Body, which included the fleet carriers *Zuikaku* and *Shōkaku,* as well as the light carrier *Zuihō*. Desron10, which included the heavy cruiser *Kumano* and eight destroyers, including *Yukikaze*, watched over Admiral Nagumo's flattops. *Yukikaze* held station near *Zuikaku*, just forward of the carrier's starboard beam.

Along with the Main Body was the Advance Force, which orbited the smaller carrier *Jun'yō* and included battleships, cruisers, and destroyers. Vice Admiral Kondō Nobutake commanded the Advance Force from the bridge of the heavy cruiser *Atago*. Finally, Abe commanded the Vanguard Force from the towering pagoda of the battleship *Hiei*. They confronted the US Navy's carriers *Enterprise* and *Hornet*, with their escort of battleships, cruisers, and destroyers, in the Battle of the Santa Cruz Islands (Japanese, Battle of the South Pacific). It represented the fourth major aircraft carrier battle in the Pacific, after Coral Sea, Midway, and the Eastern Solomon Islands.

Early in the morning on October 25, Admiral Yamamoto received word from the Seventeenth Army that Henderson Field had been taken late the previous evening. "Banzai! – a little before 23:00 the Right Wing captured the airfield,"[15] the report trumpeted. Several hours later, the Imperial Army retracted the statement and admitted that the airfield remained in US custody. But Yamamoto, acting on the original report, had put the Imperial Navy in motion. The action started when, on the morning of October 26, bombers from the *Enterprise* discovered Admiral Nagumo's strike force and forced carrier *Zuihō* to retire after severely damaging her flight deck.

Later that morning, Imperial Navy planes discovered carrier *Hornet* and hit her repeatedly with bombs, which caused numerous fires throughout the flattop, and torpedoes, which caused her to list. Later, after *Northampton*'s heroic efforts to tow her, Japanese torpedo planes struck again, knocking out her remaining power. The US Navy attempted to scuttle her, "to prevent her from falling into the hands of an enemy cruiser–destroyer force rapidly approaching this area."[16] *Hornet* sank in 2,700 fathoms early on October 27, after the Imperial Navy finished the job. Imperial Navy planes attacked *Enterprise* later in the morning of October 26, and she "received 2 bomb hits forward and a number of near misses."[17] But, she lucked out. A dense rainsquall had hidden *Enterprise* and sheltered her from the earlier attack wave that badly mauled *Hornet*. The battle raged through the day, and US planes, not only from *Enterprise* and *Hornet*, but also from Henderson Field and Espiritu Santo, targeted other ships in the Imperial Navy fleet and badly damaged the carrier *Shōkaku*.

Despite the widespread carnage on the water that day, *Zuikaku* remained untouched in the battle, as did her escort, *Yukikaze*. Of the other destroyers, *Amatsukaze* and *Tokitsukaze* left the battlefield with the damaged *Shōkaku*. *Maikaze* and *Hamakaze* escorted the burning *Zuihō* as she fled. *Teruzuki* overheated pursuing the enemy alongside the cruiser *Kumano*. And *Arashi* withdrew to the rear of the formation. *Yukikaze* alone remained in the strike force, untouched by US bombs, torpedoes, or strafing bullets. It was with these experiences in the Pacific that *Yukikaze* began to gain the reputation in the Imperial Navy as "unsinkable."

The Battle of the Santa Cruz Islands might be considered a tactical victory if a strategic loss for the Imperial Navy, considering that the Seventeenth Army's ground offensive ultimately failed to take Henderson Field and the Imperial Navy delivered no fresh troops. But the "lucky ship" *Yukikaze* sailed through the ocean battlefield untouched. Two weeks later that reputation as unsinkable was put to the ultimate test north of Guadalcanal.

* * *

Despite General Maruyama's setback at Henderson Field and the inconclusive finish to the Battle of the Santa Cruz Islands, the Imperial Army continued to send reinforcements to Guadalcanal via the Rat Transports. Between November 2 and 10 alone, some sixty-five destroyers and two cruisers brought troops to the western part of the island. Meanwhile, the US continued to send in reinforcements and supplies of its own. In the waters north of Guadalcanal, as troop transports made their way toward the island, an important naval convergence occurred.

Rear Admiral Scott left Espiritu Santo for Guadalcanal on November 9 with troop transports and escorting cruisers and destroyers. Similarly, Rear Admiral Turner left Nouméa for Guadalcanal on November 8 with troop transports, with Rear Admiral Callaghan's cruisers and destroyers. Meanwhile, to the north, Admiral Kondō prepared to depart Truk for Guadalcanal with eleven high-speed transports and accompanying warships, with Rear Admiral Abe in the vanguard as the bombarding Raiding Force. If Admiral Kondō could punch through US defenses, he carried in his ships 58 artillery pieces, 75,000 shells, and a month's rations for some 20,000 soldiers. It might make the difference for the Imperial Army – the future of the Guadalcanal campaign hung in the balance.

On November 12, US transports began unloading troops and supplies at Lunga Point under sporadic harassing by Japanese artillery and aircraft. That day, Admiral Turner received aircraft intelligence of a sizable Imperial Navy task force headed toward Guadalcanal – Admiral Kondō's force was on its way. With few options, Turner ordered Admiral Callaghan to escort his transports safely to sea and then engage the Imperial Navy task force. He did exactly that.

That night, Callaghan separated from his transports two hours before midnight and, with an easterly nine-knot breeze and clear skies, headed northward to engage Admiral Abe's heavy Raiding Force. Callaghan's battle formation placed four destroyers in the vanguard, followed by four cruisers and four more destroyers in the rear. Abe's Raiding Force consisted of two fast battleships, one light cruiser, and eleven destroyers. Admiral Abe represented the sharp tip of Kondō's spear thrusting toward Guadalcanal. Admiral Abe's mission was to knock out Henderson Field once and for all with a heavy naval bombardment of Type 3 incendiary fragmentation shells, reminiscent of "The Bombardment" courtesy of *Haruna* and *Kongō* on October 14 under Admiral Kurita.

In the early morning hours of November 13 – after Abe's Raiding Force had entered the squall, lost formation, turned north, and then turned south again, now in three separate groups – the US and Imperial Navy forces met. But only one navy was genuinely surprised by the encounter. Coming from the south, on the cruiser *Helena*, wedged smack in the middle of the US battle column, the new onboard SG radar "reported a contact at 0124, bearing 312° T, range 27,000 yards. One or two minutes after this Radar Plot reported that three separate groups of targets were distinguishable."[18] Radar had unmasked the Japanese in the darkness.

Captain Gilbert Hoover of *Helena* immediately reported the radar blips to Admiral Callaghan, who had oddly chosen *San Francisco*, a warship without SG radar, as his flagship. The *Fletcher*, too, had SG radar, and picked up Admiral Abe's Raiding Group six minutes later, as did the destroyer *O'Bannon*. In other words, before Abe even knew the US Navy was in the vicinity, the commander of *Fletcher*, Captain William Cole,

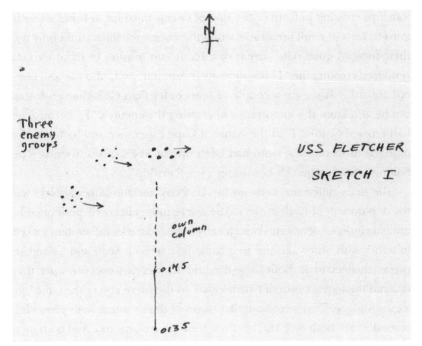

Figure 6.2 A sketch of the initial radar display from the destroyer *Fletcher* as the two forces converged off Guadalcanal early in the morning of November 13, 1942. National Archives, "USS FLETCHER - Report of Action (Enc A)." Fold3 File #267968693. National Archive Identifier 134025505. Courtesy of the National Archives.

knew that the "Enemy forces were apparently in three groups, one of which had crossed ahead of our column from port to starboard. The second was on the port bow of our column and the third on the port beam."[19] For this brief moment, the US Navy possessed a clear tactical edge, but it wasn't adequately exploited (see Figure 6.2).

It would be a night full of missed opportunities for both sides. Both Admirals, Callaghan and Abe, were competent men. Both men had graduated from their respective naval academies in 1911, so they represented the same tactical vintage. They largely viewed the oceanic military landscape the same way – they wanted their ships in tight formation and they wanted to cross the enemy's "T," even though new analysis suggests that Admiral Callaghan likely sought to bring his cruisers in close and pummel the two Imperial Navy battleships. Crossing the "T" was a naval warfare tactic common in the nineteenth and twentieth centuries. Basically, it allowed the warships crossing in front of the line of enemy warships to bring all their guns to bear in a full broadside, while the enemy warships could only use their forward guns. The advent of aircraft and missiles in naval warfare rendered crossing the "T" obsolete. Rear Admiral Scott, who was also present aboard *Atlanta*, was a couple of years older than Callaghan and Abe, but he also knew the importance of crossing the enemy's "T," because he had crossed Gotō's "T" at the Battle at Cape Esperance and had won the night. It turns out that Gotō had been one of Abe's closest friends. The Solomon Sea was quickly becoming a small world.

The main difference between the US Navy and the Imperial Navy was the deployment of its destroyers: Abe's were more effectively positioned to navigate independently and launch early torpedo attacks, rather than tucked in tightly with other warships in a battle line, as both Scott and Callaghan proved inclined to do. Both Callaghan and Abe were just over fifty when they entered the waters north of Guadalcanal, so they were also of the same biological vintage. They were at similar stages of their careers, both promising rear admirals. Both men had cut their teeth on cruisers, too. And both men struck dignified poses in full-dress uniform, model navy men representing two proud traditions. But both men were about to be thrust into one of the least dignified and most confusing battles of the war, an absolute melée. One of the two men lost his life that night, while the other lost his career.

When Callaghan learned Abe's position and disposition, he decided to engage the enemy, but still gave no firing instructions or orders. Suddenly, *Cushing*, the lead destroyer, sighted two Imperial Navy destroyers, *Yūdachi* and *Harusame*, crossing from port to starboard at a range of 3,000 yards. (As you may recall, these two destroyers had not followed Rear Admiral Takama when he prematurely turned *Asagumo* to the north in the aforementioned rainsquall.) Importantly, Japanese watchmen also saw *Cushing*. "Enemy sighted,"[20] the report came to Admiral Abe. Then, from *Hiei*'s towering bridge, the lookout shouted, "Four black objects ahead ... look like warships." Now, the Japanese knew the Americans were out there.

To avoid hitting the two destroyers and to unmask her torpedoes, *Cushing* peeled off, taking *Laffey*, *Sterett*, and *O'Bannon* with her, causing a pileup in the battle line. But, whatever element of surprise Admiral Callaghan may have enjoyed with SG radar was now lost. Now, Admiral Abe desperately needed time to get the Type 3 incendiary shells down to

the magazines and the armor-piercing shells up to the turrets of his battleships, whose gunners had already prepared for the fiery Henderson
Field bombardment. For a moment, it looked like the Midway nightmare
might play out all over again, this time on the decks of *Hiei* and *Kirishima*.
Captain Hara of *Amatsukaze* wrote, "On the decks of the two battleships
there was pandemonium. Almost every hand had left his battle station to
help cart away the Type 3 shells. There was a stampede in the magazines,
men pushing and kicking to reach the armor-piercing shells stored deep
inside."[21] But still the US warships didn't fire. "Mysteriously,"[22] remembered Captain Hara, "for eight long minutes, no shells came from the
enemy." Meanwhile, the two navies continued to charge toward each
other at 40 knots, eating 1,200 meters per minute.

Once the vanguard US destroyers had peeled off, the big *Hiei* stared
directly at *Atlanta*. Immediately, *Hiei* and the destroyer *Akatsuki*, forward
of *Hiei*'s starboard bow, snapped open their searchlights and illuminated
Admiral Scott's flagship. Only seconds earlier, *Atlanta*, according to Captain
Samuel Jenkins, had been "forced to turn left almost immediately ... in
order to avoid collision with a destroyer of the van group."[23] Armor-piercing
shells (many of them likely friendly fire from *San Francisco*) quickly rained
down and riddled the cruiser with gaping holes, tearing through the bridge
and killing Admiral Scott instantly. Then, remembered Captain Jenkins,
"two heavy jolts were felt, the first possibly a torpedo hit forward, and the
second definitely a torpedo hit in the forward engine room. Both of these
were distinctly heavier and different in character from our gunfire hits."[24]
Atlanta was dead in the water and under heavy fire. The cruiser foundered
throughout the day, but by that evening the "ship sank, approximately 3
miles West of Lunga Point, in about 80 fathoms of water."[25] The cruiser
Atlanta was one of five US warships lost that day.

But *Hiei* and *Akatsuki* took a beating from Admiral Callaghan's warships. Once ablaze, they, too, became easy targets, just as *Atlanta* had
proved. At this juncture, Admiral Abe ordered his two battleships to turn
north and escape the close-quarter carnage, fighting best left to maneuverable cruisers and destroyers. Meanwhile, *Akatsuki* was sunk, the price
she paid for illuminating her searchlights. As *Kirishima* turned northward
she caught sight of *San Francisco* and opened fire with her fourteen-inch
guns, along with *Hiei*'s the largest barrels on the water that night. The

massive shells ripped through *San Francisco*'s bridge, and *Inazuma* and *Ikazuchi*, both heavily armed *Fubuki*-class destroyers, quickly joined in – killing Admiral Callaghan and Captain Cassin Young. Badly damaged, *San Francisco* bravely kept her bow toward the battle, only later withdrawing. Somehow, the tough cruiser stayed afloat. Regardless, both US admirals were dead in the first twenty minutes or so of the battle.

Meanwhile, *Yūdachi* found herself paralleling the US column, which was now cutting through the middle of the Japanese ships. She quickly managed to get her fish in the water. On the cruiser *Helena*, they observed that the cruiser *Portland* "appeared to be out of control and on questioning reported a torpedo hit jammed her rudder."[26] One of *Yūdachi*'s fish had found her. The destroyers at the vanguard of the US column that had peeled away to avoid *Yūdachi* and *Marusame* fared no better than *Atlanta*, *San Francisco*, or *Portland*. The lead destroyer, *Cushing*, was "heavily hit by enemy fire at about 0200 … and was stopped, lying dead in the water with no power on the ship."[27] The destroyer had to be abandoned. Ashore, US Marines observed that she "burned the day of the thirteenth,"[28] until "there was a large explosion" and observers saw "no further sign of the ship." She had gone down.

Yukikaze was in the thick of the fighting. She first took aim at *Barton*, who she reportedly left ablaze and with fouled steerage. Aboard *Fletcher*, Captain William Cole observed that, at 01:56, *Barton*, after having been hit by *Amatsukaze*'s torpedoes, "exploded and simply disappeared in fragments."[29] The *Monssen*, just behind *Barton*, was visibly "low in the water."[30] *Yukikaze* suffered her first casualty in the fighting when strafing machine-gun fire over her upper works killed a sailor. *Yukikaze*, her five-inch guns blazing, scored hits on *Laffey*'s turret after the US destroyer had strafed *Hiei*'s upper works with machinegun fire, and the US destroyer burst into flames. *Yukikaze* fired 374 rounds of 5-inch shells during the fighting, and some found their targets that night. *Laffey* was among the US ships "lost in action."[31] According to her commanding officer, "About five minutes after the order to abandon ship was given, the ship blew up with a terrific explosion and sank immediately." *Sterett* and *O'Bannon*, who trailed *Laffey*, survived the melée but were damaged, *Sterett* badly. Eventually, *Yukikaze* withdrew northward with the cruiser *Nagara*.

Amatsukaze had also dashed into the melée. After launching her torpedoes, she readied another spread, these bound for *Juneau*'s hull. Almost four minutes after the Torpedo Chief had launched the fish, "a large, reddish flame rose from our target. It was the American cruiser *Juneau*."[32] Later, *Amatsukaze* came under heavy fire from *Helena*, whose radar had "picked up a destroyer on our starboard quarter firing at us and opened fire on it at a range of 7200 yards."[33] Aboard *Amatsukaze*, *Helena*'s first shell "exploded at the fire director station,"[34] while the second "pierced the deck slightly below the bridge and exploded in the radio room," killing everybody in it. The brave *Helena* then turned her attention to *Asagumo*, *Murasame*, and *Samidare*, who had engaged the US cruiser in a fierce gun battle. *Helena* survived, but ended up badly damaged in the exchange. As Hara's *Amatsukaze* withdrew, she passed *Yukikaze*, which Admiral Abe had tasked with assisting the mauled battleship *Hiei*. *San Francisco* had managed to shoot two eight-inch holes through *Hiei*'s belt and disable her rudder. While passing, the signalmen aboard *Yukikaze* exhorted, "Heartiest congratulations to *Amatsukaze*. We're heading to assist *Hiei*."[35] Even Captain Hara, as the destroyers passed at 1,000 meters, couldn't help but comment that *Yukikaze* "had not received a single hit" during the thick fighting that night.

The fighting had lasted about half an hour and extracted a toll from both sides. The Japanese lost the destroyers *Yūdachi* and *Akatsuki*, while the US lost the cruisers *Atlanta* and *Juneau*, five destroyers, and two admirals. The Japanese proved to be outstanding night fighters, but SG radar had leveled the playing field. As Captain Gilbert Hoover, commanding officer aboard *Helena*, wrote, the "value of the Sail George Radar cannot be overemphasized ... every possible effort should be made to at least equip flagships with it."[36] With radar, the US Navy had evened the odds in their nocturnal battles with the Imperial Navy.

But the Naval Battle of Guadalcanal was anything but over. The battleship *Kirishima*, the cruiser *Nagara*, and seven destroyers raced northward at high speed to get out of range of US aircraft, from both carriers and from Henderson Field, with the coming sunrise, while *Yukikaze* and *Teruzuki* tended to the mauled *Hiei*, whose rudder was damaged, and the ship was turning in a continuous circle (see Figure 6.3).

When *Yukikaze* approached *Hiei*, her deck was covered in blood and body parts, as well as shredded pieces of metal. Admiral Abe was wounded and his chief of staff, Suzuki Masakane, was dead. *Hiei* just turned in circles. Captain Nishida Masao, *Hiei*'s commander, then drew

Figure 6.3 The battleship *Hiei* under way in Tokyo Bay on July 11, 1942, just four months before the Naval Battle of Guadalcanal. NH 73075 Courtesy of the Naval History & Heritage Command.

on experience from the 1935 Fourth Fleet Incident when his cruiser *Ōi* had towed the destroyer *Hatsuyuki* for three days and nights to safety. According to Itō Masanori, Captain Nishida recommended, seemingly impossibly, given *Hiei*'s weight, that *Yukikaze* tow *Hiei* from harm's way. By 10:30, the two tethered vessels had made ten miles to the north of Savo Island and Kamimbo Bay on Guadalcanal – it would take *Yukikaze* three weeks to reach the safety of Rabaul at an irksome two knots. It was at this moment that US aircraft from Henderson Field, Espiritu Santo, and the carrier *Enterprise* appeared over the wounded *Hiei*.

The battleship took a pounding. At 16:00, Admiral Abe transferred his flag to *Yukikaze*, and *Hiei*'s sailors fled to the two destroyers. *Yukikaze* sent a message to Combined Fleet Headquarters: "Should we abandon *Hiei*?"[37] The response came back: "Tow her with all your might!"[38] According to Itō, with no air cover and no reinforcements, *Yukikaze* continued to attempt to tow the rudderless gray hulk. US planes continued to pummel the battleship from the air. Just as night began to fall on November 13, *Yukikaze* took a near miss, injuring Torpedo Chief Shirato Toshizo in the head and cracking one of her boilers. Aboard *Hiei*, Captain Nishida ordered the battleship's large Kingston valves opened in order to sink her. He intended to stay with the vessel. Only after receiving Admiral Abe's direct orders did Captain Nishida, tears streaming down his face, abandon the precious *Hiei*.

Famous for her elegant bridge, *Hiei* was the first Japanese battleship lost in the war. She was the first in her class built in Japan, and those in the Imperial Navy adored her. In the 1930s, *Hiei* had served as Emperor Hirohito's Imperial Flagship, with lavish palatial accommodations built inside, and from which he conducted several Imperial Navy Grand Maneuver reviews. *Hiei* enjoyed strong symbolic ties to the living-god Emperor and the Imperial State he embodied. The episode ruined Abe and Nishida's navy careers. Admiral Yamamoto was absolutely livid and removed both men from active service. Eventually, Torpedo Chief Shirato recovered in the hospital and Wireless Operator Saitō Kazuyoshi replaced him as Torpedo Chief. As for *Yukikaze*, she steamed back to the Kure shipyard, where engineers placed a massive steel band around her boiler, where it stayed for the rest of the war.

* * *

During the night of November 15, Admiral Kondō regrouped in another bid to bomb Henderson Field, but an even more determined US task force awaited him. *Kirishima, Hiei*'s sister ship, found herself in the sights of new battleship *Washington*'s sixteen-inch guns and *Kirishima* eventually went down. On this occasion, all attempts to destroy Henderson Field, and resupply Seventeenth Army in Guadalcanal, had ended in failure.

But the Japanese continued to run Rat Transports to Guadalcanal. In one of the most skillful displays of seamanship and naval prowess of the war, Rear Admiral Tanaka Raizō soundly defeated a superior US force in the Battle of Tassafaronga (Japanese, Battle of Lunga Point) on the night of November 30. During the epic engagement, Tanaka's ghostlike destroyers, many heavily laden with some 200 supply drums each and scores of Imperial Army soldiers, managed to sink one US cruiser and maul three others. But, despite Tanaka's brilliance, the writing was on the wall at Guadalcanal.

So much had been spent on Guadalcanal. The Japanese had lost two battleships, one light carrier, three heavy cruisers, one light cruiser, eleven destroyers, and six submarines, while the Allies had lost two aircraft carriers, six heavy cruisers, two light cruisers, and fourteen destroyers – all in an attempt to hold, take, or retake Henderson Field. The Japanese had lost 24 warships at 134,839 tons, while the Allies lost 24 warships at 126,240 tons. And, of course, these numbers don't include the ghastly number of human lives lost in the fighting for the crab-infested, inhospitable island.

Regardless of such extravagant investment, Japan's war planners decided to cut their losses early in 1943. When it was time to evacuate

Japan's Seventeenth Army from Guadalcanal in Operation Ke, Rear Admiral Tanaka led the way by delivering 600 men under Major General Matsuda Iwao on the night of January 14. The Matsuda unit served as the rear guard as destroyers evacuated the Seventeenth Army from the killing grounds of Guadalcanal. The first evacuation occurred on February 2–3 and involved one light cruiser and twenty destroyers. They managed to evacuate 4,935 men. The second run occurred two days later and rescued 3,921. Of course, *Yukikaze* was among the destroyers transporting the Seventeenth Army to safety. After the first two transports, Rear Admiral Hashimoto Shintarō and Koyanagi Tomiji, Imperial Navy officers in charge of the evacuation, began having second thoughts about the third and final effort. Surely, they thought, the enemy would be waiting in anticipation this time, possibly setting a trap.

At Imperial Navy headquarters at Buin (on Bougainville Island), a lively discussion ensued regarding whether to use high-speed motorboats for the final evacuation. Combined Fleet Headquarters had become alarmed by recent destroyer losses. But, at the meeting, Captain Kanma, *Yukikaze*'s commanding officer, and the captain of the destroyer *Hamakaze*, shouted together "It's obvious this is a job for the destroyers!"[39] Headquarters decided in favor of the destroyers, and many in the Imperial Navy fervently believed that, with the unsinkable *Yukikaze* present, the final evacuation would be a success. The final evacuation on February 7–8 liberated 1,796 men from Guadalcanal and Russell islands.

In all, the navy evacuated 10,652 soldiers from Guadalcanal. Admiral Nimitz marveled at the ability of the Japanese to remove their troops from Guadalcanal, right out from under the noses of superior US air and surface forces. "Until the last moment it appeared that the Japanese were attempting a major reinforcement effort,"[40] he recalled. "Only the skill in keeping their plans disguised and bold celerity in carrying them out enabled the Japanese to withdraw the remnants of the Guadalcanal garrison. Not until all organized forces had been evacuated on 8 February did we realize the purpose of their air and naval dispositions."

Tactically, it was a highly skillful operation. But, as Winston Churchill had observed of the evacuation of Dunkirk, "wars are not won by evacuations."[41]

CHAPTER 7

Defending the Solomon Sea
and Bismarck Barrier

After we returned to our classroom, we wrote letters to sailors ... I tried as
hard as I could to write letters that would make them happy.

Schoolgirl Nakane Mihoko in her diary

AFTER *YUKIKAZE* and the other destroyers had evacuated Imperial
Army troops from Guadalcanal in early February 1943, the war
in the South Seas took on an even more desperate tenor. With the
skies filled with Allied planes from Henderson Field and elsewhere, the
Japanese needed to defend the islands and airstrips they still possessed
in the northern Solomon Islands and Bismarck Barrier. The war therefore shifted to the Papuan Peninsula, New Guinea, and the northern
Solomon Islands, where General Douglas MacArthur had started gain-
ing ground against Imperial Army forces.

In response, Imperial Headquarters sought to "wear out" the Allied
advance through ferocious fighting in appalling conditions. While reinforcing Imperial Army troops at Lae, in southern New Guinea, *Yukikaze*
participated in the Battle of the Bismarck Sea in late February 1943,
where Allied strafing and skip-bombing wreaked havoc on Imperial Navy
transport vessels and their screening destroyers. Without adequate air
cover, Imperial Navy warships were like fish in a barrel.

Following the debacle in the Bismarck Sea, *Yukikaze* continued with
heavy troop transport duties, constantly reconfiguring the Japanese
defense of the Bismarck Barrier. Later that fall, *Yukikaze* also traveled
back to Japan, where she dry-docked at Kure for maintenance and
badly needed upgrades. At this juncture, her upgrades focused on

strengthening her anemic antiaircraft capabilities, but engineers also installed radar-detecting electronics that proved effective on the battlefield, particularly at the Battle of Kolombangara.

Yukikaze's stay at Kure, where sailors had an opportunity to venture ashore before returning to the next front, the Mariana Islands, presents an opportunity to talk about the ways in which Japanese subjects created a spiritual and nationalistic umbilical cord with Imperial Navy warships and their sailors. In particular, women and children, whether by sewing garments or writing letters, by living frugally and waiting in long food lines, or by collecting badly needed metals, contributed to life on the Emperor's warships. They celebrated as Imperial Headquarters sent more young men to the front, waving flags at train stations across the country, and they mourned when many of those same men returned in small wooden boxes. Often, nothing returned at all, actually, only a name and an official letter.

It's simply impossible to understand life aboard Imperial Navy warships without exploring this emotional tether to the home islands – it's the story of a nation gripped by total war. Imperial Navy warships required these connections as badly as they did the bunker fuel that had started the war in the first place.

* * *

In late 1942, while fighting raged in the perilous waters surrounding Guadalcanal, Japan's war planners sought to refresh the Papuan campaign with the strategic goal of capturing Port Moresby, an Australian-controlled colonial town on the south side of the Papuan Peninsula facing the Coral Sea. In May 1942, Imperial Headquarters tried to land troops there, and the ensuing naval struggle resulted in the battle that bears that sea's name. Even though the Imperial Navy boasted a slight edge on the water that day, sinking the US flattop *Lexington* during the Battle of the Coral Sea, it failed to land forces at Port Moresby. It proved a regrettable outcome for Japan. As the war entered 1943, and Guadalcanal fell into Allied hands, not occupying Port Moresby became a serious barrier in Japanese attempts to hold New Guinea and contain the Allied advance up the Solomon Islands. Once again, it all came down to airstrips and control of the skies. It was virtually suicide for surface vessels to navigate in daylight without robust air support.

With the airspace in the southern Solomon Sea congested with Allied aircraft using Henderson Field, the forward bases on the Papuan Peninsula, New Guinea, New Britain, and New Ireland took on added significance for Japan. Indeed, Allied war planners had identified two routes to Tokyo and, ultimately, victory in the Pacific: one was the Marshalls–Marianas–Iwo Jima route and the other was the New Guinea–Leyte–Luzon–Okinawa route.

Knowing this, on September 30, 1942, Imperial Headquarters agreed to a New Operational Policy that, among other components, had directed "With Rabaul as a ... bastion, stockpile munitions and use Japanese garrisons already posted in the Bismarck Archipelago, Bougainville and the Gilberts and Marshalls, to delay and wear out the expected Allied offensive."[1] Increasingly, Japan's strategy became less about a decisive battle and more about wearing the United States out through suicidal violence, in the hope of forcing the soft and luxury-addicted Yankees to tire and sue for peace.

To achieve these ends, the Japanese had constructed a formidable barrier of archipelagic outposts throughout the northern Solomon and Bismarck seas, with Rabaul, on New Britain, positioned as the centerpiece. But Buna, Gona, Salamaua, and Lae on the northernmost reaches of the Papuan Peninsula proved vitally important as well, as did Cape Gloucester on New Britain and Kavieng on New Ireland. For Japan, holding the Bismarck Barrier became essential to protecting the home islands from an Allied march northward through the Philippines, where General Douglas MacArthur still ached to fulfill his promise to return.

After the Guadalcanal campaign, escort duties in these waters occupied most of *Yukikaze*'s time. Three days after the final Guadalcanal evacuation, on February 10, *Yukikaze* escorted the damaged destroyer *Maikaze* to Truk in the Caroline Islands. Then, she spent her time escorting the armed transport *Gokoku-maru* along the coast of New Britain. On the last day of February, the Imperial Navy again slated her to escort troop transports, this time to Lae to reinforce beleaguered Imperial Army soldiers in southern New Guinea. Without adequate air cover, it represented a risky operation – Allied planes from Milne Bay and Port Moresby could easily reach any transports, as they frequently did. But, by the end of February, the Japanese had become desperate to hang onto Lae, along with Wewak and Madang, some of the last solid toeholds in New Guinea. General MacArthur, by contrast, became more committed than ever to evicting them. Resupplying those troops in Lae became *Yukikaze*'s next dangerous mission.

* * *

After the Battle of the Coral Sea, the Imperial Headquarters had not given up on capturing Port Moresby. From newly constructed airstrips in Rabaul and elsewhere in New Britain, Japanese bombers harassed Allied installations in Port Moresby throughout the early summer of 1942. On July 20, the Japanese made a move to retake Papua when the cruisers *Tenryū* and *Tatsuta*, with three screening destroyers, delivered three troop transports carrying Colonel Yokoyama Yōsuke's advance force from Rabaul to west of Buna, on the northern portion of the Papua Peninsula. The next day they proceeded to Buna. Less than a month later, Major General Horii Tomitarō arrived in Buna with the main body of Imperial Army forces and, after additional convoys had unloaded, brought Japanese troop strength to just over 11,000 men. Basically, at this juncture, the Allies and Japanese were opposite one another on the central portion of the peninsula, separated by the formidable spiny ridge of the Owen Stanley Range.

The Kokoda Trail offered passage through the rugged, high-altitude peaks, which a thick rainforest blanketed in the lower elevations and sponge-like moss covered in the upper reaches. Crossing the peninsula was no picnic. It took Horii's forces six weeks to reach about thirty miles east of Port Moresby, "from where they could see the fires of Moresby."[2] Then, however, a freshly reinforced Australian garrison pushed them back, and they retreated "weeping tears of blood" as they withdrew into the inhospitable mountains. There, only starvation, disease, and sniper fire awaited them. Eventually, the Allies, led by the Australians, chased them all the way back to Buna.

The Imperial Navy's attempt to take Milne Bay, on the tip of the peninsula, also met with frustration. General MacArthur had beaten the Japanese to the strategically important haven, and by June Allied engineers had started work on an airfield. On August 25, as Major General Horii's troops assembled in Buna for the miserable march over the

Owen Stanley Range, the Imperial Navy escorted two troop transports to Milne Bay and managed to disembark some troops before B-17 bombers chased the transports and the escorts back out to sea. These forces, with some reinforcements, fought tenaciously around Milne Bay, but could never establish a foothold or capture the critical airfield. It proved yet another brutal reminder that naval operations and amphibious landings without proper air support were nearly always doomed to failure.

With the Japanese halted on the Kokoda Trail and at Milne Bay, General MacArthur went on the offensive. On November 30, he ordered Lieutenant General Robert L. Eichelberger "to take Buna, or not come back alive."[3] His goal was to take Papua by evicting the Japanese from Buna, Gona, and Sanananda and, thereby, secure the Dobodura Plain to the west of Buna for his own airfield. The Allies paid for Papua dearly, because the Japanese valued their airstrip engineered between Buna and Cape Endaiadère, from where fighter planes could harass Port Moresby and Milne Bay, and then safely reach Salamaua and Rabaul to refuel and rearm. Fighting raged throughout December, with disease ravaging both sides. Colonel Yokoyama wrote telling his superiors in Rabaul, "Food short. Local resources, which we had to eat, also short. Medical supplies for sick also short. Therefore malnutrition has broken out. This causing losses from death without even fighting. Request urgent air transport."[4]

But few supplies proved forthcoming across the B-17-infested airspace between Rabaul and Buna. The situation became increasingly intolerable. "With the dawn the enemy starts shooting all over again,"[5] wrote one demoralized Japanese soldier. "All I can do is shed tears of resentment. Now we are waiting only for death. Even the invincible Imperial Army is at a loss." The Australians managed to take Gona on December 9. On January 2, 1943, Eichelberger entered Buna. Sanananda fell to the Australians on January 18. What remained of the tattered Japanese forces withdrew by barge across the treacherous Dampier Strait, though many of the severely wounded "left their souls for an eternity on Buna Beach."[6]

The Papuan campaign proved a costly affair for both sides, as deadly as any battle fought in World War II. In the wake of these defeats, the Imperial Army sought to harden the Munda–Rabaul–Lae line in southern New Guinea. In January and February, the Imperial Army started depositing elements of General Adachi Hatazō's Eighteenth Army at

Lae. The Twentieth Division from Taiwan and the Forty-First Division from northern China also redeployed to help hold the second-largest island in the world. Between the middle of January and the middle of February, they departed Palau and successfully landed at Wewak in New Guinea. From there, they advanced on the strategically important Madang and began construction of an airfield. But infantry in Lae would have to be reinforced even further if the Imperial Army had any hope of halting the Allied advance up the Papuan Peninsula into New Guinea. It was the task of *Yukikaze* and seven other destroyers to see that the Fifty-First Division, under the command of General Nakano Hidemitsu, and its heavy equipment and supplies, all carefully assembled at Rabaul, arrived safely at Lae. Like so many of *Yukikaze*'s missions, a Japanese victory might reshape the contours of the war.

* * *

Engineer Masuda Reiji served on the destroyer *Arashio* during the mission to resupply the troops at Lae. The Imperial Navy had drafted the young merchant mariner in 1942, and he found himself quickly transferred to the South Seas. Initially, around Guadalcanal, he served aboard the destroyer *Asashio*. Indeed, he was on *Asashio* when the destroyer assisted with the evacuation of the Seventeenth Army from Guadalcanal, alongside *Yukikaze*. After Guadalcanal fell into Allied hands, the Imperial Navy's leadership transferred Masuda to *Arashio* and redeployed the vessel northward to the Bismarck Barrier, where, alongside *Yukikaze*, she transported elements of Nakano's Fifty-First Division and their heavy artillery to Lae. "If we could get those troops and their heavy weapons there,"[7] thought Masuda, "they could turn back the Allies." The Fifty-First Division possessed considerable artillery and ammunition, all badly needed firepower to drive General MacArthur back from New Guinea.

Planners slated 8 destroyers and 200 aircraft (from airstrips in Rabaul, Gasmata, and Lae), to watch over the 8 transport vessels as they departed Rabaul in the dead of night on March 1. Before the convoy departed, Nakano, commander of the Fifty-First Division, gathered the officers together and, looking at *Yukikaze*, reportedly said, "So this is *Yukikaze!* No matter where she fights, she simply can't be sunk."[8] The unsinkable destroyer's reputation was now well established, even among Imperial Army circles.

Sheltered by a storm front and friendly Bismarck waters, the transports enjoyed an uneventful first day as they plied the waters north of New Britain, but Allied reconnaissance planes spotted the convoy late in the afternoon. "Convoy of 14 ships north of New Britain … westerly course … six of the vessels destroyers," the planes reported to General MacArthur's headquarters. On the morning of March 2, as they entered Dampier Strait, on the western edge of New Britain, B-17, B-25, and Beaufighter bombers, with crews trained for strafing and "skip-bombing," spotted the convoy and descended for the kill. General George C. Kenney commanded the air operation.

Unprepared for the low-altitude bombing and strafing runs, the Japanese warships adjusted course, anticipating to comb the tracks of the torpedoes they thought were coming. (Combing the tracks of torpedoes refers to adjusting course so that the warship's bow or stern faces the incoming spread of torpedoes, rather than facing them broadside. This narrows the surface area for the torpedoes to make contact.) Instead, however, they found themselves shattered by hits and near misses from bombs skipping across the surface. (Skip bombing was an innovation that allowed bombs, released at low altitudes, to skip across the surface of the water like flat stones and strike the side of an enemy vessel. Although dangerous, it greatly increased the odds of a hit over high-altitude bombing.) Before the clock struck noon, Allied planes had sunk one transport, the *Kyokusei-maru*, and badly damaged two others (see Figure 7.1). *Yukikaze*, who transported Nakano and his staff, along with *Asagumo*, rescued some 950 soldiers and sailors from the water and proceeded to deliver them at high speed to Lae. Nakano, some thirty officers, and a battalion's worth of men disembarked in the early morning hours of March 3 (eventually these men evacuated Lae in September by crossing over Mount Salawaket, where they suffered even more casualties). Both *Yukikaze* and *Asagumo* then sped back to the convoy and their escort duties. They arrived just in time for the main Allied air attack.

On March 3, Allied planes again descended on the convoy and its escorts with devastating skip-bombing and strafing runs. "Suddenly,"[9] as Masuda recalled, "we were attacked by more than a hundred and thirty planes. Our side had only forty. We didn't have a chance to beat them." He remembered, "They would come in on you at low altitude, and they'd

Figure 7.1 Allied aircraft execute a low-level bombing run against a Japanese transport vessel, probably the 2,883-ton *Taimei-maru*. Official US Air Force Photograph, National Archives, Catalog D23285AC.

skip bombs across the water like you'd throw a stone." The technique wreaked havoc among the Japanese transport vessels. "All seven of the remaining transports were enveloped in flames. Their masts tumbled down, their bridges flew to pieces, the ammunition they were carrying was hit, and whole ships blew up."

Arashio fired madly at the Allied planes, but eventually two 500-pound bombs mauled the destroyer. "Our bridge was hit ... Nobody could have survived. The captain, the chief navigator, the gunnery and torpedo chiefs, and the chief medical officer were all killed in action." Neither were soldiers spared: "We were carrying about fifty men from the landing force, one hundred and sixty army men, and three special newspaper correspondents. They, too, were killed in action." Miraculously, the engineers in the bowels of the destroyer survived.

Most of *Arashio*'s survivors evacuated to Masuda's old ship, *Asashio*, but Masuda and a handful of others from engineering tried to rescue the foundering vessel. But the Allied strafing runs continued. "We tried to abandon ship, but planes flying almost as low as the masts sprayed us with machine-guns. Hands were shot off, stomachs blown open. Most of the crew were murdered or wounded there. Hundreds were swimming in the ocean. Nobody was there to rescue them. They were wiped out, carried away by a strong current running at roughly four or five knots." Men leapt overboard, "saying it was better to take a chance on being saved from the ocean than to remain on such a ship of horrors."

Then, that night, as their warship drifted, an Imperial Navy destroyer came to their aid from the darkness. It was *Yukikaze*. "Eventually," explained Masuda, "about seventeen of us did survive, when that night, near midnight, the destroyer *Yukikaze* came to our rescue." Men aboard *Yukikaze* shouted into the darkness: "'Ahoy! Ahoy! This is *Yukikaze!*' We answered as loudly as we could, '*Arashio* here!'" The men were then plucked from the sinking *Arashio* and raced to Rabaul.

Asashio was not alone in meeting her fate in what became known to the Japanese as "Dampier's Tragedy" (known to the US Navy as the Battle of the Bismarck Sea). The Allied strafing runs injured Admiral Kimura Masatomi, commander of the convoy, and his flagship *Shirayuki* was eventually scuttled. *Tokitsukaze* was hit next, and *Yukikaze* was forced to evacuate the officers and crew, including General Adachi, commander of the Eighteenth Army, and his Chief of Staff, Yoshihara Kane.

Yoshihara was in his cabin consulting with Staff Officers when the bombing runs had started. Suddenly, loud explosions and machinegun fire rang out. When he finally made his way to the bridge, the captain explained, "We've had it."[10] Yoshihara looked across the water at what remained of the convoy. He remembered, "Already, the ships had been reduced by half their number, it seemed. And of those ships that were still on the surface, more than half were sending up smoke and flames. I was speechless with amazement because our losses were greater than I could possibly have expected."

Of the evacuation to *Yukikaze*, Yoshihara recalled, "Although every ship in the convoy had suffered a group attack from the enemy planes, this ship had not been visited by one enemy aircraft; like a military observer, it had merely fired at the enemy planes." Eventually, Allied planes sank or badly damaged all the transports, as well as four of the escorting destroyers. The remaining destroyers, including *Yukikaze*, scurried over the water, looking for oil-covered survivors. Some 3,664 Japanese were killed in the Battle of the Bismarck Sea, while the four remaining destroyers managed to rescue 2,427 and return them to Rabaul. Unable to satisfactorily reinforce Lae, New Guinea was all but lost. General MacArthur was one step closer to the Philippines and then Japan.

* * *

After Dampier's Tragedy, *Yukikaze* continued to escort troops throughout the northern Solomon Islands. Between early March and May, she hauled or escorted Imperial Army soldiers to Kolombangara (New Georgia), Rekata (in the Santa Isabel Islands), Finschhafen (New Guinea), and Cape Gloucester (New Britain). On April 16, she arrived in Truk in order to escort, with the aid of the newly launched cruiser *Agano* and two destroyers, the flattops *Zuikaku* and *Zuihō* to the home islands. She arrived in Kure on May 8.

When she eased into the Hashirajima Anchorage near Kure it marked five months that *Yukikaze* had been away from a Japanese port. After more hard escorting duties, she returned to Kure on September 2, where workers dry-docked her for over a month in order to undertake extensive repairs and refitting. In the yard, *Yukikaze* had critical modifications made to her armaments. These visits to Kure represented two of the thirteen times that *Yukikaze* returned to Japanese ports for various durations and reasons during World War II. She found herself in the yard only twice during the entire war.

During her visits to Kure in May and September, *Yukikaze* underwent modifications that enabled her to adapt to the constantly changing nature of Pacific battlefields. In retrospect, the cruel lessons from the smashing on the Bismarck Sea drove many of these updates. During the May visit, for example, *Yukikaze* had a twin 25 mm antiaircraft mount added forward of the bridge on the bandstand; a triple 25 mm mount replaced the double mount aft of the funnel. Equally importantly, she had a radar-detecting device installed on her mast, an electronic system that Japanese engineers called "reverse radar."

This clever device represented the Imperial Navy's response to the increased use of radar on US warships, which had evened the odds of night fighting in the Solomon Islands. Basically, the device detected the distance and direction of radar waves emanating from enemy ships, and presented the information on a screen on the bridge, not unlike radar. Importantly, it could discriminate radar waves from ordinary radio waves, even at great distances. Though not the game-changer radar proved to be for the Allies, reverse radar proved decisive for *Yukikaze* in the days ahead, particularly in the fighting around Kolombangara. While in dry dock, *Yukikaze* had her X-Turret (the raised one closest to the funnel) replaced by two triple-mounted 25 mm antiaircraft mounts. Engineers also fixed Type 13 radar (originally designed for antiaircraft roles) to her mainmast and Type 23 radar (originally designed for gunnery control) to her foremast, and outfitted her with improved sonar and hydrophones (mostly borrowed from German U-boats). It proved an extensive refitting – the pre-September 2 and post-September 2, 1943 destroyers struck strikingly different profiles. In some respects, they were very different warships fighting in very different wars. *Yukikaze* had originally been designed to assist in a decisive battle against the US Navy, but engineers modified her for more robust antiaircraft and antisubmarine escort duties.

Obviously, the adaptations represented the Imperial Navy's reluctant retreat from the Alfred Mahan-inspired idea that destroyers would be used in an old school, Tsushima Strait-like shootout with the US Navy, hammering it out with big naval guns. Instead, destroyers would be deployed in a more Julian Corbett-like fashion, in antiaircraft and antisubmarine roles, usually while escorting troops, supplies, and raw materials. But there is another important point here: her frequent trips to Kure and Yokosuka for updates and refueling demonstrate that, although a blue-water fighter, *Yukikaze* remained tethered to the home islands throughout the war. Her sailors did, too. In this manner, the home islands played a critical part in the war effort, even on the ocean.

Throughout the war, a national umbilical cord of spiritual and material connections linked sailors to the home islands, ones that served to buoy young men on the front. It also sustained their loved ones at home, particularly as information from the front grew scarce and its accuracy increasingly suspect. Such connections also had the secondary effect of rendering Japan's citizens emotional participants in the effort of fighting a total war. Women and children far from China and the ocean battlefields of the South Seas had come to internalize the war through daily activities on the home front. Indeed, women and children led the way in the emotional internalization of the war effort. Since the Meiji years, women were seen as representing the moral fortitude of the nation, and this intensified during the war.

In 1943, by the time such men as engineer Masuda returned to Japan after Dampier's Tragedy, the country had started to feel the war more painfully. Throughout the war, the Imperial State had waged a domestic campaign, largely through neighborhood associations and education, to make women and children emotional participants in the war effort. Women and children connected Imperial Navy sailors to the home front in a manner that reveals the importance of Confucian family values in sustaining the Imperial State during war – what became the "family state." During the many "spiritual mobilization campaigns," the government encouraged citizens – but mainly women, because Confucianism, starting with such texts as Kaibara Ekken's seventeenth-century misogynistic masterpiece *The Greater Learning for Women*, viewed women as more prone to luxury – to avoid extravagance. But they were also encouraged to make 1,000-stitch belts for servicemen to wear in battle, the famous *haramaki*, as well as to write uplifting and patriotic letters to them.

Women also led metal collection drives for neighborhood associations, and oversaw food rationing, savings-bond campaigns, air-defense drills, and labor service drives. Usually, women represented families at neighborhood association meetings, and the Home Ministry placed the pressure for compliance squarely on their overworked shoulders. Since the Meiji years, women had served as the moral nucleus of the Imperial State, and now they would serve as the moral nucleus of the Greater East Asian War effort.

After the Pearl Harbor operation, the war slowly came home to Japanese citizens. At first, changes verged on the ridiculous, with the clunky Japanese "center ball" replacing the English "strike" in baseball terminology, for example. But the hunger pangs of food rationing quickly followed the changing names of baseball pitches, and the war began to alter Japanese life at home. Such staples as miso, salt, and soy sauce were among the first to be rationed, just as food was rationed aboard Imperial Navy vessels. People felt compelled to do their part, too. With no beef or pork available from the community council, Sakamoto Tane, a housewife from Kōchi on Shikoku, recorded in her diary, "I have the feeling that little by little there will be shortages but that in war, we must aim for frugality even in small ways and we must be careful about waste – for the sake of the country."[11] This *kuni no tame*, "for the sake of the country," became a common refrain.

Eating less was the least Japanese women such as Sakamoto could do, given the heroic victories by the Imperial Navy in the South Seas. "Today a special news report at four o'clock [said that] our navy, once again, had produced great military results,"[12] she wrote in her diary. "It referred to the sea battles around Java, Surabaya, and Batavia. Truly we can only be grateful for, and excited by, our imperial forces' magnificent power." Patriotic housewives followed the war closely at home, not just in the papers but also on the radio, cheerfully depriving themselves and their children of protein and calories, making similar sacrifices to that of the Emperor's soldiers on the front. This synchronicity of deprivation proved important – women and children deprived themselves to synchronize with hunger in the Imperial Navy and, later, the Imperial Navy sacrificed its magnificent ships to synchronize with the burning nation. Along with over 7 million other radio listeners, Sakamoto relished news of the early naval victories in the South Seas, ones that became increasingly rare by 1943 – events like the bruising in Dampier Strait became far more common, and it wasn't broadcasted.

Housewives also organized military sendoff celebrations and helped eulogize the "heroic spirits" of the fallen, as the nation's sons, or whatever remains they could recover, returned to their villages in small wooden boxes as ashes. The Imperial State referred to them as "shattered jewels" for making the ultimate sacrifice for their country. But a housewife such as Sakamoto, by living frugally, eating less, waving flags at train stations to send away more of the nation's sons, collecting metal, and eulogizing the endless stream of "shattered jewels" as they returned home, believed she helped elevate the fighting spirit of Emperor's soldiers. "The 100 million of our citizens cannot but expect to elevate even higher the 3,000-year tradition of our fighting spirit and our iron will,"[13] she wrote. Through such actions, the country became one in spirit, "with the single heart of the 'One Hundred Million,' the greatest military power." It was a contribution to the Imperial State and "put the Sage Mind at ease by achieving the goals of this sacred war," whatever those goals might have been by late 1943.

Japanese citizens, but particularly women and children, came to assume a collective responsibility for the war and the mental wellbeing of the Sage Emperor, in whose name Japanese waged war. Daily life reflected the cruel rhythms of the war. Every month began with "Remembrance Day," or the eighth of the month, the day that the Imperial Navy bombed Pearl Harbor. It was December 7 in Hawai'i, but Japan synchronized the war, no matter the front or time zone, according to Japanese standard time – Tokyo served as the organizing center of the Greater East Asian War. Then, there were the endless air-raid drills, which only grew more frequent and violent as the war progressed.

A stifling number of citizens' associations and brigades helped internalize the war for most people: Neighborhood Associations, Housewives Associations, Household Labor Brigades, National Service Brigades, and Serving the Country Brigades popped up everywhere like wild chrysanthemums. It wasn't long before the government started mobilizing teenagers for labor, such as in September 1943 when fourteen-year-old girls were required to report for work. By March 1944, the Girls' Volunteer Corps bursted at the seams with nearly 3 million members. Mass relocations also occurred, with all nonessential people being encouraged to relocate to the countryside, including the nation's children.

Despite the increase in labor, rice production soon plummeted in Japan, and the Allied war on Japanese shipping drastically curtailed the amount of rice imported from throughout the empire. Already, in 1942, women spent an average of four and a half hours per day waiting in line for food, a situation that grew worse as the war progressed, though, predictably, the wealthy faired better. With malnutrition came a slew of workplace diseases such as tuberculosis, neuralgia, rickets, and exhaustion. Folks in the countryside had fuller bellies because they raised their own food, and by 1945 most city dwellers found themselves teetering on the brink of starvation.

By 1943, the cities themselves became eerily bereft of the voices of children as the Imperial State encouraged city-dwelling parents to evacuate their children to the countryside, not unlike what happened in cities such as London during the Blitz in 1940. When the war ended in August 1945, some 1.3 million children had abandoned Japan's major cities, over half of those moving in with relatives, but others relocating to country inns or Buddhist temples. While the children were away, teachers encouraged them to keep diaries, tracking their transformation into what authorities called "splendid little citizens," preparing for the "decisive battle" with the hated Americans. Teachers taught hygiene and civic morality, as well as the virtues of Japan's past heroes, most of them heroic because they had willingly given their lives in the name of imperial loyalty. Children composed poetry on Japan's divinity and superiority to other nations. Like women, they too served as an emotional link to sailors and soldiers at the front, writing letters of support to the Emperor's forces.

In her diary, nine-year-old Nakane Mihoko from Tokyo remembered that, on Imperial Rescript Observance Day, "When I went to school in the morning, the beautiful rising-sun flags on each house were fluttering in the morning breeze. There was a ceremony at school."[14] She recalled that, "After we returned to our classroom, we wrote letters to sailors. I did as I always did. I tried as hard as I could to write letters that would make them happy." When not writing letters to Imperial Navy sailors, such "splendid little citizens" as Nakane sent off new conscripts to the front. Nakane remembered sending off a son from the Maeda family: "we shouted 'Maeda banzai!' three times. He boarded the train. When that happened, the band started playing. It was very merry."[15] Inevitably, the remains of many of those conscripts returned in wooden boxes. On May 10, 1945, Nakane wrote, "In the afternoon we welcomed the spirits of departed heroes"[16] back to Japan. This was the war through the eyes of a child.

Later, she revealed how she felt "grateful to them"[17] for their having made the ultimate sacrifice. Such was the cycle of little Nakane's conditioning as a "splendid little citizen." Given that the daily rhythm of her life was shaped by war, even the hardest tasks, such as stacking wood, were made easy when "I thought of the soldiers,"[18] and the sacrifices they were making. When she did, sacrifices on the home front became far easier. In an abstract but quite real way, she became connected to the sailors and soldiers on the front, and they to her. They were always hungry, sailors and children alike, but their bonds became cemented by the obligations, gratitude, and sacrifices expected of all Japanese citizens, even the tiniest and most innocent among them. Nakane confided in her diary, "I want to do my best to become a splendid citizen." With warships such as *Yukikaze* battling in the Pacific against overwhelming enemy forces, she believed in her heart that it was the least she could do.

* * *

On June 30, 1943, as part of Operation Cartwheel, the Allies started the campaign to take New Georgia by quickly capturing Rendova Island. In doing so, they sought to neutralize the Japanese airstrip on Munda Point, on the west coast of New Georgia. In response, Japanese war planners sought to reinforce and resupply troops around New Georgia in order to keep the airstrip out of enemy hands. In support of this response, Imperial Navy planners ordered a supply mission to navigate "The Slot" from Rabaul and land 1,200 troops at Vila on Kolombangara Island, to the northwest. Commanders slated Desron2, commanded by the fifty-one-year-old Admiral Isaki Shunji from his flagship *Jintsū*, the intrepid cruiser of the Rat Transports fame, to escort the troop relocation to Vila. The torpedo maestro Vice Admiral Tanaka, former master of *Jintsū*, had been relieved for his outspokenness. As always, it's the nail that sticks out of the wood that gets hammered on the head, and Tanaka stood out. *Yukikaze, Mikazuki, Hamakaze, Kiyonami,* and *Yūgure* accompanied the stalwart cruiser on the critical reinforcement mission.

For their part, the Allies sought to ambush the Japanese and, to do so, mobilized a task force under the command of Admiral Walden Lee Ainsworth. He sought to prevent the Japanese from landing reinforcements and supplies, as well as to sink enemy ships. He commanded three cruisers, *Honolulu, St. Louis,* and the New Zealand vessel *Leander,* with ten destroyers. Captain Francis X. McInerney commanded the vanguard destroyers, the formidable *Nicholas, O'Bannon, Taylor, Jenkins,* and *Radford.* The situation had the makings of a cruiser–destroyer brawl.

On the night of July 12–13, the Allied task force approached Kolombangara on a northeasterly course. *O'Bannon,* a *Fletcher*-class destroyer and one of the most decorated US warships in World War II, shared the vanguard. Her captain, Donald J. MacDonald, recorded that "the moon was in the first quarter phase, moonset was at 0212 L/13, visibility was good, estimated at approximately 7 miles, the sea was calm, the wind was force 3 from the southeast."[19] It was a pleasant enough night, but Captain MacDonald had fought in the Solomon Islands long enough to know that the night presented perfect conditions for Japanese night-fighting tactics, which relied heavily on early visual detection and an ample helping of torpedoes.

As Captain MacDonald reported, that night, at around 00:45, "word was received from Task Group Commander over the TBS circuit that there were six enemy ships bearing 310° T, distance 20 miles, from us."[20] According to *Radford*'s commander, Captain W. K. Romoser, shortly after this report, the "Task Group [was] directed to form battle disposition"[21] and increase speed to 28 knots with 600 yards distance between vessels. As *O'Bannon* charged toward the Imperial Navy vessels, "radar contact was established on a large pip bearing 300° T, distance 24,500 yards,"[22] and it became clear that "a cruiser was [the] second ship in the column." Indeed, Admiral Isaki had positioned *Jintsū* second in the Japanese battle column.

Admiral Ainsworth ordered Operation A, and the US destroyers in the vanguard, including *O'Bannon* and *Radford*, fired five torpedoes after making their simultaneous turn and attempting to cross the "enemy's bow,"[23] a classic crossing of the "T" maneuver. *O'Bannon* trained her fish on the "2nd ship in column," Admiral Isaki's flagship. Two minutes later, the Allied cruisers opened up with their big guns at 9,500 meters distance. *Jintsū* had illuminated her searchlights, which, according to Captain Romoser, were "used as visual point of aim in conjunction with 'FD' radar ranges while salvos were rocked back and forth across target with 200 yard spots."[24] The US tactic was to pummel the Japanese warships with the big naval guns while navigating just outside optimum Type 93 torpedo range.

The US Navy estimated the range of the Type 93 torpedo to be approximately 5,000 meters. In reality, the Type 93 had an effective range of closer to 22,000 meters at the highest speed setting and could travel that range at close to 50 knots. But the US thinking was that, by opening up a naval barrage at 10,000 meters, the Allied warships could hit the Imperial Navy task force while safely operating outside the range of Japanese torpedoes, the underwater missiles of World War II. Indeed, prior to the night action, Admiral Ainsworth had discussed with the task force the "night anti-aircraft cruising dispositions"[25] and "method of reversing the action by the use of simultaneous turns." He deployed such evasive maneuvers to avoid the Type 93 torpedoes. Ever since the humiliation at the Battle of Tassafaronga, where the feisty Tanaka had savaged Allied vessels with torpedoes, the Allies tried to keep their distance from Japanese torpedo men.

By 1943, along with the doctrine of staying out of torpedo range, the US Navy had also come to rely heavily on radar, particularly for night action. In the first year and a half of the war, superior Japanese lookouts had generally aced the US Navy in night fighting. On Imperial Navy warships, officers assumed that keen lookouts, groomed for the critical posts since having their eyes identified as superior to those of other cadets, could spot the masts of warships at 10,000 meters, well within torpedo range. But radar could see objects further than that – it proved one of the most important technological breakthroughs of the war. But it also had its limitation in close-quarters fighting, as we shall see.

Famously, the Imperial Navy was slow to develop radar, but the Japanese had begun experimenting with a technological advancement of their own, an electronic system engineers called "reverse radar." Reverse radar couldn't see ships as radar could. But it could detect radar waves or electronic pulses, which were now constantly emanating from US warships. In fact, reverse radar could detect radar waves from as far away as 100 kilometers or more. In April 1943, engineers outfitted *Yukikaze* with reverse radar and, in the early morning hours of July 13, even before her lookouts spotted enemy masts, she had long since detected Admiral Ainsworth's task force charging northward. Japanese reverse radar had likely detected the Allied ships before Allied radar had picked up the Japanese vessels, in fact.

The destroyer *Mikazuki* led the Imperial Navy escort force as it approached Kolombangara, followed by Admiral Isaki's flagship *Jintsū*. *Yukikaze* brought up the rear of the formation. Japanese lookouts, their eyes bloodshot with fatigue, scanned the horizons for the Allied task force they already knew was coming. There was a nervous air on the bridge of the unsinkable destroyer. "Would the new reverse radar system even work?," many wondered. Then, at 00:55, Japanese lookouts spotted the Allied task force coming over the southern horizon. The crewman operating *Yukikaze*'s reverse radar was a well-known wireless operator in the Imperial Navy who later became known as a master reverse-radar operator. In fact, after the Battle of Kolombangara, Admiral Ozawa Jisaburō reassigned this particular crewman to operate the reverse radar on his flagship, the big flattop *Zuikaku*.

The Japanese may have known that the Allies were coming, but the Allies fired the first shots. In the first 20 minutes of the engagement, *Honolulu* fired 1,110 6-inch shells and 123 5-inch shells, while *St. Louis* fired 1,360 6-inchers and *Leander* 160. As *Radford*'s commander reported, after the opening salvo, *Jintsū* was enveloped by flames and then "exploded, and disappeared from radar scope." The big guns of the US cruisers had mauled *Jintsū*, quickly sinking the four-stacker and killing Admiral Isaki with it. About ten minutes later, *Radford*'s "Sound gear picked up torpedoes" in the water, which prompted the destroyer to rapidly change course. *Radford* evaded the Type 93 torpedoes in this initial Japanese salvo, as did *Jenkins*.

Meanwhile, aboard *Yukikaze*, Lieutenant Commander Shimazui Takemi, who served as overall commander of Desron16, had immediately assumed command of the Imperial Navy escort after Admiral Isaki's demise. He held fast as the destroyers charged the enemy at full throttle. Quietly, Shimazui calculated that his highest-percentage shot was to bring *Yukikaze* and the other destroyers within 3,000 meters, virtually point-blank range. Each destroyer had eight Type 93 bolts to fire in one salvo, so they had to count. Imperial Navy torpedo tactics were straightforward: once a destroyer had launched eight torpedoes from one side, the warship quickly came about while crews reloaded the tubes to fire again, a dangerous and time-consuming process.

In June 1943, in fighting around Santa Isabel Island, Imperial Navy commanders, overconfident of the abilities of their secret weapon, had fired their torpedoes prematurely, which frustrated their efforts. Similarly, on November 14–15, 1942, at the Naval Battle of Guadalcanal, Imperial Navy destroyers had prematurely fired thirty-four torpedoes at *South Dakota*, and not a single one struck the battlewagon. By contrast, on November 30, 1942, at the Battle of Tassafaronga, Admiral Tanaka had clobbered the US Navy with torpedoes alone, but only after he had dashed to within

5,000 meters of his targets. As *Yukikaze* sped toward Admiral Ainsworth's task force that night, Shimazui understood that, although the Type 93 torpedo served as a long-range weapon, it proved far more effective in close-in combat. This sort of combat – that is, close-in fighting, the kind that required courage – suited Japanese sensibilities anyway.

Calmly, Lieutenant Commander Shimazui confirmed the speed and heading of the US task force and prepared his fish. He peered back at Captain Kanma, also an experienced torpedo man.

"Let's continue within 4,000 meters,"[26] responded Kanma. The Japanese charged ahead at thirty knots.

Someone on the bridge could be heard asking, "Are we still waiting on the torpedoes?"

Another voice pleaded, "Can we please fire, sir?"

But still the Imperial Navy destroyers plowed ahead. Tension filled the bridge.

Saitō Kazuyoshi, the new Torpedo Chief aboard *Yukikaze*, had never fired a torpedo in combat. His expression was of a man who faced certain death. He asked, "Permission to fire, please sir!"

But Shimazui wouldn't budge and waited until the task force was within 5,000 meters. He then gave the order to fire. With this order, decades of torpedo tradition aboard *Yukikaze* came to fruition to execute the strike. Since long before Kolombangara, Imperial Navy brass had considered *Yukikaze*'s torpedo preparedness to be among the best in the fleet. Every morning, torpedo men doted over their fish, almost "as if they were their own children." One of *Yukikaze*'s first captains, Wakita Kiichirō, a stern patriarch at home, had instituted the practice of polishing the torpedoes daily aboard *Yukikaze*, a practice that was performed without fail. It's not surprising that, in July 1941, Imperial Navy Headquarters transferred Captain Wakita to command the 21st Torpedo Squadron, comprised of *Chidori*-class torpedo boats. Nonetheless, his relentless attention to detail still permeated the torpedo culture aboard *Yukikaze*.

That is precisely what happened in the early morning darkness of July 13. At 4,800 meters, eight torpedoes leapt from *Yukikaze*'s amidships launchers, as well as from the other destroyers, and within minutes one slammed into *Leander*. Shouts of "Banzai!" could be heard from *Yukikaze*'s deck. As Admiral Ainsworth wrote in his Action Report, "The LEANDER received her torpedo hit at about 0124 as she was completing the turn. This torpedo seems to have been the only one to reach the cruiser formation, although the destroyers, then on the starboard quarter of the cruiser formation, had to do some sharp maneuvering to avoid several of them."[27] Immediately, several of the US destroyers peeled off to aid the stricken *Leander*, which retreated to Auckland and, later, shipyards in Boston. (The *Leander* was in a shambles, but with herculean efforts returned to the Pacific in the autumn of 1944.)

While the remaining US warship opened fire, the Imperial Navy destroyers began their turn for a second torpedo attack. Now the lead vessel, *Yukikaze* received the brunt of this fire, but miraculously escaped damage. *Hamakaze*'s commander, Captain Kamii Hiroshi, watched in amazement as enemy fire surrounded *Yukikaze*, columns of water splashing everywhere, but the warship didn't receive a single hit. *Yukikaze* ran northeast at thirty-two knots while the enemy shells splashed to her stern, probably deflected slightly by the freshening southwesterly wind.

For the US commander, radar created more confusion than clarity at this point in the engagement. It took Admiral Ainsworth precious time to determine that the Imperial Navy destroyers on his radar screen weren't "cripples" fleeing the battlefield or his own vessels, but rather that the "enemy contact was closing rapidly"[28] and "four ships were headed toward us" on an attack pattern. Suddenly, after the Japanese had made their turn, Admiral Ainsworth transformed from predator to prey. As Admiral Ainsworth began his turn and unmasked the big guns of his cruisers, Shimazui launched his second salvo of torpedoes.

Yukikaze had launched her first torpedoes at 01:20, and her second at around 01:50, a mere thirty minutes later. Japanese records indicate that the distance was 4,500 meters for the second salvo, while Admiral Ainsworth thought the charging destroyers were still at 15,000 yards. This led Ainsworth to speculate that the "Jap ships may have fired in radar control," but they did not. The more likely explanation is that the Japanese destroyers had gotten far closer than Ainsworth knew because of confusion between friend and foe on the radar screen. In his Action Report, Admiral Ainsworth reported that torpedoes struck the *St. Louis* at 02:08 and the *Honolulu* at 02:11, and that the *Gwin* "received a torpedo hit about three minutes later." By contrast, the *Radford* noted, at "0215 GWIN

Figure 7.2 The bow of *St. Louis*, showing torpedo damage received during the Battle of Kolombangara. She was photographed while under repair at Tulagi on July 20, 1943. Official US Navy Photograph, National Archives, Catalog #: 80-G-259410.

reported hit by a torpedo,"[29] at "0218 HONOLULU reported hit by a torpedo," and at "0233 ST LOUIS reported hit by a torpedo" (Figure 7.2). Regardless of the exact time, all three ships were badly damaged by seriously fast action and accurate torpedo fire. The *Gwin* went down, while the *Honolulu* eventually returned to Hawaii and the *St. Louis* to the Mare Island Naval Shipyard (near San Francisco) for extensive repairs.

Importantly, the mission was a success for Japanese war planners: the Imperial Navy successfully deposited 1,200 Imperial Army troops at Vila to guard the Munda Point airstrip on New Georgia. As usual, however, it proved too little too late. Japan's ability to project military power was ebbing, not flooding. On August 5, 1943, after desperate jungle fighting, Munda fell to the Allies. By the end of September, all Japanese forces on New Georgia had been killed, evacuated, or taken prisoner. The Allies had taken another small step toward the Japanese homeland.

CHAPTER 8

The Mariana Islands and the Collapse of Japan's Defensive Sphere

Shifted periscope to port bow, and saw destroyer heading at us, zero angle on bow, with practically nothing but bow wave showing.

Captain Herman Kossler during the Battle of the Philippine Sea

JAPAN'S GOD OF WAR continued to shelter *Yukikaze* as the fighting dragged on in the Pacific, but the same can't be said of the Emperor's forces in general. The magnificent warships of the Imperial Navy, in particular the Special Type destroyers, disappeared far faster than they could be replaced. And fewer destroyers meant weakened escorts for oil tankers and troop transports, exposing them to Allied attack. Japan subsequently began to lose merchant shipping at a staggering pace.

In the summer of 1943, *Yukikaze* patrolled the forward Imperial Navy base at Truk until US planes destroyed it. She then escorted flattops throughout the Western Pacific and Mariana Islands. With the Solomon Islands, Papuan Peninsula, and New Guinea lost, islands such as Tinian and Saipan, in the Marianas, likely only distant names to most Japanese, took on added significance in the defense of the home islands. The lumbering, but bomb-laden, Flying Fortresses could reach Japan's largest cities from Saipan.

At the end of 1943, Captain Terauchi Masamichi, a large and intimidating man, assumed command of *Yukikaze*, after Captain Kanma, like commanders before him, burned out. Captain Terauchi had come from another lucky ship, the destroyer *Inazuma*, before it had sunk. With Terauchi in command, *Yukikaze* entered the dangerous 1944–1945 period of the war with a man known for his tenacious fighting spirit. But

Captain Terauchi's desire for tactical victories didn't always reflect the desires of Imperial Navy brass.

By 1944, dark clouds had gathered over Japan's entire empire, including the Western Pacific. Japan had staked much of its development since the Meiji Restoration on its empire, and the sprawling Greater East Asian Co-Prosperity Sphere stood on the brink of historical oblivion. Most importantly, oil began to disappear from Japanese tank farms, largely a result of successful Allied submarine and bomber raids on Japan's merchant marine fleet. Increasingly desperate, engineers resorted to distilling fuel from pine roots to fill aircraft tanks. This is the period of "gradual decline," as Japan entered the Dark Valley of the war.

By early summer 1944, the US Navy eyed Saipan in order to blow a gaping hole in Japan's Absolute National Defensive Sphere. And the horrifying Imperial Army banzai charges on the island only portended what the Allies would be up against as they approached the home islands. To assist with the defense of Saipan, the Imperial Navy mobilized to meet US Task Force 58 at the Battle of the Philippine Sea, where Japan's carrier-based air wing was all but destroyed in the infamous Marianas Turkey Shoot.

In very real ways, Imperial Navy culture shifted at this moment. After the fighting in the Mariana Islands, the Imperial Navy, once known for its tactical discipline, its dependency on the element of surprise, its preference for night-fighting, and its elaborate strategic planning, began resorting to suicide tactics, more in line with the Imperial Army's culture of sacrifice. After the Marianas campaign, the Imperial Navy fought less for tactical victories than to satiate Japanese history's appetite for glory, posterity, and an honorable death. If Japanese cities and subjects were to burn, so must the Imperial Navy's magnificent warships.

* * *

What does it mean to be a "lucky ship" during the bloodiest war the world has ever known? *Yukikaze* had escorted the big flattop *Zuikaku* at the Battle of the Santa Cruise Islands and they were left untouched. Captain Hara of the destroyer *Amatsukaze* had marveled that *Yukikaze* remained unscathed during the naval brawl at Guadalcanal, while the US Navy pummeled other Imperial Navy warships. The Eighteenth

Army's Chief of Staff, Yoshihara Kane, had commented, after Dampier's Tragedy, "Although every ship in the convoy had suffered a group attack from the enemy planes, this ship had not been visited by one enemy aircraft; like a military observer, it had merely fired at the enemy planes." Similarly, Captain Kamii Hiroshi of *Hamakaze* had remarked that artillery explosions surrounded *Yukikaze* at Kolombangara, but the unsinkable destroyer emerged with little more than a scratch. How is such luck even possible in the context of industrial-scale killing?

For Imperial Navy warships fighting in the Java Sea, the Solomon Islands, and along the Bismarck Barrier between 1941 and late 1943, surviving depended on the skill and training of the officers and crew, as well as the seaworthiness and battle preparedness of the warship. *Yukikaze* excelled on all these fronts: her officers proved plenty competent and her sailors performed well. They also maintained their vessel carefully, and she was always ready to fight. Other than striking a reef in the strong currents at Tawi-Tawi, in the southern Philippines, *Yukikaze* navigated the tides, currents, and reef-infested waters of the South Seas with salty acumen. She also avoided the almost daily onslaught of attacks by enemy submarines, airplanes, and warships. To a certain degree, then, she earned her good fortune through skilled seamanship and tenacious fighting. But seamanship doesn't explain everything.

After two years of heavy fighting in the South Pacific, Allied forces had managed to slash their way deep into the Solomon Islands and had taken the Papuan Peninsula and a large swath of New Guinea. By the summer of 1943, Japanese warships and troop transports dared travel only by night in the Solomon Islands, given the Allied command of the skies. In this atmosphere, surviving proved more complicated than simple preparedness: it also required a healthy sprinkling of luck. Just as many in the US Navy considered the cruiser *Helena* and the destroyer *O'Bannon* to be lucky ships, at least until they weren't, Japanese sailors aboard *Yukikaze* said of the little warship *un ga yoi*, or her "luck is good." It turns out that fate is a fickle mistress, however. For some to benefit from good luck, others must not.

On the night of July 20, 1943, the Imperial Navy's Eighth Squadron, commanded by Rear Admiral Nishimura Shōji – whom we'll meet again at Leyte Gulf – eased down The Slot along the west coast of Choiseul

Island, heading once again toward Kolombangara. They were involved in yet another troop transport run, providing more young men for the Solomon Islands grinder. Comprised of the big cruisers *Suzuya* and *Maya*, the light cruiser *Tenryū*, and four destroyers led by *Yukikaze*, the Eighth Squadron packed a pretty serious punch, with plenty of big 20.3 cm (8-inch) guns and scores of torpedoes. Stubborn fighting still raged around the islands of Choiseul, Kolombangara, and Vella Lavella, but the Eighth Squadron remained buoyed by the victory over Admiral Ainsworth's task force a week earlier.

Admiral Nishimura knew from recent night fighting that slipping within close torpedo range remained the key to success against the US Navy, not an artillery duel with heavies. Imperial Navy cruisers such as *Suzuya* and *Maya* carried twenty-four Type 93 torpedoes each, not to mention what the four destroyers carried. *Yukikaze* had identified signals with her reverse radar, and the Japanese anticipated a fight. With this in mind, Admiral Nishimura navigated southward with *Yukikaze* ahead of *Hamakaze* in the right column, and *Yūgure* ahead of *Kiyonami* in the left column. *Suzuya*, *Maya*, and *Tenryū*, the cruisers, held the center column in that order.

In navy circles, officers and sailors alike knew Admiral Nishimura as the *Mihari no Kamisama*, or the Lookout God. He had chosen *Suzuya*, a *Mogami*-class warship, for his flag. Good lookouts in the Imperial Navy could see as far as 8,000 meters or more, but none further than Nishimura, who reportedly identified ships as far away as 10,000 meters. He sometimes held competitions aboard his commands to identify the best lookout, and then he went head to head with the winners, always besting them with his keen eyes. Nishimura believed that early identification of the enemy was the secret to success on the water, and, before radar anyway, he was right.

That night, Admiral Nishimura hoped to spot the enemy warships, adjust course, slip within 3,000 meters (as the Japanese had with Admiral Ainsworth's task force), release the fish in the water, and then disappear safely northward. It was a simple plan. But, on this night, the Allied ships never came over the horizon and the signals on *Yukikaze*'s reverse radar eventually faded. It was 02:50 (Japan Time), and Nishimura's force needed to turn around and return to Rabaul or they would be caught on open water in daylight, a dangerous time for Imperial Navy warships.

When an Imperial Navy squadron changed course, commanders used two basic techniques to safely reverse the direction of their battle dispositions or columns. In what commanders called a "simultaneous turn," the ships in the right column turned 180 degrees to starboard, as did the ships in the middle column. Meanwhile, the ships in the left column turned to port. When all the ships finished the maneuver, they were heading in the opposite direction, but their relative position within the three battle columns had reversed. Now, the warships that once held the right column held the left.

Conversely, in what commanders called a "general straight angle turn," the ships in the right and middle columns swung around to port, while the ships holding the left column turned inside to starboard. This technique had the advantage that, when the ships completed the 180-degree turn, the warships held station in the same relative positions in the three columns as they had prior to the turn, simplifying orders in the heat of combat.

Usually, Admiral Nishimura ordered the second, the "general straight angle turn," which would have put *Yukikaze* and *Hamakaze* in the right column as they headed north up The Slot, now off Santa Isabel Island. To everybody's surprise, however, Nishimura ordered a "simultaneous turn," which meant that *Yukikaze* and *Hamakaze* held the left column as they passed Santa Isabel. Now, the destroyers *Yūgure* and *Kiyonami* held the right column as the Eighth Squadron headed north up The Slot.

Before the Eighth Squadron had even completed its turn, however, Allied bombers came flying low and fast over the foothills of Santa Isabel on a skip-bombing run, the same technique they had used at the Battle of the Bismarck Sea. A US Marine Grumman TBF Avenger from Guadalcanal sank *Yūgure* with a direct hit, while US Army B-25s sank *Kiyonami*. The battle concluded in a flash, and only the screams of drowning, oil-covered sailors pierced the once tranquil night. Had Nishimura ordered the "general straight angle turn," as he typically did, *Yukikaze* and *Hamakaze* would have been the targets of the skip-bombing raid. But he didn't, and *Yukikaze*, safely off the port beam of the formidable *Suzuya*, lived to fight in the Marianas, in Leyte Gulf, and at Okinawa. Some 240 men from *Kiyonami* died in the water that night, as did another

228 from *Yūgure*. That's what it means to be a "lucky ship" in the context of total war. *Kiyonami* and *Yūgure* were not lucky ships.

* * *

In August 1943, *Yukikaze* withdrew to the Imperial Navy fortress at Truk Lagoon, where she underwent repairs and refits. When workers had completed those repairs in September, Imperial Navy brass assigned the destroyer to guard duties around Truk, before she traveled to the home islands for even more substantial refits, which I've detailed already. The lagoon at Truk served as a principal naval anchorage for the Imperial Navy Combined Fleet, often home to the battleships *Musashi* and *Yamato*, the flagship of Admiral Yamamoto. The admiral spent considerable time at Truk until, on April 18, 1943, US P-38s, acting on Magic-decrypted intelligence, shot down his Mitsubishi G4M bomber and Zero escort planes while they were traveling between Rabaul and Bougainville Island. Ostensibly, he had made the trip to boost troop morale.

With his fiery death, morale faded even more. His grieving colleagues cremated him in Buin, and a solemn *Musashi* transported his remains to Tokyo. After his dark state funeral on June 5, the gloom that plagued Imperial forces in the South Seas began spreading throughout the entire nation. Admiral Yamamoto had celebrated triumphs and anguished over tragedies, but there was always something about the admiral's panache and unbridled confidence that gave the Imperial Navy a ray of hope in their war of desperation. Now that ray of hope had vanished.

Truk Lagoon remained a formidable naval base, however. Civil engineers had fortified the islands surrounding the main lagoon with elaborate bunkers, pillboxes, trenches, and networks of reinforced caves. They also built roads, some five airstrips, a seaplane base, a torpedo-boat base, submarine repair facilities, a radar station, and a complex communications hub for directing the battleships, aircraft carriers, cruisers, destroyers, tankers, cargo ships, submarines, minesweepers, and tugboats that frequented the turquoise waters. The surrounding landscape and seascape protected the lagoon, as did the substantial manmade fortifications. Its impenetrability led some to call it the "Gibraltar of the Pacific," while others compared it to the safe haven at Pearl Harbor.

Truk served the Japanese until Operation Hailstorm in February 1944, when US planes from the Marshall Islands destroyed the Imperial Navy facilities there, including a substantial number of ships and planes. Today, for scuba divers, these wrecks make the lagoon among the most exciting diving destinations in the world. It's a veritable Imperial Navy graveyard, one of several in the Pacific.

After her refits at the Kure Naval Yard, on October 11 *Yukikaze* escorted the light carrier *Ryūhō* to Singapore. By this time, the South China Sea had become a dangerous place for Imperial Navy carriers, and *Yukikaze* played a vital role in guarding the flattop. Twice *Yukikaze* observed what spotters believed to be enemy submarines, but both sightings turned out to be false alarms. *Ryūhō*, weighed down with a load of manganese, nickel, and rubber, returned to Japan safely, with the unsinkable destroyer at her side.

After the fighting around Guadalcanal, a near miss had cracked one of *Yukikaze*'s boilers, and mechanics had placed a large steel band around it to keep it together. On these escort runs, *Yukikaze* easily reached thirty-five knots during performance tests, prompting loud cheers from officers and crew on her deck. In November 1943, *Yukikaze* provided escort cover again, this time back to Truk with the destroyer *Amatsukaze*, the light carrier *Chitose*, and the transports *Yasukuni-maru* and *Irako*. *Yukikaze* patrolled the waters around the watery fortress until December 7, when she returned to Yokosuka with *Chitose* and *Irako*.

Two days before her departure, while patrolling about ten miles south of the lagoon, *Yukikaze* reported encountering an enemy submarine. It was her second confrontation with an enemy submarine of the war. On spotting the submarine, *Yukikaze* immediately launched depth charges and, not long after, officers and crew observed the bright sheen of oil spreading on the surface of the water.

The normally cautious Lieutenant Commander Shimazui, overall commander of Desron16, looked at Captain Kanma with a grin on his face. "Looks like we got them!" he said. Kanma responded, "It certainly does."

He then recorded the same in his command log. Along with *S-37* in the Java Sea, this was the second Allied submarine that *Yukikaze* had tangled with. On the US side, there are no records of an Imperial Navy vessel sinking an Allied submarine on December 5, though several hunted the waters around Truk. It was not uncommon for destroyers to report that a submarine had been sunk when in fact their quarry had escaped, which may have happened in this instance. It may also have been one of a handful of Allied submarines that simply went missing during the war. We'll probably never know.

On December 7, *Yukikaze* escorted a convoy bound for Yokosuka. From there, she made the trip to Kure, her homeport, to spend New Year's Day there. Her officers and crew, exhausted from the constant fighting, welcomed the opportunity to spend even a brief respite with family. It proved badly needed rest, but it also proved inadequate to recharge Captain Kanma's depleted batteries. In the Imperial Navy, it was not unusual for captains to lose excessive amounts of weight, and Kanma had as well, a dangerous amount. Typically, Imperial Navy destroyers didn't have vice-commanders, only three lieutenants under the captain: Chief Navigator, Torpedo Chief, and Gunnery Chief. In the event that a destroyer captain was killed or incapacitated, the senior commissioned officer among the three lieutenants assumed command responsibilities.

The captain oversaw everything that occurred inside and outside the warship, and the responsibility proved overwhelming for many men. Destroyer captains didn't sleep much, for example. If the opportunity presented itself, they might down a cup of saké and catch a quick catnap, but that was about it. Even men in excellent health eventually succumbed to the demands of commanding a destroyer. Earlier, physicians had hospitalized Captain Tobida with serious chest pains. Captain Kanma, after his retirement, suffered serious chest pains as well.

In December 1943, while *Yukikaze* tugged at her mooring lines at Kure, Imperial Navy brass relieved Captain Kanma, and Captain Terauchi Masamichi became master of the unsinkable destroyer. If Kanma epitomized the expression "navy neat," with his tidy appearance and thoughtful demeanor, then Captain Terauchi was quite the opposite. He was more of a buccaneer. Perennially disheveled, Captain Terauchi had a dreadful appearance at times, with a large brow that never ceased sweating, no matter the temperature. At well over 200 pounds, he was a giant man for his day, and could barely navigate *Yukikaze*'s narrow stairwells. He proved a daunting figure on the bridge, and every fiber of his being exuded the Imperial Navy's tenacious fighting spirit.

Captain Terauchi was well known in navy circles, mainly because, when it came to drinking parties, he reigned supreme. Indeed, rumor had it that he had been confined to the rank of captain for nine years because of his notorious drinking habit. But Captain Terauchi didn't seem to mind – being a destroyer captain suited his personality. Well acquainted with fighting in the Solomon Islands, he had served aboard *Inazuma*, a *Fubuki*-class destroyer. Many also considered *Inazuma* a lucky ship, and she survived until May 1944, when the Allied submarine *Bonefish* blew her stern off near Tawi-Tawi, just before sortieing for the Battle of the Philippine Sea. *Inazuma* fought around Guadalcanal, Buna, and Bougainville Island between 1941 and 1943, where *Yukikaze* also operated, and Imperial Navy brass viewed Captain Terauchi as a skilled and lucky destroyer captain. He was a perfect fit for *Yukikaze*.

What does it mean to be a lucky captain? Once, while transporting troops north of Buna in December 1942, *Inazuma* dropped her hook off the coast to give officers and crew some badly needed rest. It was 02:00 and extremely dark – it seemed safe enough. No sooner had *Inazuma* set anchor than three B-17 bombers descended on the destroyer. With no time to spare, *Inazuma* weighed anchor and Captain Terauchi ordered full throttle. As the ship got under way, 500-kilogram bombs exploded on both sides of *Inazuma*, but the destroyer managed to escape unscathed. *Yukikaze*'s officers and crew viewed these kinds of stories as evidence that Captain Terauchi was a good fit for the unsinkable destroyer.

When Terauchi first transferred aboard *Yukikaze*, the Torpedo Chief, Saitō Kazuyoshi, announced that, "Once again, *Yukikaze* has been blessed with a famously lucky captain. It's testimony that *Yukikaze* is a ship that can't be sunk."[1] This represented the same sentiment that the officers and crew had felt when Captain Kanma became captain a year and a half earlier. Then, the Torpedo Chief of *Amatsukaze*, Morita Tomoyuki, who later became captain of that destroyer, had announced much the same. At the dawn of 1944, Imperial Navy brass had blessed *Yukikaze* with yet another lucky commander, and she would need him.

* * *

The Japanese empire had not been similarly blessed with good fortune. Dark clouds obscured the rays of light emanating from the rising sun in

1944. Since the dawn of the nineteenth century, Japanese nationalists had stressed the vast, resplendent light of imperial rule. This had constituted the meat of their case for overthrowing the Tokugawa shoguns in 1868 and replacing samurai rule with a constitutional monarchy under the youthful Meiji Emperor. Often, historians attribute the birth of the twentieth-century Japanese empire to the engagement with Western imperialism in the nineteenth century: empires were markers of modern nations and Japan needed one to be modern. But it's more complicated than simply copying the West. The Japanese had started colonizing the northern island of Hokkaido as early as the seventeenth century, and, not unlike Manifest Destiny in the history of the United States, traces of expansionism were in the DNA of Japanese civilization from earlier times. Nation-making and empire went hand in hand.

Rhetoric of imperial expansion also colored the birth of imperial nationalism in the late eighteenth and early nineteenth centuries. It's well documented that Japan's early nationalists stressed ancestral connections to the Emperor. As Kamo Mabuchi wrote, "To know the *kokutai* [the national essence] is to know the ancestors and, thus, to exhaust loyal intention to the emperor."[2] But less known is the early connection to imperial expansion. Aizawa Seishisai, another nineteenth-century imperial nationalist, trumpeted, "Our Divine Land is where the sun rises and where the primordial energy originates ... Japan's position at the vertex of the earth makes it the standard for the nations of the world. Indeed, it casts light over the world, and the distance which the resplendent imperial influence reaches knows no limit."[3]

Twentieth-century military leaders had made this lofty nineteenth-century language reality with the establishment of the Greater East Asian Co-Prosperity Sphere. During the first year of the Pacific War, it must have felt like Japan really was situated at the "vertex of the earth" and a "standard for the nations of the world" as its Imperial Navy made quick work of Allied warships, leaving only oil slicks where vessels had once been.

By the early twentieth century, nationalists such as Kita Ikki, building on earlier rhetoric, became even more vocal about the need for Japanese expansion. He spent several years in China involved with the overthrow of the Qing Dynasty and returned to Japan in 1919. On his return, he wrote, *A Plan for the Reorganization of Japan*, in which he outlined the need for an Asia liberated from the shackles of Western empire. A reinvigorated Japan, through the creation of its own empire, promised to lead Asia out from the darkness of Western oppressors.

This became the intellectual rationale for kicking the French out of Indochina, the British out of Singapore and Borneo, the Americans out of the Philippines, and the Dutch out of the East Indies – which, by 1943, Imperial forces had done. "Truly, our seven hundred million brothers in China and India have no path to independence other than that offered by our guidance and protection,"[4] he wrote in 1919. Had the government not executed him in 1937, he might have thought he was right in 1942, before Midway and Guadalcanal, that is.

Japan needed to become a charismatic authoritarian state led by the Emperor, fulfilling what Kita called the "Shōwa Restoration," a nostalgic nod to earlier times. By suspending the Meiji Constitution, Japan could avoid the "malign influence" of the Diet and self-interested political parties. Kita's ultra-nationalist, antidemocratic, antiparty voice became increasingly influential as Japan entered the 1930s, particularly among young, idealistic officers in the Imperial Army. Such young officers increasingly believed they needed to take political matters in their own hands. The important point is that Japan's meteoric economic, political, and military rise after the Meiji Restoration had been tethered from the beginning to a limitless "resplendent imperial influence." It was as implicit to the modern Japanese state as steam trains and the Emperor himself, and those who called for "little Japanism," such as the journalist Ishibashi Tanzan, were quickly relegated to the margins or silenced.

The beginning of 1943 represented the apex of Japan's "resplendent imperial influence," however. By the beginning of 1944, Japan's imperial project, the one that was supposed to liberate much of Asia from Western oppression, had stalled and entered a period called *jiri hin*, or "gradual decline." Japan had not liberated Asia at all, but rather had established a rapacious, extractive empire of its own, one dedicated to the unbridled exploitation of labor and raw materials. But the destruction of Japan's merchant fleet and the rapid decline of the amount of raw materials such as oil, rubber, manganese, and iron ore reaching the home islands crushed Japan's economy, and severely limited its ability to make war with an adversary with a seemingly endless supply of labor and

natural resources. Admiral Yamamoto had learned of American industrial potential while studying at Harvard and during his two postings as
naval attaché in Washington, D.C., and had therefore opposed the war.
But he proved duty bound to start it and was now dead.

By 1944, the oil supply had dwindled so markedly that Japanese scientists began searching for new methods to produce high-octane petroleum, mainly for aircraft to be used for Special Assault missions. One of
the most destructive answers scientists designed – destructive for Japan's
already ravaged forests, that is – was the pine-root oil project.

Using a technique discovered by increasingly desperate Imperial Navy
chemists, engineers began manufacturing high-octane fuel from the
resins derived from pine roots. But the project was desperately flawed
from the outset: producing such fuel required substantial human energy
from an already exhausted nation, and exacerbated further destruction
of forestlands already heavily denuded for other wartime and industrial
purposes. On average, one gallon of pine root oil required two and a
half days of heavy labor and many tons of freshly extracted pine roots.
One Mitsubishi A6M Zero held 137 gallons in its primary fuel tank, and
an additional 87 gallons in its drop tank. Needless to say, the number of
trees that had to be destroyed to fly a single fighter aircraft for an hour
or two was astonishing.

Despite the fact that the Japanese already suffered widespread food
shortages, the Emperor's subjects rose to the occasion and built some
34,000 pine-root stills, producing some 70,000 barrels of pine root crude
a month from Japan's beleaguered arboreal oilfields. The amount of
fuel produced from such pine-root stills never came close to supplying
the Emperor's forces with the industrial juice necessary to beat the Allies,
but it did scar the once green archipelago for generations.

Between 1941 and 1945, loggers felled some 14,000 square miles,
or about 15 percent of Japan's forests. Two-thirds of that loggers clear-
cut. Immediately after the war, one observer remarked, "Monumental
piles of roots and stumps lined many of the roadways. Mountainsides
were stripped bare of every tree and sapling."[5] The number of trees cut
down throughout the Greater East Asian Co-Prosperity Sphere proved
equally staggering. In the end, the role of Japan's empire had never
been the promotion of racial harmony, nor was it about some imperial

resplendent light. Rather, it was about unmitigated industrial extraction. In the final analysis, establishing and defending this extractive empire was always *Yukikaze*'s war.

Through Imperial Navy eyes, the oil-supply problem never boiled down to a simple lack of tankers, either. It's not just that Allied submarines and bombers had sent a large portion of Japan's merchant and tanker fleet to Davy Jones's Locker by 1944, though they indisputably had. Equally important was that the vessels that remained proved outdated and dangerously slow. On top of that, the Imperial Navy had lost an appalling number of destroyers by 1944 – fifty-six newer destroyers between 1941 and 1943 alone – meaning that convoys that required six escort destroyers typically had four, and convoys that required four escort vessels typically had two.

The US Navy was now ascendant in sea control. Records illustrate the hardship caused by insufficient destroyer escorts as the Allies penetrated deeper into Japan's maritime sphere. The Allies sank some twenty-seven Japanese oil tankers in the first two years of the war between 1941 and 1943. They easily exceeded that number – thirty-three Japanese tankers sunk in all – in the first three months of 1944 alone. This downward death spiral, with the Imperial Navy unable to defend its sea-lanes of communication and military transports, became *Yukikaze*'s 1944 oil-covered nightmare.

* * *

On January 10, 1944, *Yukikaze* departed Moji, Japan. *Chitose*, the light carrier, represented the main strength of the task force that arrived in Singapore on January 20. Five days later, *Yukikaze* escorted *Chitose* and convoy Hi-32 on the return voyage, loaded with oil and bauxite, a mineral with high aluminum content. Along the way, one enemy aircraft appeared, presumably a scout plane from the Chinese mainland, but *Yukikaze*'s new vertical-angle antiaircraft mounts made an effective showing. No other aircraft or submarines showed up, and the mission proved relatively uneventful.

February witnessed much the same escort work. This time, however, *Yukikaze*'s new destination became the Mariana Islands, particularly the stronghold of Saipan, part of Japan's Absolute National Defensive

Sphere. Since the beginning of the war, the Imperial Navy's wartime strategy had always depended on a network of bands to guard its precious natural resources in the South Seas, historian Morison's "perimeter of steel." But as the US Navy penetrated those outer bands in the Solomon Islands and Bismarck Barrier, the Imperial Navy transitioned from offense to defense – ultimately, the defense of the home islands.

Saipan was different than the strongholds in the Solomon Islands and the Bismarck Barrier, however. The German Empire had controlled Saipan until the Japanese relieved it of the sizable island in 1914, during World War I. Japan, of course, had fought on the side of the Allies, and the League of Nations formally awarded Saipan to Japan as part of the South Seas Mandate in 1919. Starting in the 1920s, Japanese, Taiwanese, Koreans, and Okinawans began to settle on the island, largely as labor to develop sugarcane plantations. Eventually, the South Seas Development Company built refineries on Saipan, as well as ports, wharfs, roads, a power station, schools, and a Shinto shrine. As the war shifted to the Marianas in 1944, some 30,000 Japanese lived on Saipan, as well as a handful of native inhabitants. The fighting would be different on Saipan because Japanese families had lived on the islands for decades.

At the beginning of 1944, the Pacific Theater took on a new, more frenetic pace, and the Emperor's forces began fortifying Saipan, Guam, and Tinian, most part of the Absolute National Defensive Sphere and all unthinkably close to the home islands (at least insofar as long-range bombers were concerned). Driven by US domestic politics and the war schedule in Europe, the Allies had hastened the tempo of the Central Pacific campaign, taking Makin and Tarawa in the Gilbert Islands in November 1943, and eventually, as part of Operation Cartwheel, isolating the stronghold at Rabaul. The Allied landings at Tarawa proved a bloodbath, and this forced Allied war planners to rethink some aspects of the Pacific island-hopping strategy. Yet, Saipan couldn't be avoided – it was too big to just hop over, and the Allies had long desired the Marianas for bomber bases.

Imperial Headquarters called on the navy to do whatever it could to fortify the northern Marianas, and *Yukikaze* began escorting transports of troops, fighter planes, munitions, and aviation fuel to the First Air Squadron on Saipan and Tinian, a slightly smaller island to the southwest. In a manner, *Yukikaze* had started escorting Japan's wartime

Figure 8.1 Matsuzoe Takeshi's "Destroyers Escorting a Transport Convoy" postcard (author's collection).

manufacturing full circle, bringing the oil and bauxite from Singapore to Japan, where workers transformed it into aviation fuel and airplanes, which *Yukikaze* then transported to the Marianas for the defense of Saipan and Tinian (see Figure 8.1). In 1944, as *Yukikaze*'s record attests, the war had stretched the capabilities of the extractive empire to its absolute limits.

In February, the principal threat to Japanese shipping in the Mariana Islands became Allied submarines, particularly their use of the German "wolf pack" hunting techniques (see Figure 8.2). Such wolf packs lurked in the waters around well-known Japanese navigational routes, and *Yukikaze*, accompanied by *Chitose* and the destroyer *Hatsushimo*, had to be particularly vigilant when they departed Kagoshima on February 20 bound for Saipan and Tinian. No sooner had they got under way than *Yukikaze*'s reverse radar detected a large number of enemy signals to the south. Eventually, *Yukikaze* confirmed the existence of enemy warships, and the convoy made for the base at Ulithi, an atoll in the Caroline Islands. Once the coast had cleared, the vessels made way for Saipan and arrived on February 26. They unloaded their cargo and returned to Yokosuka on March 4. It was a quick turnaround.

Figure 8.2 Suzuki Gyosui's "Antisubmarine Company in the Growing Darkness – Attacking the Enemy's Strength" postcard (author's collection).

Once again using flattops to transport badly needed war materiel, on March 29, *Yukikaze* escorted the carrier *Zuihō* out of the naval yard at Yokosuka. In Ise Bay, the small convoy rendezvoused with the carrier *Ryūhō* and her escort, the destroyer *Hatsushimo*, and they departed for Tinian to once again further strengthen the First Air Squadron in the face of the pending US invasion. On April 2, near Guam, the Japanese spotted what they thought was a US wolf pack, but on further investigation no boats were encountered. After delivering their supplies, *Yukikaze* made for the home islands and returned to Kure without incident on April 8. But *Yukikaze*'s new intensified escort duties were only getting started. By 1944, the nature of her participation in the war in the Pacific had changed.

On April 20, Imperial Navy brass ordered *Yukikaze* to escort *Yamato* and the cruiser *Maya* into the South Seas, which she did, arriving at Lingga Roads in Borneo on May 1. In part, the decision to have *Yukikaze* guard the battleship and heavy cruiser evidences the trust the Imperial Navy placed in the unsinkable destroyer and the supposedly unsinkable battleship, but also the fact that it was quickly running out of escort destroyers. *Yukikaze* spent eleven days at Lingga Roads before traveling to Tawi-Tawi, arriving on May 15.

With the increased pressure on Japanese cargo ships and tankers, Imperial Navy planners didn't have the oil or aviation fuel to train for pending missions in home waters, so they decided to train closer to Borneo and the refining capabilities at Balikpapan. Here, the warships from Japan rendezvoused with flattops that operated near Singapore and began staging for the next attempt at a decisive battle with the US Navy. The war effort had entered dire straits for the Japanese and nothing came easily. On May 14, while escorting tankers bound for Balikpapan, the US submarine *Bonefish* blew the stern off Captain Terauchi's former command, the destroyer *Inazuma*, killing 161 sailors. The other destroyer on the scene, *Hibiki*, managed to pull some 125 sailors out of the oily waters and transported them to safety.

Yukikaze arrived at Tawi-Tawi on May 15, and three days later damaged her propeller on the reef guarding the inner anchorage. She spent most of late May and early June escorting the carrier *Taihō* to and from the anchorage, while the flattop trained her inexperienced flight crews for the coming engagement in the Philippine Sea. At this juncture, many Imperial Navy warships were burning unrefined bunker fuel extracted directly from Borneo. Because she had ruined one of her propellers, *Yukikaze* could only limp along at a cumbersome twenty-five knots. It proved a speed that wouldn't suffice in a blue-water surface fight with high-speed carriers. Instead, battle planners relegated her, along with four other outdated destroyers, to escort the tankers that would refuel the warships en route in preparation for the decisive battle. Ironically, guarding these tankers, *Yukikaze* witnessed more action than most destroyers on the front line.

* * *

Vice Admiral Ozawa Jisaburō, commander of the Combined Fleet, had transferred his flag to the carrier *Taihō* on April 15, and the flattop served as the command center for the battle codenamed Operation A-Go. Even *Musashi* and *Yamato* sortied for what many in Imperial Navy Headquarters viewed as the decisive battle they'd been anticipating since the outbreak of war. The Combined Fleet departed Tawi-Tawi on June 13, and six days later, about 500 nautical miles west of Saipan, *Taihō* hoisted the Z battle flag – the flag that Admiral Tōgō had hoisted on *Mikasa* at the Battle of Tsushima in the Russo-Japanese War and that Admiral Nagumo had hoisted on *Akagi* before the attack on Pearl Harbor – signaling the beginning of operations. It was a heady, all-or-nothing moment.

Captain Terauchi, enraged that his destroyer had been relegated to escort duties, thought it better to sink than not participate in the decisive battle to come, but *Yukikaze* soon had her hands full. *Yukikaze* was tasked with guarding the precious oil tankers from attacks by US submarines. Without replenishment en route to the Philippine Sea, the Combined Fleet wouldn't have the fuel to fight. US submarines infested these waters, and *Cavalla*, a *Gato*-class boat, had spotted *Yukikaze*'s tanker convoy on June 17.

Lieutenant Commander Herman J. Kossler, captain of *Cavalla*, established radar contact with the convoy at 23:03 on June 16. About a half hour later, *Cavalla* determined by radar that "two large ships about 1500 yards abeam, with three escorts"[6] made up the convoy. The convoy maintained a course of about 120° T, while zigzagging about thirty degrees to either side, rightfully wary of what lurked beneath the waves. At 03:40, *Cavalla*, now completely cloaked by darkness, surfaced to periscope depth and identified the convoy as containing a "medium and large tanker, with a large tanker on the port flank,"[7] likely the Kawasaki-style tankers, including the lead tanker *Genyō-maru*, in *Yukikaze*'s charge.

But, as *Cavalla* readied torpedoes, "sound reported fast screws just abaft port beam, closing us. Through periscope made out an Asashio Class destroyer heading in our direction."[8] In all likelihood, the destroyer was *Yukikaze*. *Cavalla* managed to evade the destroyer, and by 04:02 "had good set up on target, torpedo run about 3000 yards, with about five minutes to go before firing when sound reported screws on port bow."[9] The tenacious destroyer was back. "Shifted periscope to port bow, and saw destroyer heading at us, zero angle on bow, with practically nothing but bow wave showing,"[10] wrote Captain Kossler. Immediately, *Cavalla* "flooded negative and went deep." For the next half hour or so, the destroyer loitered, remaining "fairly close" to the targets. By 05:06, however, *Cavalla* had surfaced and the coast was clear, but so were the targets. *Yukikaze* and the four additional screening destroyers had successfully fended off an attack on the tankers, which might have nipped the Battle of the Philippine Sea in the bud.

How can we be sure the destroyer was *Yukikaze*? Of the five destroyers charged with screening the tankers, none were *Asashio*-class vessels. All were older and slower warships, and hence war planners had tasked them with staying behind to guard the tankers. The only destroyer that *Cavalla*'s Executive Officer might have mistaken for an *Asashio*-class boat was the *Kagerō*-class *Yukikaze*. US Navy officers, using identification cards and waterline models, had become fairly adept at identifying Imperial Navy warships, and the *Kagerō*-class boats were only one generation removed from the *Asashio*-class boats, and struck a strikingly similar silhouette, particularly at night. In all likelihood, *Yukikaze* had successfully chased *Cavalla* away. Historians often characterize the Battle of the Philippine Sea (Japanese, Battle off the Mariana Islands) as an aircraft duel, which it surely was in many respects. But submarines decided that summer day on the water, and *Yukikaze*'s encounter was only the beginning.

It turns out that *Cavalla* didn't have to wait long for another crack at Japanese ships. By the morning of June 19, she had given up chasing the tankers and headed for her previously assigned patrol station. At 10:42, her JP hydrophone "reported water noises on about the same bearing"[11] as a previously spotted Japanese plane. As a result, Captain Kossler "kept a careful periscope watch in that direction." Ten minutes later, when Kossler raised his periscope once more, the "picture was too good to be true."[12] He explained, "I could see four ships, a large Carrier with two Cruisers ahead on the port bow and a Destroyer about one thousand yards on the starboard beam. The Carrier was later identified as Shokaku class, and the Cruisers as Atago class." Although the escorting destroyer posed some challenges, Captain Kossler decided that the risk was worth it. "When sighted and during the attack she [the carrier] was in the act of taking on aircraft of the small single engine low wing type," Captain Kossler observed.

The flattop was the venerable *Shōkaku* herself, one of two remaining veterans of the Pearl Harbor attack (*Zuikaku* was the other), and she was vulnerable because the "forward part of her flight deck was jammed with planes, my guess at least thirty maybe more." *Cavalla* struck. Captain Kossler wrote, the boat "fired spread of six torpedoes ... After firing fifth torpedo flooded negative and went deep, firing the sixth on the way down." He remembered that the "first torpedo hit at 50 seconds, and the second and third at 8 second intervals after that." The other three torpedoes missed, but *Cavalla*'s blow proved deadly. The 844-foot carrier eventually exploded and sank. *Urakaze*, the escorting destroyer, dropped 106 depth charges over the course of the next 3 hours, "56 of which were fairly close,"[13] noted Captain Kossler, but *Cavalla* dove deep and escaped with only minor damage.

Cavalla wasn't the only US submarine hunting Japanese flattops that day in the Philippine Sea. At 08:09 that same morning, *Albacore*, another *Gato*-class boat, had formulated a "final bearing"[14] on one of two Imperial Navy carriers spotted and had "fired six from the bow tubes" at between 6,000 and 8,000 yards. *Taihō*, the new pride of the Imperial Navy, was *Albacore*'s target. Once *Albacore* had launched her torpedoes, wrote Captain James W. Blanchard, the submarine "went to deep submergence with three destroyers heading our way, and many planes overhead."[15] Three minutes after launching her torpedoes, *Albacore* "heard and felt explosion, definitely not a depth charge. Time of run correct for hit with No. 6 torpedo."

As the Imperial Navy destroyers dropped depth charges over the submarine, the officers and crew of *Albacore* continued to hear large explosions underwater. The submarine finally went to periscope depth at 12:01 and surfaced at 13:12, but made no visual contact with the target and continued its patrol. But one of *Albacore*'s six torpedoes had holed *Taihō* on the starboard side, near her fuel tanks, initiating a series of events that led to the flattop's sinking late that afternoon. Out of a crew of 2,150 on *Taihō*, 1,650 men lost their lives that day.

With *Yukikaze* and other Imperial Navy warships and transports rushing back and forth to Saipan in the spring of 1944, the Japanese had effectively upped their force levels on the island to 31,629, including 6,160 Imperial Navy combatants. This was nearly twice what US intelligence suggested, turning the invasion of Saipan into a bloodbath. The US Navy and Imperial Navy had met in the Philippine Sea while the battle raged on nearby Saipan. Because the battle still raged, Admiral Raymond A. Spruance had tethered Task Force 58 to Saipan to watch over the US invasion forces. Task Force 58 "must cover Saipan and our forces engaged in that operation,"[16] he insisted. But Admiral Ozawa had never been interested in attacking US logistical support on Saipan – he wanted his elusive decisive battle with the US carriers. (It's worth interjecting at this point that earlier, at the Battle of Savo Island, Admiral Mikawa had shown little interest in troop transports and later, at Leyte Gulf, Admiral Kurita wasn't interested in troop transports, either. He wanted Admiral William Halsey's Third Fleet carriers.) With superior planes, superior pilots, and good hunting by submarines, the US carried the day on June 19 on the Philippine Sea.

That day, Grumman TBF Avengers from the US carrier *Belleau Wood* found the carrier *Hiyō*, the third Japanese carrier lost that day. The US flattop had spent the better part of the day intercepting bogies, but sixty miles was the closest Japanese planes ever got to her. Bearing 250° T, the first wave of planes "came straight in on this bearing and were intercepted almost a hundred miles out. The next group came from this same direction, but circled to the south before closing. They were intercepted at sixty miles. The next group tried circling to the northwest, but they too were intercepted at over sixty miles."[17] The "Great Marianas Turkey Shoot," as US servicemen later called the battle, was on. The master of *Belleau Wood*, Captain J. Perry, hailed June 19 as the "greatest naval air fight of the war,"[18] and for the US it was decisive.

The next day, search planes from the carrier *Lexington* spotted the Combined Fleet fleeing northward on a course of 315° T. It was nearly 16:00, and Admiral Marc Mitscher, commander of the carriers, knew the sun would set just before 19:00. Nonetheless, he sent 226 planes to chase the Japanese carriers anyway, 99 of which were lost, most on the return flight, requiring that 160 pilots and crewmen be fished from the ocean that night and the next day.

Belleau Wood participated in the action. On Mitscher's order, her "deck loads were launched immediately and this ship sent four TBF's with torpedoes and an escort of six fighters." Only three fighters of *Belleau Wood*'s strike package of six fighters landed on the carrier safely that night. *Yorktown* and *Hornet* received two others, and a sixth pilot was fished out of the water the next day after being shot down by mistake.

Of the four torpedo planes, one landed aboard *Lexington* and the remaining three ditched in the ocean. With the exception of one man, Lieutenant George P. Brown, the pilots and crews were all successfully rescued. As Captain Perry wrote, "The planes from this ship definitely sank one enemy aircraft carrier … by making three observed torpedo hits."[19] By the time *Belleau Wood*'s TBF had launched her torpedo, *Hiyō* was reeling from two bomb hits; but the torpedo bored into her engine room and doomed the flattop. She sank stern first.

The Imperial Navy lost three carriers at the Battle of the Philippine Sea, as well as over 400 carrier aircraft and their precious, if poorly trained, pilots. US fighters had utterly destroyed Japan's naval air wing. After June 1944, Japan had only enough planes, thirty-five operational ones, to arm one of its light carriers. The flattops of the mighty Combined Fleet, which had redefined modern naval warfare at Pearl Harbor, were finished and could only serve as a decoy force in future operations.

But *Yukikaze* and the other escorting destroyers still had work to do. Earlier, they had managed to chase off US submarines, but, on the final day of the battle, US aircraft – Grumman TBF Avengers, Curtiss SB2C Helldivers, and Grumman F6F Hellcats from the carrier *Wasp* – set the oilers *Seiyō-maru, Gen'yō-maru,* and *Hayasui* ablaze with aerial bombing on June 20 1944. This represented three of the six oilers that had refueled the newly reconstituted Combined Fleet before the Battle of the Philippine Sea.

Uzuki, a *Mutsuki*-class destroyer, evacuated men from the *Gen'yō-maru* and scuttled the oiler with her main guns. *Yukikaze* evacuated the *Seiyō-maru* and scuttled the oiler with a single torpedo. It was the first time that Torpedo Specialist Nishizaki Nobuo, then a sailor aged sixteen, had fired a torpedo at another vessel. He remembered how the torpedo leapt from its launcher and smashed into the side of the 10,000-ton vessel with a roar, just below the waterline. "Black smoke then consumed the vessel and it disappeared from the surface of the water,"[20] he wrote. He continued, "My hair stood on end the first time I fired the venerable Type 93 torpedo."

Watching the fish slam into the side of the *Seiyō-maru* gave Nishizaki full appreciation of what torpedoes were capable of, particularly if one was to ever find *Yukikaze*'s lightly armored sides. That night, when the aerial attacks stopped and the antiaircraft batteries from the Imperial Navy went silent, the black water calmed. As Nishizaki stared across the dark expanse, a voice said, "Those enemy planes will come again tomorrow. For now, just eat while you can. Just eat." The next day, *Yukikaze* and the other destroyers escorted the surviving oilers as far as Guimaras Island in the Philippines.

But *Yukikaze* wasn't idle for long. Within days, *Yukikaze* and other destroyers escorted another tanker convoy from Guimaras Island to the Kure Naval Arsenal. Only two days out, while *Yukikaze* galloped through the water with a pod of dolphins at her bow, a lookout shouted "periscope!" Immediately, excitement spread throughout the destroyer as the crew prepared to engage a US submarine. It turned out, however, that the lookout had been mistaken. It wasn't a submarine at all; rather, it was a person adrift in a small raft. Immediately, *Yukikaze*'s master, at this time Captain Terauchi Masamichi, ordered "Prepare the cutter!," and sailors prepared to launch one of *Yukikaze*'s two amidships auxiliary craft. Nishizaki was one of the twelve men required to man the oars.

As they approached, *Yukikaze*'s sailors saw that the raft was a makeshift craft; nothing more than lashed together scraps of wood. The raft drifted slowly on a westerly course. On the aft portion of the raft sat a silent, disheveled man with a long beard. Lined up inside the raft lay ten or so men, their emaciated bodies looking mummified from the relentless exposure to the sun. "Only their beady eyes moved about their otherwise expressionless faces,"[21] Nishizaki recalled.

Eventually, the unshaven man explained that he was from a transport vessel, the 5,000-ton *Tarushima-maru*. Hydrophone Operator Noma Mitsue, also aboard *Yukikaze*, remembered that the men had subsisted on potatoes, carefully cutting them into quarters to share them, along with rainwater. The sailors didn't know this at the time, but the US submarine *Whale* had sunk the crippled *Tarushima-maru* with a torpedo five months earlier. Improbably, they had drifted ever since. Eventually, *Yukikaze*'s sailors got the men safely aboard the destroyer. As *Yukikaze* once more got under way, the rescued men looked like they might recover, but three died two days later from lack of proper medical attention.

* * *

Did the Romans know that, in 410 CE, when the Visigoths, led by Alaric, sacked the city of Rome, their vast empire, at least as it sprawled to the west, was collapsing? Did the "licentious fury of the tribes of Germany and Scythia,"[22] as historian Edward Gibbon labeled them, know that they had snuffed out one of the most powerful civilizing forces in history?

In 1279, after the Battle of Yamen, when Kublai Khan formally established the Yuan Dynasty, did Southern Song elites realize that Chinese rule of the empire had been ceded to the Mongols for a century? Was it lost on British Royalty that, in 1997, when Hong Kong, an imperial prize from the Opium War, was transferred back to China, it signaled the end of the empire and the ascendancy of another in the east?

Certainly, it couldn't have been lost on Japanese war planners in Imperial Headquarters that, with the defeat of the Imperial Navy at the Battle of the Philippine Sea and US forces in control of Saipan by July 9, Tinian by August 1, and Guam by August 10, the United States had breached the Absolute National Defensive Sphere and the empire was collapsing before their eyes. It was over.

Once the Mariana Islands were in US hands, the United States could commence the next stage of the war – the invasion of the Philippines. Although war planners had made an early case for the invasion of Formosa (Taiwan), by October 3 the Philippines had become the next US objective and the future launching pad for Operation Downfall – the invasion of the Japanese homeland and the end of the Pacific War. Fleet Admiral Chester W. Nimitz was onboard and the invasion of the Philippines was slated to occur at Leyte Gulf on October 20.

Not surprisingly, this was *Yukikaze*'s next destination as well.

CHAPTER 9

The Leyte Theater

All ships, general attack!
Admiral Kurita Takeo's order to attack during the Battle off Samar, part of
the Leyte Gulf Operation

THE SITUATION JAPAN FACED in the late summer of 1944 requires us to step back for a moment, to put 1944 in historical context. Japan was on the cusp of losing not only the war, which was dramatic enough, but also an empire that had required seventy-five years to build. Simultaneously, however, it was also on the cusp of a half-century of postwar demilitarization, democratization, economic recovery, rebuilding, and finding a new place in Asia and the world. Japan teetered between a nagging, gnawing history and a frightening, unknown future, both of which demanded sacrifices. The empire had required untold lives and treasure, and it had elevated some, mainly the Japanese and their collaborators, at the cost of so many others, principally their colonial underlings. Japan's empire was intertwined with the DNA of its national identity, a critical piece to the puzzle of its unique version of modern civilization. It would not be surrendered easily.

Like the Western empires Japan had emulated in the late nineteenth century, the Greater East Asian Co-Prosperity Sphere, Japan's empire in its full metastasis, had been a source of resources and fertile ground for economic investments. It had simultaneously been a site of dreams of Asian harmony and nightmares of racial supremacy. The empire was as much a part of Japan's modern experience as trains, the Meiji Constitution, and the Emperor himself. And, in 1944, it was slipping away like sand through a child's fingers.

To understand how Japan got to this juncture – how *Yukikaze* found herself fighting a desperate war, where nothing but death awaited her officers and crew; where, from the bridge of the destroyer, only black storm clouds loomed on Japan's horizon – we look back at the breakdown of diplomatic negotiations with the United States in 1941 and the beginning of the war. Why exactly did Japan decide to go to war with the United States and place in harm's way the Imperial Navy's warships and their gallant sailors, Japan's best and brightest? Japan had never intended the war to drag on into 1944. And yet, in the fall of 1944, the war did still drag on, and, to fight it, *Yukikaze* sailed into one of the most important naval battles of World War II – Leyte Gulf. As we'll see, Leyte Gulf witnessed a change in Imperial Navy thinking, particularly among high-ranking officers.

Less about possible futures, ones earned on ocean battlefields, Leyte was about words such as "legacy" and "history" – these notions now motivated the Imperial Navy as much as any Mahan-style decisive victory ever had. Like the Imperial Army and the Japanese nation as a whole, the precious Imperial Navy, with its magnificent battleships, many of which had yet to fire a shot in anger, would have to be sacrificed on the altar of history, along with their brave sailors, their blood cleansing the path toward the unknown future. And *Yukikaze* witnessed it all.

* * *

"At this moment, our Empire stands on the threshold of glory or oblivion,"[1] announced Prime Minister Tōjō Hideki on December 1, 1941, after Japan's Privy Council had finalized the decision to go to war with the US. Emperor Hirohito had sat silently during the deliberations that day, while a Japanese armada, unlike anything the world had ever seen before, sailed for Hawai'i. But, after the Battle of the Philippine Sea in the summer of 1944, and the near-complete destruction of the Imperial Navy's air wing, it was all but certain which future it would be – oblivion.

An empire a century in the making is a lot to gamble away with the roll of a die. That's how Foreign Minister Tōgō Shigenori had described the brinksmanship between Japanese diplomats and Secretary of State Cordell Hull in November 1941, on the eve of the attack on Pearl Harbor. "The success or failure of the pending discussions will have an immense effect on the destiny of the Japanese Empire,"[2] he told the ambassador in Washington, Nomura Kichisaburō. "In fact, we gambled the fate of our land on the throw of this die." In the middle of the nineteenth century, Japan had largely been isolated from the world and ruled by men with unused swords and shaved pates. But, after the Meiji Restoration of 1868, the island country had learned an important lesson: modern nations build and defend empires. Subsequently, Japan's oligarchy sought to construct one, which they did with dazzling and, to many Western observers, alarming speed.

Not long after the Meiji Restoration, Japanese gunboat diplomacy in Korea had led to war with China's Qing Dynasty in 1895, and Japan emerged victorious after throttling the newly modernized Beiyang Fleet at the Battle of the Yalu River. But the Great Powers, not thrilled with upstart Oriental members, intervened and deprived Japan of its war spoils. The Russian Empire was among the Great Powers that denied Japan its spoils in 1895, and the Russians found themselves, during the Russo-Japanese War of 1905, similarly humiliated at the hands of Japan's skilled land and sea forces, particularly at the Battle of Tsushima Strait, one of the most famous naval battles ever fought. As a consequence, Russia reluctantly ceded its lease on the valuable South Manchurian Railway, which became the cornerstone of the Japanese empire, a launching pad for the invasion of Manchuria proper in 1931 and much of coastal China in 1937.

Japan's victory over the Russian empire caught the eye of colonial observers. The Viceroy of British India, George Curzon, acknowledged that the "reverberations of that victory have gone like a thunderclap through the whispering galleries of the East."[3] Whispering galleries? The Japanese used megaphones to broadcast those reverberations. Mohandas Gandhi, at the time an unknown lawyer in South Africa, speculated that "so far and wide have the roots of Japanese victory spread that we cannot now visualize all the fruit it will put forth."[4] He wrote that, "When everyone in Japan, rich and poor, came to believe in self-respect, the country became free. She could give Russia a slap in the face ... In the same way, we must, too, need to feel the spirit of self-respect." Japan's victory over Russia became a rallying cry for Asian liberation, which Japan twisted and used as a rallying cry for yet more extraction-based empire building.

Whether recognized openly or not, after the victory over Russia, Japan was now a Pacific Power. Theodore Roosevelt, who brokered the peace deal at Portsmouth that ended the Russo-Japanese War (and earned him a Nobel Peace Prize for his efforts), wrote to Senator Philander C. Knox that Japan is "a most formidable military power. Her people have peculiar fighting capacity. They are very proud, very warlike, very sensitive."[5] When it came to Japan, he confided to the future Secretary of State and Attorney General, "there is no more continuing important feature" of US foreign policy than containing the spread of the Japanese empire. In large part, that statement held true through World War II. It was certainly President Franklin D. Roosevelt's approach to dealing with Japan.

Regardless, Japan proved unusually difficult to contain. As Japanese modernity marched headlong into the twentieth century, so did the empire, with the annexation of Korea in 1910 and the invasion of Manchuria in 1931. In 1932, Japan established the puppet state of Manchukuo in Manchuria and, after formal condemnation by the League of Nations' Lytton Report, withdrew from that world body, seven months before Nazi Germany did. Six years later, Imperial Army forces poured into China proper after the "China Incident" (the Marco Polo Bridge Incident of 1937), and much of coastal China was in Japanese hands shortly thereafter.

After being snubbed by the Allies at the Paris Peace Conference following World War I, in which the Japanese delegation had unsuccessfully pushed for a racial equality clause, Japan pivoted away from Europe and the United States and toward Asia, and thereafter wore a national chip on its shoulder regarding Western arrogance. When the killing was finally over, in 1946, Emperor Hirohito reportedly told aide Kinoshita Michio, "The Western powers rejected the Japanese people's outcries for the principle of racial equality that Japan's delegation demanded at the peace conference after the First World War ... Acts like anti-Japanese immigration legislation in California and the whites-only policy of Australia were enough to outrage the Japanese people."[6]

There's little doubt that this outrage colored Japanese negotiations with the United States, and the Japanese public decried the stifling "encirclement" perpetrated by the Western powers. It's undeniable that there was always a certain, "How do you like me now?" element to

Admiral Yamamoto's audacious Pearl Harbor attack. Not just among Japanese, but even an African American taxi driver in the United States could muse after Pearl Harbor, "But one thing you've got to give those Japs, they showed the white man that a brown hand could handle a plane and machine gun too."[7] Japan's empire always had a strong odor of this palpable Asian indignation.

By the end of November 1937, the Emperor's forces had secured Shanghai. Less than two weeks later, Nanjing, capital of the Republic of China, fell to Japanese troops and became the site of one of the most notorious massacres of the war. Marauding Imperial Army soldiers repeatedly gang-raped women, burned buildings, and murdered civilians and soldiers alike with near complete impunity. By the end of 1938, Canton had also capitulated, but victory in the interior of China proved elusive for Japanese war planners. Before war even broke out with the United States, Imperial Japanese forces were already overextended and bogged down in what became the "China question." Solving the China question became a serious sticking point with US negotiators on the eve of Pearl Harbor. It became an impasse that ultimately proved insurmountable. On their respective continents of Pacific affairs, the two sides were actually worlds apart.

In Tokyo, frustrations grew as the war in China calcified into a quagmire, and Japanese war planners came to view severing Chinese supply lines in French Indochina as the key to Japan's heretofore elusive victory. Arms and supplies offloaded at Haiphong ports traveled through Hanoi and eventually to Kunming, in China's interior. By late September 1940, after diplomatic wrangling and military arm-twisting with the Vichy government, Japan had boots on the ground in Indochina and had largely halted supplies bound for Kunming. General Tōjō, who served as War Minister at the time, explained, "We should not miss the present opportunity or we shall be blamed"[8] by future generations for not taking advantage of the current situation. The future was at stake, and Japanese war planners had sought to break the quagmire in China by securing Indochina, but it came at a high diplomatic cost.

Japan's expansion into Indochina became yet one more sticking point in the gummed-up negotiations with the United States to avoid war between the two Pacific powers. Tokyo saw Indochina as the key to solving the China question, while Washington saw it as more Japanese aggression, pure and simple. It emerged as one of many problems of perception between the two nations. The Japanese viewed themselves as colonizers in the Pacific, much like the United States in the Philippines, the British in Malaya, the French in Indochina, and the Dutch in Indonesia. Washington saw the Japanese as aggressors and conquerors. It proved a daunting discrepancy shaped by decades of condescension, arrogance, and racism on both sides, and one that could never be surmounted during the countdown to war.

On September 24, 1940, the Roosevelt administration responded to Japan's move into Indochina with a complete embargo of iron and steel and, the next day, a sizable loan to China. Tempers flared in Tokyo, and, on September 27, Japan joined the Axis Powers, catching US policymakers offguard. At this juncture, President Roosevelt still remained preoccupied with affairs in Europe and preferred to drag negotiations on with Japan and avoid a military confrontation. But, on April 13, 1941, Japan entered a Neutrality Pact with the Soviet Union, once again surprising the United States, and nominally freeing the Imperial Army to divert its attention from the northern border to the "treasure houses" in the south. When Hitler betrayed Joseph Stalin and invaded the Soviet Union on June 22, 1941, Tokyo was divided regarding how to respond. Prime Minister Konoye Fumimaro favored negotiating with the United States in order to obtain Japan's objectives, while Foreign Minister Matsuoka Yōsuke pushed for joining Germany against Britain and Russia, even at the risk of war with the United States. This proved one of many moments when the European Theater reached around the globe to direct affairs in the Asia–Pacific Theater, making World War II very much a world at war.

The problem was that the oil and other natural resources that Japan desperately needed were in the south, not the north, making an attack in Siberia nearly pointless. Joachim von Ribbentrop, Nazi Germany's Minister of Foreign Affairs, tried to link the two in order to convince Japan to attack Russia in the north in order to aid Operation Barbarossa. He argued that the collapse of the Soviet Union "offers to Japan the unique opportunity to free herself from the Russian threat and to give the Japanese Empire security in the north, which is a necessary prerequisite to her expansion in the south in accordance with her vital needs."[9] Once the Axis defeated the Soviet Union, he continued, the United States would realize the "absolute futility of entering into the war on the side of England," solving Japan's dilemma with the United States altogether. Though tempted, the Japanese government never bit. The Imperial Army had already tangled with the clever General Georgy Zhukov once along the Manchukuo border, at the humiliating battles of Lake Khazan in 1938 and Khalkhin Gol in 1939, and had little appetite for more of what he had dished out.

President Roosevelt knew the Japanese ambassador in Washington, Nomura, a former admiral in the Imperial Navy, and the two met privately in an attempt to halt the drift toward war. Roosevelt reportedly told his old acquaintance, "There is plenty of room in the Pacific area for everybody ... It would not do this country any good nor Japan any good, but both of them harm to get into war."[10] The two men agreed, but the war in Europe kept poking at the sore spots in the Pacific. It presented opportunities for Japanese war planners, and redoubled President Roosevelt's attention in the Atlantic.

Regardless, the President continued to push for negotiations in the Pacific. On July 1, 1941, he told Harold Ickes, US Secretary of the Interior, "It is terribly important for the control of the Atlantic for us to keep peace in the Pacific. I simply have not got enough Navy to go round."[11] With Western Europe firmly in Nazi hands in 1941, and Britain's Prime Minister Winston Churchill clamoring for more aid, this was the US predicament in a nutshell – drag along Japan in order to focus on Europe, then deal with Japan later.

But, for a variety of reasons, Japan didn't want to be dealt with later. The next day, Japan's Privy Council met, again with the Emperor present, and determined that, in order to resolve the China question, establish the Greater East Asian Co-Prosperity Sphere, and bring "security and preservation to the nation,"[12] the Emperor's forces needed to advance into the South Seas. The Privy Council added that "The Imperial Government will carry out the above program no matter what obstacles may be encountered." On July 23, 1941, in a first step, Japanese forces threw diplomatic niceties to the wind with Vichy France and moved into southern Indochina in preparation for the advance into the South Seas. At stake were the oilfields of the Dutch East Indies, the rubber plantations of British Malaya, and the tin mines and rice fields of French Indochina.

Hawks in the Roosevelt administration pushed for a robust response, including a complete oil embargo; but the President believed an oil embargo, in particular, would unnecessarily push the Japanese to war. Roosevelt's reading of Japan's position corresponded to that of the US military, including Admiral Harold Stark. On July 21, only two days before the Japanese expanded their foothold in French Indochina, Stark had forwarded to Roosevelt a Navy Department memorandum that submitted that Japan was unlikely to expand beyond Indochina, unless the United States cut off oil exports. "An embargo,"[13] the memorandum concluded, "would probably result in a fairly early attack by Japan on Malaya and the Netherlands East Indies, and possibly would involve the United States in an early war in the Pacific."

Others, including General George Marshall, concurred with Stark's opinion. Japan's dependency on oil imports meant that an oil embargo represented a red line for the Imperial State. As an alternative to an oil embargo, on July 26 the United States froze Japanese assets, and the War Department recalled General Douglas MacArthur to active duty. "If there is going to be trouble in the Far East,"[14] Roosevelt told an aide, "I want Douglas to be in charge." General MacArthur began making plans to head for the Philippines as Commanding General of American forces in the Far East.

Without a doubt, one of the most twisted parts of the breakdown of negotiations between the United States and Japan related to how export licenses were approved in the US government. Export licenses fell under the Foreign Funds Control Committee, which Dean Acheson, the Assistant Secretary of State, chaired. Not only arrogant, Acheson was a hawk, and argued, while Roosevelt and Churchill met in Newfoundland aboard the *Prince of Wales*, that the President's earlier asset-freeze order was vague, and so he refused to release Japanese funds for any purchases, including oil. Demonstrating a fatally flawed understanding of Japan's national culture, he asserted that "no rational Japanese could believe that an attack on us could result in anything but disaster for his country." He ignored protests from the State Department's Far Eastern Division and Treasury, crowing in his memoirs, "Whether or not we had a policy, we had a state of affairs,"[15] a state of affairs that, as Admiral Stark, General Marshall, and President Roosevelt accurately predicted, triggered Japan's southern advance and led to war with the United States.

Careful observers in Japan knew that the oil embargo meant war, even if Acheson didn't. Wilfrid Fleischer, editor of the *Japan Advertiser*, commented that, with the oil embargo, "Japan must move quickly to consummate her conquests in Asia or face economic ruin and defeat ... The Japanese are now with their backs to the wall and they must carry on with the struggle they have so rashly embarked upon or renounce their dreams of empire in Asia. The die has been cast."[16] As we have seen, with empire being so closely tied to Japan's quest for modernity and Great Power status, the idea of renouncing "their dreams of empire" was simply out of the question. That would have meant that the entire Meiji project, Japan's history since 1868, was a failure. The US Ambassador in Tokyo, Joseph Grew, also saw war coming after the oil embargo. "The vicious circle of reprisals and counter reprisals is on,"[17] he wrote. "The obvious conclusion is eventual war."

The oil embargo caught Japan completely off guard. Earlier, on June 20, the United States had limited some oil exports to Japan from Atlantic and Gulf Coast ports, but shortages in the eastern states, not a reprisal for Japanese aggression, had spurred the cuts. Shutting down oil exports to Japan proved devastating. Consequently, on September 6, in a last-minute attempt to halt the slip toward war, Prime Minister Konoye sought to arrange a summit with President Roosevelt. Ambassador Grew was in favor of the summit, believing the Prime Minister's intentions to be sincere; but hawks in the Roosevelt administration opposed any such meeting. Henry Stimson, US Secretary of War, feared that "such a conference if actually held would produce concessions which would be highly dangerous to our vitally important relations with China."[18] In the end, the US State Department placed so many preconditions in front of the meeting that it never took place.

Consequently, the diplomatic situation between the two countries continued to deteriorate. By August 1941, Secretary Hull was convinced of the Japanese that "Nothing will stop them except force,"[19] which was hardly an open-minded approach to diplomacy. After meeting with Hull on August 6, Ambassador Nomura cabled to Tokyo, "Judging from the impression I received today, it seems utterly impossible now by explanation to bring the authorities of the American Government to understand the true intention of Japan, and it was clearly perceived that the United States is already determined to face any situation that may be brought about."[20] The negotiations were jammed tight by late summer. Washington sought to buy time because of the war in Europe, while Tokyo thought that time was being wasted because November and December presented the best opportunities for landing operations in the South Seas. By January the northeast monsoons would have arrived, making landings more difficult. Having failed to produce a diplomatic breakthrough in Washington, Konoye resigned as Prime Minister, and the hardliner General Tōjō formed a cabinet on October 17, 1941.

In a particularly urgent appeal, on November 3, Ambassador Grew cabled Washington that, if negotiations failed, "Japan may go all out in a do or die effort to render herself invulnerable to foreign economic pressure, even to the extent of committing national hara-kiri. For those of us who are in direct touch with the atmosphere from day to day realize that this is not only possible *but probable*" (emphasis in original).[21] Grew warned Washington that Japan's decision-making "cannot be gauged by any Western measuring rod. It would be hazardous to base our national policy on the belief, held in certain quarters, that our economic pressure will not drive Japan to war." War with Japan could come with "dangerous and dramatic suddenness," he warned. Never have such astute diplomatic observations been ignored by such smart men with such deadly consequences. Ambassador Grew saw the cultural, economic, and political drivers that pushed Japan to the South Seas – the particular Japanese drivers – while the key members of the Roosevelt administration remained clouded by their own arrogance toward the Japanese and their myopic focus on affairs in Europe.

In some respects, a war of national desperation is how Emperor Hirohito also viewed the coming conflict. In August, when the Emperor had questioned Admiral Nagano Osami, who later served as Commander in Chief of the Imperial Navy, regarding whether the Imperial Navy could achieve speedy victories over US and British naval forces as it had over the Russians in 1905, Nagano responded with unusual candor: "A victory like the one in the Battle of the Japan Sea is out of the question, and

I cannot tell you whether Japan will win or not."[22] Later, the Emperor confided to Kido Kōichi, Lord Keeper of the Privy Seal, "This means that Japan is going to fight a war of desperation." In many respects, that's precisely what happened. Japan started its war with the United States out of desperation, and then fought it desperately to the bitter end.

On November 5, Japan's Privy Council met again in the presence of the Emperor. Prime Minister Tōjō railed against those who urged patience and peace. "To adopt a policy of patience and perseverance was tantamount to self-annihilation. Rather than await extinction, it was better to face death by breaking through the encircling ring and find a way for existence."[23] With this impassioned appeal for national survival, on November 7 the Privy Council set the Pearl Harbor attack date: Admiral Yamamoto's audacious assault would take place December 8 (Japan time). The Privy Council decided to pursue a diplomatic resolution until November 25, after which time Japan would pursue a military solution. While the Privy Council met in Tokyo, the US Joint Board of the Army and Navy met in Washington. General Marshall and Admiral Stark continued to argue that defeating Germany was the primary objective, and therefore war with Japan should be avoided. But events had gotten in front of them by this point.

The "reprisals and counter reprisals" that so alarmed Ambassador Grew continued. On November 24, the US Navy (with Army concurrence) warned Pacific commanders that "Chances of favorable outcome of negotiations with Japan very doubtful. This situation coupled with statements of Japanese Government and movements their naval and military forces indicate in our opinion that a surprise aggressive movement in any direction including attack on Philippines or Guam is a possibility."[24] Two days later, Secretary Hull met with Nomura and diplomat Kurusu Saburō in order to reiterate the old US demands, rather than take up a Japanese proposal for a cooling-off period. This, despite the fact that decrypted intercepts alerted US policymakers to the fact that Japanese diplomats were under a strict deadline for manufacturing a breakthrough.

President Roosevelt had liked the idea of a cooling-off period, and jotted down his own ideas for a *modus vivendi* in the Pacific, but Secretary Hull never presented the plan to the Japanese contingent. After the meeting with the two exasperated Japanese diplomats, Hull told Stimson, "I wash my hands of it."[25] So had the Japanese. The Imperial Navy strike force had started making way for Hawai'i on November 26. Japan's Privy Council met on December 1 and formally approved the decision to go to war. At the meeting, Prime Minister Tōjō asked whether Japan's empire was on the threshold of glory or oblivion. He continued, "I am convinced that the whole nation, presenting a united front and laying down their lives for the sake of the country, will surely deliver us from the present national crisis."[26]

That's where events stood in the first days of December 1941. In Washington, hawks in the Roosevelt administration remained smug in their condescension that the Japanese would never be so uppity, never be so foolhardy, and never be so irrational as to challenge Western supremacy in the Pacific, even if US Navy analysts insisted otherwise. They had washed their hands of the negotiation, willing to take their chances with battleships. Meanwhile, in Tokyo, the Privy Council continued to conjure images of Western encirclement and the magical thinking of Japanese spiritual superiority, and contended that the only way to resolve the nagging China question was to open yet another military front in the South Seas. Surely, they reasoned, war, not diplomacy, would break the constricting hold of Western encirclement and grant Japan its rightful place in the sun. Their blinders secured firmly in place, both sides careened toward total war.

The breakdown in negotiations would pit three (including the British) of the greatest navies ever built against one another in the world's largest body of water. By the summer of 1944, three years later, countless people had died in the Pacific – they had drowned, been dismembered, blown to pieces, devoured by sharks, ravaged by tropical disease, displaced by war, murdered and raped by marauding armies, malnourished by lack of food, and left to rot in filthy POW camps. But, nothing could be done about all that now – that was all water in *Yukikaze*'s wake, almost like a dream in how quickly it had all taken place. As *Yukikaze* departed Brunei in October 1944, the outcome of the naval war in the Pacific teetered on one last epic battle. This is where history stood as *Yukikaze* made way for Leyte Gulf in the Philippines, where the largest naval battle ever fought took place.

* * *

In the last days of June 1944, after the drubbing in the Philippine Sea, Japan's Combined Fleet limped back to the Inland Sea and the temporary safety of home waters. The only functioning fleet carrier left was *Zuikaku*, the sole survivor of the Pearl Harbor raid. From the vantage point of air power, the Imperial Navy was finished. But Japan still had a powerful battleship and cruiser fleet, even if it lacked adequate air support to protect it. Sortieing big warships without air support was tantamount to suicide, just ask Admiral Sir Tom Spencer Vaughan Phillips, who went down with the *Prince of Wales* on December 10, 1941, after Japanese planes made short work of the battlewagon. Early in the war, the Imperial Navy had written the playbook on sinking big ships with lots of small planes, but now they had little alternative but to fight unprotected as fall approached.

The leviathans *Yamato* and *Musashi* represented the core strength of the Imperial Navy fleet with their eighteen-inch guns. The battlewagons *Nagato*, *Kongō*, *Haruna*, *Fusō*, and *Yamashiro* also packed formidable punches with their fourteen- and sixteen-inch guns. Combined Fleet Headquarters had relegated two other battleships, *Ise* and *Hyūga*, to dry dock in order to be converted into makeshift "aircraft cruisers." Ten heavy cruisers, several of them powerful *Takao*-class ships, rounded out what the Imperial Navy had left. These battleships and cruisers participated in what Imperial Navy planners named Operation Shō, or "Victory" – what became known as the Battle of Leyte Gulf.

Leyte Gulf was a complicated, geographically dispersed naval battle, waged underwater, on the surface, and in the skies, and its narrative rhythm resembles that of a tragic Kabuki play, with its slow start, a build up of narrative tension, and the dramatic ending. As with most Kabuki plays, Leyte might be divided into five acts for ease of narration. Act one began with the Palawan Passage Ambush, as Admiral Kurita Takeo's Center Force made its way toward the Sibuyan Sea from Brunei and US submarines ambushed his warships, sinking two cruisers and damaging others. The Air Battle of the Sibuyan Sea represented act two, when US carrier-based aircraft descended on the fleet as it made its way toward San Bernardino Strait and Leyte Gulf, killing the heroine *Musashi*.

Then, Admiral Nishimura Shōji's Southern Force engaging US warships in the Battle of Surigao Strait represented the harrowing act three, when his force of aging dreadnought battleships was destroyed. When Admiral Halsey ordered the Third Fleet northward after pummeling the Center Force in the Sibuyan Sea, that became act four – the Battle off Cape Engaño and the complete destruction of Japan's "decoy" carrier force. And, finally, came the decisive act five, when Admiral Kurita's Center Force engaged US escort carriers off Samar northeast of Leyte Gulf, ultimately deciding to break off the attack and hunt Halsey's carriers. *Yukikaze*, our intrepid destroyer, had supporting roles in acts one, two, and five.

In the late summer of 1944, as the Imperial Navy licked its wounds from the Battle of the Philippine Sea and contemplated Operation Shō, many obstacles prohibited launching what remained of the Imperial Navy against advancing US land and sea forces, but none more debilitating than the reason Japan had waged war in the first place – oil. Adequate fuel oil didn't exist in the home islands, nor could the remaining tankers safely transport it in the submarine-infested waters south of the home islands.

In order to prepare for the next battle, the remnants of the Combined Fleet therefore made for the Lingga Island anchorage south of Singapore, closer to the Balikpapan oilfields and refineries. There the Imperial Navy trained night and day, without rest, preparing for the next mission: a final, desperate attempt at a decisive battle to stave off US troop landings in the Philippines. The remaining fleet carrier, *Zuikaku*, the light carriers *Chitose* and *Chiyoda*, as well as the three smaller, repurposed carriers, *Zuihō*, *Ryūhō*, and *Jun'yō*, stayed behind in the Inland Sea. With precious few planes, they best served as decoys to lure Admiral Halsey's Third Fleet carriers away from Admiral Kurita's naked Center Force as it approached Leyte Gulf. The swarms of US bombers had yet to arrive from Saipan to menace Japanese waters, and they could hold in the Inland Sea in relative safety, at least for the time being.

Rear Admiral Kurita, whom we first met in the waters around Guadalcanal, was the overall commander of the force of five battleships, ten heavy cruisers, two light cruisers, and fifteen destroyers that comprised the Center Force in Operation Shō. On October 20, Kurita's warships departed Lingga Island and entered the relative protection of the Brunei anchorage. Two days later, the fleet departed Brunei and made way for the Philippines. Without scout planes or combat air patrols, the warships proved easy pickings for US submarines and, on October 23, the submarines *Darter* and *Dace* sank *Atago* and *Maya*, respectively, while they were under way in the Palawan Passage. Kurita was forced to swim for his life, an inauspicious start to the action. *Darter* also badly damaged *Takao* in the ambush. Even before Kurita's Center Force reached the Sibuyan Sea, in other words, US submarines, in act one, the Ambush at Palawan Passage, had diminished Kurita's overall strength. It was a bad start.

Rear Admiral Kurita's Center Force planned to rendezvous with two other forces navigating alternative routes to Leyte Gulf from the south. Vice Admiral Nishimura, the "Lookout God," commanded the vanguard of the Southern Force, comprised of two battleships, one heavy cruiser, and four destroyers. Vice Admiral Shima Kiyohide commanded the disjointed rear of the Southern Force, comprised of two heavy cruisers, one light cruiser, and four destroyers. Hoping to meet the Southern Forces at Leyte, Admiral Kurita raced through the Sibuyan Sea with *Yukikaze* in Circle Formation 2 on the starboard aft quarter of *Kongō* and *Haruna*. They navigated about fifteen kilometers ahead of Circle Formation 1, which orbited the flagship *Yamato* and her sister ship, *Musashi*. Neither formation had combat air support, carrier-based planes or otherwise, but they stubbornly pressed ahead anyway.

Before departing Lingga, Admiral Kurita had tried to lay reservations to rest among his officers and staff regarding the Leyte operation. Many senior officers had grumbled, "We do not mind death, but we are very concerned for the honor of the Japanese navy."[27] They continued with an appeal to the Imperial Navy's glorious history: "If the final effort of our great Navy should be spent in engaging a group of empty cargo ships, surely admirals Tōgō [Heihachirō] and Yamamoto [Gonnohyōe] would weep in their graves."

Admiral Kurita was on the same historical wavelength, but had something else in mind. "I know that many of you are strongly opposed to this assignment,"[28] he began. "But the war situation is far more critical than any of you can possibly know." He then conjured the logic of sacrifice that had come to consume the Imperial Navy after the fall of the Solomon Islands and the breach of the Bismarck Barrier. He said, "Would it not be a shame to have the fleet remain intact while our nation perishes?"

It's an important question for understanding the remainder of *Yukikaze*'s operations in the Pacific, because all of them, in one form or another, involved the logic of sacrifice and, frankly, suicide. This makes *Yukikaze*'s story all the more miraculous: it's one thing to survive a war in which you're trying to stay alive; it's quite another when you're content with dying for the Imperial State and your family.

In Admiral Kurita's mind, the Leyte operation would be the naval equivalent of a banzai charge, suicide by US carriers, an act of sublime sincerity designed to match the resolve of the nation, which in a matter of months would burn to the ground from US incendiary and, eventually, atomic bombs. Japan had arrived at the moment of "national hara-kiri," as Ambassador Joseph Grew had described the nation's resolve in late 1941. It was part of the pillow words of war explored earlier, and Admiral Kurita's warships would join the references to Divine Wind, Special Assaults, Special Attacks, Floating Chrysanthemums, and Shattered Jewels that became commonplace in the summer of 1944. As World War II pounded, ground, and burned to a crescendo in the Pacific, Japan's Imperial State would sacrifice everything – including its prized warships and sailors.

Surely, in the milieu of frenzied death, the Imperial Navy's grand war machines, the monuments to Japan's Great Power status, the ships venerated on popular postcards and succored by the Emperor himself, would have to be sacrificed as well. Admiral Kurita may have reminded his officers in the same speech that "there are such things as miracles," but the rush to Leyte Gulf to engage the numerically superior US Navy, with its twelve fleet carriers and countless bombers and fighter aircraft, was as much about sacrificing warships as anything else. It was a naval banzai charge – any good Imperial Navy officer knew that waiting for a "miracle" hardly constituted effective tactical thinking. It was an act of desperation, much like the war itself had been, a tragic Kabuki play's dramatic finale.

* * *

On October 24, as Admiral Kurita crossed the Sibuyan Sea in act two of Leyte Gulf, waves of US torpedo planes and bombers descended on his warships, hitting several and causing them to reduce their speed to a

Figure 9.1 Task Force 38 aircraft attack the Japanese battleship *Musashi* and a destroyer in the Battle of the Sibuyan Sea, October 24, 1944. NH 63432. Courtesy of Naval History & Heritage Command.

dawdling twenty knots. Consequently, Kurita reduced the fleet's speed to eighteen knots. In the attacks, a torpedo holed *Musashi* and the magisterial ship peeled off with a small escort, forced to fend off the aerial onslaught. US planes pursued and destroyed *Musashi*. She took no fewer than nineteen torpedo hits and seventeen bomb hits – a lioness brought down by swarming, buzzing gnats in the Sibuyan Sea (see Figure 9.1).

But the Kabuki play continued to gain momentum. Undeterred, Admiral Kurita's remaining warships continued eastward, resolute in their determination to meet the Southern Force at Leyte Gulf and pound the enemy transports. However, the waves of US torpedo planes and bombers that descended on the fleet proved debilitating, and Admiral Kurita feared that his warships would sink before nightfall in the hail of torpedoes and bombs. At 15:55, he ordered the fleet to come about to a westerly course in order to temporarily move out of the range of enemy aircraft. He reported to Combined Fleet Headquarters that, "As a result of five aerial attacks from 06:30 to 15:30, our damages are not light ... If we continue our present course our losses will increase incalculably, with little hope of success for our mission."[29] He therefore ordered his ships to "withdraw outside the range of enemy air attack for the time being."

It proved a fateful decision, because it meant Admiral Kurita's warships never rendezvoused with the Southern Force on schedule the next morning, jeopardizing the already desperate battle plan and sentencing Admiral Nishimura's smaller force to certain death in act three. But it also had the unintended consequence of tricking Admiral Halsey into thinking his carrier-based planes had knocked Admiral Kurita completely out of the fight, freeing him to pursue Admiral Ozawa's decoy carriers in the north.

In the Air Battle of the Sibuyan Sea, the United States had launched 259 air sorties of Hellcats, Helldivers, and Avengers at Kurita's Center Force. The Imperial Navy, with no combat air patrol, lost one battleship, four heavy cruisers, and four destroyers, all before they were even within 100 nautical miles of Leyte. Imperial Navy antiaircraft fire downed eighteen US planes, a miserably low number given the hundreds that swarmed Kurita's warships on October 24. But the US Navy took its knocks, too.

The Imperial Navy had placed Admiral Ōnishi Takijirō in charge of the Fifth Base Air Force in the Philippines, which, after the numerous aircraft lost at Truk and the Palau Islands, consisted of a little over 100 aircraft. Though none of them protected Admiral Kurita's ships, many of Ōnishi's planes flew conventional bombing raids, such as the Luzon-based plane that planted a single 550-pound bomb on the flight deck of the carrier *Princeton*. She eventually sank when her torpedo magazine exploded, threatening to take the aid-rendering cruiser *Birmingham* with her (see Figure 9.2). The violent explosion aboard the *Princeton* mauled the deck of *Birmingham*, and the "dead, dying and wounded, many of them badly and horribly, covered the decks,"[30] recalled one eye witness aboard the cruiser.

The best chance the Imperial Navy ever had of stopping the US landings at Leyte had always been Admiral Kurita's Center Force. After he had come about on the evening of October 24, a US reconnaissance plane reported his apparent withdrawal from the action, and the US aerial attack stopped. The halting of the air attack emboldened Admiral

Figure 9.2 *Princeton* burning soon after a Japanese bomb hit her while operating off the Philippines on October 24, 1944. This view, taken from *USS South Dakota* (BB-57), shows the large smoke column passing aft following a heavy explosion in the carrier's hangar deck. Official US Navy Photograph, National Archives, Catalog #: 80-G-287970.

Kurita, who, with no more bombs raining down on his warships, ordered his fleet to come about once more on the original easterly course toward the San Bernardino Strait. When a subordinate reminded Kurita that Combined Fleet Headquarters had not responded to his request for land-based air support, Kurita said only "That's alright. Let's go!"[31] It was now 17:14 and the cruiser *Kumano* was on point and *Yukikaze* guarded the rear. Two hours later Combined Fleet Headquarters responded to Kurita as follows: "Believing in divine help, resume the attack!"[32]

As Admiral Kurita plied eastward that night, he received an ominous radio transmission from Admiral Nishimura. He radioed that, with the thirty-year-old dreadnoughts *Fusō* and *Yamashiro*, he planned to "storm the center of the eastern shore of Leyte Gulf at 04:00 on the 25th"[33] as scheduled, but now well before Admiral Kurita could ever hope to arrive. Nishimura's mission had always been a particularly dangerous one. Because *Fusō* and *Yamashiro* were relatively slow and lacked the firepower of the newer battleships, Kurita had detached Nishimura to take a southern route to Leyte Gulf, through the Surigao Strait. Had his arrival coincided with that of Admiral Kurita, the fourteen-inch guns of the old dreadnoughts might have contributed to dislodging the enemy from Leyte; but, as they arrived on their own, even with the reinforcement of the cruiser *Mogami* and four destroyers, the US Navy ripped Nishimura apart. But, making act three of the Kabuki play all the more dramatic, Admiral Nishimura had lost his son in the Philippines, a promising young man who had graduated at the top of his class from the Etajima Naval Academy, and he was now ready to give the ultimate sacrifice, too.

Nishimura approached Leyte cautiously, hoping to pull off a victory under impossible odds. As he approached, the cruiser *Mogami* catapulted a single scout seaplane to reconnoiter the area. The pilot radioed: "Sighted four battleships and two cruisers to the south of the bay. There are also about eighty transports off the landing area. There are four destroyers and several torpedo boats near Surigao Strait. In addition there are twelve carriers and ten destroyers in position forty miles southeast of Leyte."[34] These sentences represented the only intelligence that any Japanese commander received during the entire Leyte action.

The US Navy mauled Admiral Nishimura at the north entrance of Surigao Strait. Early in the morning of October 25, torpedo boats sank two of his destroyers and damaged a third. With enemy radar blips lighting up his screen aboard *Yamashiro*, Nishimura ordered a single-column attack toward Leyte. His last transmitted message was "Enemy destroyers and torpedo boats on both sides of the north entrance to Surigao Strait. Our destroyers have been torpedoed. *Yamashiro* hit by one torpedo but able to proceed."[35] She didn't proceed for long. When a third torpedo slammed into *Yamashiro* and ignited her magazines, she later exploded and sank, after *Fusō*, taking Admiral Nishimura to reunite with his beloved son. (For the first two years of World War II, the US Mark 14 [launched from submarines] and Mark 15 [launched from destroyers] torpedoes were plagued by repeated mishaps, rendering them all but useless. By Leyte Gulf, however, most of the problems had been remedied, and the torpedo proved an effective weapon in battle.)

Aboard *Fusō*, Rear Admiral Masami Ban had assumed command of what remained of the warships. It wasn't long before bombs had ignited fires aboard both *Mogami* and *Fusō*. The old dreadnought's guns blazed until she rolled over and sank early that morning. The US Navy's response had been rapid and overwhelming. "We didn't want them to pull another Savo Island on us,"[36] remarked Rear Admiral Jesse Oldendorf, the commander in charge. His disposition and numerical superiority assured that the Imperial Navy wouldn't pull off any surprise victories in the Philippines.

Vice Admiral Shima's warships arrived in the immediate wake of Nishimura's near complete annihilation. With the heavy cruisers *Nachi* and *Ashigara*, and the old light cruiser *Abukuma*, Admiral Shima's ragtag force made over thirty knots but arrived late. As Shima entered Surigao, he saw what appeared to be two burning ships, an ominous sign of what awaited him. Quickly, Shima's cruisers veered right and fired eight torpedoes at the enemy ships on radar, but then retired from the scene. While retiring, the cruiser *Nachi* collided with the burning *Mogami* as she limped southward, her speed reduced. But the day's fighting had ended. Of Admiral Nishimura's warships, only the destroyer *Shigure* made it back to Brunei. With at least nine lives, *Mogami* fought valiantly, but was finally destroyed by US aircraft as she fled. Except for the mopping-up phase in the Mindanao Sea, the Battle of Surigao Strait, act three of the Leyte Kabuki drama, was largely over before breakfast.

Early that same day, on October 25, at about the same time Admiral Nishimura battled in the Mindanao Sea and Surigao Strait, Kurita's fleet had entered the narrow San Bernardino Strait, which is less than two miles across and runs eight knots. The fast water and possible concealed enemy (Kurita didn't know that Halsey's carriers had chased Ozawa northward) pushed the remnants of the Imperial Navy to its limits. Accordingly, the Center Force organized into a night-search formation.

As they passed through the narrows, Kurita's warships waited anxiously for a US Navy ambush, but it never materialized. *Yukikaze* navigated in the rear on the right side of the ships. Sailors were on edge as they scanned the dark horizon for any sign of enemy ships. Lookouts could just make out the mountains on the west coast of Samar Island to the south, and radar and anti-radar systems buzzed as they scanned the airwaves for signs of enemy communications. Kurita was 100 nautical miles from Leyte Gulf, the location of the US troop landings and his rendezvous with infamy.

As the sun rose on October 25, Kurita braced himself for Halsey's aerial attack and ordered an antiaircraft formation, with *Yukikaze* moving to the vanguard. But Halsey's planes never came, because he was pursuing Admiral Ozawa north of Leyte. Using the Imperial Navy carriers as decoys had turned out to be a stroke of genius. Earlier, on October 19, Admiral Ozawa had proposed the idea to Admiral Toyoda Soemu, Commander at Combined Fleet Headquarters and architect of Operation A-Gō (the Battle of the Philippine Sea) and Operation Shō (the Battle of Leyte Gulf). "I propose to maneuver my ships from the north in such a way that they will lure the enemy task force away from the battle area and thus reduce pressure on the Kurita fleet."[37] It worked swimmingly. In act four of the Leyte Kabuki drama, Admiral Halsey, driven by ambition, prematurely abandoned the fight with Kurita's battleships and cruisers to pursue Admiral Ozawa, taking valuable air support with him. Admiral Halsey pounded Ozawa's carriers, sinking them all in the coming days, including the venerable *Zuikaku*. He had successfully taken Halsey's Third Fleet out of the fight – perhaps the "miracle" that Admiral Kurita had hoped for was at hand?

Before turning south toward Leyte, Kurita continued eastward into the Pacific about twenty nautical miles off Samar Island. He then cut south. As the morning progressed, the cloud cover began to thicken and reduced overall visibility. Squalls began to form over the water. The wind speed was eight knots and slowly whitecaps began brushing the surface of the water in white strokes. With no reconnaissance from the air, the conditions placed a weighty burden on Kurita's escort destroyers to spot lurking submarines.

Then, suddenly, at 06:45, lookouts aboard the flagship spotted four masts coming over the southeast horizon and an enemy reconnaissance plane buzzed over Kurita's fleet. Admiral Kurita radioed Combined Fleet Headquarters, "By Heaven-sent opportunity, we are dashing to attack the enemy carriers."[38] The moment for miracles – and sacrifices – had come for Admiral Kurita's Center Force.

On the horizon sailed six US escort carriers in a circle disposition, screened by three destroyers and three escort destroyers. This was Task

Force 77.4.3 – or Taffy 3 – under the command of Rear Admiral Clifton Sprague. Stationed off Samar Island, Taffy 3, like the two other escort carrier groups, provided critical air support for the landing operations on Leyte. It wasn't Admiral Halsey's fast fleet carriers, but Kurita didn't know that yet. In rapid succession, the escort carriers in Taffy 3 began running to the southwest at nineteen knots. Kurita's warships made over twenty-five knots as they quickly closed the gap with the spooked Taffy 3.

Torpedo Specialist Nishizaki remembered that, as *Yukikaze* turned south along the eastern coast of Samar with the Center Force, a "large squall obscured the warships in complete darkness for a considerable period of time."[39] At daybreak, however, the squall dissipated and visibility slowly improved. He recalled that, "to the east, in the red glow of the horizon, we spotted three masts." Immediately, Captain Terauchi thundered from *Yukikaze*'s bridge, "Prepare to attack." Upon seeing the numerous masts, the sailors aboard *Yukikaze* thought that this represented a once in a lifetime chance to engage Halsey's fast fleet carriers. Admiral Kurita's order then came down the wireless: *Zengun totsugeki seyo* – "All ships, general attack!" With this, the Center Force charged the enemy carriers at full speed in the final fifth act. By Nishizaki's recollection, at this stage of the battle, the US carriers, for whatever reason, had yet to launch their aircraft.

As Nishizaki and the other torpedo men readied for the attack, the group leader shouted "Make no mistake, we've caught them by surprise!" His words buoyed their confidence for the coming battle. It was Nishizaki's first experience with launching torpedoes in combat. "I felt the blood pulsing through my veins as the destroyer danced wildly in the building seas," he wrote. The US destroyers made smoke, he recalled, which skillfully obscured the carriers. As Admiral Kurita's destroyers pressed the attack to within 10,000 meters, the dye from enemy shells splashed columns of water in red, yellow, and green all around the speeding ships. When *Yukikaze* approached within 10,000 meters of the US carriers, Torpedo Chief Saitō Kazuyoshi ordered "Prepare for torpedo attack on the second carrier in the enemy column!"

Nishizaki recalled the sequence of events that led to the torpedo attack: pressure increased in the torpedo tubes and the starter valve clicked open. He observed that the first destroyer in their column,

Urakaze, had launched four torpedoes as she came about hard to starboard. Then, the second and third destroyers in the torpedo squadron fired. It was now *Yukikaze*'s turn. Nishizaki explained that, "On the launchers, in order to get the angle of fire correct, the red and black sighting pins needed to be properly aligned, but no matter how many times I tried, moving the launcher to the right and left, I couldn't get them aligned."

"Calm down!," shouted the Torpedo Chief. "Make it count."

Suddenly, the sighting pins clicked into place and *Yukikaze* launched her torpedoes over her port beam. Then, as one of the Torpedo Chiefs stared at his stopwatch, the others waited in quiet anticipation to see whether their Type 93 fish had found their target. "Now," somebody whispered. Just then, there was a reddish-brown explosion on the horizon. It seemed clear to the torpedo men aboard *Yukikaze* that at least one of their fish had found its mark. "Banzai!," shouted the Torpedo Chief, his hands in the air, and the men followed suit. Euphoric, Nishizaki exclaimed aloud, "We did it!"

Yukikaze and her sister destroyers, *Urakaze*, *Isokaze*, and *Hamakaze*, had trained their torpedoes on two *Casablanca*-class escort carriers, the *St. Lo* and *Kalinin Bay*. Both escort carriers ran on the northernmost side of the US formation and represented the easiest targets for the destroyers. They proved no match for the speed of the *Kagerō*-class warships. The commander of the *St. Lo*, Captain Francis McKenna, wrote in his Action Report, "Cruisers could be seen dead astern firing full broadsides. Salvos were short astern. The *St. Lo* was laying smoke which was holding close to the water."[40] Early in the fighting, the little carrier had managed to evade the incoming ordnance.

But the Imperial Navy cruisers and destroyers were "observed still closing," he recalled, getting within optimal torpedo range. He remembered that one Japanese destroyer off *St. Lo*'s starboard quarter had closed to within 6,900 yards before releasing its fish. Once their torpedoes had been released, the Imperial Navy destroyers peeled off to withdraw to the northwest toward Leyte Gulf. A pilot from the *St. Lo* first saw the fish heading toward the escort carrier on the port and starboard beams, and he alerted the crew. "Shortly thereafter a number of them were sighted from the ship, apparently nearing the end of their run, as they were porpoising."[41]

The pilot, Lt. Leonard Waldrop, "strafed one which exploded in the wake of the *Kalinin Bay*, another exploded a short distance on the port quarter." It was likely that these explosions near the two escort carriers are what the sailors aboard *Yukikaze* witnessed when they shouted "Banzai!" No doubt they thought their Type 93 torpedoes had found their mark. The *Kalinin Bay* escaped, but the *St. Lo* did sink that morning, not from Japanese torpedoes but because of a kamikaze attack by a Mitsubishi Zero pilot, who planted his plane and bomb squarely on *St. Lo*'s flight deck.

As numerous aircraft descended on the escort carrier *St. Lo*, Captain McKenna remembered, "one of them, when about abeam to starboard went into a right turn toward the *St. Lo*. The after starboard guns opened on him, but with no apparent effect. This plane, a Zeke 52, with a bomb under each wing, continued his right turn into the groove, and approached over the ramp at very high speed." The aircraft then smashed into the deck. "There was a tremendous crash and flash of an explosion as one or both bombs exploded. The plane continued up the deck leaving fragments strewn about and its remnants went over the bow."[42] Although initially the "Captain's impression was that no serious damage had been suffered," the attack proved fatal and eventually the *St. Lo* sank.

The Imperial Navy fought tenaciously off Samar. Once close enough, the battleship *Yamato* opened fire with her eighteen-inch guns. It was the first time her big guns had fired at the enemy during the entire war. As Taffy 3 fled to the southwest, the US screening destroyers made smoke to the north of them, but the carriers on the windward side of the formation, namely *Gambier Bay* and *Kalinin Bay*, were exposed by the freshening northeast breeze. According to the *Gambier Bay*'s commanding officer, Captain Walter Vieweg, the escort carrier took "heavy and disastrous fire"[43] from the eight-inch guns of the cruisers that closed fast from the northeast.

The big ordnance from Kurita's battleships also "fell dangerously close to the ship's side and may have caused some underwater damage not immediately apparent." As we've seen, near misses could be as dangerous as direct hits. About an hour into the battle, at 08:16, a shell hit *Gambier Bay*'s forward engine room below the waterline. Then, a hit to the pilothouse knocked out forward steerage. Eventually, all ship's power was lost. By 08:50, "two or three enemy cruisers had closed and were firing into the ship at point blank range." Fires raged as the *Gambier Bay* listed badly to port. She capsized and sank twenty minutes later.

As the battle commenced, the US escort carriers, including the harried *Gambier Bay*, had successfully launched their aircraft, which scattered the Imperial Navy warships out of formation. Admiral Kurita's poorly executed general attack order had placed the Center Force in disarray, but Kurita's attack had always been more of a banzai charge than an attempt to cross Sprague's "T" in order to win a tactical victory. Soon, the Center Force found itself spread out over some fifteen nautical miles and, in some instances, out of VHF communication range. (VHF, or very-high-frequency radio, typically operates within line of sight, so it can be obscured by the ocean's horizon, or by islands and mountains. At twelve meters above the water [say, on the bridge of a destroyer], the ocean's horizon is just over thirteen kilometers distant.) The screening US destroyers also launched their torpedoes with exceptional accuracy, and at one point forced *Yamato* to come about in order to comb their wakes by running away from the scene of the action. By the time the threat had abated, *Yamato* was some thirty miles from the center of the battle. Throughout the beginning of act five, the Battle off Samar, Admiral Kurita continued to believe that he had engaged the bulk of Halsey's Third Fleet of fast carriers. Instead, Admiral Kurita had engaged Sprague's Taffy 3, but Kurita fought blindly without eyes in the sky that day.

The *Johnston* was one of the US destroyers trying to protect the vulnerable escort carriers to windward. The fourteen-inch guns of *Kongō* or *Haruna* likely scored the first hits on the *Johnston*. After launching torpedoes and firing numerous five-inchers at Kurita's Center Force, several hits badly maimed the destroyer. As the Gunnery Officer, Lieutenant Robert C. Hagen, the senior-most surviving officer, remembered, "It is believed we were hit by three fourteen inch projectiles, followed thirty seconds later by three 6 inch projectiles."[44] He continued, "These hits knocked out the after fire room and engine room, all power to the steering engine, all power to the after three inch guns and rendered the gyrocompass worthless." Immediately, the sailors scrambled aft to steer the warship manually and gunners fired the functioning guns. Miraculously, the *Johnston* then found temporary shelter in a "providential rain storm."

It wasn't long before the *Johnston*'s radar was operational and she began to fire back at the Imperial Navy ships. No sooner had the *Johnston* narrowly avoided a collision with the destroyer *Heermann*, while exiting the squall, than "there suddenly appeared out of the smoke a battleship of the KONGO class, seven thousand yards distant, on our port beam." *Johnston* quickly established a solution and took the battleship under fire. The *Johnston* fired forty rounds and "several hits were observed on the pagoda structure." While the *Johnston* continued to the southwest with the remainder of Taffy 3, Japanese cruiser and destroyer divisions surrounded the US destroyer. The *Johnston* frantically took a column of Japanese destroyers under fire until a "most amazing thing happened" – the lead Japanese destroyer turned away. Following the lead destroyer, "all remaining six Jap destroyers turned ninety degrees to the right and the range began to open rapidly." But, the respite proved short-lived, as *Johnston* still had other cruisers and destroyers to contend with and alternated fire at the cruisers on the port side and the destroyers closing to starboard.

"Finally at about 0930 we found ourselves with two cruisers dead ahead of us, several Jap destroyers on our starboard quarter and two cruisers on our port quarter." According to Hagen, "At this fateful time numerous Japanese units had us under very effective fire, all of those ships being within six to ten thousand yards of us." The hail of shells knocked out the remaining engine room and fire room, the ship lost communications, and most guns were not operational. "As the ship went dead in the water and its fate long since inevitable, the Captain gave the order to abandon ship at about 0945." The men boarded lifeboats as the gallant *Johnston* began to roll over. At this moment, "a Japanese destroyer was observed to close the range to one thousand yards to insure the ships [*sic*] final destruction." It was *Yukikaze*.

Torpedo Specialist Nishizaki remembered that, as *Yukikaze* approached the stricken *Johnston*, he could see a white flag hoisted on her mast. Sailors had cleated a lifeboat to her stern. Many sailors had started boarding the lifeboat, after the order came to abandon ship. Seeing this, *Yukikaze*'s Machinegun Chief, for whom, as Nishizaki commented, "hostility toward the enemy came naturally,"[45] ordered "Open fire!" and a handful of bullets hit the painter that held the lifeboat to the *Johnston*.

Just then, Captain Terauchi thundered from the bridge, "Cease firing on those trying to escape!" Assured that *Johnston* was finished, *Yukikaze* then departed without slaughtering the US sailors, as often happened on both sides. By this time, Admiral Kurita's order to abandon the fight at Leyte Gulf had arrived. He was not about to sacrifice his mighty battleships, symbols of a Great Power nation, in a banzai charge against lowly escort carriers and transport vessels. He was after Halsey's Third Fleet carriers, his fifth and final act.

* * *

"Did we not just have carriers right before our eyes?,"[46] thundered the voice of Captain Terauchi from the bridge of *Yukikaze*, after he received Admiral Kurita's order to withdraw. As the US forces began a strategic retreat southward, Kurita had decided not to pursue them, and instead turned toward Leyte Gulf, his original objective. However, rather than engage the transports at Leyte Gulf, Admiral Kurita, in one of the more controversial decisions of the war, ordered the Center Force to turn north and hunt Halsey's carriers. Not finding them, he eventually ordered that the Center Force return to Brunei. Torpedo Specialist Nishizaki recalled that, as Kurita's warships fled through the San Bernardino Strait into the Sibuyan Sea on October 26, Halsey's carrier-based planes, as well as B-24 bombers from Indonesia's Morotai Island, began carpet-bombing the Center Force warships from high altitude. He remembered that the bombs rained down and caused towering white splashes and wicked seas, and sank the cruiser *Noshiro*.

Had *Yamato*, *Nagato*, *Kongō*, and *Haruna* stormed into Leyte Gulf and shelled what remained of the US troops and transports with their big guns, they could have wreaked havoc on the entire operation, killing hundreds. Admiral Kurita's decision to break off the attack was a profound one, but one that's largely misunderstood. Leyte was as much about sacrificing the Emperor's warships on the altar of history as it was about killing US soldiers and sailors. Later, when asked about the decision, and the controversy that surrounded it, Admiral Kurita blamed the decision in part on fatigue. "I did not feel tired at the time but, under great strain and without sleep for three days and nights, I was exhausted both mentally and physically," he explained. But Kurita also acknowledged that he had become obsessed with finding Halsey's Third Fleet, and was not thrilled with the idea of attacking the transports at Leyte Gulf. "The destruction of the enemy aircraft carriers was a kind of obsession with me, and I fell victim to it," he confided in conversations with Itō Masanori.

But Halsey's whereabouts remained unknown and therefore represented a dangerous element in the Leyte battle plan. "Leyte Gulf was stationary, the enemy task force was not and so the chances of finding it were an unknown quantity. If one says it was an error in judgment for me to have reversed course for an unknown quantity, then I have no excuses." As Kurita's critics would have it, he should have attacked his known, static target, the US transports in Leyte Gulf, rather than chase the specter of Halsey's carriers, the unknown element. At the time, Admiral Kurita thought otherwise.

But this explanation represented Kurita's tactical voice, his somber postwar voice, his reconciliatory voice after the killing and sacrificing of the war had ended. To really understand Kurita at Leyte Gulf, it's his voice before the battle at the Brunei anchorage, not after the battle in his living room, which really matters. "Would it not be a shame to have the fleet remain intact while our nation perishes?" It's an important question, one that only the bards of Japan's history can answer.

As the curtain closed on the Kabuki play of Leyte Gulf, the imperial heroes of Japan's martial past, the tragic nobility of Japan's sublime history, convened as judge and jury to answer Admiral Kurita's question, and they answered, "Yes, it would be a shame, Admiral." And so Kurita sailed away from Leyte that way, leaving the US landings largely unmolested, to search out the phantoms of Halsey's Third Fleet. What he found instead was infamy in naval history.

CHAPTER 10

Dangerous Homewaters and *Shinano* Destroyed

A periscope can be seen if it comes up in the daytime.

Hydrophone Operator Noma Mitsue on the sinking of the carrier *Shinano*

IF IMPERIAL NAVY BRASS had begun to move in the direction of sacrificing warships, rather than using them to strategic advantage in a desperate war, Leyte Gulf might be considered successful. The Imperial Navy suffered devastating losses at Leyte, including the loss of *Musashi*, *Yamato*'s sister ship. The battlewagon never saw the kind of big-gun brawl she was designed for, just as the Imperial Navy never really saw the Mahan-style decisive battle it had been built for – World War II was an industrial war, with industrial requirements.

None of the Leyte losses proved more dramatic than the sinking of the heavy cruiser *Suzuya*, particularly as remembered by sailors aboard *Yukikaze*. The big cruiser took many sailors to their watery grave, their terrified faces peering through sealed portals as the mangled ship went down. Some sailors did miraculously escape the galvanized coffin and tried to swim to *Yukikaze* and safety, and the destroyer mounted a valiant rescue attempt. Nonetheless, of the thirty-two warships that had left on October 22 for Operation Victory at Leyte Gulf, only fourteen returned to Brunei. And there, once in the anchorage, they were pummeled anew by Allied planes. There would be no quarter for the Imperial Navy, anywhere.

While in Brunei, *Yukikaze* lost a machinegunner to Allied raids, and officers held a formal funeral for the sailor on deck. It provides an interesting window onto life in the Imperial Navy, even in late 1944 as its world began to collapse around it. It was a navy defined by traditions, and the funeral exposes a navy desperately trying to hold onto some of them. But Brunei quickly became too dangerous for Japan's warships, and, less than one month after the defeat at Leyte, Imperial Navy Headquarters decided to bring the ships home. Making for home waters, they navigated through the submarine-infested South China Sea, and even more ships were lost.

Shortly after arriving at Yokosuka, Imperial Navy Headquarters ordered *Yukikaze* and the remainder of Desron17 to escort the giant flattop *Shinano* as she tried to escape Yokosuka for Kure. War planners feared that Allied reconnaissance planes had spotted her. Like with so many other Pacific battles, *Yukikaze* had a front-row seat to the US Navy's sinking of World War II's largest carrier. *Shinano*'s escorting destroyers tried desperately to save the flattop, but in the end she sank, taking her captain with her: she proved woefully unprepared, in every sense of the word, for the intensity of late-1944 fighting, even in Japan's home waters. The naval battles of the Pacific had come home to Japan. It's one thing to lose carriers in such exotic places as the Coral Sea, Midway Atoll, and the Mariana Islands; it's quite another to lose one 100 kilometers from Wakayama Prefecture, basically in your backyard.

But, that's precisely where the war stood in the fall of 1944.

* * *

After bearing away from Leyte Gulf, Admiral Kurita's Center Force, still searching for Admiral Halsey's carriers rather than the consolation prize of US troop transports, pushed north about 100 nautical miles looking for the US flattops, which had just finished throttling Admiral Ozawa's bait force. By sunset, when Admiral Halsey's Third Fleet had still not been spotted, Kurita decided to turn west through the San Bernardino Strait and into the Sibuyan Sea in order to reach the safety of Brunei Harbor.

The trip back through the Sibuyan Sea witnessed a veritable hailstorm of 500- and 1,000-pound ordnances, which rained down on Admiral Kurita's ships from US bombers. In this storm of flashes, explosions, and fiery black columns of water, a bomb hit the cruiser *Noshiro* and she went down. *Yamato* received several hits and near misses and took on some 3,000 tons of seawater while she ran at best possible speed with the extra weight. The bombs roiled and rocked the sea, transforming it into a boiling, confused mess. Torpedo Specialist Nishizaki, aboard *Yukikaze*, remembered being absolutely terrified, as he didn't know whether the next 1,000-pound bomb would find his little destroyer or not.

In order to evade lurking submarines, Admiral Kurita's warships took a circuitous route back to Brunei through the dangerous, shoal-ridden waters west of the Spratly Islands and the South China Sea; they then ran at sixteen knots, their best speed, given the damaged warships, toward the relative safety of Brunei Harbor. A thick trail of fuel oil meandered behind the broken fleet like blood behind a wounded animal. On October 28, at 21:30 in the evening, the warships ghosted into Brunei Harbor. But Leyte would not soon be forgotten. It had seared itself into the memory of *Yukikaze*'s young Hydrophone Operator, Noma Mitsue.

Initially, Noma had felt the thrill of battle as Admiral Kurita's Center Force engaged the US escort carriers off Samar. Mistakenly thinking they had found Admiral Halsey's Third Fleet, the Imperial Navy warships charged at flank speed toward the escort carriers. He remembered being on *Yukikaze*'s bridge, wearing only a sailor's cap rather than a combat helmet, even as fifty-caliber bullets whizzed overhead and pinged loudly off the mast. "It was amazing,"[1] he recalled in later interviews. He watched in awe as the battlewagons *Yamato*, *Nagato*, *Haruna*, and *Kongō* hurled their massive shells toward the enemy. He also gazed in astonishment as the heavy-cruiser *Tone* burst into flames after repeated attacks by enemy aircraft, though the ship managed to survive.

Of the torpedo elements in Admiral Kurita's Center Force, *Yukikaze*'s group had followed *Yahagi* into the battle, while the other destroyers had followed *Noshiro* – both were *Agano*-class light cruisers. "At the time," he remembered, "I thought that I was really experiencing a World War II naval battle." For the young sailor, it was "like watching a movie," one choreographed for an Imperial Navy victory in a traditional-style artillery duel. But, when US aircraft arrived, the realities of naval warfare began to take a firm grip on Noma. Early in the battle, he became alarmed when he saw that a torpedo had misfired from *Noshiro*'s port side. As the cruiser raced into battle, the torpedo protruded dangerously from the launcher's tube. As he looked through his binoculars, Noma worried that if the torpedo dropped and floated, it would surely detonate when *Yukikaze* or one of the other destroyers inadvertently struck it.

But it was the sinking of *Suzuya* that scarred Noma's memory of the Battle off Samar. In the late morning of October 25, scores of carrier-based torpedo-bombers had descended on the big cruiser, and near misses had fouled her port screw and detonated torpedoes armed in their launchers. The explosions mauled the deck, blocked egress passages below deck, and caused fires throughout the ship. Initially, recalled Noma, commanders had ordered *Yukikaze* to render aid and rescue sailors from the water. But, as she approached, the officers could see that another destroyer, likely *Okinami*, sought to render assistance as well. As *Yukikaze* approached, Noma witnessed something that he'd not soon forget. In fact, for the remainder of his life, whenever somebody mentioned the name *Suzuya*, the specter of the ill-fated cruiser and her sailors returned to haunt him.

Noma could see that US planes had thoroughly crunched and snarled *Suzuya*'s deck and that, as a morbid ensign of death, a sailor's corpse dangled from the cruiser's mast. Presumably, one of the blasts had blown the man skyward and he became tangled in the electronics and rigging. But the snarled deck had also trapped hundreds of sailors below deck. Before the battle, sailors had secured the warship's portholes, and sealed subdivided bulkheads and watertight doors – something resembling Condition Zebra. Condition Zebra is typically set when a warship sounds to general quarters and represents the maximum degree of subdivision and watertight thoroughness that a warship can attain. It helps contain flooding and fire to one section of the warship.

But, on *Suzuya*, sailors (probably from the engineering department) had desperately opened these portholes and their hands waved and their faces protruded from the openings as they begged for help. Pitifully, the portholes proved too small for even their heads to fit through. As he watched the scene in horror, Noma next heard a loud explosion and *Suzuya* disappeared, taking her screaming, begging sailors with her.

"I didn't think there could be anything so cruel," he thought. "*Yamato* went 'boom' and sank after a big explosion, but it took *Suzuya* a long time to go down. With the upper deck mangled and the lower decks pitch black, only narrow rays of light shone through the portals and allowed men to look through them or wave their hands. Now that's cruel," he said.

Some of *Suzuya*'s sailors attempted to swim to safety. As these men approached, *Yukikaze* stopped her engines to avoid sucking the men under and slicing them up in the water.

"You only have to swim a little more!," shouted sailors aboard *Yukikaze*.

"I can't swim because my leg's broken," came one reply, as men tried hopelessly to tread water.

The height of a destroyer's freeboard was quite tall, and many men in the water attempted to ride waves up the side of the destroyer, presumably grabbing cargo nets or rope ladders that sailors had thrown over the sides. Noma watched these men in anguish. He remembered that, when they finally tired and began to drown, air bubbled to the surface from their gaping mouths. It was only then that Noma knew they were dead – he also knew that some day that gaping, gurgling mouth might be his.

Suzuya's cruel fate had befallen many warships and sailors on both sides at Leyte Gulf. For the Imperial Navy, only four battleships, two heavy cruisers, one light cruiser, and seven destroyers returned from Leyte. On the return voyage, *Yukikaze* had navigated in the vanguard, on the right side of the formation just aft of the starboard quarter of *Yahagi*. Nearly all of the warships in Admiral Kurita's Center Force had received some sort of damage, all except one, that is – *Yukikaze*.

Brunei had once been a safe haven for the Imperial Navy, but it now proved a tempting target for US bombers. On November 6, US planes began area-bombing Brunei, and one of *Yukikaze*'s machinegunners, the young Ōzaki Ryōichi, died from shrapnel wounds he sustained to his chest. Because the unsinkable destroyer sustained so little damage during the war, it was one of the precious few times that Torpedo Specialist Nishizaki witnessed a burial at sea. It was a particularly sad day for him.

He and Ōzaki had history. Earlier in the war, he had gotten to know the young sailor while they were together in Singapore, when the two men had ducked into a coffee shop to evade nosy military police. In the coffee shop, they discovered the simple delights of strawberry shortcake with whipped cream. As they savored the treat, Ōzaki said, "I didn't know that the world had such delicious things!"[2] Even after the war, every time Nishizaki saw strawberry shortcake, he remembered the young gunner's enormous smile on that sweet day in Singapore, early in the war.

But Ōzaki was dead now, mangled from shrapnel wounds. Aboard *Yukikaze*, a Sailor First Class who was also a Buddhist priest performed the appropriate rites by chanting sutras for the mourning officers and crew. Crew members then hoisted the flag at half-mast, while an honor guard formally presented arms. In the background, a naval ensemble played the patriotic bugle call *Kuni no shizume*, "Guardians of the Land," a patriotic piece originally written and arranged by the Meiji court musician Shiba Fujitsune. As the sailors stood at attention in front of Ōzaki's coffin, the lyrics floated through the freshening ocean breeze:

> May the guardians of our land's peace,
>
> the gods and spirits enshrined here,
>
> fly through the heavens to view
>
> the bustle of today's festival,
>
> and protect our sovereign's reign ...[3]

The sailors then consecrated Ōzaki's body to the sea. The honor guard held both sides of the flag-draped coffin, and artillerymen fired two blanks from *Yukikaze*'s guns. The honor guard then slowly walked the coffin to a hole in the gunwales of the destroyer and slipped the coffin overboard, where it slowly disappeared into the harbor. As the coffin sank, the sailors followed Captain Terauchi in a formal salute to their fallen comrade. This type of scene became more common as the remnants of the Combined Fleet remained anchored at Brunei, sitting ducks for increasingly accurate US bombers.

After being harried by the kind of raids that killed Ōzaki for nearly three weeks, Imperial Navy Headquarters made the decision to evacuate Brunei and bring the remnants of the Combined Fleet home. On the evening of November 19, the fleet began the dangerous journey back to Japan. Desron17, comprised of *Urakaze* (the flagship, with the commander of Desron17, Captain Tanii Tamotsu), *Yukikaze*, *Isokaze*, and *Hamakaze*, cruised on both sides of the battlewagons *Yamato* and *Kongō* as the ships headed north in the gathering darkness at a loathsomely slow pace of sixteen knots. They proved easy targets.

Just after midnight on November 21, in calm seas with good visibility, the US submarine *Sealion*, patrolling in the Taiwan Strait, began tracking the warships on radar. Captain Eli Thomas Reich, the commander of the

Balao-class submarine, wrote in his War Report "three pips, very clear and distinct"[4] and moving slowly. The weather presented good conditions to hunt battleships: "Overcast sky, no moon, visibility about 1500 yards, calm sea," he wrote. As *Sealion* moved closer, the pips became better defined on the screen. The radar clearly outlined "Two large pips and two smaller pips" on its screen at 35,000 yards, "the greatest ranges we have ever obtained on our radar," the Captain noted.

The targets continued on a course of 60° T, inching along at a slow sixteen knots and, surprisingly, were "not zigzagging," as might have been expected. As *Sealion* glided closer, the winds increased and the seas began to build, and the radar screen began to make out the escort ships on the port and starboard beam of the two battleships. When *Sealion* got ahead of the column at 02:56, she turned and launched six torpedoes at the second battleship at 3,000 yards. She then quickly "came right with full rudder to bring the stern tubes to bear" and launched three additional torpedoes at the third ship in the column at about 1,800 yards. The crew then waited, watching the seconds pass on the Torpedo Chief's stopwatch.

Captain Reich reported that, four minutes after launching the first salvo, *Sealion*'s crew "saw and heard three hits on first battleship – several small mushrooms of explosions noted in the darkness." Then, they "saw and heard at least one hit on second battleship – this hit gave a large violent explosion with a sudden rise of flames at the target, but it quickly subsided." Still, the ships continued, and Captain Reich came to believe that he had only hit the armored belt of the battleships and failed to sink them. He had set the torpedo depth at a relatively shallow eight feet, hoping he might serendipitously bag a destroyer while going for the big battleships. As it turned out, he did.

The conditions had turned against Captain Reich, however. The weather had shifted and the seas began to build. At 04:06, as the submarine raced at flank speed to intercept, Captain Reich noted "Sea and wind increasing all the time – now about force 5 or 6 [typically, between 20 and 27 knots, with 4- to 13-foot waves] – taking solid water over bridge, with plenty coming over conning tower hatch." *Sealion*'s radar indicated that the Imperial Navy column had split into two groups, with the second heading astern. It turns out that this was the badly damaged *Kongō* and her destroyer escort making for safe haven. *Sealion* went after the wounded *Kongō*, launching three additional torpedoes, which slowed the warship to eleven knots.

At 05:24, Captain Reich reported that, after a brilliant explosion – it "looked like a sunset at midnight" – the battleship pip could be seen getting smaller on the radar screen until it disappeared, leaving only the destroyers, including *Yukikaze*, "milling around vicinity of target," searching in vain for survivors in the howling thirty-knot wind. Captain Reich considered chasing the other Imperial Navy warships north, but heavy seas had swamped *Sealion* and the chase had overheated her engines, so she decided to break off the pursuit, eventually submerging. It was a good night, nonetheless. *Sealion* sank the battleship *Kongō*, whose artillery barrage had so terrorized US soldiers on Guadalcanal in the early morning hours of October 14, 1942, and the stalwart destroyer *Urakaze*, flagship of Desron17, in her raid.

Eventually, on November 25, the battered remnants of the Combined Fleet entered Bungo Channel and arrived in the navigable waters off Iyo on Shikoku Island. Only three battleships, three cruisers, and six destroyers raised Hashirajima in the Inland Sea that morning. Nishizaki remembered, "When I saw the inland mountains of Japan I knew I was home."[5] Imperial Navy warships might be named after Japan's natural features, but they were no substitute for the real thing. The next day, *Yamato* departed for Kure, while *Yukikaze*, *Hamakaze*, and *Isokaze*, the tattered remnants of Desron17, escorted *Nagato*, who had taken four direct bomb hits and eight near misses, to Yokosuka. There, the battleship remained until the end of the war, until the atomic bomb tests at Bikini Atoll in 1946 destroyed her.

Although the officers and crew of Desron17 were exhausted, the Imperial Navy immediately placed the destroyers on patrol duty – the Kii Province offing (the coast off Wakayama Prefecture), the Enshū Sea (south between Shizuoka and Nagoya), and Sagami Bay (west of Yokosuka) had become rife with US submarines. Nowhere on the globe proved safe waters anymore for the once-dominant Imperial Japanese Navy, not even home waters. Then, only three days after arriving in Japan, Imperial Navy Headquarters mobilized the three destroyers – exhausted, leaderless, and beaten – to escort the super-carrier *Shinano* on her maiden voyage. The Imperial Navy billed the massive flattop as Japan's last hope in an increasingly desperate war.

* * *

Engineers built the carrier *Shinano* on a repurposed *Yamato*-class battleship hull. At 872 feet in length over all, she was a big ship, even by later Cold War standards. (The US *Essex*-class carriers [in commission 1942–1991] were 820 feet, and displaced 30,000 tons, while the *Midway*-class carriers [in commission 1945–1992] were 968 feet, and displaced 45,000 tons.) Engineers built her deck with composite steel designed to withstand 500-kilogram bomb blasts, even those delivered by speeding dive-bombers, the kind that had wreaked such havoc at Midway. Like the carrier *Taihō*, her bridge and funnel sponsoned from the starboard side of the flight deck amidships. She bristled with 16 12.7 centimeter (5-inch) Type 89 guns in 8 twin mounts, and over 100 of the ubiquitous Type 96 25 millimeter antiaircraft guns in 35 triple mounts. Aircraft could be refueled on the flight deck, eliminating the dangers experienced at Coral Sea and Midway of refueling below in the hangar. With her magnificent flight deck, the Imperial Navy viewed *Shinano* as a floating airbase within the Pacific, an island unto herself, and the new centerpiece of a reconfigured Combined Fleet that could challenge the US Navy's advance toward Japan after the fall of Saipan.

But *Shinano* required relocation from Yokosuka to Kure because navy brass believed a US reconnaissance plane had spotted her. On November 27, Captain Abe Toshio of *Shinano* met with the destroyer captains of Desron17 to discuss the upcoming mission. He explained that the plan to relocate *Shinano* involved departing at night under cover of darkness, racing through the Inland Sea and into the Kii Channel on a westerly course, and then on to relative safety. As Nishizaki recalled, however, the destroyer captains adamantly opposed the proposal. They had learned much from the war about escort duties, particularly over the last year. They had other ideas.

"With escorting aircraft,"[6] the Desron17 captains explained, "depart early in the morning instead. It's safest breaking through submarine-infested waters during the day!" They'd be completely blind at night, they argued.

But Captain Abe countered that the orders came from Imperial Navy Headquarters and could not be countermanded. With the inevitability of the changing tides, on November 28, at 18:00, *Shinano* eased out of Yokosuka with her ragtag destroyer escort. *Hamakaze* held the point position, while *Isokaze* navigated on the left flank and *Yukikaze* navigated on the right, all holding position about 1,200 meters from the flattop. *Shinano* carried 2,175 officers and crew on her unceremonious maiden voyage, as well as about 300 shipyard workers and 40 civilian contractors. She had no proper aircraft for combat air patrol or bombers, only six Shin'yō, or "Sea Quake," suicide boats and fifty suicide flying bombs, the newly designed MXY-17 Ōka, or "Cherry Blossom," a rocket-powered kamikaze aircraft usually carried within range of its target by a Mitsubishi bomber. Neither the Shin'yō nor Ōka suicide machines were useful in the mission to relocate the behemoth *Shinano*. The flattop was just transporting those weapons to Western Japan, where they could later be used in Operation Floating Chrysanthemum against US landings at Okinawa. What she needed was a combat air patrol. With the exception of her three-destroyer escort, she was naked in submarine- and bomber-infested waters, and at night.

The destroyer captains were rightfully wary because they knew that Imperial Navy vessels would not be the only ones navigating in the darkness of the Inland Sea that night. And they weren't disappointed. Late that evening, the US submarine *Archerfish*, commanded by Captain Joseph F. Enright, picked up the big flattop and its escorting destroyers on radar and cautiously moved in. For the remainder of that evening and early into the next morning, *Archerfish* tried to maneuver into firing position, but the Imperial Navy vessels ran faster than the submarine.

As Enright wrote in his Action Report, "From here on it was a mad race for a possible firing position. His speed was about one knot in excess of our best, but his zig plan allowed us to pull ahead very slowly."[7] But, when Captain Enright raised his periscope to watch, keen-eyed Imperial Navy spotters saw him. Early in the morning on November 29, as the vessels crossed the Enshū Sea (south between Shizuoka and Nagoya), lookouts reported seeing a black shape on the horizon, what appeared to be a periscope.

Immediately, *Hamakaze*, at the lead of the formation, rushed over to investigate. At this juncture, although *Hamakaze* and *Isokaze* apparently communicated with one another, neither destroyer communicated with *Yukikaze* (by error, oversight, or malfunction of equipment), which continued southward on the flank of *Shinano*, rather than peeling off to search for the submarine, with her sister ships. This diminished the effectiveness of the antisubmarine search. In many ways, the failure of the remaining three members of Desron17 can be attributed to the earlier loss of *Urakaze* in the Taiwan Strait. Aboard *Urakaze*, the Desron17 commander, Tanii Tamotsu, had served as the organizational glue that held the destroyers together and allowed them to operate in a carefully choreographed fashion. As the three destroyers sought to protect *Shinano*, they largely operated independently of one another, eventually dooming their mission to failure. Before their departure, they had never decided on an overall Desron17 commander, and had failed even to craft an escort plan for the trip to Kure. With *Hamakaze* and *Isokaze* searching for *Archerfish*, *Yukikaze* and *Shinano* ran in a southerly direction at flank speed, right into *Archerfish*'s waiting crosshairs.

Onboard *Shinano*, lookouts had also seen the suspicious shape, but they continued southward anyway. Some inexperienced lookouts even dismissed the periscope as a cloud formation. Dutifully, *Yukikaze* continued to hold station with the flattop. At that precise moment, *Archerfish* adjusted course southward, taking advantage of the carrier's zigzagging, and intercepted *Shinano*. At 03:17, with *Shinano* making a "late favorable zig," *Archerfish* maneuvered into optimum firing position. Captain Enright wrote "Starting firing all bow tubes, Mk 14 torpedoes, set depth 10 feet – First gyro 28° right, track 100, spread from cards, aft to forward." The target was at 1,400 yards, virtually point-blank range. Not long after the first torpedo was fired, Captain Enright wrote "Heard and observed first hit just inside stern near props and rudder. Large ball of fire climbed his side." The fish had found their mark.

Sleeping aboard *Yukikaze*, Torpedo Specialist Nishizaki felt the impact of the explosion while tucked in his swinging hammock. Suddenly, the order came from above deck, "Prepare depth charges!" Nishizaki flew from his hammock, donned his steel helmet and flak vest, and ran to the aft portion of the destroyer, where the depth-charge launcher was located. "Ready to prepare to launch, sir!," he shouted toward the Torpedo Chief. As *Yukikaze* raced into the darkness, Nishizaki heard

"Kaboom! Kaboom! Kaboom!," as three more torpedoes slammed into the side of *Shinano*. Huge columns of fire and water rose from the side of the flattop. Then, piercing the darkness, came an ominous lamp signal from *Shinano*: "Torpedo hits on starboard beam." The big carrier had taken four torpedo hits on her starboard side.

Bred for antisubmarine warfare, *Yukikaze* dashed to where she thought *Archerfish* lay hidden. The Torpedo Chief shouted "Prepare to fire … Fire!" Quickly, Nishizaki hit the fire button with all his strength. Then, "Pashoom! Pashoom! Pashoom!" The depth charges flew some fifty meters into the sky from the firing rack in quick succession. The next instant, a concussive "Kathoom!" as the charges exploded under-water, raising the entire aft section of the destroyer from the water. Hydrophone Operator Noma, whose well-trained ears had heard *Archerfish*'s torpedoes pass near *Yukikaze* before they hit *Shinano*, remembered he had just arrived on the bridge when he received word that a massive pillar of fire had erupted near the carrier's last known location. According to Noma, the three destroyers immediately started dropping depth charges around the suspected location of the US submarine.

Noma recalled that, when the depth charge detonated, because of the presence of *Noctiluca scintillans*, a bioluminescent marine microor-ganism, in the surrounding ocean, the water erupted and convulsed in explosive bubbles of blues and whites. Even though he was in the midst of battle, he momentarily forgot about the war. He thought "That's sure beautiful," but then the reality of war quickly returned. Sailors began looking over the sides for signs of oil and debris, but none were seen. Then, the order came to cease firing. Meanwhile, aboard *Archerfish*, Captain Enright remembered receiving a "total of 14 depth charges. Closest one was perhaps 300 yards away." *Yukikaze* and her sister ships had shot blindly into the dark. *Archerfish* slid away after launching one of the most legendary torpedo strikes of the entire war.

Four torpedoes had slammed into the side of *Shinano*, but engi-neers had fitted her flight deck to a *Yamato*-class battleship hull. Surely, thought Nishizaki, four torpedoes couldn't sink her. He was reassured by the sound of *Yukikaze* easing back to a more deliberate cruising speed. He went below decks, climbed back into his hammock, and began to doze off. His last thought was "After all, she's the largest aircraft carrier in the world." He then slept for a couple of hours. Everything was quiet again except for the rhythmic turns of *Yukikaze*'s screws.

But when he woke up and returned above deck at 06:00, he could see that *Shinano* now listed badly to starboard, about 20° after the starboard boiler room had flooded. She had also reduced speed. An officer aboard *Yukikaze* said "They'll flood the port side ballast compartments with seawater. She'll regain her balance soon. There's no problem." But there was a problem. By 08:00 it had become clear to everybody that *Shinano*'s list had worsened. Despite Captain Abe's protests and requests for a delay, *Shinano* had left Yokosuka with few watertight doors installed, and many holes through the bulkheads and compartments for electrical wires, conduits, and ducting had never been sealed – a single torpedo hit could flood the entire flattop. Engineers had yet to even conduct air tests of her compartments. Most of her sailors were inexperienced, too.

Captain Abe gave new orders to the destroyer captains: "Use the destroyers as tugboats to get *Shinano* as far as Shionomisaki [a promontory in southern Wakayama Prefecture]. We'll run her aground there." On hearing this, experienced sailors aboard *Yukikaze* could only respond "What a fat-headed idiot!" The saltier sailors thought the whole idea was ludicrous.

But orders were orders, and two *Kagerō*-class destroyers, *Hamakaze* and *Isokaze*, vessels that displaced less than 5,000 tons between the two of them, attempted to tow with a wire rope some 70 nautical miles to Japan's coast a flooded aircraft carrier that displaced over 65,500 tons. Captain Abe ordered that *Yukikaze* keep a look out for more submarines that might come to finish the job. Knowing there wasn't much time, sailors got to work immediately. They unwound the wire rope from *Shinano*'s winch, transported it by tender to the destroyers, ran it through the hawseholes, and wrapped it around the funnels. Once *Shinano* gave the signal, the destroyers engaged their engines and the wire rope cinched and tightened. As the destroyers pulled, the wire rope that had formed a catenary underwater broke the surface and snapped tight. But, even as the destroyers gave more power to the engines, *Shinano* didn't so much as budge. Dark, black smoke poured from *Isokaze* and *Hamakaze*'s stacks as they pulled with all their combined might, the wire rope as tight as a piano string. It groaned as it wrenched tighter and tighter around the destroyers' funnels. But still the carrier wouldn't move.

Just then, somebody shouted, "Be careful! It's going to break!"[8] In an instant, the sailors heard a loud snap and the wire rope parted. It was flung into the air and then came crashing down like a whip, slicing the head clean off a sailor from *Hamakaze* who was aboard one of the tenders. It was a gory conclusion to a nightmarish episode. By 10:00, Captain Abe reluctantly gave the order "All persons evacuate!"

Nishizaki and Noma watched in horror as sailors, shipyard workers, and civilians alike began leaping from the carrier's listing flight deck into the water. The sinking flattop sucked many of them under. Captain Abe ordered that he be tied to the flagpole at the bow of *Shinano*, and, bound there, he went down with the ship. Noma remembered the "rescue work was terrible. We never knew when torpedoes would hit us. With the coming of dawn, make no mistake that the US submarines surely watched us. They had moved just outside depth charge range."[9] The big flattop sank about sixty-five nautical miles south of Wakayama Prefecture.

At 06:10, Captain Enright had thought it safe enough to go to periscope depth. "Nothing in sight,"[10] he reported. "Our target by all rights should have been down long ago," he penned in his Action Report. Nobody in the US Navy believed that he had sunk a super-carrier, as *Shinano*'s existence was a well-kept secret. US Navy brass credited Enright with sinking a smaller *Hiyō*-class carrier during the war; after the war, however, when *Shinano*'s existence became known, he was awarded the Navy Cross.

As for *Yukikaze* and her sister ships, they fished as many men out of the water as they could, packed them aboard, and made way for Kure. Noma said of the incident, "If only they had listened to the destroyer captains and run during the day. A submarine periscope can be seen at one nautical mile. That's well within the range of the three destroyers. A periscope can be seen if it comes up in the daytime."[11]

* * *

Though tragic, there was something fitting about *Shinano*'s sinking, something congruous with the state of Japan's war of desperation. The Battle of Saipan ended on July 9, 1944. Some 30,000 Imperial Army soldiers died on Saipan, as well as an additional 7,000 Japanese civilians, many of those during mass suicides. The fall of Saipan and nearby Tinian precipitated

Prime Minister Tōjō's resignation, as well as regular B-29 bomber vis-its over the Japanese homeland with their incendiary payloads. Among the most infamous was Operation Meetinghouse on March 9–10, 1945, when hundreds of B-29s of the US Army Air Force dropped 1,665 tons of napalm on Tokyo, leaving 100,000 Japanese burned to death and some 16 square miles of city charred. Earlier, General Douglas MacArthur, fulfilling his promise to return to the Philippines, landed at Leyte Gulf on October 20. It precipitated what, by some estimations, remains the largest naval battle ever fought by the two implacable foes – the Battle of Leyte Gulf, which ended on October 26.

After the Battle of Leyte Gulf, Admiral Ōnishi Takijirō and the Kamikaze Special Attack Corps sought to heap as much damage on the US Navy as possible in November and December 1944, as US troops and supplies poured into Leyte. With the Imperial Navy basically destroyed, the Imperial Army had sought to reinforce and resupply its garrisons on Leyte in order to challenge the still vulnerable US forces there. Ormoc, the largest port city on Leyte, proved the logical destination for Japanese convoys and their screening destroyers. Under General Yamashita Tomoyuki, the Japanese ran nine convoys throughout November and early December and delivered some 34,000 Imperial Army troops to bol-ster their forces on Leyte. Only by cutting off Ormoc could US forces truly secure Leyte, and that's exactly what happened. On December 7, while operating in Ormoc Bay, one of the first choreographed kamikaze attacks nearly sank the US destroyer *Lamson*, and did sink two of her sister ships.

Captain John V. Noel of the *Lamson* had come to believe that Japanese kamikaze pilots found US warships by "homing on our SC radar."[12] As he explained in his Action Report, "while off the west coast of LEYTE bogies would be detected at thirty to seventy miles heading <u>directly</u> toward us." He concluded that "this seems to indicate that the enemy is using a radar receiver which indicates direction by the intensity of the incoming sig-nal." Once they are close, the signal becomes too strong and therefore "saturated," at which time they begin searching visually. This was likely the reverse-radar device.

One of these suicide planes, a "Tony," or Kawasaki Ki-61, homed in on *Lamson* as she escorted a group of amphibious vessels retiring from

Ormoc Bay. The amphibious vessels had just delivered elements of the 77th Infantry Division under Major General Andrew D. Bruce to eradicate the Japanese presence on the island. To avoid the forward guns and antiaircraft placements, the suicide plane "approached from astern (220° relative) and deliberately struck the bridge structure at the forecastle deck level."[13] Captain Noel explained of the kamikaze attack, "the plane strafed as it approached and carried one or more small bombs which exploded just forward of the base of the forward stack." As became typical of kamikaze strikes, "a large fire with flames reaching as high as the radar antenna quickly enveloped the bridge causing many casualties." Japan's suicide pilots gave Captain Noel a crash course on what the war would be like as US forces approached the home islands, particularly in the fighting around Okinawa.

Although there was some talk of scuttling the ailing destroyer, the *Lamson* limped to the Puget Sound Navy Yard in Bremerton, Washington, where it underwent repairs and returned to action in June 1945. In the fighting around Ormoc Bay, the United States lost three destroyers, including the *Ward* and *Mahan* during the December 7 landings, and one high-speed transport, while the Imperial Navy lost six destroyers, including the experimental *Shimakaze*, twenty small transport vessels, and a host of smaller vessels. But, with the Imperial Navy and Army crushed on Leyte, General MacArthur's push toward Manila could begin. With the aid of their Filipino allies, US troops began the slow, arduous, and bloody task of rooting out the Imperial Army and retaking the Philippines.

It proved plodding work. The campaign for Mindoro and Marinduque, south of Milan in the west-central Philippines, began in December 1944 and only concluded the next summer, when Filipino guerillas began mopping-up activities on those two islands at the end of June. Mindoro airbases became critical in the liberation of the north. The campaign to liberate Luzon started in March 1945 and took some four months to complete. In April, US forces liberated Palawan and Zamboanga, in the southwestern Philippines. The campaign in the Southern Visayas started in February and ended in early summer. Mindanao, the largest island in the southern Philippines, wasn't safe until July. It proved relentless fighting against Imperial Army dead-enders, but it had to be done in order to slowly march northward for the undertaking of Operation Downfall, the invasion of Japan proper and the end of the war.

There was also hard work to be done in the South Seas. With the help of Australian and British allies, key areas in Borneo, once critical geography in Japan's oil independence, took well into the summer of 1945 to liberate: Tarakan in June, Brunei Bay in early July, and Balikpapan in late July. Far to the northeast of the Philippines, the bloody fighting on Iwo Jima, in the southern Ogasawara Islands, had finally concluded on March 16. Strand by strand, Japan's dreams of autarchy came unraveled. Piece by piece, the empire a half-century in the making crumbled. The miracle of modern Japan had turned into a feverish nightmare. And these pieces of the Greater East Asian Co-Prosperity Sphere weren't tumbling like dominos, either. They yielded slowly and painfully, like decayed teeth. They died a little bit at a time with every drowned or mutilated soldier, no matter the flag they carried. Now, the war was measured less in days and hours than in charred landscapes and bloated, sunbaked bodies.

As *Yukikaze* and the tattered remnants of the Combined Fleet entered Japanese waters in November 1944, in their wake lay what quickly became the ruins of Japan's oceanic empire. Nothing remained now, only death and destruction. Native populations once promised liberation from Western empires now hunted down their former Japanese masters and brutally killed them. Allied prisoners rotted and died in abandoned POW camps. In late 1944, flamethrowers became the weapon of choice for burning out Imperial Army soldiers holed up in fortified caves. The Pacific reeked of napalm and cooked flesh.

But *Yukikaze* continued to fight in the midst of this stench and ruin. In the spring of 1945, however, she fought not for tactical advantages. She searched no more for the gallant decisive battle with the US Navy, one precipitated by the hoisting of the Imperial Navy's legendary Z flag. Really, she didn't even fight for the Emperor and the Imperial State anymore. Now, she and her remaining warships, including the battleship *Yamato*, sought the elusive *Hagakure*-style nobility that could be found only in death. They sought the silence of the sea. They sought forgiveness from history. The Imperial Navy's complete destruction required a crescendo worthy of the desperate war it had fought tirelessly for over three years. But what would World War II's crescendo on the Pacific look like?

Japanese history is replete with crescendos – dramatic endings that place an exclamation point on historical closure. They punctuate the rhythms of Japanese history, marking openings and closings. Whenever there is a major paradigmatic shift, the episodic change from the classical to the medieval periods, for example, a stunning act often punctuates the moment in telling, often bloody fashion. It washes away what had been before, like holy water does blood from a sacrificial altar. But it's not just that the event is dramatic, often moving and sad; it's also pregnant with meaning, highly emblematic, and analytically useful when understanding change across time. The event says something; it speaks of its age. Students of Japanese history know these crescendos well.

In the twelfth century, for example, in the waning days of the Genpei War and the epic struggle between the Taira and the Minamoto families, the decisive Battle of Dan-no-Ura occurred in April 1185. Largely a naval battle fought in Shimonoseki Strait, the Minamoto family emerged victorious. The leading general of the Taira family, Taira no Tomomori, reported the results to his mother, Taira no Tokiko, the widow of supreme patriarch Taira no Kiyomori and now known by her Buddhist title, the Lady Nii. She was also the grandmother of the child Emperor, Antoku.

As Tomomori approached the imperial barge, its banners fluttering and flags snapping in the wind, he said "As far as I can see, we are finished."[14] Hearing this, the Lady Nii, adorning herself in Buddhist garb and imperial regalia, picked up the child Emperor. "I may be a woman," she said, "but I will not let the enemy take me." She then stepped up onto the gunwales of the barge. "Where are you taking me, Grandmother?," asked young Emperor Antoku. Looking into the Inland Sea, she said "Down there, far beneath the waves, another capital awaits us." With Antoku in her arms, the Lady Nii "plunged into the fathomless deep" and the Kamakura period began.

With Emperor Antoku's death, Japan began centuries of samurai rule, starting in the coastal city of Kamakura, where the Minamoto family established the first *bakufu*, or shogun's government. With the advent of samurai rule, Japan lurched into the medieval period and its Zen-inspired, aesthetic renaissance of Noh drama, tea ceremonies, black-ink painting, and sculpture. Feudalism replaced imperial rule from the capital, and samurai replaced aristocrats as the masters of the land. But endemic civil war erupted in Japan after a fourteenth-century succession struggle in the imperial family. It occurred when Emperor Go-Daigo sought to create a new, reenergized era of imperial rule in 1333. In response, powerful samurai families, most prominently the Hōjō, who had replaced the Minamoto in the capital of Kamakura, arrested Go-Daigo and actively patronized a more compliant member of the imperial household, the Emperor Kōgon. The samurai in Kamakura promptly exiled Go-Daigo.

But Go-Daigo wasn't finished making trouble. With the help of a loyalist samurai by the name of Kusunoki Masashige, Go-Daigo escaped exile, entered Kyoto triumphantly, and started the Kenmu regime in 1333. But, after only three years of Go-Daigo's rule, the disgruntled Ashikaga Takauji rebelled. Famously, Kusunoki Masashige loyally came to the Emperor's side. On a hot summer day in 1336, at the Battle of Minato River, the armies of Kusunoki Masashige and Ashikaga Takauji met to decide the fate of the realm. Takauji had twice the troops on the field that day, and by the evening Masashige, defeated and wounded, fled with his younger brother, Masasue, to a nearby farmhouse. The words spoken by the siblings before they committed *seppuku*, or ritual suicide, remain among the most famous in Japan's imperial loyalist tradition.

Masashige asked his brother what his last wish might be. "I should like to be reborn seven times into this world of men,"[15] replied Masasue, laughing loudly, "so that I might destroy the enemies of the court." Masashige agreed and then explained that he, too, would like to be reborn again and again, so that he might kill the Emperor's enemies. The two brothers then disemboweled themselves, mustered the strength to stab each other with their swords and, in a celebrated scene, laid their heads "on the same pillow." Masashige's defense of Emperor Go-Daigo, against a numerically superior foe, became the stuff of legends in Japan during World War II. Kamikaze pilots worshipped Masashige, and his crest became the namesake and emblem of the "Floating Chrysanthemum Operation" to defend Okinawa in April 1945.

Indeed, prior to the Okinawa operation, sailors drew Kusunoki's floating chrysanthemum crest on the first exhaust funnel of several of the participating destroyers. Hydrophone Operator Noma remembered that in one instance they even wrote the characters *hi-ri-hō-ken-ten*, a supposed motto of Kusunoki's that emphasized the "superiority of impe-rial authority over any law," but he couldn't remember exactly on which destroyer, thinking it might have been *Isokaze.* "So, with a white pen, we drew Kusunoki Masashige's chrysanthemum mark on the ship's funnel. Because we had done so, no one thought we were returning from the operation. Neither did I."[16] There are some accounts that explain that Captain Terauchi wouldn't allow Kusunoki's mark to be drawn on his vessel's funnel, barking "We'll proceed as we always do." These accounts also insist that Captain Terauchi prohibited sailors from sending any last letters, hair, or finger nails to their family members. But Torpedo Specialist Nishizaki Nobuo clearly recalled being told when the last mail came. He also remembered being ordered to write his death note.

Then, after centuries, as the medieval period shuttered to a close, the first great unifier, Oda Nobunaga, after one of his lieutenants betrayed him, committed ritual suicide as fires raged around him in the Honnōji Temple to avoid the shame of capture. Nobunaga was a clever but exces-sively cruel man, and his successors, though perfectly capable of acts of brutality when necessary, focused more on diplomacy in their efforts to unify the realm in the aftermath of centuries of civil war precipitated by Go-Daigo's defeat. With Nobunaga's death the medieval period died, too, and the pages of history, once again, turned as the Tokugawa shoguns came to power and Japan entered the early modern period. With early modernity, Japan's cities and urban populations blossomed with the commercialization of the economy, nowhere more so than the Yoshiwara pleasure district in Edo (now Tokyo). The aesthetics of the *ukiyō,* or the "floating world," dominated literature and woodblock print-making and, although despotic, Japan enjoyed unparalleled peace and stability under Tokugawa rule.

But the political rigidity of Tokugawa rule couldn't survive the fluidity of the economic and social changes sweeping the country, nor did the shoguns have an answer to the arrival of Commodore Matthew C. Perry in the battleship *Missouri* in 1853. He had come to "open Japan," but his arrival set in motion the eventual fall of the Tokugawa shoguns in 1868. In their place, an Imperial Restoration under the Meiji Emperor occurred, ushering in a revolution in Japanese life. Suddenly, *bunmei kaika,* or "civilization and enlightenment," became the slogan of the day, and Japanese men, donning formal jackets and top hats, began to taste the delights of Western civilization.

The Meiji government even abolished previous social castes – such as samurai status, replacing hereditary military privilege with a conscript army – precipitating a violent reaction by more conservative elements, namely Saigō Takamori, a leading figure in the overthrow of the Tokugawa shoguns. The lavish lives of Meiji oligarchs chafed against his plain clothing, simple foods, and "revere heaven, love mankind"[17] philosophical slogan. "Civilization is the upholding of justice; it has nothing to do with outward grandeur, palatial magnificence or gorgeous clothing or general ostentation of superficial appearances," he said. This led to the Satsuma Rebellion against the fledgling Meiji government in 1877 and Saigō's eventual ritual suicide, once the Meiji conscript army had defeated his band of disgruntled samurai. His final poem read as follows:

> Having fought in the Emperor's cause,
> What joy to die like the tinted leaves that fall in Tatsuta
> Before they have been spoiled by autumn rains.

When Saigō slid that sword into his belly and was decapitated, the last vestiges of Japan's feudal order died and, once again, the pages of history turned.

These are some pretty big *hakama* pants to fill, and the wispy, bespectacled General Tōjō Hideki, even though he was an architect of the war and tried to commit suicide after Japan's surrender, proved not up to the task in the eyes of history. He was a lamb, but a scrawny one of poor quality. Emperor Hirohito, though clearly sharing responsibility for the war, often stood on the margins and was pushed relentlessly by the aggrieved Imperial Army warmongers in the government. One historian described Hirohito as a "silent spider positioned at the center of a wide, multisided web,"[18] pushing the Imperial State toward total war. Surely, he could have done more to stop the slide toward war, particularly in negotiations with the United States, but a spider he was not, more like a ladybug, and he would not do either for history's thirst for tragic sacrifice.

No, as fighting in the Pacific ground to a close, something bigger was required. This point is important: the heads of Japan's war planners swam in this history of epochal sacrifice. It weighed down their decision-making. It clouded their rationalism. They knew these tragic heroes intimately. How does an admiral make tactical and strategic decisions with these historical giants screaming in his ears? The wartime epoch's sacrificial altar needed the blood of something with true grandeur, something spectacularly emblematic of Japan's entire post-Meiji modern experience – industrialization, empire, and war for autonomy and respect from the Great Powers. Really, in the Pacific, only one thing proved grand enough to play the role of Taira no Tokiko, Kusunoki Masashige, and Saigō Takamori in order to turn the page of history, and it wasn't a person at all – it was the largest battleship ever constructed, the very one named after the Land of the Gods. History required a new tragic hero, the unsinkable, unconquerable, indomitable, super-dreadnought-class *Yamato* at its altar.

One of the last poems attributed to the semi-mythical Prince Yamato Takeru reads as follows:

> Ah, Yamato, fairest of all lands,
> Girt with mountains like a many-layered hedge of green!
> How dear to me is the beauty of Yamato![19]

In the spring of 1945, the battleship *Yamato* would step in as sacrificial proxy for the divine land, its cherished namesake, and be slaughtered.

CHAPTER 11

Yamato and the Specter of History

A kamikaze spirit permeated the entire navy.
Admiral Kusaka Ryūnosuke, Chief of Staff of the Combined Fleet

B Y THE TIME US forces began landing on the beaches of Okinawa
on April 1, 1945, the Imperial Navy's proud warships mostly rested
on the bottom of the ocean. Of the big battlewagons, only *Haruna* and
Yamato were operational, and an escort of a light cruiser and a handful
of destroyers guarded the latter. *Yukikaze* was one of these escort ships.

While General MacArthur trudged up the Philippines in a grueling
fight for every inch of reclaimed territory, US war planners launched
Operation Iceberg, the invasion of Okinawa. It was the final stage before
the invasion of Japan proper. In response to Iceberg, five days after US
troops started coming ashore on Okinawa, Imperial Navy Headquarters
launched the Floating Chrysanthemum air attacks. Kamikazes constituted the bulk of these planes and they, of course, were never meant
to return home. Japanese planners threw all their airpower at Okinawa,
and spared nothing for *Yamato*'s combat air patrol, her escort, and their
run to Okinawa. But, for *Yamato*, success never meant returning home,
anyway. The big battleship, too, was slated a Floating Chrysanthemum:
an ephemeral blossom, a springtime manifestation of brilliance, one
ready to be whisked away forever by the currents of history.

Two of *Yukikaze*'s sailors, Nishizaki Nobuo and Noma Mitsue, provide us with first-hand accounts of Operation "Heaven One," *Yamato*'s
final mission. Interestingly, the officers and crew aboard *Yukikaze* and
several of the other escort warships viewed *Yamato*'s suicide run as not

a kamikaze raid at all, because kamikaze tactics typically had a strategy behind them. Though a grisly tactic for sure, kamikazes were essentially smart bombs or guided missiles, not guided electronically, of course, but by the hands of pilots. They slammed their planes into US ships to deter the landings at Leyte or Okinawa. There was a strategic goal with kamikaze tactics – halt or slow US landings, and bloody the Americans' nose to make them think twice about invading Japan. That's what makes kamikaze so horrifying: they were horrifyingly purposeful.

Yamato's Floating Chrysanthemum mission had a different air about it. Controversy surrounded the Heaven One operation from the outset. The captain of the cruiser *Yahagi* begged to be allowed to menace US supply lines, rather than needlessly (as he saw it) sacrifice his warship along with *Yamato*. At least menacing supply lines had strategic value, he reasoned. Exasperated by *Yamato*'s fate, Captain Hara exclaimed during the pre-operation meeting that "The realistic thing for us to do is to attack the enemy's overextended supply lines."[1] But Imperial Navy brass wasn't answering to realism; they answered instead to ghosts, ever-present watchers like Tōgō Heihachirō and Yamamoto Gonnohyōe, founders of the Imperial Navy. They listened to such martial heroes as Kusunoki Masashige, symbols of imperial loyalty. They knew what they were to do. They focused on the historical legacy they hoped to leave behind in the wake of a lost world war.

The time for tactics and strategies ended at the Battle of the Philippine Sea. It was time to bring the lamb of history *Yamato* to the altar and pay homage to the martial heroes of Japan's past.

* * *

By the time of the US landings in the Kerama Islands, west of Okinawa, on March 26, 1945, the Imperial Navy was out of oil, out of warships, and basically out of the fight. Japan had under a dozen fighting ships left. Of the once-proud battleships, only *Yamato* still worked. *Musashi* sank in the Sibuyan Sea on October 24, 1944, on her way to Leyte Gulf. *Nagato* was largely derelict after Leyte, and an internal explosion had sunk her sister ship, *Mutsu*, on June 8, 1943. Of the *Kongō*-class quadruplets, only *Haruna* still floated, and even then only until US planes sank her at her moorings on July 28, 1945. The US Navy sank both *Fusō* and *Yamashiro* at the Battle of Surigao Strait on October 25, 1944.

Left from among the plucky cruisers was the *Agano*-class *Yahagi*, and eight destroyers supported her, including three *Kagerō*-class vessels, *Yukikaze, Isokaze,* and *Hamakaze*. The US Navy had sunk all the fast aircraft carriers that had participated in the Pearl Harbor raid, as well as the next-generation flattops, *Taihō* and *Shinano*. The two newly built *Unryū*-class carriers, *Katsuragi* and *Amagi*, never embarked aircraft and never left Japanese waters. Without meaningful air support, the ten functional warships couldn't hope to stem the rising Allied tide in the Western Pacific, but they could be sacrificed on the altar of history. Admiral Kurita had asked, before the Leyte Gulf operation, "Would it not be a shame to have the fleet remain intact while our nation perishes?" But the nation's woes had only just begun when Admiral Kurita asked that question. That was before Operation Meetinghouse and the burning down of Tokyo, for example. Never was Admiral Kurita's question more apropos than on April 1, 1945, when the US invasion of Okinawa began.

Newly renamed the Second Fleet, the surviving Imperial Navy warships would be put forward as part of what war planners called *kikusui sakusen*, or the "Floating Chrysanthemum Operation," named after the chrysanthemum crest of Kusunoki Masashige, the loyalist samurai hero of the fourteenth century. The operation included hundreds of kamikaze planes organized into ten waves, designed to target US warships off the coast of Okinawa. That spring, the global context was ripe for history making. By April 1945, the Red Army stood at Berlin's doorstep and the United States was knocking loudly at Japan's, and the bloodletting known as World War II, the hungry meat grinder of industrial modernity, had entered its final and most frenzied stage.

The four principal US commanders who oversaw Operation Iceberg, the invasion of Okinawa, were Admiral Raymond Spruance (Fifth Fleet), Vice Admiral Marc Mitscher (Task Force 58, the fast carrier force), Vice Admiral Richmond Turner (Task Force 51, the amphibious Joint Expeditionary Force), and, overseeing land operations, General Simon Bolivar Buckner (Tenth Army). Okinawa, much like the Gilberts, Marshalls, Marianas, and Iwo Jima was a Central Pacific affair, and the command structure reflected that fact. It hardly mattered in April 1945 anyway because the Philippines continued to keep General MacArthur and the Seventh Fleet plenty occupied to the south. Japanese military planners sought to make the Americans pay dearly for every inch of reclaimed territory, and they adhered to that grisly strategy until the bitter end.

The US armada that descended on Okinawa was nothing short of astonishing. The number of Admiral Turner's ships involved with the amphibious phase alone numbered 1,213, representing 45 different classes and categories. That's not counting Admiral Mitscher's additional eighty-eight warships and the twenty-two contributed by the British Royal Navy. This armada, after landings in the Kerama Islands and undertaking minesweeping operations in late March, delivered 2,380 US Navy assault troops, 81,165 US Marines, and 98,567 US Army soldiers to southwestern Okinawa, on the beaches north of the capital of Naha.

Among the Marines who landed on the beaches of Okinawa that Easter Sunday, April 1, 1945, was Eugene Sledge. Many US Marines slated for Operation Iceberg, including Sledge, had, only months before, come from the battlefields of Peleliu Island, which had witnessed some of the most savage fighting of the Pacific campaign. Fought between September 15 and November 27, 1944, the Battle of Peleliu, in the Palau Chain and therefore part of the broader Mariana effort, had taught Sledge and other Marines that the fighting in the Pacific was otherworldly in its cruelty. Sledge wrote that Pacific fighting was "not the dispassionate killing seen on other fronts or in other wars."[2] He mused, "This was a brutish, primitive hatred, as characteristic of the horror of war in the Pacific as the palm trees and the islands." The ferocity of the killing became as exotic as the South Pacific landscape itself.

Amphibious landings could be particularly terrifying. On September 15, Sledge recalled, the beaches of Peleliu became a "nightmare of flashes, violent explosions, and snapping bullets."[3] He wrote that "Most of what I saw blurred. My mind was benumbed by the shock of it." He became terrified of artillery shells in particular, what he called the "invention of hell." On the battlefield, he wrote, "Fear is many faceted and has many subtle nuances, but the terror and desperation endured under heavy shelling are by far the most unbearable."[4] But there would be plenty of shelling between the two bitter enemies, and plenty of acts of unthinkable violence.

At one point, Sledge watched as a fellow Marine extracted gold teeth from a Japanese soldier who was still alive. "He put the point of his kabar [the KA-BAR is a seven-inch combat knife issued by the US Marine Corps] on the base of a tooth and hit the handle with the palm of his hand. Because the Japanese was kicking his feet and thrashing about, the knife point glanced off the tooth and sank deeply into the victim's mouth."[5] Determined to get the tooth, the "Marine cursed him and with a slash cut his cheeks open to each ear. He put his foot on the sufferer's lower jaw and tried again. Blood poured out of the soldier's mouth. He made a gurgling noise and thrashed wildly." Finally, Sledge shouted "Put the man out of his misery," which, thankfully, somebody did with a bullet to the head. Both sides perpetrated such acts of gratuitous cruelty as the fighting in the Pacific approached the Japanese homeland.

Japanese aren't ruthless killers by nature, and neither are Americans. And yet, surrounded by palm trees under the burning tropical sun, they killed each other with unspeakable ferocity. It felt pent up. Relentless government campaigns on both sides to dehumanize the Pacific enemy had paid off in spades – Japanese gladly killed the blood-sucking "American demons," while the Americans eagerly eradicated "Louseous Japanicus," an insect infestation for which "flame throwers, mortars, grenades and bayonets have proven to be an effective remedy."[6] Peleliu reified this dehumanization, amplified it, and taught Sledge that "Time had no meaning; life had no meaning. The fierce struggle for survival in the abyss of Peleliu eroded the veneer of civilization and made savages of us all. We existed in an environment totally incomprehensible to men behind the lines – service troops and civilians."[7] But he hadn't seen Okinawa yet.

Sledge departed Peleliu on October 30 aboard the merchant troop ship *Sea Runner*. As he climbed the cargo netting onto the ship, he thought, "at least I was crawling up out of the abyss of Peleliu!"[8] Nearly 1,400 US troops died taking Peleliu, just under 8,000 more were injured, and nearly all the 11,000 Imperial Army soldiers stationed there died trying to hold the outcropping of coral. Next, Sledge and the other Marines traveled to Pavuvu, in the Solomon Islands, to prepare for Okinawa.

But the respite was short-lived. On March 21, aboard the *McCracken*, a *Haskell*-class attack transport, Sledge anchored at the Ulithi Atoll, on the western edge of Caroline Islands, formerly one of *Yukikaze*'s haunts. The sprawling lagoon provided nearly enough room to stage the colossal number of men and vessels required for the Operation Iceberg. "We lined the rails of our transport and looked out over the vast fleet in amazement,"[9] wrote Sledge. "We saw ships of every description: huge new battleships, cruisers, sleek destroyers, and a host of fast escort craft. Aircraft carriers were there in greater numbers than any of us had ever seen before." But no kelp grew on the bottoms of the "biggest invasion fleet ever assembled in the Pacific" because they didn't stay long at Ulithi. The *McCracken* and other vessels weighed anchor six days later and made their way to the landing beaches of Okinawa.

Though anticipating a brawl like that at Peleliu, where the Japanese opposition proved stiff, the landings on Okinawa were completely different. Sledge wrote of the April 1 landing operation that "Images of the maelstrom at Peleliu had been flashing through my mind, but on Okinawa there was practically no opposition to the landing."[10] Though delightfully surprised, Sledge suspected that "it wasn't at all like the Japanese to let us walk ashore unopposed on an island only 350 miles from their homeland." He knew his enemy well. Something was coming.

In fact, Imperial General Headquarters had shifted tactics on opposing large amphibious landings, and General Ushijima Mitsuru, in command of the Thirty-Second Army on Okinawa, used a new playbook. Rather than attempt to "annihilate"[11] the enemy on the beachhead, as had occurred on such islands as Tarawa, Saipan, and Peleliu, the Imperial Army allowed the United States to "land in full" and then be "lured into a position where he cannot receive cover and support from the naval and aerial bombardment." The enemy forces could then be "wiped out." The Imperial Army would fight for Okinawa, but the first show of Japanese force came from the sky.

Admiral Ugaki Mitome, referring to the opening of Operation Floating Chrysanthemum, wrote on April 6 that "We carried out night attacks against the enemy around Okinawa and an extensive search in the morning."[12] By the end of the operations, "We didn't know the result of our attack except the reports of 'I am crashing onto a carrier,' but, judging from the enemy telephones in hurried confusion and requests for help, it was almost certain that we destroyed four carriers." If the naval battles in the Pacific taught one thing, it should have been that a pilot's determination of "almost certain," particularly with regard to

Figure 11.1 Scene on *Bunker Hill*'s flight deck, looking aft, while her crew fought fires caused by kamikaze hits, off Okinawa on May 11, 1945. Official US Navy Photograph, National Archives, Catalog #: 80-G-323712.

sinking carriers and battleships, was hardly ever certain. Regardless, the Floating Chrysanthemum planes came in ten massive waves in an attempt to halt the US landings. In all, nearly 700 Japanese aircraft participated in opposing Operation Iceberg that day, and about 355 of those were kamikaze planes (see Figure 11.1).

The day of the April 6 Floating Chrysanthemum attacks, Ugaki noted that a fresh Force 5 or 6 northeasterly wind brushed whitecaps on the waters near Okinawa, complicating the missions. (Force 5–6 winds are approximately 17–27 knots, with accompanying waves ranging in height from 4 to 13 feet.) He wrote that "Visibility on the sea wasn't good, clouds fully covering the sky. But there was no waste of our attacks, as those who couldn't find enemies carried out special attacks around Okinawa," dropping bombs on men like Sledge. As a result of the ten waves of attacks, wrote Ugaki, the "sea around Okinawa … turned into a scene of carnage, and a reconnaissance plane reported that as many as 150 columns of black smoke were observed."

Ugaki's kamikaze forces had indeed created some carnage on the water that day, sinking three destroyers, two ammunition ships, and one LST (Landing Ship, Tank) – and burning, dismembering, and killing sailors aboard those vessels – but nothing like he had originally hoped. Mainly, destroyers involved with the radar picket around the landing beaches received the brunt of the waves of kamikaze attacks because they made first contact and engaged the enemy with antiaircraft fire. Destroyers such as *Bush* and *Colhoun* survived wave upon wave of suicide attacks before eventually succumbing. Five kamikaze planes reportedly smashed into the destroyer *Emmons* before she went down. The ammunition ships *Logan-V* and *Hobbs-V* also sank that day, as did *LST-447*. Surely, the black columns of smoke that so impressed Japanese reconnaissance planes billowed from the dozen or so other warships damaged and nearly sunk that day. But the "scene of carnage" unleashed by Japan's youthful suicide pilots did nothing to stem the Allied invasion, so it would be left to *Yamato* to make her last stand.

* * *

Operation Ten-Gō, or "Heaven One," complemented Operation Floating Chrysanthemum. Indeed, as zealous kamikaze pilots ended their tragically short lives in the waters around Okinawa, *Yamato* and the rest of the Second Fleet got under way. Her orders from Imperial Navy Headquarters read simply "On April 8 at dawn, the Second Fleet should charge into the enemy anchorage off the coast of Kadena on Okinawa Island. Fuel will be enough for one-way only. Know that this is a Special Assault Operation."[13] It couldn't be anything else. The last warships of the Imperial Japanese Navy were to make their way toward the Kadena Anchorage off Okinawa and, once there, *Yamato* was to either fight to the death and sink or be beached and used as an artillery placement. The April 8 date corresponded to a general assault planned by Japan's Thirty-Second Army on Okinawa that had up to this point hidden in the north and south, away from the landing beaches. The Imperial Navy's dramatic crescendo was near. It was also the Buddha's birthday.

The night before they set sail, April 5, aboard *Yukikaze*, Torpedo Specialist Nishizaki remembered that the officers had opened the canteen, where sailors drank their fill of saké and relished a variety of

delicious sweets. Typically, the ship's canteen sold all kinds of daily neces-
sities, such as towels, tissue, and toothbrushes, at a low price, but on this
night, the saké flowed freely. He remembered that, no matter the department – engineering, boiler, electrical, or torpedo – all the men sat in a
circle together, enjoying the libations on the eve of their certain deaths.

When Nishizaki entered, an officer shouted "Hey, sailor, sing a verse
from 'Lodge by the Lakeside.'"[14] Nishizaki enthusiastically joined the
party and began belting out the melancholy lines from the 1940 hit by
the fetching Takamine Mieko. The next thing Nishizaki knew, he was
being offered drinks both by the Torpedo Chief and by the Engineering
Chief. But Nishizaki was still young and couldn't hold his alcohol very
well, and had to retreat above deck for fresh air.

The next day, April 6, the Second Fleet relocated from the Mitajiri
Offing to the Tokuyama Offing and, while there, regrouped. At 08:00,
Nishizaki recalled a ship-wide announcement aboard *Yukikaze*. "The
last mail departs this vessel today at 10:00. Pass any mail to your group
leader." Then another announcement: "Also, now is a good time to write
your death note." Nishizaki debated writing one for his mother, but, in
the end, he wrote nothing.

Similar soul searching occurred aboard *Yamato*. Ensign Yoshida
Mitsuru was a sailor aboard the battleship as it made its final preparations for Operation Ten-Gō. Yoshida had waited impatiently for
"*Kamikaze Yamato*" to set sail, training with the other sailors and, during
spare moments, thumbing through a biography of the Enlightenment
philosopher Baruch Spinoza to idle away the hours. The night before
the fateful mission, the officers and crew drank saké together, becoming "one in body and spirit."[15] He prepared to die with men he didn't
know, but, because they were together on *Yamato*, essentially their giant,
navy-gray tomb, they will "form a single corpse"[16] consecrated by the
ocean. Yoshida noted with irony that every single thing *Yamato* did at
this juncture, from refueling to setting sail, B-29s observed from overhead. He wrote "Are the American forces already intent on predicting
the hour of our sailing?" On April 6, at 16:00, the Second Fleet departed
the Tokuyama Offing, coordinating its departure between Operation
Floating Chrysanthemum and the Thirty-Second Army's assault planned
for April 8.

The situation was grim, but the Second Fleet was buoyed by one fact: the unsinkable destroyer *Yukikaze* would navigate alongside *Yamato*. Captain Hara, master of *Yahagi*, recalled a song that had once been popular in the forward bases of Truk and Rabaul, celebrating two unsinkable destroyers, one of them his former command. It hardly mattered that the US submarine *Blackfin* had holed that warship, *Shigure*, just over two months earlier in the Gulf of Siam. The verses went,

> Sasebo's *Shigure* and Kure's *Yukikaze*
> Immortal and indestructible destroyers!
> You fulfill the miracle dream of sailors,
> Two ships which always return from battle.[17]

As the warships got under way, Ensign Yoshida marveled at the Second Fleet. "The final task force sortie of the Japanese navy,"[18] he said. "Ten picked vessels – the best." They weren't actually picked, they had only survived so far, somehow, but the escorting warships impressed him, nonetheless. Fate had picked them, maybe. "Full of spirit and biting through the pure white crests of the waves: our escort ships," including *Yukikaze*, now sortieing to their death. "The arrow has been loosed," he wrote. The Second Fleet "pushed onward with a single purpose, defying the currents." It, too, felt like a force of nature.

Admiral Toyoda Soemu, Commander-in-Chief of the Combined Fleet, passed along his farewell address to the brave sailors. Echoing General Tōjō and others before him, he explained that the "fate of the empire hangs in the balance."[19] The Second Fleet would orchestrate an attack on the enemy off Okinawa, "unparalleled in its heroic bravery." He continued, "We have done this to exalt the glorious tradition of the surface forces of the Imperial Navy, gathering together the might of the Imperial Navy for this one battle, and to transmit its glory to posterity."

The last line is key, as it was to history that Admiral Toyoda spoke, not to the future of the young sailors about to sacrifice their lives in the name of the "glorious traditions" of the Imperial Navy and Japanese history. The Imperial Navy knew that the "enemy's military strength is colossal,"[20] but wouldn't be deterred. Indeed, the Second Fleet hadn't been under way for long before radar and radar-detecting devices aboard *Yamato* picked up US submarines. These were *Threadfin* and, a little while later, *Hackleback*.

Threadfin probably could have expedited *Yamato*'s glorious death. As the Second Fleet departed, the *Balao*-class submarine stealthily patrolled the approaches to the Bungo Channel. Captain John Joseph Foote, *Threadfin*'s commander, wrote that, on the evening of April 6, the submarine's radar distinguished four pips that became distinct from the multiple islands in the area. Two minutes later, "we had two large ships and at least four smaller ones on the PPI screen."[21] Captain Foote noted in his Action Report that "We were in a favorable attack position for either the large ships or the DD's." But *Threadfin* would let the Second Fleet slip by this time.

Apparently, even the US Navy understood the symbolic power of the occasion, and sinking *Yamato* with a torpedo delivered by a stealthy submarine just wouldn't do. "We had specific written orders to clear initial contact reports before attacking," explained Captain Foote. *Threadfin* reported the contact and could only watch as the Second Fleet sailed by. Captain Foote hoped for permission to engage the enemy warships, but it never came. "THREADFIN's chance for the Hall of Fame passed before the contact report was cleared," he wrote. The thirty-one-year-old submarine commander could only watch: "Enemy force formed up – two large ships in column with typical circular screen of six light vessels, circle spacing about two miles – approximate base course 140°(T), speed 25 knots." It was *Yamato* on her way to history's altar.

The Second Fleet hadn't been under way for long when *Asashimo*, a screening destroyer on the right of the formation, experienced engine trouble and dropped back for repairs. The next morning, on April 7 at 09:45, Yoshida began what would be *Yamato*'s last watch. "The clouds lower steadily; the ceiling: 1,000 meters. Wind velocity: over twenty knots. Sudden showers."[22] These conditions set the stage of *Yamato*'s death.

Just before noon, word came from Amami-Ōshima lookouts: "250 carrier-based enemy planes headed due north; keep close watch."[23] On *Yamato*'s bridge sat Admiral Itō Seiichi, the commanding officer of Operation Ten-Gō. After hearing the report of the enemy planes, he smiled and said only "We got through the morning alright, didn't we?" Yoshida remembered of Itō that "From now on, until the ship capsizes, he will sit, arms folded, like a rock amid the smoke of the guns and the rain of the bullets. All those around him will be killed or wounded, but he will move not at all."

Yamato measured over 863 feet in length. Her main battery of 9 460 millimeter (18.1-inch) guns shot a 3,200-pound (that's the weight of a 2022 Toyota Camry) shell well over 20 miles. She displaced over 72,000 tons fully laden. Her engines propelled the giant at over twenty-seven knots, and the steel plating protecting those big engines ranged between eight and sixteen inches thick. Her compliment of souls was 2,767. She was, in historian Morison's words, a "singularly beautiful ship."[24] For all her power and might, however, with no air cover, *Yamato* was a sitting duck. Morison pondered, "In view of what had happened to another naked fleet, Admiral Kurita's in the Battle for Leyte Gulf, it seems inexplicable that the now unified Japanese air command should have hurled all its available fighters against TF 58 and the amphibious forces 6 and 7 April, instead of covering these ships." It's inexplicable only if you believe that the Second Fleet performed anything other than a suicide mission.

Even Admiral Kurita, who had held out hope for "miracles" at Leyte Gulf, knew that the Imperial Navy was in the midst of a Banzai-charge frenzy, and said as much at the outset of the Leyte effort. Captain Hara, master of *Yahagi* during Operation Ten-Gō, recalled an officers' meeting on *Yahagi* before the Second Fleet set sail. Admiral Komura Keizō, commander of Desron2, of which *Yahagi* served as the flagship, briefed the assembled captains on the upcoming mission. He explained the Imperial Navy Headquarters orders and then added that "this is not even a kamikaze mission, for that implies the chance of chalking up a worthy target."[25] Rather, he explained, Ten-Gō was nothing short of a "genuine suicide sortie," plain and simple. Already – and particularly after her early withdrawal from Leyte Gulf – *Yamato*, the pride of the Combined Fleet, had gained a reputation as a "floating hotel for idle, inept admirals."[26] It was time to change her reputation and rewrite her epitaph.

In a later conversation among officers regarding the merits of Operation Ten-Gō, Admiral Itō, who commanded the operation, ended the discussion by saying "I think we are being given an appropriate chance to die."[27] As if reading from the *Hagakure* itself, he reminded the Imperial Navy officers that a "samurai lives so that he is always prepared to die." Admiral Kusaka Ryūnosuke, Chief of Staff of the Combined Fleet, said of the admiral that "Itō was prepared for certain death when he took command of the shrunken Second Fleet. Having been a deputy chief of staff for so long, he evidently felt acute responsibility for our continuous defeats. Few people retained common sense in those days. A kamikaze spirit permeated the entire navy." It's this "kamikaze spirit," or more accurately a suicide frenzy, that explains the inexplicable after the defeats suffered in the Mariana Islands. The Imperial Navy was committing collective *seppuku,* or ritual suicide, while the nation burned under the punishing visits of the B-29s.

On the morning of April 7, as the Second Fleet began to turn south toward Okinawa, US Navy commanders, fully apprised of *Yamato*'s heading, debated who should wield the sacrificial knife to slice her throat. Oh, at this moment, how the ancient Japanese bards hungered for Rear Admiral Morton Deyo to unleash the battleships *Tennessee, West Virginia, Maryland, New Mexico, Colorado,* and *Idaho* to fight *Yamato* on her own turf, in a classic engagement, her ensign snapping in the freshening breeze, her colossal guns blazing, just as her creators had intended. But, in the end, history had other points to make, and Admiral Mitscher snatched the knife, launching the first planes against the battleship late in the morning.

Task Groups 58.1 and 58.3 launched 280 planes that morning, with 53 of them failing to find the target. Task Group 58.4 launched an additional 106 planes, for a total of 333 aircraft descending on the sacrificial battlewagon. They found her, antiaircraft guns blazing with Type 3 antiaircraft rounds, thirty-two minutes after noon. In quick succession, *Yamato* received two bomb hits and one torpedo hit, and *Yahagi* drifted dead in the water after a torpedo holed her engine room. *Hamakaze* sank after repeated hits. Aboard *Yahagi,* Captain Hara, who had always questioned the wisdom of Heaven One, remembered that *Yahagi* "shuddered as a torpedo caught her portside, amidship just below the waterline ... *Yahagi* stumbled crazily for a few minutes and then shuddered to an abrupt and horrifying halt."[28] *Yahagi* was dead in the water twelve minutes into the engagement (see Figure 11.2).

As bombs rained down and torpedoes slammed into the last remnants of the Second Fleet that afternoon, Captain Hara remembered from the bridge of the sinking *Yahagi* that *Yamato* fought on bravely, and "Destroyers *Yukikaze* and *Fuyutsuki* flitted nimbly about in a valiant effort to protect the huge ship."[29] By 14:06, *Yahagi* was so low in the water

Figure 11.2 Japanese cruiser *Yahagi* under air attack during Operation Ten-Gō on April 7, 1945. Official US Navy Photograph, National Archives, Catalog #: 80-G-316084.

that "waves were lapping the deck of the command post where Admiral Komura and I now stood alone." They removed their shoes and jumped into the water. Over the course of the early afternoon, although aircraft from US Task Force 58 sank or rendered inoperable *Hamakaze, Yahagi, Isokaze, Asashimo,* and *Kasumi, Yukikaze,* still unscathed, continued to fight, her twenty-four antiaircraft guns red hot. Columns of water dyed an eerie black from gunpowder exploded skyward in every direction.

When the action started, Nishizaki had entered the torpedo room with Petty Officer Uchida Mokichi just as the US aircraft descended from the cloud cover. "The third and fifth waves were the most violent,"[30] recalled Nishizaki. Between aerial assaults, the torpedo men aboard *Yukikaze* prepared the torpedoes to be discharged overboard, so that enemy strafing didn't detonate them. When the planes came, Nishizaki heard bullets whizzing over his head and clanging against the metal ship. It was then that Nishizaki heard Uchida groan and collapse in front of him. "Sir!,"[31] Nishizaki shouted. He then felt a searing, burning pain in his left thigh, as if three burning prongs had been thrust into his leg. "I'm hit!," he shouted, and then collapsed. As Nishizaki lay on the floor of the torpedo room, he began to lose consciousness. Bullets from strafing aircraft had found their way through a ventilation window into the torpedo room. As he faded, he had a glimmer of his neighborhood barber back home who had lost a leg in an earthquake.

Soon, medics came to take Petty Officer Uchida away. As they carted him off in a stretcher, Nishizaki said "Hang in there!," but it was the last time he saw Uchida alive. "Uchida was a truly good soul,"[32] wrote Nishizaki, "and it's the nature of war that it would cut the life of such a good person short." Then, a group of sailors helped Nishizaki to the sick bay. He remembered that there was blood everywhere, soaking the deck. When he arrived, Nishizaki observed that there were already about ten sailors inside the small room. In agonizing pain and near death, some of the sailors called out for their wives and children; others called out for their mothers. But, as Nishizaki wrote, "not one of them called out *Tennō heika, banzai!* ["May His Majesty, the Emperor, live ten thousand years!"] A person on the brink of death doesn't call out for the Emperor, they call out for their family."[33]

In the sick bay, the medical staff was completely overwhelmed. Knowing that another wave of US planes was imminent, Nishizaki decided that he'd rather die in the torpedo department than in the packed sick bay, so he limped back toward his station. Thankfully, an officer named Maruyama, from the accounting department, with a temporary medic armband, showed up.

"Hey, Nishizaki, what's up?," he asked.

"I've been hit," Nishizaki responded.

Maruyama proceeded to cut open Nishizaki's combat trousers with a scalpel, and, with sanitized gauze and a pair of tweezers, began poking around in the hole in Nishizaki's leg, looking for bullet fragments. "The pain was unbearable," Nishizaki remembered.

"Hey, Maruyama, is it okay?,"[34] asked Nishizaki, gasping from the pain.

Maruyama looked up and said "the bones haven't been damaged but, because there are four bullet fragments lodged around the opening of the wound, I'm covering it with gauze." He then bandaged Nishizaki's leg.

But the pain continued to be unbearable. Nishizaki decided to remove the bandage and have a look. When he did, he saw bullet fragments in the wound, one of which protruded about one centimeter and, whenever it touched his pants, it chafed against a nerve and the pain proved unbearable.

When Maruyama came around again, Nishizaki, pointing to his leg, said "the pain is unbearable, take the remaining fragments out."

But Maruyama responded, "I've got too many patients. With something like this … you do it yourself." He took out from his first-aid kit forceps, tweezers, and several pieces of disinfected gauze. "Use these," he said. "Afterwards, if you don't change the gauze, it'll get infected," he warned. He then walked out the door. Taking deep breaths, Nishizaki, mustering all his strength and courage, began removing the bullet fragments from the gaping wound in his own thigh.

Meanwhile, Captain Terauchi's head was thrust out the conning tower of *Yukikaze*, his face coal black from the tainted seawater, with only the whites of his eyes shining through. Torpedo Chief Saitō Kazuyoshi implored Captain Terauchi, "Old friend, it'd be so unfortunate were you to die in battle today. Please, move so that enemy bullets don't hit you."[35] Captain Terauchi and Torpedo Chief Saitō were atop the conning tower, spotting bombs and torpedoes.

As Ensign Yoshida observed from *Yamato*, such destroyer tactics were hair-raising to watch: "The captain sits atop the forward conn and is responsible for the front half of the ship; the senior officer sits atop the aft deckhouse, responsible for the stern half."[36] Together, they "spot each torpedo and bomb coming toward them and, tracking them with the naked eye, take evasive action." It was low-tech, complicated business in the heat of battle, but somehow *Yukikaze* mostly dodged the bombs and torpedoes.

But *Yamato* took a beating. One bomb exploded in the antiaircraft radar compartment, utterly destroying it. Ensign Yoshida, inspecting the scene, wrote, "Just as I begin to think that everything must have been blown away, I notice a chunk of flesh smashed onto a panel of the broken bulkhead, a red barrel of flesh about as big around as two arms can reach ... It must be a torso from which all extremities – arms, legs, head – have been ripped off ... The smell of fat is heavy in the air."[37] Yoshida pondered, "How did they die, those beings who only a moment ago were so real?" Hitting US aircraft proved virtually impossible, given their velocity and the angle of attack. Trying to shoot down the US planes with the 25 millimeter guns was "like chasing after butterflies with our bare hands," he observed. And the US aircraft kept coming, wave upon wave. Whereas the Imperial Navy had no aircraft, the US Navy seemed to have an endless supply of them to throw at the ten hapless warships.

As *Yamato* began to list, Ensign Yoshida took solace in the escorting destroyers on both sides of the battleship. He wrote that "*Fuyutsuki* to starboard and *Yukikaze* to port, dashing along and breaking through curtains of water several times taller than they, signal to us in *Yamato*: 'Everything in order.'"[38] He continued, "Of the nine ships assigned to protect us, these two are the only ones doing their job ... The others are either lying on the bottom or listing from their wounds." But *Yamato*'s own list only grew worse, despite efforts to correct it. Yoshida wrote that "The horizon stands at right angles to the narrow lookout ports; chops my range of vision into two parts, black and white; presses in on me ... List: 80 degrees." Sailors began to abandon ship, including Yoshida. At 14:23, listing some 90°, *Yamato* exploded into a giant mushroom cloud when her magazines detonated. She remains the largest, most stunning battleship ever constructed (see Figure 11.3).

Before Heaven One had been launched, the assembled captains had agreed to "head to the Kadena offing to attack, no matter how many ships might be lost."[39] So, even after *Yamato*'s dramatic explosion, *Yukikaze* continued to charge south, cut from her tether to the floundering battleship. Sailors swam in the waters around the remaining destroyers, and Captain Terauchi, hell bent on taking the battle to Okinawa, said "Pick

Figure 11.3 *Yamato* maneuvers under attack as a bomb explodes off her port side during Operation Ten-Gô on April 7, 1945. L42-09.06.05 Courtesy of the Naval History & Heritage Command.

up only the strong sailors. Wounded sailors are to be left. Only people that can stand and fight on Okinawa are to be saved."[40] Nishizaki remembered other officers repeating these orders while they pulled men from the water. It was cruel thinking for cruel times, and *Yukikaze*'s master sought to continue southward. Even the commander of the destroyers, Captain Yoshida Masayoshi aboard *Fuyutsuki*, insisted that the remnants of the Second Fleet continue to Okinawa.

But then came new instructions from Imperial Navy Headquarters. They ordered the remaining warships to return. Now came the recognition that Heaven One was over, and the remaining destroyers began to pull exhausted sailors from *Yamato* and the other warships out of the water. "Make space on deck," ordered Captain Terauchi from the bridge. It's unknown how many sailors *Yukikaze* rescued, but her deck was pure black, "like ants covering sugar,"[41] piled with exhausted, defeated men, among them *Yamato*'s Executive Officer, Nomura Jirō.

Nishizaki remembered the rescue operation well. "Close off the port beam,"[42] he recalled, "heads that looked like melons floated between the waves. Their breathing sounded like a traditional sea whistle." Nishizaki explained that, while rescuing sailors in the water, the propellers of the destroyer needed to be stopped, so the ship often drifted abeam into the breaking waves. Without helm control, the vessel rolled badly.

"During this," explained Nishizaki, "sailors put on cotton gloves, non-slip shoes tied tightly, and grabbed a piece of four-meter line. One by one, sailors were brought aboard in this manner," he remembered. "We also used a bamboo pole and a life ring to rescue sailors in the water. They climbed up the side of the ship using a rope ladder. In the end, it was up to them … they had to want to live." With the vessel stopped, these were hellish conditions to work in. It was Nishizaki's first experience rescuing sailors from oil-covered water. Of the rescued, only their eyes and teeth were white. Once on board, their clothes were cut off and thrown in the water. They were given eye drops, and many vomited up oil. The rescued sailors were brought to the washroom, where steam was used to remove the oil.

While rescuing sailors, Nishizaki had a sailor grab his line, but the young man struggled to hang on. Looking closer, Nishizaki noticed that the sailor had lost his right arm and so tried to save himself using only his left. Nishizaki then noticed that a large noncommissioned officer had grabbed onto the one-armed sailor's legs. As hard as he tried, Nishizaki could not haul both men in.

"Let go! Let go!,"[43] he shouted to the noncommissioned officer. But he wouldn't.

Quickly, Nishizaki grabbed a nearby gaff and struck the noncommissioned officer's arm as hard as he could, and the man disappeared into the waves. "I ended up saving only the one-armed young sailor," wrote Nishizaki. Not long afterwards, a corpse with a white shirt like the one worn by the noncommissioned officer floated to the surface of the ocean. Horrified, Nishizaki thought it might be the corpse of the man. "It's been seventy-four years," wrote Nishizaki in his memoir, "and not one day has gone by on which I haven't thought of that episode."

Yukikaze was also tasked with scuttling the badly damaged *Isokaze*, her sister ship, after rescuing her sailors. In order that the *Kagerō*-class destroyer not fall into enemy hands, *Isokaze*'s master, Captain Shintani Kiichi, ordered that the vessel be sunk. "From *Yukikaze*'s Number 1 torpedo launcher we fired a torpedo, but it failed to find its target. The second time we used the guns and sank her," wrote Nishizaki. It was one of the hardest things he had to do.

Meanwhile, Captain Hara of *Yahagi* had resigned himself to death while floating in the ocean. "After all," he wrote, "a samurai lives so that he is always prepared to die. I could wait quietly for death, without regret or remorse."[44] He fell asleep, his head resting on a drifting log. He woke to the sound of a cutter from one of the destroyers. "Suddenly, I was terrified," he wrote. "I wanted desperately to live." Finally, Hara untied himself from the log and started splashing, which caught the attention of the cutter. When the boat approached, Hara realized that "I was too weak even to grab the side of boat, but four strong hands quickly hauled me in." Eventually, the cutter brought Hara to the destroyer *Hatsushimo*, where Captain Masazō Sakō greeted him. *Hatsushimo*'s crew had successfully rescued Admiral Komura as well, and he rested comfortably in the captain's cabin. The three other remaining destroyers, *Yukikaze*, *Fuyutsuki*, and *Suzutsuki*, had already left for Sasebo. Captain Masazō briefed Hara on the condition of the warships, adding that "*Yukikaze* is not badly damaged, but she lost three men killed by strafing."[45] Operation Ten-Gō was officially over, but the ground fighting on Okinawa was just getting started.

* * *

The fighting on Okinawa didn't subside until the end of June, when General Ushijima Mitsuru and his Chief of Staff, General Chō Isamu, committed suicide. The United States lost over 12,000 men on Okinawa, while the Japanese lost somewhere in the neighborhood of 110,000, which included conscripted Okinawans, many of them children. Under pressure of the Imperial Army, scores of Okinawans, who had little affection for their Japanese conquerors, committed group suicide, many mothers leaping from cliffs with their children. Not unlike *Yamato*, they became *gyokusai*, or "shattered jewels," with hand grenades that Japanese soldiers had distributed in advance. Okinawa was the last stand of the Imperial Navy's frenzied, suicidal death.

Basically, the war was over, but not for *Yukikaze*.

CHAPTER 12

Surrender and the Enduring Dangers
of *Yukikaze*'s Haunt

The war situation has developed not necessarily to Japan's advantage.

Emperor Hirohito in his surrender message of August 15, 1945

AFTER *YAMATO* SANK, the surviving destroyers limped back to Sasebo. Eventually, Imperial Navy Headquarters ordered *Yukikaze* and her fellow survivor, *Hatsushimo*, to Maizuru Harbor, on the Japan Sea coast, where they spent the remaining months of the war evading heavily mined waters and repeated bombing raids by Allied planes. *Yukikaze* did so successfully, while *Hatsushimo* did not. After hitting a mine, she was beached.

Near Maizuru, the officers and crew of *Yukikaze* eventually hid the unsinkable destroyer under camouflaging of tree limbs and netting, and repeatedly ventured to shore, like ragged castaways, looking for provisions, only to be rebuked by exhausted and angry villagers. They wanted nothing to do with the war or the Imperial Navy. Nobody did, particularly after Japan surrendered on August 15, 1945. After the defeat, association with Japan's war machine in any way was now toxic, a fact that colored the manner in which historians have engaged, or, more often than not, simply not engaged, with the military dimension of Japan's wartime experience.

The days after the surrender were confusing. Rumors swirled over what would happen to the young men aboard *Yukikaze*, one of the few Imperial Navy survivors. Some said that the unsinkable destroyer would be exhibited in America, a miraculous survivor, an oddity of the war, while others claimed that everybody aboard would be castrated. Importantly, in the immediate wake of the surrender, after being ordered to do so, Torpedo Specialist Nishizaki collected all the documents, orders, and records from *Yukikaze* and burned them in the forest – erasing her official history forever. He regretted it for the rest of his life. He viewed it as a betrayal of his fellow sailors, and of the destroyer herself.

But *Yukikaze* still had work to do, even after 1945. Next, engineers removed her guns and torpedo tubes, and the unsinkable destroyer became a troop transport, repatriating defeated Japanese soldiers from around the Asia–Pacific region – thousands of them. Her sailors wanted to go home; it had been a long war, but *Yukikaze*'s war wasn't over yet. In fact, it proved far from over, because, after completing her troop repatriation duties, the Allies designated her a "Vessel in Special Custody" and she became war reparations to China. In this sense, *Yukikaze* became not a lamb on the altar of history, as tragic *Yamato* had been, but rather a lamb on the altar of postwar diplomacy and looming Cold War politics. Once in Shanghai, she saw limited action in China's Civil War, and was eventually evacuated to Taiwan after the establishment of the People's Republic of China on the mainland. Once in Taiwan, she saw far more action in the Republic of China's navy for decades, protecting the Taiwan Strait from the threat of communist incursions. The People's Republic always viewed Taiwan's Republic of China as a renegade "bandit clique," one that would eventually be reincorporated with the mainland.

Even if you don't count her enduring cultural legacies in literature, gaming, film, and Japan's Maritime Self-Defense Force, *Yukikaze*'s war was a long one. Only in 1970, after over thirty years of service, was she finally scuttled.

* * *

Yukikaze, Hatsushimo, and *Fuyutsuki* ghosted into Sasebo on the morning of April 8, 1945. Not long after them, *Suzutsuki* limped into the harbor in reverse. During the battle, a bomb (or, by some accounts, a torpedo) had landed squarely in the forward section of the destroyer, ripping apart the two forward gun turrets, sparking a massive blaze, and sinking half of the bow. On seeing *Suzutsuki*'s commander, Captain Hirayama Toshio, Captain Terauchi belted out "So you're lucky, too, my old friend!"[1] It was a moment of levity in an otherwise desperate situation.

They were lucky indeed. In Operation Heaven One, *Yamato* had embarked with 3,332 souls. Only 276 survived, among them the young

Figure 12.1 *Yukikaze* under way off Sasebo in January 1940. Photograph donated by Kazu-toshi Hando in 1970. NH 73052 Courtesy of Naval History & Heritage Command.

Ensign Yoshida Mitsuru. At least eleven torpedoes holed the goliath, as well as six bombs and countless near misses. US aircraft also repeatedly strafed her decks. Seven torpedoes and twelve bombs hit *Yahagi*, and she lost 446 sailors out of her compliment of 949. Of the eight accompanying destroyers, only half, *Yukikaze, Fuyutsuki, Suzutsuki,* and *Hatsushimo*, survived the battle, while *Isokaze, Hamakaze, Asashimo,* and *Kasumi* did not; some 535 sailors were killed and hundreds more wounded (see Figure 12.1).

Yukikaze sailed with 350 men aboard, and strafing by Grumman F6F Hellcats killed 3 and wounded an additional 15. The Second Fleet's antiaircraft fire shot down ten US aircraft during the battle, killing twelve men. The United States successfully rescued many others. With *Amatsukaze*'s scuttling near Xiamen (Amoy) on April 10, *Yukikaze* became the last *Kagerō*-class destroyer, the last warship of her kind. Of the original Desron16 that invaded the Philippines on December 8, 1941, *Tokitsukaze* sank in March 1943 at the Battle of the Bismarck Sea, *Hatsukaze* sank in November 1943 off Bougainville after a collision, and *Amatsukaze* was scuttled in April 1945 off Xiamen (Map 12.1).

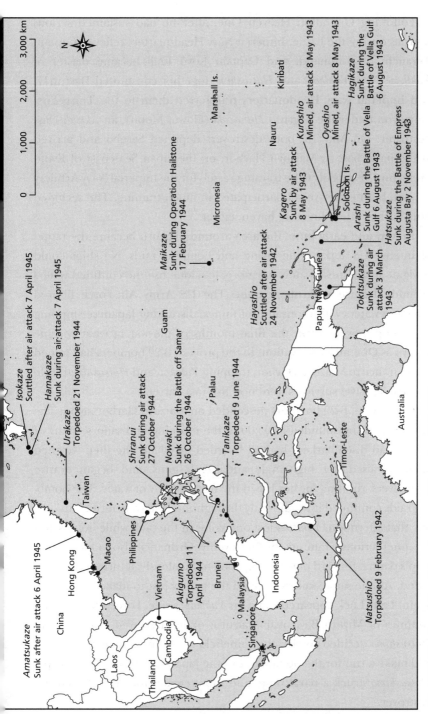

Map 12.1 The fate of *Kagerō*-class destroyers, 6 December 1941–1945

Following Operation Heaven One, after he had sustained serious injuries during the battle, Imperial Navy Headquarters relieved Captain Terauchi of command, and Captain Koyō Keiji became master of *Yukikaze*. Now *Yukikaze* and *Hatsushimo* together constituted Desron17, and Imperial Navy Headquarters transferred them to the Thirty-First Squadron under the flagship *Hanazuki* (Flower Moon), an *Akizuki*-class destroyer. On May 15, both destroyers departed Sasebo and arrived at the naval base at Maizuru Harbor, on the Japan Sea coast of Kyoto Prefecture, ostensibly to be training vessels for the Imperial Navy Artillery School, but neither vessel participated in much training. The secluded little harbor offered no safe haven, either.

In May and early June, the area around Maizuru became the target of intense US aerial mine laying and bombing raids. No ships could navigate in Japanese waters anymore, let alone use the confined waters around Maizuru to artillery train. The US Army Air Force littered Japanese waters with thousands of mines, disrupting Japanese shipping and troop movement in the final months of the war in what became known as Operation Starvation. In the process, B-29 bombers had mined the entrance to Maizuru Harbor, trapping *Yukikaze* and *Hatsushimo* inside the bay. The two survivors were now fish in a barrel.

On May 30, B-29 bombers descended on Maizuru Harbor again. The air raid warning sounded at 05:00 in the morning and sailors, many of whom had disembarked, had all boarded by 06:30. She then weighed anchor, raised her high-angle antiaircraft guns, and began evasive maneuvers, running for her life in the narrow body of water. The bombing raids continued intermittently throughout the day, petering out only late that afternoon. *Yukikaze* lost one sailor in the raid, while bombs and shrapnel seriously injured another twenty. Ordnance also lodged in the ship's pantry, forward of the bridge but, miraculously, it turned out to be a dud. All the same, sailors flooded the pantry just to make sure. Once again, Lady Luck appeared to be on *Yukikaze*'s side. Forced to leave the confines of Miyazu Bay, near Maizuru, or be destroyed, *Yukikaze* and *Hatsushimo* decided to risk the minefield at the mouth of the harbor and make a run for the open water of the Japan Sea. During the escape, *Hatsushimo* struck a naval mine and the crew was forced to beach the destroyer.

But *Yukikaze* did make it. Once outside the minefield, *Yukikaze* raced north, stopping just outside Ine Harbor, near the damaged *Jingei*-class submarine tender *Chōgei*. Although *Chōgei* had departed Maizuru for Ine Harbor the day before, US bombers had found her the next day and a well-placed bomb had completely destroyed her bridge. She had sought refuge north of Aojima Island, just outside the harbor. *Yukikaze* berthed just off the Ōjima promontory, due west of *Chōgei*. But *Yukikaze* arrived in the dead of night, and didn't see the damaged submarine tender until the next morning.

Once there, officers and crew began the work of trying to camouflage the 388-foot destroyer before the morning light brought the next wave of B-29 bombers. She represented the last of her kind, and US forces had slated her for extinction – there just weren't a lot of other Imperial Navy targets around. It was a familiar nocturnal rhythm for the destroyer's crew, much like the fighting in the Solomon Islands and the Bismarck Barrier, only now she hid in home waters. Under cover of night, sailors disembarked and walked on mountain roads to gather camouflage material. Nishizaki remembered that the gunnery department cut down small trees and shrubs, while the torpedo department procured fishing nets from the Ine Village fishing cooperative. Being part of the torpedo department, Nishizaki was among the men who approached the fishing village late that night.

After climbing the breakwater and hiking up a small mountain road, they approached the house of the elder of the fishing cooperative. A voice asked, "It's the dead of night. What time do you think it is?"[2]

"We have a warship near this secluded place, so surely, come tomorrow, the B-29s will be back. Because of this, is it possible that we might seek quarters in this village tonight?," asked Nishimura.

"I see. I see. It's your fault then," the old man answered. Nishimura was momentarily taken aback by the remark. Although the war wasn't over yet, this – "It's your fault then" – would be Japan's postwar refrain in a nutshell toward the entire war effort, not just the generals and admirals who led it, but also the young men who fought and died in it. It became Japan's way of paying the wages of guilt that followed the bloodiest conflict the world had ever seen – militarists had held Japan captive, forced the public into a war most people never supported, and conscripted young men to fight for a cause they never believed in. When General MacArthur arrived in Japan on August 30, 1945, and began the US occupation, he in effect liberated the Japanese people from themselves, or at least from Japan's military dictatorship. When it came to the initial popularity of the war, the waving flags, the patriotic music, the warship reviews, the anthem, and the Emperor astride his white horse, a national amnesia swept the nation.

In this way, many Japanese, including Emperor Hirohito, never took responsibility for a war that actually had been popular when it first broke out, when Japan convulsed in the feverish throes of "victory disease." But after the killing had stopped, because the war was the fault of the military establishment that had fought it, not the public that had raged in the press against the "Western encirclement" in 1941, Japan's participation in World War II became a marginal subject, an anomaly in an otherwise vibrant democracy, a dark valley from which the country now began to emerge. In this manner, the United States less defeated Japan than liberated Japan from its own military leaders. The remarks of the old man in the fishing village presaged this shift in attitude, the beginnings of historical amnesia, particularly as the war caused more and more hardship and suffering at home.

Ultimately, though, Nishizaki procured from the crotchety old man the fishing net he required to camouflage the destroyer. He recalled of that day, "If you think about it, we woke up early to enemy bombers, navigated in frantic circles around the narrow Miyazu Harbor, crossed the naval mine field and created a berth near Ine Village, and properly camouflaged the vessel. In reality, it was over twenty hours that amounted to a full day of hard fighting. Dinner had been a favorite, *shiruko*, but I didn't eat much. On the deck covered in morning dew, I fell asleep as if I had died."[3] (*Shiruko* is a traditional Japanese sweet porridge of crushed *azuki* beans, served in a bowl with *mochi*, or Japanese rice cake.) He awoke to the cool morning air. "I felt like I was in the jungle with all the camouflage covering of fish nets and branches the vessel." It was only then that Nishizaki saw the decapitated *Chōgei* nearby, her bridge blown away.

Over the course of the next few months, *Yukikaze*'s officers and crew came and went from the camouflaged destroyer, but May 30 was

Yukikaze's last battle, at least as *Yukikaze*. After the atomic bombings of Hiroshima and Nagasaki on August 6 and 9, respectively, at precisely noon on August 15, the "Broadcast of the Jeweled Voice" announced to Japanese subjects Japan's surrender to the Allies. The Emperor had recorded the announcement the day before on a phonographic record with NHK technicians, and the Imperial Household played the jeweled voice on NHK radio the next day. They then played Japan's national anthem, *Kimigayo*, to bolster patriotic sentiment.

The Emperor announced: "After pondering deeply the general trends of the world and the actual conditions obtaining in our empire today, we have decided to effect a settlement of the present situation by resorting to an extraordinary measure." In one of the great understatements of the war, he said, "Despite the best that has been done by everyone – the gallant fighting of the military and naval forces, the diligence and assiduity of our servants of the state, and the devoted service of our one hundred million people – the war situation has developed not necessarily to Japan's advantage." He then continued, "We have resolved to pave the way for a grand peace for all the generations to come by enduring the unendurable and suffering what is insufferable," defeat at the hands of the Allies. Japan's war of desperation against the menace of Western encirclement and oil starvation was finally over.

Two days after the Emperor's announcement, *Yukikaze*'s sailors removed her camouflage. Nishizaki remembered that rumors swirled aboard the destroyer about what would happen to them next now that Japan had surrendered. "The Americans would surely hang the admirals and generals by their necks," men whispered in the galley. "They'll castrate noncommissioned officers," he heard another sailor say on deck. These were among the rumors swirling in the cramped confines of the warship, no doubt fueled by years of propaganda about the savagery of the American devils.

The Allies did hang war criminals after the war. The Military Tribunal for the Far East sentenced seven Imperial Army figures to death and sixteen other prominent figures to life in prison, only two of whom hailed from the Imperial Navy. The Allies hanged the seven, which included General Tōjō, on December 23, 1948, at the Sugamo Prison. The Tribunal leveled the indictments against those defendants who "intended to and did plan, prepare, initiate, or wage aggressive war"[4] against the Allies. With the Tribunal's indictments, any legitimate strategies in the South Pacific, such as the quest for energy autarchy, were relegated to a "plan or conspiracy" of aggression and lawlessness. Basically, the Allies relegated Japan's experience during the first half of the twentieth century (between April 1928 and September 1945 as the indictments stated) to a "war of aggression and a war in violation of international law." In a word, the Tribunal rendered much of Japan's modernity criminal.

Many sailors aboard *Yukikaze* assumed that their unsinkable destroyer would be brought to America and paraded and exhibited before throngs of people, a war prize from a defeated nation. That never happened. What did happen was that, slowly but surely, starting in order with enlisted men, the demobilization of the Japanese war machine began. Aboard *Yukikaze*, the department heads gave the sailors a pittance farewell payment, saying "Don't ever forget the pride and glory of having fought together on the destroyer *Yukikaze*."

Then, one day shortly after the surrender, the Torpedo Chief asked Nishizaki to do something he regretted for the rest of his life. "Hey, Nishizaki, we need to complete some unfinished business," he said in a hushed voice. "Go burn the secret documents stowed aboard the ship. It's your duty, and be sure to do it alone where nobody can see you."

Dutifully, Nishizaki wrapped the documents in *furoshiki* cloth and headed into the mountains, finding a place where he didn't think the villagers would see the smoke. There, in a hand-dug hole, he burned operational directives, secret mission orders, and various personnel records. "*Yukikaze*'s history, the proof that we had lived, I turned to ashes that day," he wrote. He then buried the ashes in the hole. As he did so, he heard the voices of fellow servicemen, both dead and alive, in his head: "Are you still cooperating with the military?" Japan had surrendered. The war was over. It was our fault. And yet you're still doing the Imperial Navy's bidding? It's a question that haunted him for the rest of his life.

* * *

After the surrender, the officers and crew brought *Yukikaze* to Maizuru Harbor, where engineers transformed the fighting ship into a demobilized troop transport vessel. Engineers removed the two main gun turrets to make room for temporary quarters for soldiers being brought home. Captain Satō Seishichi replaced Koyō Keiji as commander in November 1945. Three months later, on February 11, 1946, she began the arduous task of transporting Japan's half-starved soldiers and, often, their families, home from fronts around the former Greater East Asian Co-Prosperity Sphere, starting with a trip to Shantou, China, after a brief stopover at Sasebo. Millions of Japanese had surrendered to the Allies, and they needed to be brought home, at least those not forcibly conscripted to dismantle the infrastructure of their former empire, or laboring in Stalin's gulags, or dangling by their slender necks after quick trials.

"Of course, I wanted to hurry to the home where my mother waited,"[5] wrote Nishizaki about the end of the war. "But, at the time, professional soldiers feared General Headquarters and didn't want to reveal their place of employment. Plus, no matter what, I felt strongly about being there to meet *Yukikaze*'s destiny." Nishizaki remembered that many ships, US and Japanese, were converted to demobilized troop transports, including the repaired submarine tender *Chōgei*, *Yukikaze*'s makeshift berth mate at the end of the war.

During the demobilization, Nishizaki became Deck Chief and oversaw the complex task of the repatriation of soldiers back home. In Nishizaki's recollection, by the end of December 1946, a period of about ten months, *Yukikaze* had been to China's Shantou (just east of Guangzhou, formerly Canton) once, Huludao (on the coast of Manchuria, in Liaodong Bay) five times, Rabaul (in Papua New Guinea) twice, Port Moresby (on the Papuan Peninsula) once, Saigon twice, Bangkok twice, and Naha (in Okinawa) four times. In all, *Yukikaze* repatriated 13,056 Japanese in 15 missions. In many respects, the war still wasn't over for *Yukikaze*.

In order to accommodate soldiers and, oftentimes, entire families, particularly coming from places like Manchuria, *Yukikaze*'s crew published the *Yukikaze News*, a makeshift newspaper designed to comfort soldiers and family that had been on the front for years by relaying snippets of postwar news. *Yukikaze*'s crew remained well disciplined throughout the repatriation, which wasn't always the case on other vessels. Volunteers aboard the destroyer went so far as to create the "*Yukikaze* Orchestra," which performed songs such as "Welcome to the Demobilized *Yukikaze*," a ditty that Takahashi Ei and Asahina Hideo co-wrote for demobilized and demoralized soldiers.

Once, while returning from Huludao, a woman gave birth to a child aboard *Yukikaze* and Captain Satō became the child's godfather. He named the baby boy Hakata, which was *Yukikaze*'s destination. Even though the war was over, people's lives continued – children were born and the nation lived on. An officer aboard *Yukikaze* recalled that, during one repatriation mission, an angry demobilized soldier, after seeing unblemished *Yukikaze*, blurted out, "Where was this ship, and what was it doing, while our country was in so much peril? There isn't even so much as a bullet hole!" But the officers and crew had been instructed not to discuss *Yukikaze*'s substantial operational history, so they sheepishly kept their heads down as they brought the soldiers home by the thousands. Where had she been? During the war she had been everywhere; after the war, nowhere.

On December 30, 1946, after nearly a year of repatriating Japanese soldiers and families, the occupation authorities designated *Yukikaze* a "Vessel in Special Custody" and in May 1947 an Allied survey of naval vessels chose her as a "model ship" (see Figure 12.2). While *Yukikaze* tugged at her mooring lines at the Shibaura Wharf, an Allied surveyor remarked, "I've never seen a naval vessel from a defeated nation in this kind of impeccable order!" It was her final commendation, after hard fighting at nearly every major naval battle in the Pacific. The next month, *Yukikaze* traveled to Yokosuka, where she prepared for being made war reparation. The Allies allowed Japan to keep one coast guard patrol vessel, as well as five coastal defense ships, thirty-five sub-chasers, and a host of smaller patrol vessels. The Allies – namely the United States, the United Kingdom, the Soviet Union, and China – distributed the remaining 134 vessels of the Imperial Navy by lottery. *Yukikaze* was allotted to become part of Chiang Kai-shek's Republic of China Navy.

On July 6, 1947, *Yukikaze* departed Nagaura Bay, in Kanagawa Prefecture, for Shanghai, under the command of Captain Higashi Hideo. As she made way, shouts of "Banzai!" and "Japan's best ship!" came from the dockworkers. The Chief Navigator, Nakajima Tenji, compared *Yukikaze*'s role as war reparation to the Republic of China to that of the timeless loyalty of retainer Ōishi Yoshio, who sacrificed everything to avenge his lord, Asano Naganori of Akō domain – the storyline of the

Figure 12.2 View of *Yukikaze*'s deck, looking aft from her bow. Taken in Tokyo on May 26, 1947, where she was exhibited to representatives of the leading Allied powers. The escort ship *Shisaka* is at right. Both ships were employed repatriating Japanese nationals from overseas, and were stripped of armament for this service. They were later transferred to the Chinese Navy. Note *Yukikaze*'s deck plating, with raised plates attached for nonskid purposes, and her anchor- and line-handling equipment. Photographed by Kaye Calmus. Photograph from the Army Signal Corps Collection, National Archives, Catalog #: SC 286589.

famous "forty-seven samurai" saga of the early eighteenth century. Once again, she joined the ranks of Japan's immortal historical giants, men such as Kusunoki Masashige, the ones that had haunted the Imperial Navy throughout the war. *Yukikaze* could never break free from these tethers to history. With them firmly in place, she then sailed for Shanghai.

* * *

As she departed Nagaura Bay for Shanghai, *Yukikaze*'s past four years of total, unrestricted war fanned out in her wake, slowly disappearing beyond the horizon. The familiar sound of her engines, turbines, and turning screws comforted the sailors. But in front of her spanned two distinct courses, ones that serve as an ideal ending place for this biography of a warship. Seen from today – that is, the first quarter of the twenty-first century – those two courses, and their accompanying waypoints, offer two vantage points from which to view *Yukikaze*'s complex legacy, as well as the broader lessons of World War II in the Pacific.

The first course is her service as *Dan Yang*, the eventual flagship of the Republic of China Navy. On this heading, the Chinese Civil War and the Cold War in East Asia served as her waypoints in the dangerous waters of the Taiwan Strait. She had known these waters as *Yukikaze* – this is where she watched the US submarine *Sealion* hole the battleship *Kongō* and the destroyer *Urakaze* in the final year of the war. Once the Allies had turned *Yukikaze* over to Generalissimo Chiang Kai-shek, leader of the Nationalist government, the destroyer immediately became embroiled in the Civil War between the Guomindang Nationalists and the Chinese Communist Party (CCP), which had simmered throughout the Greater East Asian War.

Chiang had always perceived that "the Japanese were the disease of the skin and the Communists were the threat to the heart,"[6] and that perception shaped his approach to the war. He never proved fully able to focus on expelling Japan's Imperial Army from China, even after the creation in 1937 of a "united front" against the Japanese, because of his obsession with ridding China of Mao Zedong and the CCP. On several occasions, Chiang demonstrated a preference for butchering Communists rather than Japanese, such as when Nationalist troops wiped out Red Army soldiers in the 1941 "Wannan Incident" in Anhui Province.

In 1943, Chiang had published a pamphlet titled *China's Destiny*, in which he outlined a vision for postwar China – it did not include the Communists in any way whatsoever. The Communists retorted that Chiang sought to "establish his own dictatorship by destroying the CCP and other progressive forces in China,"[7] basically creating a "fascist China." The two sides found no common ground, not even in the urgency of expelling the marauding Imperial Army.

By 1945, after initially urging cooperation between China's Nationalists and Communists, the US government had thrown its full support behind Chiang and refused to cooperate with the Communists, setting the stage for the contours of the Cold War in East Asia. In May 1945, Chiang, speaking in the temporary capital of Chongqing, asserted that "Japan is our enemy abroad, and the CCP is our enemy at home."[8] Even with Imperial Army troops ransacking China, he said, "our central problem today is how to destroy the CCP." This remains the principal reason why Mao won the war of public perception in China and eventually defeated the Nationalists in the Civil War. For most Chinese, the Japanese represented more than a flesh wound. Chiang proved totally tone deaf.

Further demarcating Cold War lines, on August 9, 1945, when the Soviet Union declared war on Japan, Mao ordered his Red Army to "cooperate with the Soviet Red Army"[9] in the north, although it would be an overstatement to say that the relationship between the CCP and the Soviet Union was cooperative. On August 28, Mao and his lieutenant Zhou Enlai traveled to Chongqing in an attempt to democratize politics and unify Nationalist and Communist troops under a single banner, but the negotiations broke down. It wasn't long before the two sides began to clash throughout the country.

But Mao began focusing his attention on the north, under the strategy of "maintaining a defensive posture in the south while waging an offensive in the north."[10] By October 19, the Communists had decided to "go all out to control the entire Northeast."[11] Even after General George Marshall visited China in a last-ditch effort to bring the two sides together, the Nationalists and Communists could not reconcile their differences, particularly regarding the nationalization of the Red Army under Generalissimo Chiang's command. In March 1946, fighting broke out between the Nationalists and the Communists in Siping, a strategically important city in southern Manchuria – a prelude to the Civil War that boiled over that summer.

Yukikaze arrived in Shanghai as tensions heated up between the Nationalists and Communists, but, without big guns, she wasn't much of a fighting ship. Officially, *Yukikaze* became *Dan Yang* (DD-12), named after the city of that name, on May 1, 1948. A handful of the Japanese warships that the Allies had turned over to the Republic of China's naval engineers were rearmed relatively quickly, such as *Xin Yang* (formerly the Imperial Navy escort destroyer *Hatsuume*) and *Hui'an* (formerly the Imperial Navy escort ship *Shisaka*). They played minor roles in the Civil War.

Prominently, *Dan Yang* evacuated Shanghai for Keelung, Taiwan, in 1948, reportedly with Generalissimo Chiang aboard, as well as untold amounts of gold and national treasure bound for Taiwanese museums. But a lack of workers and proper facilities meant that the Republic of China Navy delayed *Dan Yang*'s rearming until 1951, after she was in Zuoying in southern Taiwan. At this juncture, it became imperative that *Dan Yang* rearm in order to become a Cold Warrior in the ongoing struggle between the People's Republic of China on the mainland and the Republic of China on Taiwan.

Initially, dock workers rearmed *Dan Yang* with repurposed Japanese weapons, mostly old shore mounts from World War II, including the familiar Type 96 25 mm antiaircraft gun, the Type 89 12.7 cm (5-inch) high-angle gun on the forward turret, and the Type 98 10 cm (4-inch) gun on the two aft turrets. She was also outfitted with updated electronics. After the destruction of *Chongqing* (formerly *HMS Aurora*, an *Arethusa*-class light cruiser), *Dan Yang* became the flagship of the Republic of China Navy. *Chongqing*'s officers and crew had defected to the Communists on February 25, 1949, in the waning months of the Civil War, and the Nationalists returned the favor by sinking the cruiser the next month in Huludao Harbor.

In 1953, *Dan Yang* visited the Philippines on a diplomatic mission and undertook a blockade of the People's Republic of China, intercepting Polish and Soviet tankers in the process. In 1956, engineers replaced her repurposed Japanese armaments with US guns, specifically three Mark 12 127 mm (5-inch) guns (the main guns of the *Fletcher*-class destroyers), two 76 mm (3-inch) guns, ten 40 mm Bofors guns, and a healthy complement of depth charges.

Fully armed, *Dan Yang* quickly became embroiled in Cold War affairs. After the Nationalists had evacuated to Taiwan, war planners in the People's Republic began strategizing a seizure of the renegade island. On June 14, 1949, Mao sent a telegram to People's Liberation Army commanders in Eastern China to "pay attention to seizing Taiwan immediately."[12] He ordered the People's Liberation Army to be ready to "occupy Taiwan in the coming winter." But military setbacks on Jinmen Island (formerly Quemoy) and Dengbu Island (off Zhejiang Province) forced war planners to postpone the Taiwan invasion until the summer of 1951. Then, the Korean War required Mao's full attention, and the Taiwan invasion got placed on the back burner yet again, particularly after the Nationalist secret services unearthed a Communist spy ring in Taiwan, robbing the People's Republic of its intelligence in Taipei. For the three years of the Korean War (1950–1953), the People's Republic shelved the Taiwan invasion, even though the Nationalists continued to harass coastal areas of the mainland.

The end of the Korean War set the stage for the First Taiwan Strait Crisis. In 1953, the People's Liberation Army established an East China Military Region headquarters for the purpose of retaking several small Nationalist-controlled islands off the coast of Zhejiang Province, particularly Dachen and Yijiangshan. Mao considered the two islands strategically vital, given their location near Shanghai and the mouth of the Yangzi River. Eventually, the planning included using Fujian shore batteries to shell military installations on Jinmen Island. Simultaneously, the People's Republic began a public relations campaign to emphasize the fact that "We must liberate Taiwan."[13] The stage was being set for the first step in retaking Taiwan. It wasn't just to retake the Chinese territory stolen by Generalissimo Chiang's "bandit clique," but to strengthen Mao's notion of "continuous revolution" within China. Mao stressed that he had designed the campaign to liberate Taiwan to "raise the political consciousness and political alertness of the people of the whole country; we mean to stir up our people's revolutionary enthusiasm."

People's Liberation Army shore batteries pounded installations on Jinmen on September 3 and 22, 1954, which accelerated negotiations between the governments in Taipei and Washington, D.C. for a mutual defense treaty. On December 2, 1956, Washington and Taipei signed the mutual defense treaty, committing the United States to the use of force to defend Taiwan in the case of a Communist invasion. Now, the Taiwan Strait was placed squarely in the crosshairs of Cold War geopolitics and the continuous threat of a nuclear holocaust. These stormy seas represented *Dan Yang*'s new home waters.

On August 23, 1958, the People's Liberation Army again shelled Republic of China military installations on Jinmen Island and the Mazu Islands, once again as a first step toward liberating Taiwan from the Nationalists. This became known as the Second Taiwan Strait Crisis,

and witnessed a far more robust US response from President Dwight
D. Eisenhower. The next day, Nationalist naval forces clashed with the
Communists around Dongding Island in an effort to halt a People's
Liberation Army amphibious landing. The People's Liberation Navy
dispatched six torpedo boats to attack Nationalist supply vessels near
Jinmen's Liuluo Bay. During this fighting around Dongding, *Dan Yang*
unmasked her main guns against the Communists and helped stymie the
amphibious landing. By September, the United States had waded into
the conflict, bringing a veritable armada to the Taiwan Strait, including two aircraft carrier groups, in order to provide armed escorts for
Nationalist ships approaching Jinmen. The United States also supplied
the navy with better, updated weaponry.

In 1958, the mutual defense treaty of 1954 necessitated a strong US
response, precipitating the first genuine nuclear crisis of the Cold War.
Dan Yang navigated the Taiwan Strait alongside a new generation of war-
ships in the US Seventh Fleet, such as the *Essex*-class carrier *Lexington*.
And a new generation of supersonic aircraft supported the big flattop,
such as F-100D Super Sabres, F-101C Voodoos, F-104A Starfighters, and
B-57B Canberras. Gone were the B-17 Flying Fortresses, the Grumman
F6F Hellcats, the Douglas SBD Dauntlesses, and the Mitsubishi A6M
Zeros, aircraft that, only fifteen years earlier, had ruled the skies over the
Pacific. But, once again, *Yukikaze* – or, rather, *Dan Yang* – found herself
in the middle of dangerous geopolitical affairs, this time in the Cold
War, and under the threatening clouds of the potential use of nuclear
weapons.

Mao had sought to "teach the Americans a lesson"[14] because they had
"bullied us for many years." He had hoped to "bring about the awakening
of many people, and will make them determined to fight against the impe-
rialists," but instead he set the table for Cold War tensions in the Taiwan
Strait that persist to this day. Most serious observers agree that, if there is to
be a World War III, it will likely start in the Taiwan Strait, though Russia's
invasion of Ukraine would be a contender flashpoint as well.

The Republic of China Navy retired *Dan Yang* in December 1965 and
decommissioned her one year later. After a typhoon damaged *Dan Yang*
in the summer of 1969, she was scrapped. By December 31, 1971, nothing remained of the destroyer formerly known as *Yukikaze*. But Taipei,

in a diplomatic gesture, did return the helm and one anchor to Japan. They are displayed at the Technical School of the Japan Maritime Self-Defense Forces in Etajima. The left propeller is displayed at the Republic of China Naval Academy in Kaohsiung City.

In this biography, *Dan Yang* represented the physical embodiment of *Yukikaze*, the rivets, welds, and galvanized steel assembled in Sasebo, the blood and sweat soaked into her teak deck, and her sleek hull and raised bridge. While the other *Kagerō*-class destroyers rested quietly on the bottom of the sea, *Dan Yang*, with her Republic of China Navy ensign, remained to fight in new waters with new allies, such as alongside the carrier *Lexington* (CV-16) during the Second Taiwan Strait Crisis. But, in 1971, *Yukikaze*'s physical story ended. Taiwanese workers had dismembered the unsinkable destroyer and her story was over.

* * *

But history isn't just about material things moving through time. It's also about the power of ideas as they move through time, and still floating around Japan's postwar world was the name *Yukikaze*, and what that name represented – essentially, where this book started, with her name. Today, far fewer people associate the name *Yukikaze* with melancholic laments in the tenth-century *Kagerō Diary* or the *Kagerō*-class destroyer of World War II than with more recent military science-fiction thrillers.

If you google "Yukikaze," these are the names that top the list, such as Kambayashi Chōhei's *Yukikaze*, first published as a series of short stories in *S-F Magazine*, "a magazine of science fiction & fact," and later released by Hayakawa publishing in 1984. Kambayashi's work takes place in the early twenty-first century, when an alien force known as JAM has invaded Earth by utilizing a space portal, the "Passageway," which mysteriously appeared over Antarctica. Through the Passageway, "JAM came swarming out of it to launch their first strike."[15]

In response, the United Nations creates a military force to repel the invasion and pursues the JAM invaders back through the Passageway, establishing bases in the JAM home world. The JAM home world is a planet named Faery, and the Faery Air Force, which includes a fighter codenamed "Yukikaze," continues the campaign against JAM. Lieutenant Fukai Rei pilots "Yukikaze," an advanced fighter with AI capabilities, basically a "supercomputer with wings," and he fights against the JAM enemies, who plant clones throughout the Faery Air Force, which becomes the focus of the plot. In the series, "Yukikaze" is a highly advanced, and highly intelligent, tactical reconnaissance plane, a force for good defending Earth against crafty alien invaders. But her pilot is coldhearted, emotionless, computer-like. On Faery, the Faery Air Force defends an "Absolute Defense Line," not unlike *Yukikaze* the destroyer did during World War II.

Science-fiction writers quickly refashioned *Yukikaze* to fit Japan's postwar milieu, where any discussions of Japan's participation in World War II became fraught, always a tricky subject. She became a fantastical FFR-31MR/D Super Sylph fighter battling heroically to save the world against JAM invaders, not unlike the situation in which the real *Kagerō*-class destroyer had found herself in 1945. But after Japan's surrender, which necessitated acknowledging that Japan had waged a "war of aggression," not a desperate struggle to free itself from Western encirclement in order to acquire oil, the Imperial Navy turned from hero to villain, and admiring Imperial Navy warships became socially less acceptable. Indeed, perusing Imperial Navy magazines in quiet corners of bookstores in Japan became something akin to thumbing through soft porn, almost a little creepy.

"I see. I see. It's your fault," the old fisherman had told Torpedo Specialist Nishizaki, and that's how most Japanese people came to view all things military in the postwar period. In this context, military science fiction offered a space to explore the forbidden, to talk about the bravery of *Yukikaze*, celebrate her heroic exploits, relish her defying the odds, and all without talking about an Imperial Navy warship, or really talking about Japan's lost "war of aggression," at all.

Certainly, this is the feeling one gets from *Space Battleship Yamato*, a popular 1974 series that aired in the United States as *Star Blazers*, about a space battleship, named *Yamato* – one carefully drawn to resemble the actual battleship and resurrected from what had been her ocean grave (oceans have long since dried up in the series, exposing the warship) – during an interstellar war. In the series, space battleship *Yamato* attempts to retrieve a technology that can reverse the effects of radiation on Earth, after bad guys called the Gamilas have bombed the home world. In the original series, *Yukikaze* appears as an *Isokaze*-class torpedo destroyer under the command of Captain Mamoru Kodai. But *Yukikaze* doesn't live long, ironically. Disobeying orders, she charges ahead and sacrifices herself in Operation M, crashing onto the surface of the planet Enceladus while providing cover for the battleship space-ship *Kirishima*.

Captain Kodai explains to Admiral Okita Juzo while he's pummeled providing cover for *Kirishima*, "I'll fight, and I'll fight, and I'll go on fight-ing, even if I helm Earth's very last ship."[16] (Of course, this should all sound a little familiar, a loose riff on *Yukikaze*'s valiant efforts to save the fast battleships *Hiei* and *Kirishima* during the Naval Battle at Guadalcanal on November 12–13, 1942.) These names should all be familiar by now, and it's fascinating that the writers should have chosen to sacrifice the one destroyer that actually survived World War II in the Pacific – per-haps they sought to give her the tragic, noble death she always deserved, rather than the infamy of surviving World War II on the Pacific.

Then there is the *Kantai Collection*, or *KanColle*, which launched in April 2013 as an online game platform designed by Tanaka Kensuke, but eventually expanded into its own multimedia empire, with manga printed versions, animated films, and an assortment of collectable mer-chandise, some of it quite steamy. The computer game runs on Flash, which means it's mostly played on computers at home, rather than portable devices. In the *Kantai Collection*, Fleet Girls, who can only be described as barely pubescent pole dancers, represent the former war-ships of the Imperial Navy, each one taking on the personality of one of the warships. *Yukikaze*'s Fleet Girl is a brunette who glides atop the ocean on heels that look like rudders, complete with red antifouling paint. Her head is the destroyer's conning tower, with a pillbox hat that resembles a bridge and radar cones for earmuffs. She speaks into a voice tube, com-mon in *Kagerō*-class destroyers, too. She's holding big eye binoculars, has a torpedo launcher for a backpack, and main guns in the form of a large shoulder bag.

But, before the reader dismisses *KanColle* as another example of the sleazy side of Japanese *otaku* culture, it's important to acknowledge that in some respects the series comes closer to representing the Imperial Navy warships than both Kambayashi's *Yukikaze* and Matsumoto's *Space*

Battleship Yamato. In a 2020 interview with *Comptiq Magazine, KanColle's* creator, Tanaka, explained why he had created the series in the first place. In essence, he said, the *Kanmusu,* or Fleet Girls, represented an extension of "my own hobbies,"[17] which in the postwar years were largely forbidden. He sought to present the Imperial Navy warships he admired in a way palatable to postwar Japanese consumers, and to call his Fleet Girls sugarcoated would be an understatement.

"The vessels and fleets that once cut through waves on the sea, that dashingly strode across it. And the ships and people that struggled in difficult conditions when the war took a turn for the worse and bitterly and regretfully sank beneath the waves," he began, "I started making *KanColle* out of a desire to share their existences, making sure they weren't forgotten." In a way, Tanaka captured postwar attitudes toward Imperial Navy warships – and the war of desperation they fought – perfectly. He sought to rescue the warships of the Imperial Navy, and the manner in which they are remembered, with the life ring of Japanese animated popular culture. In an atmosphere where remembering Imperial Navy warships outside the rubric of a "war of aggression" was fraught, what better way to make them palatable to the Japanese public than dress them up in short skirts or schoolgirl uniforms, where they could battle the alien Abyssal Fleet on the high seas of make believe?

Many have pointed out the creepier aspects of the game: when Fleet Girls are hit, their clothing rips as if they've been raped, and, in some game updates, online players, known as Admirals, can even marry their Fleet Girls. This, besides the fact that, as one online blogger wrote, "countless warships featured in *Kantai Collection* were involved in Japan's wicked conquest of the South Pacific, launching raids or housing convicted war criminals."[18] Actually, no Imperial Navy war criminals were on the water in the South Pacific, at least not ones formally convicted in the Military Tribunal for the Far East, but I think we can all appreciate the sentiment.

Akky Akimoto, a journalist for the *Japan Times,* wrote that "Casual online games based on military themes and with a *kawaii* (cute) twist are currently a surprise hit in Japan. Is this related to the recent rightward tilt in national politics, or just part of Japan's creative desire to 'cutify' everything,"[19] including 60,000-ton Imperial Navy battleships.

It's a good question, as Japan has experienced a right-wing tilt in politics. But Akimoto dismisses accusations that *KanColle* is tied to a reemergence of right-wing political attitudes. "I do not believe that *KanColle* was deliberately designed to support Japan's recent reactionary tilt," he concluded. "One amusing side-effect of the game's popularity is that when you search online in Japanese for the name of a WWII battleship," wrote Akimoto, "the top results are images of *Kanmusu* girls. Real rightwingers who want to rewind history may not be so pleased about this." It's a legitimate point. Nonetheless, it's hard not to attach some of *KanColle*'s popularity to nostalgia for nationalist politics in Japan.

* * *

Not all of the postwar appearances of the unsinkable destroyer *Yukikaze* are *KanColle*'s Fleet Girls, however. Another postwar rendition, made of galvanized steel and displacing 1,700 tons, is *Yukikaze* (DD-102), a *Harukaze*-class warship launched by Mitsubishi in 1955 (see Figure 12.3). The importance of the name *Yukikaze*, and what it meant for Japan's postwar security future, wasn't just in the heads of Kambayashi, Matsumoto, and Tanaka, but also swirled around in the heads of Japan's postwar naval planners in Japan's Maritime Self-Defense Forces.

In Japan, military planners had fought and lost the war over an inability to deliver raw materials, most notably oil, to the Japanese Islands, and between 2.5 and 3.1 million Japanese deaths later, not to mention the 20 to 30 million more deaths in the sphere of Japanese military activity, Japan's security planners still faced the same challenges. Even though Japan had surrendered to the Allies, and lived sheltered during the Cold War under the safety of the US security umbrella, the necessity of securing oil for its industrial economy never abated. In fact, Japan's need for oil only intensified with the postwar reconstruction and the second "economic miracle." In this environment, securing and defending Japan's vital sea lanes of communication in the South China Sea and elsewhere became the Maritime Defense Force's principal mission.

We end with memory, and how it intersects with Japan's continuing need for resource security. In World War II in the Pacific, the Rape of Nanjing (1937–1938), Pearl Harbor (1941), and Hiroshima (1945)

(PD1)PORTLAND, Ore., June 10 -- JAPANESE FIRE A SALUTE -- The Japanese
destroyer Yukikaze fires a 21-gun national salute upon her arrival in the
Portland harbor yesterday. The smoke of her 5-inch guns hangs over the
ship. She is the first Japanese ship to come to Portland since before
World War II. The Yukikaze is the flagship of a five-ship training
squadron in Portland on a goodwill mission in connection with the annual
Portland Rose Festival. In the foreground is the U.S. destroyer Jarvis.
(AP WIREPHOTO) (fjm60130 Ogn) 1960.

Figure 12.3 Japan Maritime Self-Defense Force destroyer *Yukikaze* (DD-102) in Portland, Oregon, on June 10, 1960 (author's collection).

serve as potent sites of popular remembrance, creating unified national memories of the bloodiest conflict the world has ever seen. Such sites of remembrance also continue to fuel contemporary national grievances, a hurdle to true Asian reconciliation even to this day. But, in some respects, these sites have every right to continue to resurrect memories of World War II's utter cruelty. We need to remember. We need to teach World War II in our schools, all of it, and build and visit memorials that celebrate people making the ultimate sacrifice for liberal civilization.

But there is another kind of memory that operates in the wake of World War II, a more strategic memory – for Japan, that memory is tied to the Imperial Navy's inability to safeguard sea lanes of communication in the 1940s and bring badly needed resources, extracted from the empire, back to Japan. The island nation still desires energy independence, but now through a strategy both of pursuing alternative forms of energy, such as nuclear and hydroelectric, and through international trade deals rather than imperial autarchy. In 2012, Japan ranked second only to China as the world's largest oil importer, with most of that oil coming from Saudi Arabia, the United Arab Emirates, Qatar, Kuwait, and Iran. To bring this oil to energy-hungry Japan, tankers navigate vulnerable choke points, such as the Strait of Hormuz and the Strait of Malacca. From the Strait of Malacca, tankers bound for Japan must also navigate the waters of the hotly contested South China Sea. These choke points are the stuff of a naval strategist's nightmares.

Throughout the Cold War and the post-Cold War periods, the protection of maritime transportation routes has driven the procurement and deployment strategies of Japan's Marine Self-Defense Force, including the launching of the second-generation *Yukikaze* (DD-102). The fear that the Japanese islands could be starved of energy once again drives Japan's thinking about contemporary security challenges, and for good reason. Just as the battleship *Yamato* was emblematic of the faith of Imperial Navy planners in a decisive battle, today's *Izumo*-class light carriers, built by Japan Marine United, are emblematic of the contemporary strategy to protect chokepoints in Japan's vital sea lanes, where enemy submarines might lurk. Engineers built *Izumo* (DDH-183) and *Kaga* (DDH-184), the only two *Izumo*-class flattops, for antisubmarine warfare to support this Cold War strategy, and they were designed to hold helicopters capable of attacking subs as well as undertaking search and rescue operations.

In December 2018, however, the Japanese government approved reinforcing the flight decks of the helicopter destroyers to accommodate twelve or more F-35B aircraft, with short takeoff and vertical landing capabilities. Combined with the *Hyūga*-class helicopter destroyers, *Hyūga* and *Ise*, the warships represent a shift to a slightly more offensive posture. Today, China's People's Liberation Army and Navy have become the principal threat, with their commitment to defending contested "territorial waters" in the South and East China Sea. In response, the procurement needs of Japan's Marine Self-Defense Force shifted toward securing and protecting Japan's Exclusive Economic Zones, some 4.5 million kilometers of coastal territory, including such hotspots as the Senkaku Islands, a maritime zone with possible oil and natural gas reserves, not unlike Japan's ephemeral oil empire in the South Seas.

Once again, Japan's national and energy security is tethered to defending a vast maritime territory, one that requires a strong navy. Japan possesses territory a mere 150 kilometers from Taiwan. What makes Japan's situation particularly precarious today is not just that the island nation is surrounded by aggressive autocracies – namely, the People's Republic of China, Russia, and North Korea – but that these autocracies also possess nuclear weapons. And, given the ebb and flood of the US commitment to its Asian allies, Japan has every right to believe that it will need to take a more robust role in its own security.

At the time of writing, Japan's Prime Minister, Kishida Fumio, on the recommendation of an expert panel headed by the former ambassador to the United States, Sasae Kenichirō, is proposing to double Japan's defense spending to around $70 billion, focusing on "counterstrike capabilities." This would constitute the biggest military buildup since World War II, and should be completed by China's next Communist Party Congress, which occurs every five years. With Japanese watching in horror what has happened in Ukraine, every indication is that the national mood has warmed toward an increase in military spending.

This shift in military strategy is driven by many of the same vulnerabilities as Japan faced in 1941, which brings *Yukikaze*'s story full circle. At the dawn of the twenty-first century, Japan feels encircled by hostile enemies, and still remains as utterly dependent on imports of oil (99.7% import dependency), iron ore (99.8%), bauxite (100%), manganese (100%), wool (100%), copper ore (99.9%), nickel (100%), cobalt (100%), zinc (92%), titanium (100%), cotton (100%), wheat (93%), timber (80%), and shellfish (44%) as it was in the 1940s. Japanese policymakers eye events transpiring around Taiwan, and have grown concerned regarding Japanese territory in the region. How to secure these vital territorial waters, secure access to oil and natural gas, and protect Japan's sea lanes of communication is what keeps today's naval planners awake at night, just as it did their Imperial Navy counterparts seventy-five years ago.

But the lessons of this story transcend the experiences of one warship, one crew, and one nation. *Yukikaze*, the *Kagerō*-class destroyer, served the Imperial Navy for six years guarding oilers, escorting tankers, and conquering and defending vital waterways and territories, usually former European empires rich in natural resources such as oil. Japan's independence in the twentieth century was dependent on acquiring oil, and being subject to the whims of the United States regarding oil imports proved unacceptable. Then, in 1945, with Japan out of oil and defeated, *Yukikaze* was transferred to the Republic of China, where her Cold War service remained principally about securing the safe transport of badly needed oil and other resources to Taiwan. The oil that arrived safely in Taiwan fueled its rise to industrial prominence in the late twentieth century and secured, at least for the time being, its political independence from Beijing. Once again, in the twentieth century, being independent as a nation required being dependent on oil.

Today, with oil reserves becoming scarcer and climate change prompting debates about the future of the fossil-fuel order, securing energy has become of vital concern to all nations, but none more so than Japan and Taiwan. In 2020, 98 percent of the oil consumed by Japan and Taiwan came from abroad. During the Cold War, *Yukikaze*'s successor, the *Harukaze*-class DD-102, served Japan's Maritime Self-Defense Force by guarding vital sea lanes of communication and defending disputed territories, most of which hold the promise of energy reserves. Her struggle, too, was about escorting the oil that fuels Japan's industrial economy, and defending vital territory. This remains the preoccupation of Japan's navy to this day. In a way, no matter the master she served, *Yukikaze*'s struggle usually involved defending oil and, thereby, national independence, which serves as another lesson in this story, particularly as we lurch into the energy and climatological uncertainties of the middle of the twenty-first century.

I reckon that, decades from now, should we solve our considerable energy- and climate-related challenges, we will view *Yukikaze* not as a mechanical marvel or a brave little warship sailed by brave men during wartime, but rather as an avatar, or representation, of sorts. With smoke belching from her funnels, she guarded oilers. She fought in the Java Sea with endless rows of oil derricks in the background. As World War II and the Cold War fade into a more distant memory, *Yukikaze*, in all her incarnations, has become an avatar of our centuries-old dependency on oil, and the ghastly violence that securing oil entailed.

Acknowledgments

I T'S UNUSUAL THAT, as an academic historian, one has occasion
to write a book that weds professional interests, in this case Japanese
history, with a personal passion, in this case being on the water. But
that's precisely what this book has done.

I come from a family of boaters, a sailor and a yachtswoman to be precise, and much of what I learned about boating I learned from my mother
and father, who have spent the last thirty years living near the Salish Sea,
in Victoria and Anacortes, respectively. So I start by thanking them, Linda
Walker and Nelson Walker, for providing me with such a rich, fluid life.

I possess US Merchant Mariner Credentials as well, which would
not have been possible without my salty teacher of all things maritime,
Captain Jeffrey Sanders. The water, particularly inland seas and oceans,
is an entirely different world, and whatever successes I might have had in
these pages in capturing this dynamic environment I owe to time spent
on a boat, watching the winds, water, currents, and tides. I'm at peace
there like nowhere else. I'm also rather conservative when it comes to all
things nautical, so I've followed the mariner's convention of calling ships
by the gendered pronoun "she," which I trust won't offend anybody too
much. Ships are many things, but they are not an "it."

Several colleagues and friends kindly edited this manuscript in its
early stages. Whatever moments of elegance appear in this book, I surely
owe to them; the remaining blemishes, of course, are mine. I am grateful to Alex Bay, of Chapman University, for his truly outstanding feed-
back regarding Japan's martial traditions, particularly those born in the
medieval period. Kirk Branch, of Montana State University's English
Department, offered seasoned advice on successful narrative and

281

making the manuscript more accessible. Frank Boynton, a retired US Marine Colonel and colleague, spared me the embarrassment of making mistakes regarding military matters and nomenclature, though even his painstaking proofread couldn't possibly have caught them all. My friend Matthew Moog brought his knack for precision, his intelligent energy, and his insatiable curiosity to bear on this book, providing a proofread like I've never encountered before. Finally, in the later stages of this project, I received detailed comments and numerous corrections on the manuscript from Jonathan Parshall that constituted nothing short of a masterclass on Pacific War naval history. I'm forever grateful.

At home, my stepson, Andrew Scherffius, became an inspired sound-board and my wife, LaTrelle Scherffius, proved an endless source of narrative and topic ideas, particularly regarding how to turn an often-technical topic into a relatable one. More remarkably still, she put up with unending conversations about warships, the building of plastic models of warships, the stacks of books on warships, the dust-collecting eBay purchases of artifacts from warships, the plastering of our walls with old photographs of warships, the old charts and compasses that steered warships, the lead models that identified warships, and everything else nautical that navigated, even in the midst of a global pandemic, into our home over the past several years, as I went headlong down the rabbit hole with this topic. I don't typically fetishize military hardware, but it's just that I really like boats, all boats, and World War II had some marvelous, if marvelously deadly, ones.

I am indebted to Montana State University's Office of Research, Economic Development, and Graduate Education, the College of Letters and Science, and the Department of History and Philosophy for their unwavering support of my research program. None of this would have been possible without them.

Finally, I want to thank my students, always the best telltale for what is interesting and what is not. Thanks for setting me on the correct heading.

Notes

PREFACE

1. A. J. P. Taylor, *The Origins of the Second World War*, 2nd edition (New York, NY: Fawcett Premier Book, 1961), 22–23.
2. Mari Yamaguchi, "Japan PM Vows to Strengthen Military at Int'l Military Review," Associated Press, https://apnews.com/article/business-china-japan-united-states-europe-8aea 8040ff6a3903c85be48eabdda322. Last accessed November 13, 2022.
3. Robert Kagan, *The Jungle Grows Back: America and Our Imperiled World* (New York, NY: Vintage Books, 2018), 3–4.

1 DIVINE SHIPS OF A BLUEWATER NAVY

1. Samuel Eliot Morison, *History of the United States Naval Operations in World War II, vol.* III: *The Rising Sun in the Pacific, 1931–April 1942* (Boston, MA: Little, Brown and Company, 1984), 280.
2. Itō Masanori, *Rengō kantai no eikō* [*The Glory of the Combined Fleet*] (Tokyo: Bungei Shunjū, 1962), 274.
3. Agawa Hiroyuki, *Citadel in Spring: A Novel of Youth Spent at War*, translated by Lawrence Rogers (Kumamoto: Kurodanha Press, 2013), 106, 108.
4. Itō, *Rengō kantai no eikō*, 188–189.
5. Morison, *History of the United States Naval Operations in World War II*, vol. III, 22.
6. Brett L. Walker, *A Concise History of Japan* (Cambridge: Cambridge University Press, 2015), 244–245.
7. Haruo Shirane, ed., *Traditional Japanese Literature: An Anthology, Beginnings to 1600* (New York, NY: Columbia University Press, 2007), 201.
8. Ibid., 598.
9. *The Kagerō Diary: A Woman's Autobiographical Text from the Tenth Century*, translated with an introduction and notes by Sonja Arntzen (Ann Arbor: Center for Japanese Studies, The University of Michigan, 1997), 333. I have modified this translation slightly, from "The wind blew and snow fell" to "snowy wind." The original Japanese is 「雪風言ふ方なう降り暗がりて」.

10. H. D. Harootunian, *Things Seen and Unseen: Discourse and Ideology in Tokugawa Nativism* (Chicago: University of Chicago Press, 1988), 365.

11. H. Agawa, *The Reluctant Admiral: Yamamoto and the Imperial Navy* (Tokyo: Kodansha International, 1979), 232.

12. Yoshida Mitsuru, *Requiem for Battleship Yamato*, translated and introduction by Richard H. Minear (Annapolis, MD: Naval Institute Press, 1985), 3.

13. J. Charles Schencking, "Bureaucratic Politics, Military Budgets and Japan's Southern Advance: The Imperial Navy's Seizure of German Micronesia in the First World War," *War in History* 5, no. 3 (1988): 311.

14. Mikiso Hane, *Peasants, Rebels, Women, and Outcastes: The Underside of Modern Japan*, 2nd edition, introduction by Samuel H. Yamashita (Lanham, MD: Rowman & Littlefield, 2003), 33.

15. Hane, *Peasants, Rebels, Women, and Outcastes*, 18.

16. J. Charles Schencking, *Making Waves: Politics, Propaganda, and the Emergence of the Imperial Japanese Navy, 1868–1922* (Stanford, CA: Stanford University Press, 2005), 22.

17. Schencking, "Bureaucratic Politics," 312.

18. Schencking, *Making Waves*, 43.

19. Ibid., 111.

20. Ibid., 115.

21. Ibid., 219.

22. Julian Stafford Corbett, *Some Principles of Maritime Strategy* (Frankfurt: Outlook Verlag, 2018), 56.

23. *The United States Strategic Bombing Surveys* (European War) (Pacific War) (Reprinted by Air University Press, Maxwell Air Force Base, Alabama, 1987), 78, 108, and 72–73.

2 TORPEDOES, DESTROYERS, AND SAMURAI OF THE SEAS

1. Edwyn Gray, *The Devil's Device: Robert Whitehead and the History of the Torpedo* (Annapolis, MD: Naval Institute Press, 1975), 45.

2. Ibid., 59.

3. Ibid., 13.

4. Christopher Howe, *The Origins of Japanese Trade Supremacy: Development and Technology in Asia from 1540 to the Pacific War* (Chicago, IL: University of Chicago Press, 1996), 283.

5. David Lyon, *The First Destroyers* (Annapolis, MD: Naval Institute Press, 1996), 14.

6. David C. Evans, ed., *The Japanese Navy in World War II: In the Words of Former Japanese Naval Officers* (Annapolis, MD: Naval Institute Press, 1969), 177.

7. Ibid., 231.

8. Ibid., 232.

9. Ibid., 235.

10. Ibid., 233.

11. Ibid., 236.

12. "Limitation of Naval Armament (Five-Power Treaty or Washington Treaty)," www.ibiblio
    .org/pha/pre-war/1922/nav_lim.html. Last accessed July 29, 2023.

13. Clint Johnson, *Tin Cans & Greyhounds: The Destroyers That Won Two World Wars* (Washington, D.C.: Regnery History, 2019), 49.

14. Itō Masanori, *Rengō kantai no eikō* [*The Glory of the Combined Fleet*] (Tokyo: Bungei Shunjū, 1962), 196–97.

3 OIL EMPIRE AND JAPAN'S SOUTHERN ADVANCE

1. US Navy Technical Mission to Japan, "Characteristics of Japanese Naval Vessels, Article 12, Boilers and Machinery," Intelligence Targets Japan (DNI) of September 4, 1945, Fascicle S-1, Targets S-01 and S-05, Fascicle X-1, Target X-07 (April 1946), 7. See https://web.archive.org/web/20120423174301fw_/http://www
   .fischer-tropsch.org/primary_documents/gvt_reports/USNAVY/USNTMJ%20
   Reports/USNTMJ-200H-0416-0521%20Report%20S-01-12.pdf. Last accessed October 26, 2021.

2. Andrew Roberts, *The Storm of War: A New History of the Second World War* (New York, NY: Harper Perennial, 2011), 589.

3. Mark R. Peattie, *Nan'yō: The Rise and Fall of the Japanese in Micronesia, 1885–1945* (Honolulu, HI: University of Hawai'i Press, 1988), 51.

4. Ibid., 51, 52, 57–60.

5. Hara Tameichi, *Japanese Destroyer Captain: Pearl Harbor, Guadalcanal, Midway – the Great Naval Battles as Seen through Japanese Eyes* (Annapolis, MD: Naval Institute Press, 2011), 36.

6. Samuel Eliot Morison, *History of the United States Naval Operations in World War II, vol. III: The Rising Sun in the Pacific, 1931–April 1942* (Boston, MA: Little, Brown and Company, 1984), 280.

7. War History Office of the National Defense College of Japan (compiler), *The Invasion of the Dutch East Indies*, edited and translated by Willem Remmelink (Leiden: Leiden University Press, 2015), 1–4.

8. Ibid., 1–4.

9. Ibid., 16.

10. Itō Masanori, *Rengō kantai no eikō* [*The Glory of the Combined Fleet*] (Tokyo: Bungei Shunjū, 1962), 200.

11. Terence Kelly, *Battle for Palembang* (London: Robert Hale, 1985), 98–99.

12. Ibid., 102.

13. Ibid., 86–87.

14. Ibid., 103.

15. Ibid., 103.

16. War History Office of the National Defense College of Japan (compiler), *The Invasion of the Dutch East Indies*, 244.

17. Itō, *Rengō kantai no eikō*, 202.

18. "USS GRENADIER – War Diary, 4/12/42 to 6/10/42." National Archives Identifier 133935550. Fold3 File #267893599. https://catalog.archives.gov/id/133935550. Last accessed March 31, 2020.

4 CONQUEST OF THE SOUTH SEAS

1. "USS S-37, February 1942–March 1942." National Archives Identifier 74839471. Fold3 File #29092400. https://catalog.archives.gov/id/74839471. Last accessed March 20, 2020.
2. "USS HOUSTON, SENIOR SURVIVOR (FORMER GUNNERY OFFICER) – Report of action in the Battle of the Java Sea, 2/27/42 P J & D E I." National Archives Identifier 77543578. Fold3 File #300888147. https://catalog.archives.gov/id/77543578. Last accessed March 20, 2020.
3. Toyota Jō, *Yukikaze wa shizumazu: Kyōun kuchikukan eikō no shōgai* [*Yukikaze* Can't Be Sunk: The Glorious Career of a Fortunate Destroyer] (Tokyo: Kōjinsha, 1983), 102–107.
4. Itō Masanori, *Rengō kantai no eikō* [*The Glory of the Combined Fleet*] (Tokyo: Bungei Shunjū, 1962), 203–205.
5. "USS S-37, February 1942–March 1942."
6. Ibid.
7. Itō, *Rengō kantai no eikō*, 204–5.
8. Tameichi Hara, *Japanese Destroyer Captain: Pearl Harbor, Guadalcanal, Midway – The Great Naval Battles as Seen through Japanese Eyes* (Annapolis, MD: Naval Institute Press, 1967), 81.
9. "USS HOUSTON, SENIOR SURVIVOR (FORMER GUNNERY OFFICER) – Report of action in the Battle of the Java Sea, 2/27/42 P J & D E I."
10. Samuel Eliot Morison, *History of the United States Naval Operations in World War II, vol. III: The Rising Sun in the Pacific, 1931–April 1942* (Boston, MA: Little, Brown and Company, 1984), 284.
11. A. T. Doodson, 'Tide-Predicting Machines', *Nature* 118, no. 2978 (November 27, 1926): 789.
12. Kaijō Hōanchō Suirobu, ed., *Shōwa 19-nen: Chōsekihyō, jokan: Nihon, Nan'yō guntō, Shiberia tōgan, Manshūkoku, Shina, Tōsōtō, Minami Shinakai* [*Tide Tables, Part 1 (1944): Japan, Southern Ocean Archipelago, East Coast Siberia, Manchuria, China, Indonesian Archipelago, South China Sea*] (Tokyo: Kaijō Hōanchō, 1944).
13. "USS BONEFISH – Report of 4th War Patrol." National Archives Identifier 78543727. Fold3 File #279816061. https://catalog.archives.gov/id/78543727. Last accessed October 27, 2021.
14. H. C. Hays, "U.S. Navy MV Type of Hydrophone as an Aid and Safeguard to Navigation," *Proceedings of the American Philosophical Society* 59, no. 5 (1920): 371.
15. NHK Interview Archive, Tokkō heiki mokuhyōkan ni [On Board a Special Assault Weapon Ship]. Interview: "Kuchikukan *Yukikaze* Suisokuin: Noma Mitsue-san" ["Destroyer *Yukikaze* Hydrographer, Noma Mitsue"], October 23, 2011, https://www2.nhk.or.jp/archives/shogenarchives/shogen/movie.cgi?das_id=D0001100855_00000. Last accessed October 28, 2021.

16. "Japanese Sonar and ASDIC," in *Reports of the U.S. Naval Technical Mission to Japan* (1945–1946). Operational Archives, US Naval History Division, Washington, D.C., 1974, https://web.archive.org/web/20120501094656fw_/http://www.fischer-tropsch .org/primary_documents/gvt_reports/USNAVY/USNTMJ%20Reports/USNTMJ-200B-0343-0412%20Report%20E-10.pdf. Last accessed April 13, 2020.

5 ESCORTING CATASTROPHE AT MIDWAY

1. Ugaki Matome, *Fading Victory: The Diary of Admiral Matome Ugaki, 1941–1945*, translated by Masataka Chihaya. Foreword by Gordon W. Prange. Edited by Donald M. Goldstein and Katherine V. Dillon (Pittsburgh, PA: University of Pittsburgh Press, 1991), 111–113.
2. Agawa Hiroyuki, *The Reluctant Admiral: Yamamoto and the Imperial Navy*, translated by John Bester (Tokyo: Kodansha International, 1979), 300.
3. Official Military Personnel File for James H. Doolittle. National Archives Identifier 57283842. https://catalog.archives.gov/id/57283842. Last accessed August 15, 2020.
4. Ian W. Toll, *Pacific Crucible: War at Sea in the Pacific, 1941–1942* (New York, NY: W. W. Norton, 2012), 286, 291.
5. "USS NASHVILLE – War Diary, 4/1–30/42 (Enc A)." National Archives Identifier 133968929. Fold3 File #268391678. https://catalog.archives.gov/id/133968929. Last accessed October 28, 2021.
6. "Characteristics of Japanese Naval Vessels, Article 5, Shipboard Electrical equipment" (February 1946), in *Reports of the U.S. Naval Technical Mission to Japan* (1945–11946). Operational Archives, US Naval History Division, Washington, D.C., December 1974. https://web.archive.org/web/20120423175313fw_/http://www.fischer-tropsch .org/primary_documents/gvt_reports/USNAVY/USNTMJ%20Reports/USNTMJ-200G-0230-0662%20Report%20S-01-5.pdf. Last accessed August 15, 2020.
7. Fukuzawa Yukichi, *The Autobiography of Yukichi Fukuzawa*, translated by Eiichi Kiyooka (New York, NY: Columbia University Press, 1960), 214, 215.
8. W. Theodore De Bary, Carol Gluck, and Arthur E. Tiedemann (compilers), *Sources of Japanese Tradition, 1600 to 2000*, vol. ii, Part ii: *1868 to 2000* (New York, NY: Columbia University Press, 2006), 108–109.
9. E. B. Sledge, *With the Old Breed* (New York, NY: Ballantine Books, 2010), 34.
10. Nishizaki Nobuo, *Yukikaze no notte shōnen: Jūgosai de shussei shita kaigun tokubetsu nen-shōhei* [*A Boy aboard Yukikaze: Departing for the Front at Fifteen as a Special Navy Youth Sailor*], edited by Ogawa Mamiko (Tokyo: Fujiwara Shoten, 2019), 185.
11. NHK Interview Archive. Tokkō heiki mokuhyōkan ni [On Board a Special Assault Weapon Ship]. Interview: "Kuchikukan *Yukikaze* Suisokuin: Noma Mitsue-san" ["Destroyer *Yukikaze* Hydrographer, Noma Mitsue"], October 23, 2011, https://www2 .nhk.or.jp/archives/shogenarchives/shogen/movie.cgi?das_id=D0001100855_00000. Last accessed October 28, 2021.
12. James L. McClain, *Japan: A Modern History* (New York, NY: W. W. Norton & Company, 2002), 201–202.

13. Toyota Jō, *Yukikaze wa shizumazu: Kyōun kuchikukan eikō no shōgai* [*Yukikaze Can't Be Sunk: The Glorious Career of a Fortunate Destroyer*] (Tokyo: Kōjinsha, 1983), 114–127.

14. Tameichi Hara, *Japanese Destroyer Captain: Pearl Harbor, Guadalcanal, Midway – The Great Naval Battles as Seen through Japanese Eyes* (Annapolis, MD: Naval Institute Press, 1967), 90.

15. Jonathan Parshall and Anthony Tully, *Shattered Sword: The Untold Story of the Battle of Midway* (Washington, D.C.: Potomac Books, 2005), 149.

16. Samuel Eliot Morison, *History of the United States Naval Operations in World War II*, vol. IV: *Coral Sea, Midway, and Submarine Actions, May 1942–August 1942* (Boston, MA: Little, Brown and Company, 1984), 107.

17. Itō Masanori, *Rengō kantai no eikō* [*The Glory of the Combined Fleet*] (Tokyo: Bungei Shunjū, 1962), 206–207.

6 BARROOM BRAWL AT GUADALCANAL

1. Itō Masanori, *Rengō kantai no eikō* [*The Glory of the Combined Fleet*] (Tokyo: Bungei Shunjū, 1962), 210.

2. Ibid., 213.

3. Richard B. Frank, *Guadalcanal: The Definitive Account of the Landmark Battle* (New York, NY: Penguin, 1990), 426.

4. Samuel Eliot Morison, *History of United States Naval Operations in World War II*, vol. V: *The Struggle for Guadalcanal, August 1942–February 1943* (Boston, MA: Little, Brown and Company, 1984), 12.

5. Saburō Ienaga, *The Pacific War, 1931–1945* (New York, NY: Pantheon Books, 1978), 23.

6. Ibid., 49.

7. Yamamoto Tsunetomo, *Hagakure: The Secret Wisdom of the Samurai*, translated by Alexander Bennett (Tokyo: Tuttle Publishing, 2014), 42 of 286.

8. Ibid., 97 of 286.

9. Ienaga, *The Pacific War*, 49.

10. John W. Dower, *War without Mercy: Race & Power in the Pacific War* (New York, NY: Pantheon Books, 1986), 31.

11. Ibid., 211.

12. "USS SAN FRANCISCO – Act Rep – Torpedoing of WASP, N CAROLINA & O'BRIEN, 9/15/42 (Enc A) (1 End)." National Archives Identifier 134007281. Fold3 File #2678954823. https://catalog.archives.gov/id/134007281. Last accessed October 30, 2021.

13. Frank, *Guadalcanal*, 316–318.

14. Morison, *History of United States Naval Operations in World War II*, vol. V, 189.

15. Frank, *Guadalcanal*, 354.

16. "USS HORNET (CV8) LOSS IN ACTION. Santa Cruz 26 October, 1942." http://ibiblio .org/hyperwar/USN/WarDamageReports/WarDamageReportCV8/WarDamage ReportCV8.html. Last accessed July 27, 2023.

17. "USS ENTERPRISE – War Diary, 10/1–31/42 (Enc A–B)." National Archives Identifier 134012947. Fold3, File #267850129. https://catalog.archives.gov/id/134012947. Last accessed October 31, 2021.

18. "USS HELENA – Act off No Coast Guadalcanal, 11/13/42 (3rd Savo Is Act)." Fold3 File #268402094. National Archives Identifier 134008843. https://catalog.archives.gov/id/134008843. Last accessed November 1, 2021.

19. "USS FLETCHER – Report of Action (Enc A)." Fold3 File #267968693. National Archives Identifier 134025505. https://catalog.archives.gov/id/134025505. Last accessed November 1, 2021.

20. Tameichi Hara, *Japanese Destroyer Captain: Pearl Harbor, Guadalcanal, Midway – The Great Naval Battles as Seen through Japanese Eyes* (Annapolis, MD: Naval Institute Press, 1967), 130.

21. Hara, *Japanese Destroyer Captain*, 131.

22. Ibid.

23. "USS ATLANTA – Engagement with Jap Surface Forces off Guadalcanal, 11/12–13/42 and Loss of USS ATLANTA (Enc A–E)." Fold3 File #268537238. National Archives Identifier 134083458. https://catalog.archives.gov/id/134083458. Last accessed November 1, 2021.

24. Ibid.

25. Ibid.

26. "USS HELENA – Act off No Coast Guadalcanal, 11/13/42 (3rd Savo Is Act)."

27. "CINCPAC – Loss of USS CUSHING (Enc A)." Fold3 File #267959510. National Archive Identifier 134026735. https://catalog.archives.gov/id/134026735. Last accessed November 1, 2021.

28. Ibid.

29. "USS FLETCHER – Report of Action (Enc A)."

30. Ibid.

31. "USS LAFFEY – Report of November 16, 1942." Fold3 File #267922306. National Archives Identifier 134009504. https://catalog.archives.gov/id/134009504. Last accessed November 1, 2021.

32. Hara, *Japanese Destroyer Captain*, 136.

33. "USS HELENA – Act off No Coast Guadalcanal, 11/13/42 (3rd Savo Is Act)."

34. Hara, *Japanese Destroyer Captain*, 139.

35. Ibid., 143.

36. "USS HELENA – Act off No Coast Guadalcanal, 11/13/42 (3rd Savo Is Act)."

37. Itō, *Rengō kantai no eikō*, 220.

38. Ibid., 220.

39. Ibid., 224.

40. Frank, *Guadalcanal*, 597.

41. Winston Churchill speech to the House of Commons on June 4, 1940. https://winstonchurchill.org/resources/speeches/1940-the-finest-hour/we-shall-fight-on-the-beaches/#:~:text=We%20shall%20go%20on%20to,fight%20in%20the%20fields%20and. Last accessed July 30, 2023.

7 DEFENDING THE SOLOMON SEA AND BISMARCK BARRIER

1. Samuel Eliot Morison, *History of United States Naval Operations in World War II*, vol. vi: *Breaking the Bismarck Barrier 22 July 1942–1 May 1944* (Boston, MA: Little, Brown and Company, 1984), 25.

2. Yoshihara Kane, *Southern Cross*, translated by Doris Heath. Unpaginated. Research Centre of the Australian War Memorial in Canberra (book collection F 940.541352 T882). http://ajrp.awm.gov.au/ajrp/ajrp2.nsf/pages/NT0000411E?openDocument.   Last accessed December 4, 2020.

3. Robert L. Eichelberger, *Our Jungle Road to Tokyo* (Las Vegas, NV: Arcadia Press, 2017), 26.

4. Yoshihara, *Southern Cross*.

5. Morison, *History of United States Naval Operations in World War II*, vol. vi, 49.

6. Yoshihara, *Southern Cross*.

7. Haruko Taya Cook and Theodore F. Cook, *Japan at War: An Oral History* (New York, NY: The New Press, 1992), 301.

8. Itō Masanori, *Rengō kantai no eikō* [*The Glory of the Combined Fleet*] (Tokyo: Bungei Shunjū, 1962), 227–228.

9. Cook and Cook, *Japan at War*, 301–302.

10. Yoshihara, *Southern Cross*.

11. Samuel Hideo Yamashita, *Daily Life in Wartime Japan, 1940–1945* (Lawrence, KS: University of Kansas Press, 2015), 17.

12. Ibid., 19.

13. Ibid., 22.

14. Samuel Hideo Yamashita, *Leaves from an Autumn of Emergencies: Selections from the Diaries of Ordinary Japanese* (Honolulu, HI: University of Hawai'i Press, 2005), 278.

15. Ibid., 270.

16. Ibid., 279.

17. Ibid., 295.

18. Ibid., 276.

19. "USS O'BANNON – Engagement with Enemy surface units off Kolombangara Is, early morning of 7/13/43." Fold3 File #270727224. National Archives Identifier 135923323. https://catalog.archives.gov/id/135923323. Last accessed December 20, 2020.

20. Ibid.

21. "USS RADFORD – Night Surface Engagement off Kolombangara, 7/12–13/43." Fold3 File #269704873. National Archives Identifier 135906052. https://catalog.archives .gov/id/135906052. Last accessed December 20, 2020.

22. "USS O'BANNON – Engagement with Enemy surface units off Kolombangara Is, early morning of 7/13/43."

23. "CTG 36.1 – Night Engagement off Kolombangara, 7/12–13/43." Fold3 File #269652574. National Archives Identifier 78132687. https://catalog.archives.gov/ id/78132687. Last accessed December 22, 2020.

24. "USS RADFORD – Night Surface Engagement off Kolombangara, 7/12–13/43."

25. "CTG 36.1 – Night Engagement off Kolombangara, 7/12–13/43."

26. Itō, *Rengō kantai no eikō*, 233.
27. "CTG 36.1 – Night Engagement off Kolombangara, 7/12–13/43."
28. "CTG 36.1 – Night Engagement off Kolombangara, 7/12–13/43."
29. "USS RADFORD – Night Surface Engagement off Kolombangara, 7/12–13/43."

8 THE MARIANA ISLANDS AND THE COLLAPSE OF JAPAN'S DEFENSIVE SPHERE

1. Itō Masanori, *Rengō kantai no eikō* [*The Glory of the Combined Fleet*] (Tokyo: Bungei Shunjū, 1962), 245–246.
2. Brett L. Walker, *A Concise History of Japan* (Cambridge: Cambridge University Press, 2015), 146.
3. W. Theodore de Bary, Carol Gluck, and Arthur Tiedemann (compilers), *Sources of Japanese Tradition, 1600–2000*, 2nd Edition, vol. II (New York, NY: Columbia University Press, 2005), 621–626.
4. De Bary, Gluck, and Tiedemann (compilers), *Sources of Japanese Tradition, 1600–2000*, 960–966.
5. William M. Tsutsui, "Landscapes in the Dark Valley: Toward an Environmental History of Wartime Japan," *Environmental History*, 8, no. 2 (April 2003): 300.
6. "USS Cavalla, May 1944–August 1944." Fold3 File #29072505. National Archives Identifier 74810601. https://catalog.archives.gov/id/74810601. Last accessed February 26, 2021.
7. Ibid.
8. Ibid.
9. Ibid.
10. Ibid.
11. Ibid.
12. Ibid.
13. Ibid.
14. "USS Albacore, May 1944–July 1944." Fold3 File #32197402. National Archives Identifier 74800745. https://catalog.archives.gov/id/74800745. Last accessed February 26, 2021.
15. Ibid.
16. Waldo Heinrichs and Marc Gallicchio, *Implacable Foes: War in the Pacific, 1944–1945* (Oxford: Oxford University Press, 2017), 100.
17. "USS BELLEAU WOOD – War Diary, 6/1–30/44." Fold3 File #277721137. National Archives Identifier 78516091. https://catalog.archives.gov/id/78516091. Last accessed February 26, 2021.
18. Ibid.
19. Ibid.
20. Nishizaki Nobuo, *Yukikaze no notte shōnen: Jūgosai de shussei shita kaigun tokubetsu nenshōhei* [*A Boy aboard Yukikaze: Departing for the Front at Fifteen as a Special Navy Youth Sailor*], edited by Ogawa Mamiko (Tokyo: Fujiwara Shoten, 2019), 128–129.

21. Ibid., 133–134.
22. Edward Gibbon, *The History of the Decline and Fall of the Roman Empire*, vol. II (London: Penguin Books, 1995), 201.

9 THE LEYTE THEATER

1. W. Theodore De Bary, Carol Gluck, and Arthur E. Tiedemann (compilers), *Sources of Japanese Tradition, 1600–2000*, vol. II, Part II: *1868–2000* (New York, NY: Columbia University Press, 2006), 312.
2. Jean Edward Smith, *FDR* (New York, NY: Random House, 2008), 524.
3. Pankaj Mishra, *From the Ruins of Empire: The Intellectuals Who Remade Asia* (New York, NY: Farrar, Straus and Giroux, 2012), 1.
4. Ibid., 1.
5. Papers of Theodore Roosevelt, Manuscript Division, Library of Congress, pp. 120–126. https://web.viu.ca/davies/H321GildedAge/TR.threat.of.Japan.htm. Last accessed July 27, 2023.
6. Noriko Kawamura, *Emperor Hirohito and the Pacific War* (Seattle, WA: University of Washington Press, 2015), 25.
7. John W. Dower, *War without Mercy: Race & Power in the Pacific War* (New York, NY: Pantheon Books, 1986), 176.
8. Smith, *FDR*, 511.
9. William Leonard Langer and S. Everett Gleason, *The Undeclared War, 1940–1941: The World Crisis and American Foreign Policy* (New York, NY: Harper & Brothers Publishers, 1953), 628.
10. Smith, *FDR*, 513.
11. Ibid., 514.
12. Langer and Gleason, *The Undeclared War*, 629.
13. Smith, *FDR*, 515.
14. Ibid., 516–517.
15. Ibid., 518.
16. Langer and Gleason, *The Undeclared War*, 652.
17. Smith, *FDR*, 518.
18. Ibid., 521.
19. Langer and Gleason, *The Undeclared War*, 659.
20. Ibid., 660.
21. Smith, *FDR*, 524.
22. Kawamura, *Emperor Hirohito and the Pacific War*, 91–92.
23. Smith, *FDR*, 524.
24. Langer and Gleason, *The Undeclared War*, 898–899.
25. Smith, *FDR*, 529.
26. Langer and Gleason, *The Undeclared War*, 910.
27. Masanori Ito (with Roger Pineau), *The End of the Imperial Japanese Navy*, translated by Andrew Y. Kuroda and Roger Pineau (New York, NY: W. W. Norton & Company, 1956), 120.

28. Ibid., 120.

29. Ibid., 129.

30. Samuel Eliot Morison, *History of the United States Naval Operations in World War II*, vol. XII: *Leyte, June 1944–January 1945* (Boston, MA: Little, Brown and Company, 1984), 181.

31. Ito, *The End of the Imperial Japanese Navy*, 132.

32. Ibid., 140.

33. Ibid., 140.

34. Ibid., 135.

35. Paul S. Dull, *A Battle History of the Imperial Japanese Navy, 1941–1945* (Annapolis, MD: Naval Institute Press, 1978), 320.

36. Morison, *History of the United States Naval Operations in World War II*, vol. XII, 199.

37. Ito, *The End of the Imperial Japanese Navy*, 145.

38. Ibid., 151.

39. Nishizaki Nobuo, *Yukikaze no notte shōnen: Jūgosai de shussei shita kaigun tokubetsu nen-shōhei* [*A Boy aboard Yukikaze: Departing for the Front at Fifteen as a Special Navy Youth Sailor*], edited by Ogawa Mamiko (Tokyo: Fujiwara Shoten, 2019), 145–148.

40. "USS ST LO – Rep of Engagement with Jap Surface Forces off Samar Is, Philippines & Sinking of After Being Crash Dived by Jap Plane, 10/25/44." Fold3 File #292584087. National Archives Identifier 78698849. https://catalog.archives.gov/id/78698849. Last accessed November 4, 2021.

41. Ibid.

42. Ibid.

43. "GAMBIER BAY – Rep of Loss of USS GAMBIER BAY, 10/25/44, East of Samar Is, Philippines." Fold3 File #292238669 National Archives Identifier 78658203. https://catalog.archives.gov/id/78658203. Last accessed November 4, 2021.

44. "USS JOHNSTON – Rep of Engagement with Jap Surface Forces off Samar Is, Philippines, & Resultant Sinking of the USS JOHNSTON on 10/25/44." Fold3 File #292510767. National Archives Identifier 78668266. https://catalog.archives.gov/id/78668266. Last accessed November 4, 2021.

45. Nishizaki, *Yukikaze no notte shōnen*, 144.

46. Itō Masanori, *Rengō kantai no eikō* [*The Glory of the Combined Fleet*] (Tokyo: Bungei Shunjū, 1962), 257.

10 DANGEROUS HOMEWATERS AND *SHINANO* DESTROYED

1. NHK Interview Archive. Tokkō heiki mokuhyōkan ni [On Board a Special assault Weapon Ship]. Interview: "*Kuchikukan* Yukikaze *Suisokuin:* Noma Mitsue-san" ["Destroyer *Yukikaze* Hydrographer, Noma Mitsue"], October 23, 2011, https://www2.nhk.or.jp/archives/shogenarchives/shogen/movie.cgi?das_id=D0001100855_00000. Last accessed November 5, 2021.

2. Nishizaki Nobuo, *Yukikaze no notte shōnen: Jūgosai de shussei shita kaigun tokubetsu nen-shōhei* [*A Boy aboard Yukikaze: Departing for the Front at Fifteen as a Special Navy Youth Sailor*], edited by Ogawa Mamiko (Tokyo: Fujiwara Shoten, 2019), 145–148.

3. Yasuko Tsukahara, "State Ceremony and Music in Meiji-Era Japan," *Nineteenth Century Music Review* 10 (2013): 233.

4. "USS Sealion, October 1944–December 1944." Fold3 File #29081240. National Archives Identifier: 74845821. https://catalog.archives.gov/id/74845821. Last accessed November 5, 2021.

5. Nishizaki, *Yukikaze no notte shōnen*, 148.

6. Ibid., 149.

7. "USS Archer-fish, October 1944–March 1945." National Archive Fold3 File ##31193961. National Archives Identifier: 74801609. https://catalog.archives.gov/id/74801609. Last accessed November 5, 2021.

8. Nishizaki, *Yukikaze no notte shōnen*, 149.

9. NHK Interview Archive. Tokkō heiki mokuhyōkan ni. Interview: "*Kuchikukan* Yukikaze *Suisokuin*: Noma Mitsue-san."

10. "USS Sealion, October 1944–December 1944."

11. NHK Interview Archive. Tokkō heiki mokuhyōkan ni. Interview: "*Kuchikukan* Yukikaze *Suisokuin:* Noma Mitsue-san."

12. "USS LAMSON – Report of Operations in Support of Landings at Baybay, Leyte Island, Philippines on 12/6/44, Including AA Actions." Fold3 File #293475116. National Archives Identifier 139779002. https://catalog.archives.gov/id/139779002. Last accessed November 4, 2021.

13. "U.S.S. LAMSON (DD367), Damage Report of." Document from the private collection of Joy Martin, the daughter of Captain John V. Noel.

14. *The Tale of Heike*, translated by Royall Tyler (New York, NY: Penguin Classics, 2014), 609–611.

15. Ivan Morris, *The Nobility of Failure: Tragic Heroes in the History of Japan*, preface by Juliet Winters Carpenter (Kumamoto: Kurodahan Press, 2013), 100.

16. NHK Interview Archive. Tokkō heiki mokuhyōkan ni. Interview: "*Kuchikukan* Yukikaze *Suisokuin:* Noma Mitsue-san."

17. Morris, *The Nobility of Failure*, 195.

18. Herbert P. Bix, *Hirohito and the Making of Modern Japan* (New York, NY: HarperCollins, 2001), 179.

19. Morris, *The Nobility of Failure*, 9.

11 *YAMATO* AND THE SPECTER OF HISTORY

1. Tameichi Hara, *Japanese Destroyer Captain: Pearl Harbor, Guadalcanal, Midway – The Great Naval Battles as Seen through Japanese Eyes* (Annapolis, MD: Naval Institute Press, 1967), 262.

2. E. B. Sledge, *With the Old Breed* (New York, NY: Ballantine Books, 1981), 34.

3. Ibid., 59.

4. Ibid., 74.

5. Ibid., 120.

6. John W. Dower, *War without Mercy: Race & Power in the Pacific War* (New York, NY: Pantheon Books, 1986), 185.

7. Sledge, *With the Old Breed*, 121.

8. Ibid., 155.

9. Ibid., 178.

10. Ibid., 187.

11. Samuel Eliot Morison, *History of United States Naval Operations in World War II*, vol. xiv: *Victory in the Pacific, 1945* (Boston, MA: Little, Brown and Company, 1975), 170.

12. Ugaki Matome, *Fading Victory: The Diary of Admiral Matome Ugaki, 1941–1945*, translated by Masataka Chihaya. Foreword by Gordon W. Prange. Edited by Donald M. Goldstein and Katherine V. Dillon (Pittsburgh, PA: University of Pittsburgh Press, 1991), 572–573.

13. Itō Masanori, *Rengō kantai no eikō* [*The Glory of the Combined Fleet*] (Tokyo: Bungei Shunjū, 1962), 266.

14. Nishizaki Nobuo, *Yukikaze no notte shōnen: Jūgosai de shussei shita kaigun tokubetsu nen-shōhei* [*A Boy aboard Yukikaze: Departing for the Front at Fifteen as a Special Navy Youth Sailor*], edited by Ogawa Mamiko (Tokyo: Fujiwara Shoten, 2019), 181.

15. Yoshida Mitsuru, *Requiem for Battleship Yamato*, translated and introduction by Richard H. Minear (Annapolis, MD: Naval Institute Press, 1985), 7.

16. Ibid., 24.

17. Hara, *Japanese Destroyer Captain*, 268.

18. Yoshida, *Requiem for Battleship Yamato*, 30–31.

19. Ibid., 32.

20. Ibid., 38.

21. "USS Threadfin, March 1945–May 1945." Fold3 File #29096861. National Archives Identifier 75855041. https://catalog.archives.gov/id/74855041. Last accessed November 5, 2021.

22. Yoshida, *Requiem for Battleship Yamato*, 58.

23. Ibid., 60.

24. Morison, *History of United States Naval Operations in World War II*, vol. xiv, 202.

25. Hara, *Japanese Destroyer Captain*, 261.

26. Ibid., 264.

27. Ibid., 264.

28. Ibid., 277–278.

29. Ibid., 282.

30. Nishizaki, *Yukikaze no notte shōnen*, 190.

31. Ibid., 191.

32. Ibid., 192.

33. Ibid., 194.

34. Ibid., 195.

35. Itō, *Rengō kantai no eikō*, 267.

36. Yoshida, *Requiem for Battleship Yamato*, 65.

37. Ibid., 70–71.

38. Ibid., 91.

39. Itō, *Rengō kantai no eikō*, 268.

40. Ibid., 268.

41. Ibid., 269.

42. Nishizaki, *Yukikaze no notte shōnen*, 218–219.

43. Ibid., 224.

44. Hara, *Japanese Destroyer Captain*, 287.

45. Ibid., 288.

12 SURRENDER AND THE ENDURING DANGERS OF *YUKIKAZE*'S HAUNT

1. Itō Masanori, *Rengō kantai no eikō* [*The Glory of the Combined Fleet*] (Tokyo: Bungei Shunjū, 1962), 269.

2. Nishizaki Nobuo, *Yukikaze no notte shōnen: Jūgosai de shussei shita kaigun tokubetsu nen-shōhei* [*A Boy aboard Yukikaze: Departing for the Front at Fifteen as a Special Navy Youth Sailor*], edited by Ogawa Mamiko (Tokyo: Fujiwara Shoten, 2019), 253–254.

3. Ibid., 254–255.

4. "International Military Tribunal for the Far East," www.un.org/en/genocideprevention/documents/atrocity-crimes/Doc.3_1946%20Tokyo%20Charter.pdf. Last accessed July 29, 2023.

5. Nishizaki, *Yukikaze no notte shōnen*, 276, 281.

6. Chen Jiang, *Mao's China and the Cold War* (Chapel Hill, NC: University of North Carolina Press, 2001), 20.

7. Ibid., 22.

8. Ibid., 25.

9. Ibid., 26.

10. Ibid., 30.

11. Ibid., 31.

12. Ibid., 165.

13. Ibid., 168.

14. Ibid., 183.

15. Chōhei Kambayashi, *Yukikaze*, translated by Neil Nadelman (San Francisco, CA: Haika Soru, 2002), viii.

16. Leiji Matsumoto, *Leiji Matsumoto's Space Battleship Yamato: The Classic Collection*, translated by Zack Davisson (Tokyo: Tohan Corporation, 2019), 26.

17. "Kensuke Tanaka Interview: Comptiq Magazine June and July 2020," https://en.kancollewiki.net/Kensuke_Tanaka_Interview:_Comptiq_Magazine_June_and_July_2020. Last accessed November 13, 2021.

18. Aquagaze, "The Unfortunate Implication of Kantai Collection," https://theglorioblog.com/2014/05/01/the-unfortunate-implications-of-kantai-collection. Last accessed November 14, 2021.

19. Akky Akimoto, "'Kantai Collection': Social Game of Warships Sets Course for Big Money," *Japan Times* (February 20, 2014), www.japantimes.co.jp/life/2014/02/20/digital/kantai-collection-social-game-of-warships-sets-course-for-big-money. Last accessed November 14, 2021.

Index

INDEX